A Sorcerous Anthology: Magick and Occult Writings from the Publications of Robert Cross Smith

Copyright 2017 Topaz House Publications

No part of this book may be reproduced except brief quotations and scholarly usage except by permission of the publisher.
All medical information is for historical interest only. No guarantee is given for the efficacy of any of the practices described herein.

ISBN: 978-0-9906682-9-9

Visit Topaz House Publications at www.topazbooks.pub

A SORCEROUS
ANTHOLOGY
OR
Guide to Ancient Mysteries
BEING A
COMPLETE SYSTEM OF OCCULT PHILOSOPHY

Embellished with Fine engravings
OF HIEROGLYPHICS AND TALISMANS

By the Members of the Mercurii;
RAPHAEL, THE METROPOLITAN ASTROLOGER;
THE EDITOR OF THE PROPHTETIC ALMANACK; AND
Other Sideral Artists of First-Rate Eminence

THE FIRST EDITION
SUPERVISED AND CORRECTED, WITH NUMEROUS ADDITIONS,
BY MERLINUS ANGLICUS, JUNIOR, GENT.
Author of "Urania," The "Philosophical Merlin", "Sybilline Fragments", &c., and Member of Several Learned Societies.
Edited by John Madziarczyk

―――― "One so strong
That could control the moon, make flows and ebbs;
And deal in her command without her power."
Shakespeare, Tempest

"There are more things in heaven and earth, Hortaio
Than are dreamt of in your philosophy."
Hamlet

"Millions of spiritual creatures walk the earth
Unseen, both when we wake, and when we sleep."
Milton

Seattle
Topaz House Publications
2017

Notes on the Text

This book is composed of articles from seven publications, the majority coming from "The Familiar Astrologer" and "The Astrologer of the Nineteenth Century". These publications each had their unique style and format, and we have aimed to replicate them. Because the selections draw from multiple sources, the style of the text often changes article by article. Changes made to the original texts include enlargement and standardization of overly small text, and the alteration of names of angels and demons in gothic font to bold. The talismanic and ritual images have been redrawn, and the extraneous pictorial material that surrounded them has been removed.

Abbreviations used in the table of contents:

AN: Astrologer of the Nineteenth Century
FA: Familiar Astrologer
BF: Book of Fate
RBF: Royal Book of Fate
RBD: Royal Book of Dreams
MA: Manual of Astrology
UR: Urania, taken from "William Blake" by Arthur Symons.

Table of Contents

Introduction i

Part One: Introductions and Astrology

Biography and Introductions.

    Obituary and Horoscope of Robert Cross Smith (RBF) 1
    Introduction to "The Familiar Astrologer" (FA) 6
    Introduction to "The Astrologer of the Nineteenth Century" (AN) 8

Astrological Writings.

    Horoscope of William Blake (UR) 17
    Historical and Introductory Remarks (MA) 18
    The Mystical Signatures (MA) 41

Part Two: Divination

Geomancy

    Geomancy Part 1 (FA) 53
    Geomancy Part 2 (FA) 56
    Geomancy Part 3 (FA) 67
    Sentence of Populus and Via (FA) 69
    Sentence of Aquisitio and Amissio (FA) 79
    Sentence of Conjunctio and Carcer (FA) 89
    Sentence of Fortuna Major and Minor (FA) 99
    A Synopsis of Geomancy (AN) 109
    Examples in Geomancy (AN) 120
    Secrets in Geomancy (FA) 139
    The Oracle of Dreams (FA) 143
    Short Essay on Dreaming (RBD) 149

Physiognomie and Metaposcopy

- Palmistry, Metoposcopy, and Physiognomie 1 (FA) 175
- An Epitome or Abridgement of Physiognome (FA) 178
- Palmistry, Metoposcopy, and Physiognomie 2 (FA) 180
- Of Metoposcopy and [....] the Forehead [...](FA) 189
- Seven Planets and Signs on the Forehead (FA) 196
- Judgement of the Body by Color and Other Accidents(FA) 198
- Judgements of the Hair by Color(FA) 201
- Of the Eyes, and their Significations (FA) 204
- Of the Face (FA)205
- Of the Four Humours or Temperaments (FA) 206

Palmistry

- Palmistry, the Lines in the Hand (FA) 209
- True and Perfect Description of the Hand (FA) 210
- Prediction of the Hands in General and Particularly the Hand-Wrist(FA) 215
- A Table of the Nails (FA) 219
- Particular Rules for the Hands (FA) 222

Wheel of Pythagoras

- Ancient Divination by the Wheel of Pythagoras 1 (FA) 227
- Ancient Divination by the Wheel of Pythagoras 2 (FA) 232
- Fortunate and Unfortunate Days by the Wheel (FA) 235

Miscellaneous Divination

- Planetary Alphabet of Trithemius (FA) 237
- Ancient Augury and Soothsaying (FA) 240
- Bibliomancy (FA) 241
- A Marriage Omen (FA) 244
- Charm to Know Death (FA) 244
- Ancient Danish Calendar (AN) 245

Part Three: Low Magic

Magical Theory:

    Charms and Talismans Intro (AN) 251
    Traditions and Superstitions of Former Times Intro (FA) 251
    Singular Properties of Natural Magic (AN) 252
    The Evil Eye (FA) 255
    "Witchcraft" (BF) 258
    Animal Magnetism (FA) 259

Charms

    How to Cure Witchcraft (BF) 261
    Legendary Charm for Gathering Herbs (FA) 261
    Charm for Hooping Cough (FA) 262
    Charm to Bind or Compel Thief (FA) 262
    Charm to Stop a Bleeding Nose (FA) 263
    Charm Against Furious Beasts (AN) 263
    Charm Against General Trouble (AN) 263
    Charm Against Enemies (AN) 263
    Charm Against Peril by Fire or Water (AN) 264
    Legendary Charm against Thieves/Enemies (FA) 264
    A Safe Way to Secure a House (BF) 265
    Safeguard for Livestock and Out Buildings (BF) 266
    Safeguard for Orchards, Parks, Fields (BF) 266
    To Drive away Ghosts (BF) 267
    Protection Against Witchraft, Ill Tongue, Bad Transits (BF) 267
    To Prevent Nightmares (BF) 268
    Make a Witch Appear or Effects Cease (BF) 268
    Prevent Vermin that Destroy Poultry and Rabbits (BF) 268
    Prevent a Dog from Barking at Night (BF) 269
    To Draw Cats Together (BF) 270
    Prevent Bugs Biting in the Night-Time (BF) 270
    To Drive away Mice or Rats (BF) 271

To Prevent being Robbed on the Road (BF) 271
To Find out a Thief (BF) 272
Mighty Oration to Bring Back Stolen Goods (BF) 272

Talismans

Talismans Intro (FA) 273
Talismans Intro (AN) 274
Imperial Talisman of Constantine (FA) 275
Ring of Strength (FA) 276
Amulet or Charm for Love (FA) 276
The Spiral Semaphora (FA) 277
A Talisman for Destroying Insects and Reptiles (AN) 278
A Talisman Against Enemies (AN) 279
A Talisman for Love (AN) 280
A Talisman for War and Battle (AN) 281
Charm for Healing Diseases (AN) 281
A Curious Letter Square (FA) 284
Charm to Protect against Thieves (AN) 285

Herbs and Minerals

St. John's Wort (FA) 287
To Cause True Dreams (FA) 287
A Ring for Power (FA) 287
For Sight (FA) 287
Aconite, or Wolfsbane (FA) 287
Mullett, or Flea-Bane (FA) 287
Herbs that Act Against Spirits (FA) 288
To Make a Sad Person Merry (FA) 288
Mysterious Properties of Sunflowers (FA) 288
The Nettle (FA) 288
To Sleep without Danger (FA) 288
The Herb Celandine (FA) 289
The Herb Periwinkle (FA) 289
The Herb Henbane (FA) 289
The Lily, Astrologically Gathered (FA) 289

The Mistletoe (FA) 290
The Herb Centaury (FA) 290
Vervain, Astrologically Gathered (FA) 290
To Fascinate or Charm Dogs (FA) 290
Wonderful Properties of Sage (FA) 291
Properties of the Amethyst (FA) 291
The Coral (FA) 291
Admirable Amulet to Stop Bleeding (FA) 291
[Herb Footnote](AN) 292
To See Spirits (FA) 292
Singular Property of Pennyroyal (FA) 292
Virtues of the Mandrake (FA) 293
The Sleep of Plants (AN) 293

Mysterious Writing

Mysterious Letters Delivered by Honorius (AN) 294
Of Mysterious Writing (AN) 294
Cabalistical Words of Great Efficacy (AN) 295

Moon lore

The Influence of the Moon (FA) 299
Prognostications from the Moon's Age (FA) 301
Theory of Fortunate and Unfortunate Days (FA) 304
A Table of the Moon (FA) 305
Talismanic Effects of the Moon on Vegetables (AN) 309
Arguments Drawn from Tides (AN) 310
Application of Tides to Astrology (AN) 312

Fairy Lore

Elves in Ireland (FA) 315
The Cluricaune (FA) 319
The Banshee (FA) 320
The Phooka (FA) 321
The Fairy Land of Youth (FA) 322
Legend of O'Donoghue (FA) 323
Invocation of the Fairy Queen (FA) 325

    The Tylwyth Teg (FA) 327
    Singular Authenticated Appearance (FA) 328

Part Four: High Magic

Raising Spirits in General

    Celestial Magic Part 1 (FA) 333
    Celestial Magic Part 2 (FA) 341
    First Great Celestial Key (FA) 347
    Bonds of Spirits, their Adjurations (AN) 357
    Method of Raising and Invocating Spirits (AN) 358
    To Raise an Evil or Familiar Spirit (AN) 361

Nature and Appearances of Spirits

    Of Intelligences and Spirits (AN) 362
    Of the Names of Spirits (AN) 366
    Appearances of Spirits (AN) 370
    Forms and Appearances of Planetary Spirits (AN) 372

Incenses and Suffumigations

    Magical Suffumigations (AN) 378
    Mystical Perfumes of Planets (FA) 380

Rituals to Raise Particular Spirits

    Method of Rasing Egin, King of the North (AN) 381
    To Invoke the Spirit of Oberion (AN) 387

Necromancy:

    Method of Invocating the Dead (AN) 394
    Proceedings in the Necromantic Art (AN) 396
    Traditions Relating to Necromancy (FA) 398
    To Invocate and Converse with the Dead (FA) 400
    Another Strange Necromantic Spell (FA) 402

Magical Devices

    The Magic Bell for Invoking Spirits (AN) 403
    Description of the Urim and Thummim (AN) 404
    Composition of the Electrum Magnum (AN) 405

Magical Biographies
> Life of Henry Cornelius Agrippa (FA) 407
> Legendary Story of Thomas Perks (FA) 409

Alchemy and Natural Magic
> The Philosophers Stone, Part One (FA) 415
> Essay on the Sacerdotal Science (FA) 416
> History of Alchemy (FA) 417
> Theory of the Art (FA) 418
> Philosophers Stone, Part Two—
> Practice and Art of Alchemy (FA) 421
> [Miscellaneous Alchemical Documents] (FA) 426
> The Famous Alkahest (FA) 430
> Famous Elixer of Life (AN) 431
> Sympathetic Vial (FA) 433
> The Magical Candle (AN) 434
> Armory Unguent (AN) 434

Theosophy
> Extract from Ruben's Manuscript [Freher] (AN) 437
> Epitome of the Angelical World [Pordage] (AN) 445
> [Raphael's (?) Note on Pordage and Lee] (AN) 450
> Singular Extracts relating to Spirits and Demons [Lee] (AN) 452
> Mystic Enchantment [Eckartshausen] (FA) 469

Introduction
By John Madziarczyk

This book is a collection of articles from the occult and magical publications of Robert Cross Smith. The majority of the articles were originally published in "The Familiar Astrologer" and "The Astrologer of the Nineteenth Century". Several pieces are taken from "The Book of Fate", "Urania", "The Manual of Astrology", and "The Royal Book of Dreams". "The Astrologer of the Nineteenth Century" was created by Smith from articles first published in his weekly magazine "The Straggling Astrologer", and which were arranged by topic.

The titles "The Familiar Astrologer" and "The Astrologer of the Nineteenth Century" are somewhat deceitful, in that these publications weren't dedicated solely to astrology but had an array of contents, all related to the supernatural. They included accounts of paranormal activity, fictional writings with supernatural themes, and actual magical material. The magical material that Smith included was not trivial, but was very much in the mainstream of magical practice as it existed in the 17th, 18th, and early 19th centuries, centuries where what is sometimes called "grimoire magic" flourished. This current of magic largely died out after Smith passed on, to be replaced first by Spiritualism, then by Theosophy, and finally by magic derived from the Golden Dawn.

Virtually every topic within occultism is touched on in Smith's publications. "The Familiar Astrologer" had excerpts on the magical properties of herbs, instructions on how to summon spirits, instructions on palmistry, geomancy, physiognomy and metoposcopy, written charms, talismans, moon lore, instructions on alchemy, and more. "The Astrologer of the Nineteenth Century" contained many more articles on the same subjects, and also included two rituals for evoking particular spirits, a more in depth introduction to geomancy, more instructions on how to make particular talismans, rare mystical writings, writings on natural or sympathetic magic, and instructions on how to create a magic bell of evocation as well as how to create divinatory a device labeled "The Urim and Thummim".

Smith was born in 1795 and died in 1832, a month shy of his 36th birthday, possibly as a result of complications from one of the epidemics that passed through London in 1831. According to the obituary written by fellow astrologer Richard Morrison, or "Zadkiel", Smith was born in the area around Bristol in the United Kingdom[1]. In his own time, he was best known for the astrological almanacs he edited under the name of "Raphael", as well as for his books of geomancy based lot systems.

Smith's publications can be summarized into three categories: the books containing the geomantic lot systems, his astrological almanacs, and periodicals such as "The Familiar Astrologer" and "The Straggling Astrologer". Smith pursued all three categories of writing at the same time, so it's more profitable to look at these categories on their own, instead of going through them chronologically.

Smith started his publishing career in 1822, at the age of 27, with a geomantic lot book entitled "The Philosophical Merlin"[2]. Smith claimed the book was derived from a manuscript owned by Napoleon. Although it appeared at the same time, it was substantially different from the book known as "Napoleon's Book of Fate", which was written by Herman Kirchenhoffer[3].

Geomancy is a system of divination originally derived from making marks in the sand. It consists of first forming four figures of four lines that have potential values of one or two. These four figures are then used to derive four more figures, and then all of these are used to derive four more. Finally, three more figures are generated, two "Witnesses" and a "Judge" of the figure. Geomancy is highly integrated into astrology, and the first twelve figures are allotted to the different astrological houses, with different methods of doing so. The geomantic figures themselves, of which there are sixteen, all correspond to planets and signs.

Now, the books that Smith wrote incorporated elements of geomancy, but strictly speaking they weren't geomancy books. They were lot books. The distinction is that lot books use chance to guide the reader to pre-written answers, while geomantic instructions leave the interpretation of the chart as a whole to the practitioner. "Napoleon's Book of Fate" itself is an example of a geomantic lot system. Though based on geomancy, this competing lot book leads the reader to prewritten answers to their questions. While Smith's methods of getting to the answers in "The Philosophical Merlin" and other publications were highly novel, and actually considerably more complex than that used in "Napoleon's Book of Fate", they were ultimately still about finding answers to pre-ordained questions rather than teaching the reader a new method of interpretation.

One of Smith's innovations was the application of geomancy to dream analysis in his "Royal Book of Dreams". In this system, to get the ultimate significance of the dream the reader makes a geomantic figure, then looks up its significance in a complex chart. An abbreviated version of the Oracle appeared in "The Familiar Astrologer" and is included in this volume, as well as Smith's "Short Essay on Dreaming" from "The Royal Book of Dreams." The lot books that Smith wrote after "The Philosophical Merlin" were "The Royal Book of Fate", "The Royal Dream Book", and "Raphael's Lady-Witch". The last of these did not contain witchcraft but instead presented a geomantic lot system in combination with fantastic stories. Those interested in Smith's lot systems should consult Stephen Skinner's "Geomancy in Theory and Practice", a revision of his book

"Terrestrial Astrology", which gives an analysis of "The Philosophical Merlin", and contains a chart of its unique correspondences[4].

Smith's geomantic publications also appear to have had some sensationalism inserted into them. The "Prophetic Messenger", Smith's astrological almanac, appears to have had some as well, but that was par for the course. There were claims from the start in his geomantic publications about the fabulous origins of the manuscripts. "The Philosophical Merlin" was claimed to have been found in the wake of Napoleon's loss at the "Battle of Leipsic", while the Royal Book of Dreams was supposed to be taken from a manuscript found in a wooden box by a workman in the foundation of an ancient building. However, at least with his later publications, I would argue that there may have been more going on with these fictionalizations than meets the eye. Smith did print two series of instructions on actual geomancy, one in "The Familiar Astrologer", the other in "The Astrologer of the Nineteenth Century", but these did not appear as stand alone volumes. These instructions have been reprinted in this book, except for the parts in "The Astrologer of the Nineteenth Century" that consist of duplicate material.

Smith started his almanacs business as "Raphael" by taking over "The Prophetic Messenger" in 1826. This was a yearly publication, and Smith turned it into one that offered predictions about events in the coming year as well as predictions and advice for every day of the year. According to Ellic Howe in "Urania's Children"[5], the daily predictions were novel for the time. However, though "The Prophetic Messenger" was popular, it reportedly did not have the popularity of the more established ephemerides[6]. Smith also published "A Manual of Astrology" in 1828, which was reprinted in 1836 by the main inheritor of the Raphael mantle.

The almanac business was successful enough that after Smith's death, two associates tried to convince his widow to not publicize it by making a death mask[7]. One of them, John Palmer, was the source of the alchemical material in "The Familiar Astrologer"[8], and contributed here and there to

Smith's other publications. These two followers wanted to preserve the impression that "Raphael" was still alive, to minimize any sense of discontinuity in the almanacs. Howe documents that there were actually three groups of individuals who tried to claim the mantle of "Raphael" after Smith's death[9]. They all started almanacs with variants on the name "The Prophetic Messenger". Of these, only Palmer's publication survived. The subterfuge regarding the identity, and longevity, of "Raphael" allowed the name to live on in the almanac business into the 20th century[10]. The title was passed to a number of astrologers, along with the editorship of the almanacs associated with it.

Smith's non-almanac periodical publications were "The Straggling Astrologer", "Urania", and "The Familiar Astrologer". According to Ellic Howe, in 1824 "The Straggling Astrologer" was an already existing weekly publication[11], and Smith took it over and turned it into a variety publication on astrology, occult beliefs, and magical instructions. It also included weekly astrological prognostications, the first weekly magazines to do so [12]. "Straggling Astrologer" ran for only one year under Smith's editorship before folding, yet during that time it reprinted enough material to form "The Astrologer of the Nineteenth Century" . Smith then started "Urania", a similar publication, but a monthly one[13]. This too was short lived, reportedly having only one issue. According to Joscelyn Godwin, both "Urania" and "The Straggling Astrologer" were cannibalized to produce "The Astrologer of the 19th Century"[14], which was brought out in 1825. After the folding of "Urania", Smith took a break from publishing non-almanac periodicals.

After Smith had established himself in the almanac business, he delved back into periodical publishing with "The Familiar Astrologer". Individual copies of the original magazine are hard to come by, but the issues were reprinted in a single volume in 1828, with a second edition issued in 1831. The arrangement of the single volume fits that of successive issues of a magazine. Particularly, there are articles about Geomancy, Palmistry, and other subjects that are split into several parts located throughout the book. This would make little sense if the book was written from scratch, but much sense if that was the form in which the original material had been published. By contrast, the material from "The Straggling Astrologer" was arranged into "Circles", common themes, when it was reprinted in "The Astrologer of the Nineteenth Century".

Though Smith unfortunately died young, Smith's title of "Raphael" lived on after death, not only with the almanac, but also with the associated works written by Smith, that were republished. Many of his geomantic books were republished under the name of "Raphael", and "Astrologer of the Nineteenth Century" was plagiarized, once with the name of "Raphael", attached, once without. Famously, Lauron William de Laurence repackaged "The Astrologer of the Nineteenth Century" as, variously, "Raphael's Old Book of Magic" and "The Old Book of Magic".

However, before de Laurence pirated Smith's "Astrologer of the Nineteenth Century", Smith had already been the subject of plagiarism by one C.W. Roback. Roback, who was a man from Sweden who had emigrated to the United States[15], and who claimed to have a fantastic noble continental background[16], combined large portions of Smith's "Manual of Astrology" with "The Astrologer of the Nineteenth Century" to create "The Mysteries of Astrology and the Wonder of Magic", published in 1854. This book included a very long fictionalized biography of the author, in the style of the fantastic tales included by Smith in "The Astrologer of the Nineteenth Century". The work announces that it's issued by a London publishing house, while the author is living in Boston Massachusetts, and the book is dedicated to "The People of the United States". Despite the London imprint, it's possible that the book was only sold in the United States and never in the United Kingdom itself, which would have surely minimized the chance of readers recognizing any similarity in content between Roback's work and "The Astrologer of the Nineteenth Century".

Also intriguingly, "The Book of Fate", a reprint of a book on divination that included but went far beyond the normal geomantic lot systems of Smith's books, appeared in the 1890s. However, in characteristic form, the actual amount of material in it from Smith himself is ambiguous, as the geomantic lot system presented there includes correspondences for Neptune, which was not discovered while Smith was alive. It's possible that "The Book of Fate" was a reworking of Smith's original text by a later author, which would put it squarely in the tradition of Smith himself and others, who took previously written work and put their own spin on it.

Context of Contemporaries.

To put Smith into context with some of the other dramatis personae of the occult world of the time, Ebenezer Sibly, the astrologer and occultist, was born in 1751 and passed on in 1799[17]. His manuscripts were sold, and then resold to occult bookseller John Denley. Denley in turn lived from 1761 to 1842[18]. Francis Barrett (1772-?), who very likely knew Sibly, as they were virtual neighbors, borrowed many of Sibly's manuscripts in 1800 from Denley, copied them,[19] and released them as "The Magus" in 1801. Frederick Hockley, the crystal gazer who would be influential on Kenneth McKenzie and through him the SRIA and then the Golden Dawn, was born in 1808[20]. Smith was born in 1795. In 1822 Smith released "The Philosophical Merlin", which Joscelyn Godwin lists as being sold at Denley's store[21]. By 1824 Hockley, fifteen or sixteen at the time, most likely started his job of copying manuscripts for Denley, including those of Ebenezer Sibly[22]. 1824 was also the year that Smith took over editorship of "The Straggling Astrologer" and started publishing the occult writings that make up a substantial portion of this book.

Putting all of this in a generational perspective, Sibly and Denley were somewhat closer than the others to being of the same generation, with Denley being a decade younger. Barrett was born when Sibly was twenty one, Smith was born when Barrett was twenty three, and Hockley was born when Smith was thirteen. My personal opinion is that Hockley has been given far too much attention, solely due to his association with figures who would later influence the Golden Dawn. Smith also claimed to be associated with a group of occultists called "The Mercurii".

The "Mercurii" were supposed to be an anonymous club of gentlemen who were both occult practitioners and collectors of occult manuscripts. Many of their manuscripts were incorporated into "The Astrologer of the Nineteenth Century" and "The Familiar Astrologer". As to who the "Mercurii" were, this is a mystery, although certain people can be guessed at based on their mentions in "The Astrologer of the Nineteenth Century". Painter Richard Cosway is frequently mentioned in the book, but there's ambiguity about whether he himself was a member or whether the members simply bought his manuscripts after his death.

More solid is George Graham, who was a collaborator with Smith from the days of "The Portable Merlin", which they coauthored[23]. Graham was an "aeronaut", a balloon enthusiast, like Francis Barrett, as well as an alchemist[24]. Another possible member of the Mercurii was Alexander Tilloch, who was an inventor as well as an alchemist[25]. Tilloch, who invented a new process for printing, was deeply involved in the occult, as documented by Paul Kléber Monod in "Solomon's Secret Arts". However, like Cosway, there is an ambiguity about Tilloch's actual participation in "The Mercurii". "The Astrologer of the Nineteenth Century" reprints a talisman called "A Spiral Semiphora" that is labeled as taken from a manuscript owned by Tilloch. However Tilloch died in 1825, the same year "The Astrologer of the Nineteenth Century" was first published. It's not clear if the manuscript was gotten from Tilloch or from his estate. The same ambiguity applies to the painter Henry Fuseli. Fuseli, best known for his painting of a "Nightmare" as a demon sitting on a woman's chest, is mentioned somewhat vaguely in "The Familiar Astrologer" as a source of one of the fairy experiences recounted there, but at the time of the publication (1828), he had been dead for three years.

Another candidate for a member of the Mercurii is John Varley, also an artist and astrologer. Varley is reported to have supplied some of the horoscopes for Smith's publications[26], and to have also introduced Robert Cross Smith to William Blake[27], whose horoscope Smith later wrote. Varley collaborated with Blake on a book called "Visionary Heads", which was produced by Blake conjuring in his mind the spirits of famous historical figures and then drawing what he saw.

The "Mercurii" also included an avid but pseudonymous theosophist, that is to say a follower of Jakob Boehme, who went by the name of "Philadelphus". This person supplied very rare Behmenist manuscripts to Smith, as well as other mystical writings. Many of these appeared in "The Astrologer of the Nineteenth Century", but they also appeared in "The Familiar Astrologer" and, in one case, in "The Manual of Astrology". Another "Mercurii", going by the name of "Zadkiel" (not the astrologer), was most likely John Palmer, who supplied Smith with the texts on alchemy which were published in "The Familiar Astrologer"[28].

Part II.

The Context of Smith's Publications within the Romantic Movement

"Truth and Fiction."

"Th' Enchantresse came, she came in power,
Mistress of that transforming hour;
She breath's a wild mysterious lay,
And sang and smil'd their hate away.
O'er Truth's fair form a robe she threw,
To clothe her with attraction new,
And plucked from fictious pinions gay,
The vainer, gaudier plumes away,
Then bade her reassume her pride,

And soar as lofty, not as wide :
Each paus'd, each strange affection knew,
And wondered whence their hatred grew,
Felt fresh delight, beheld new charms,
And sunk into each other's arms.
Since, then, together will they stray,
And sing the same impassioned lay
The flower that Fiction's garden drest,
Blushes on Truth's celestial breast;
The wires that Truth has strung rejoice,
In union with Fiction's voice,
They seek the same romantic groves,
Each loves the haunts the other loves;
They climb the steep, explore the dell,
Together roam, together dwell."

—attributed to Robert Cross Smith. [29]

The above poem appeared in "Raphael's Lady Witch", and I think that it captures Smith's attitude to truth and fiction, and the fictional parts of his works very well. The "Lady Witch", published in 1831, would be the last new publication of Smith, who died the next year. It consists of a system of geomantic divination adapted for popular use surrounded by occult fiction and poetry, which claim to be accounts of visions and travels taken by Smith in his guise as "Raphael". Stories like these have caused Smith to be accused both of egoism and pandering to commercial interests, but I think a more complex dynamic is at work.

I believe that what Smith was doing with these fictional episodes in the "Lady Witch", and others, was engaging in what the Surrealists a hundred years later would call "The re-enchantment of the world". That is to say, restoring a richer interpretation of life to the world through fiction that went beyond the reductionist materialism of the day. Smith was a Romanticist, and I believe that Smith thought that the values embodied by the English romantic movement in its fiction, poetry, and visual arts were a harbinger of a new worldview. Literature can explore occult themes, and without being occult itself it can present experiences of the supernatural from a personal perspective that can make the reader interested in the real thing. The popularity of the Romantic movement, with its praise of the psychological self-examination of the human experience as well as supernatural phenomenon, could be seen as a precursor to popular acceptance of the kind of viewpoint that Smith was sympathetic to, and Smith may have believed that this viewpoint would supersede the beliefs prevalent in his day.

It's also possible that the episodes contained in "The Lady Witch" and other writings by Smith represented occult or magic experiences, or perhaps visions, of Smith's that were then fictionalized and presented to the public in order to communicate something of what occultism deals with from the inside out, so to speak. To use a degraded phrase from a few decades ago, fiction like this might expand the mind, and even lead to an experience of supernatural reality itself. Smith's accounts of his alter ego "Raphael" can be seen as a convenient vehicle for occult fiction. People, including myself, who have looked at Smith's writing and thought it egoistic might have been interpreting the tales too literally.

Some of how the occult and literature may have interacted in Smith's mind can be seen through statements in his writings. In his "Historical Introduction" to astrology published as the first part of his "Manual of Astrology", Smith declares that astrology only came into being through the combination of observation of the stars with poetry, of scientific observation with the poetic sensibility[30]. Smith also writes in "The Astrologer of the Nineteenth Century", in an article devoted to answering skeptics of astrology, "Were not the first lawgivers, the poets, the first priests, and the first philosophers—Astrologers?"[31]

Overall, with regards to fictional works in "The Astrologer of the Nineteenth Century" and "The Familiar Astrologer", what you see are a series of linked subject matters. Supernatural fiction is placed next to reports of actual supernatural happenings, which are placed next to instructions on magic, which in turn can create supernatural phenomenon. Astrology is included as a prime example of how unseen forces work in the world, acting as a gateway for the exploration of the other topics. After all, astrology itself is harmless, yet it is supernatural. If someone does a good natal chart, or makes an accurate prediction of the future, it can prove the existence of non-materialist, supernatural, phenomenon, in a way that does not obligate one to believe in things that might seem more unlikely.

I believe that the astrology, the accounts of the supernatural, the description of and instructions in magical practices, and the supernatural fiction, form a cohesive whole in Smith's work, one that attempted to portray a worldview that was an alternative to that of enlightenment materialism.

Smith also liberally quotes and praises well known Romantic and Gothic writers and poets through all of his work. For example, Smith dedicated both "The Astrologer of the Nineteenth Century"[32] and "The Manual of Astrology"[33] to Sir Walter Scott, the novelist. Walter Scott was a pioneer of Romantic fiction, authoring the medieval romance "Ivanhoe", as well as many others. Scott's fiction also included supernatural elements. Specifically, Smith's dedication to Scott (as "The Author of Waverly") states that the book is dedicated to him,

"With the most profound admiration of his unrivaled talents, which could alone have caused the intense interest now so generally evinced relative to the theory of those strange and extraordinary speculations, denominated, 'The Occult Sciences'."[34]

Smith directly mentions Scott's story "The Talisman" in his both of his introductions to the actual process of making talismans contained in "The Astrologer of the Nineteenth Century" and "The Familiar Astrologer"[35],[36]. Talking about astrology in "Raphael's Lady Witch", Smith cites Scott as an authority who believes in the reality of astrology, saying that it is

"a science which no less an authority than the celebrated author of Waverly calls an 'Divine Art.' "[37]

Lord Byron, the proto-typical Romanticist, is also praised effusively by Smith. For example, the "Lady Witch" includes a poem by Byron, on top of Smith's own poetic and prose contributions. Smith devotes six pages to analyzing Byron's horoscope in "The Astrologer of the Nineteenth Century"[38], explaining how he calculated his demise, and also mentions Byron's horoscope in his introduction[39]. In looking at Byron's horoscope, Smith reproduces a review of Byron's work in "The Mirror" which states:

"If we except Shakspeare [sp.], there is, perhaps, no writer in the English language from whose works an equal number of poetical beauties can be selected as from those of Lord Byron. He excels in the the sublime as well as the pathetic. Every theme seemed to suit his genius, and he could vary his style with his subject in a manner, and to an extent, that our literature before had given no example of."[40]

The article from "The Mirror" is followed by several quotations, including this quotation by "Albumazar", or "Abu-Mashar", an Arabic astrologer whose work was very influential on European astrology:

"His mighty star is extinct in darkness, and his ruling planet has set forever".

Smith also starts off the section of "The Astrologer of the Nineteenth Century" dedicated to charms and talismans with a quote from Act 1, Scene 1 of Lord Byron's play "Manfred".

"When the silent stars are shooting,
And the answering owls hooting,
Shall my soul be upon thine,
With a power, and with a sign?"[41]

The play itself is supernatural, and this particular selection is part of an incantation. The "Incantation" appears after Manfred has summoned the seven spirits of earth, ocean, air, night, mountains, winds, and his personal star in a ritual.

However, strangely enough, several lines are taken out, and Smith gets one of the words in the first line wrong, in that it should be "When the falling stars are shooting."

Other Romantic and Gothic writers mentioned include Charles Maturin, Keats, and William Beckford.

The second piece in "Astrologer of the Nineteenth Century" is actually a compressed, derivative, excerpt from a play based on Charles Maturin's "Melmoth the Wanderer", of which Smith writes that the book is a

"work abounding with transcendent beauty, both of the conception, of imagery, and of language: containing episode of character and intensity of interest, scarcely, if at all, to be equalled in the wide circle of romance; pictures of actual life nowhere to be found of equal and fearful effect."[42]

The novel itself is about a priest who sells his soul to the devil. The piece itself is a description of a scene from a play, "Valmondi", that the editor, presumably Smith, saw.

Keats is mentioned in "A Manual of Astrology" as

"the unfortunate Keats the poet, who fell a victim to the malicious spleen of ill-timed criticism, was born with ☿ in his horoscope in ☐ to ♅ and ♄." [43][Mercury in his horoscope in square to Uranus and Saturn].

The article on "The Evil Eye" included in "The Familiar Astrologer" contains a reference to a scene in the fantasy "Vathek" by William Beckford. In this, the supposed maliciousness of those who use the "Evil Eye" is compared to the hatred of a demon living in the Islamic hell of Eblis.[44] "Vathek" is a paradigmal example of early fantastic fiction that also has occult themes. Beckford, though, appears to not have been seriously involved with the occult.[45] "The Familiar Astrologer" book as a whole is dedicated to a lesser known author of the fantastic, George Payne Rainsford James. [46]

Romantic authors aren't the only artists referenced in the works. Visual artists, such as Henry Fuseli and John Varley are mentioned, and William Blake appears. Blake, artist, poet, and visionary, had a direct connection with Smith. "Urania" contained a horoscope of Blake, whom Smith met several times, and which has been reproduced in this book. Jonathan Barry, who points out the association between Blake and Smith in his book "Raising Spirits"[47], claims that their association came through fellow astrologer and artist John Varley, who was a friend of artist Richard Cosway. Smith's horoscope of Blake states that

"the mystical drawings of this gentleman are no less curious and worthy of notice, by all those whose minds soar above the cloggings of this terrestrial element, to which we are most of us too fastly chained to comprehend the nature and operations of the world of spirits."[48]

as well as that

"We have been in company with this gentleman several times, and have frequently been not only delighted with his conversation, but also filled with feelings of wonder at his extraordinary faculties;"

Smith particularly praised Blake's series of engravings titled "The Book of Job", one of which has been used as the cover of this volume.

However, although there was a connection between Blake and Smith, and some similarity between Blake's romantic vision and what I believe was Smith's vision of an alternative romantic worldview, there have been so many claims and counter-claims about what Blake did or didn't believe with respect to the occult, as well as to who may or may not have influenced him, that I'm reluctant to speculate on the matter.

Something that should be noted, though, is that "Philadelphus", the member of the Mercurii who supplied the theosophical material for "Straggling Astrologer" and "The Astrologer of the Nineteenth Century", wrote a note to the material published in "The Astrologer of the Nineteenth Century" where he weighs in heavily against Swedenborg. Specifically, "Philadelphus" argues that Swedenborg was mislead by evil spirits, and claims that the latter day prophet Joanna Southcote was mislead as well.[49] "Philadelphus" claims that Swedenborg's visions were evil spirits' attempt to seduce the educated and that Southcote's represented their attempt to seduce the uneducated. "Philadelphus" also condemns Blake's friend and fellow artist William Sharp for believing in Southcote.[50]

John Varley, an artist as well as an astrologer, also had his horoscope printed in "The Astrologer of the Nineteenth Century", where Smith states of him that

"This gentleman is well known among the lovers of the fine arts for his skill in that department of human talent; and it is no less well known, that he has already soared to a height far above mediocrity, [...]This skill in occult philosophy, and the predictive art, is no secret amongst the more fashionable and distinguished circles, where his predictions have conduced greatly to the revival of the belief in siderial influence."[51]

Smith was also not above pointing out prominent people in society who believed in the occult as evidence of its validity. Artist Richard Cosway stands out in this. Cosway has recently been given much attention in occult writings, but perhaps for the wrong reasons. Although Cosway was famous in his own time, he's obscure today. There's a reason for this, which is that he was not a Romantic painter, or apparently in any way unconventional in his work, but instead a very mainstream painter of miniatures and portraits in the neoclassical style, who was an occultist in his private life. His significance for Smith and others came from the fact that he was an occultist who was famous and also a member of the Royal Academy of Arts, as well as that he had a large occult library. Cosway was a great collector of magical texts, as well as a practitioner, and after his death many of his manuscripts were auctioned off, and found their way into the hands of Smith and his associates[52]. From there, many appeared in "The Astrologer of the Nineteenth Century", where they were labeled as originally belonging to Cosway.

Smith also presented a list of prominent individuals from the 17th to the 19th centuries who believed in astrology and the occult in his introduction to "The Astrology of the

Nineteenth Century"[53], as proof that competent people believed in the supernatural. He also distinguished there between popular astrology and fortune telling, and astrological charts produced by people who really knew what they were doing.

Part III

Processions of the Magical Worldview.

In a way, Smith's publications were the last flowering of the worldview that informed the grimoire magic of the 17th century, which was the standard approach to magic until the rise of Spiritualism. The first blossoming of this particular synthesis in Britain happened as a consequence of the occult publishing explosion of the mid 17th century. During that time, the invention of the printing press and the spread of literacy converged to allow for a number of translations of works into English that had previously only been available in Latin. These included Agrippa's "Three Books of Occult Philosophy", his pseudonymous "Fourth Book", a number of treatises by Paracelsus, "Natural Magic" by Giambattista della Porta, and others. The "Divine Pymander", part of the Hermetica, was translated into English for the first time by John Everard. All of the new material appears to have increased the demand for manuscript copies of grimoires, which also proliferated. New grimoires were produced as well, such as the "Lemegeton" or Lesser Key of Solomon. This grimoire, commonly known as the "Goetia", contains two documents unique to the time, the "Ars Goetia" and "Ars Theurgia Goetia". These documents were most likely compiled in Britain in the 17th century. The new occult publications served to facilitate a democratization of some of the occult doctrines of the Renaissance.

It should be noted that the Renaissance occultists inherited large parts of the worldview of their medieval forebears, such as their basic Ptolemaic cosmology, understanding of the functioning of the universe, and fundamental ideas about medicine. Renaissance thinkers modified these ideas, and in some cases, such as that of Paracelsus, modified them radically, but in general Renaissance thinkers maintained the foundations, even while putting their own spin on things. These modifications themselves underwent further change as the 16th century went on, until the chain finally broke, and the new concepts finally formed a cohesive whole that could overthrow the old. However, many of the innovations of Renaissance science would not enter into common acceptance until the late 17th century. The works of the 17th century occult publishing explosion happened after the core work had been done by people such as Galileo and Copernicus, but before the final learned break with the older worldview happened in the time of Newton. It's possible to trace a line from medieval occult practice, to that of the Renaissance, to that of the 17th century, and onwards in small, increasingly isolated, groups, to people like Smith, although very large alterations happened during each of these time periods.

Occultists in the 18th century, the heyday of the Enlightenment, responded to the challenges of the new scientific worldview in several ways. Some, like Ebenezer Sibly, attempted to turn back the clock to a kind of pre-Galilean science that accommodated both spirit and experiment, as well as to integrate the new discoveries of science back into that earlier, less materialistic, scientific worldview. Others looked to the new scientific discoveries and sought to outline how occultism was either in harmony with, or actually proved, by them. Those who pursued this strategy included people who adopted a modified scientific materialism, and tried to found a kind of materialist spirituality.

This position of accommodation is best represented by the writers of "The Conjurer's Magazine and Philosophical Miscellany", later retitled "The Astrologer's Magazine and Philosophical Miscellany", published in the 1790s. In many ways a predecessor to "The Straggling Astrologer" and "The Familiar Astrologer", "The Conjurer's Magazine" mixed astrology with reprints of magical material, accounts of supernatural phenomenon, and what would be called stage magic today. This included hidden or "occult" aspects of nature that could be used for amusement. The editors had a modified materialist outlook that saw little incompatibility between a slightly tweaked scientific worldview and the occult. Other manifestations of this approach can be seen in the many syntheses of materialism and animal or vital magnetism that happened during the late 18th and early 19th centuries.

Later on, particularly after the French Revolution and the rise of Napoleon, occultists started to challenge the idea of the materialist worldview directly. Both the strategy of turning back the clock and that of adapting materialist philosophy to spiritual purposes implicitly affirmed a faith in the scientific method, while this new trend was increasingly skeptical of the whole framework.

Occultism was not the only area that this cultural shift occurred in. The post-Revolutionary era saw the rejection of materialism and the cult of reason in many areas of life, artistic, literary, and philosophical, which became part of the basis of the romantic movement. It's significant that the areas that had the strongest movements that could be categorized as romantic, Great Britain and Germany, were also the opponents of France in the Revolutionary and Napoleonic wars, with Great Britain taking the lead in the fight against Napoleon and Germany finding itself occupied. However, the movement was not uniform, and while France itself would remain somewhat fallow with regards to literary and artistic romanticism, other countries, particularly those of Central Europe, would create syntheses that included both the ideology of the French Revolution and that of the Romantics.

It should also be noted that as the nineteenth century wore on, the ideas associated with Romanticism, as well as many of the original ideologues, became more and more conservative, but that this was not initially the case. At first, German Romantic philosophers, such as Friedrich Schlegel and Novalis, created a synthesis that was quite liberal in itself, albeit unconventional. The same could be said of the

English Romantic movement, where writers such as Samuel Taylor Coleridge pursued liberal positions before hardening into a later conservatism.

Smith, in publishing "The Straggling Astrologer" and then "The Familiar Astrologer", appeared to reflect the occultist belief in a new paradigm based on Romantic beliefs rather than accommodation with the scientific worldview based on a modified materialism, or attempting to turn back the clock as Sibly sought to do. Unfortunately, this vision was not to succeed. The supernatural climate of Gothic and Romantic fiction in the early nineteenth century United Kingdom would not yield a sustained social movement or lasting alternative worldview.

Part IV.

The Shift to Spiritualism and Beyond.

While the type of magical material printed by Smith largely disappears from the public record after his death, interest in the fantastic continued, and would prove to be the vessel that the doctrine of Spiritualism would be poured into in the 1840s. By the time the Fox sisters in upstate New York claimed to have communications with spirits, Smith's occult tradition, at least in its public form, had been dead for some time. Consequently, there was a concrete break in ideas and practice, and when occultism reformed itself in the wake of Spiritualism, it did so on completely different grounds than what had come before.

The influence of mediumship had, over all, a negative effect on the quality of occult thought, although the writings that came through, or were co-authored, by spiritualist mediums were not as uniformly bad as is sometimes presumed. Nevertheless, the philosophical worldview that had informed occultism from the 17th century to the early 19th was discarded in preference for Spiritualistcally proved occult thought. This, ironically, was often referred to as experimentally proved spirituality. Spiritualism was seen as experimental proof of spirituality because the information received by mediums was thought to prove the existence of life after death. Some of the phenomenon that were claimed to have been produced during seances were also thought to be experimental evidence of the spirit world. This trend was added to, and only partially reformed by, the rise of the Theosophical society.

Blavatsky's "Isis Unveiled" was framed as an attempt to go from science, represented by spiritualism and the investigation of psychic phenomenon, to theology. Blavatsky's own writings are certainly not without merit. However, while she attempted to reinsert elements of the western mystical tradition back into the Spiritualist context of her day, she did so in a way that was a-historical, based on the foundations of recent occult practice. Be that as it may, the most major failing of Theosophy, though, ultimately came not from Blavatsky's work in "Isis Unveiled", or from her attempts to syncretize western and eastern theological and mystical concepts, a worthy venture, but from the notion of Blavatsky's "Secret Masters". These beings resembled the spirit controls of the mediums, and in time the concept lead to the rise of spiritual writers who either outright lied about their spiritual communications, or cast their own delusions and mental illnesses as spiritual revelations. While this tendency had been present in the Spiritualist movement as well, the weight of the Theosophical Society, which did have talented writers and thinkers as part of it, caused such claims to flourish.

It's instructive to compare Robert Cross Smith's praise of the fantastic, his inclusion of fictional stories in his publications, and his fictionalized stories of finding manuscripts, with these post-Theosophical prophets and groups, as well as with the Spiritualist writers. While Smith included fantasy in his works, he also included solid occult information. On the other hand, what you see in the post-Theosophical landscape are publications that are purely fictional, that claim to be transmissions of mystical knowledge that on examination contain little that is profound. These publications might be entertaining to read, but rarely contain anything beyond the superficial, obvious, and banal.

Also instructive is to compare the fantasies of later writers with the writings of the first theosophists that Smith published in his works. These were followers of Jakob Boehme, and had little to no connection with the later Theosophical society outside of their name. They were called "Theosophists" because of their devotion to the spirit of Wisdom. Particularly, through the manuscript collection of "Philadelphus", Smith gained access to the writings of the Behmenist mystics of the Philadelphian Society, who were active in the last decades of the 17th century and the early decades of the 18th . Smith printed papers by Dionysius Andreas Freher, John Pordage and Francis Lee. These are some of the most profound writers on mysticism in the post-medieval British world. Behemenist thought, in fact, is one of the main tributaries of the western mystical tradition, although its recognition as such is only now just beginning in English speaking countries.

However, the work of the Theosophical Society not only lead to the production of fantastic stories, but also to an occult revival that provided the foundation for the most fruitful ritual magic group in the English speaking world, the Golden Dawn. In a sense, the Golden Dawn appears to have started from the same place as those attempting to graft mysticism onto Spiritualist practice did, that is to say, from zero. They did this, though, from the perspective of running a magical lodge and performing ritual magic, as opposed to figuring out where the mystical writings of the past fit into the new paradigm.

Despite some continuity with the past through the magical interests of individual members of the Societas Rosicruciae in Anglia, such as Kenneth McKenzie and Herbert Irwin, the Golden Dawn appears for the most part to have made up its practical system of magic from scratch using the writings of popular occult authors such as Eliphas Levi, as well as the more practical implications of aspects of Theosophical associated doctrine. They ultimately came up with a system that is functional, that works, and that has provided both practical and mystical results to quite a lot of people. However, their doctrine still represents a reformation of the magical worldview based on a break with the continuity of occult tradition.

This means that while Golden Dawn inspired groups might make use of grimoires, their worldview and conception of what they're doing in using them is fundamentally different from that which the original authors and users possessed. Robert Cross Smith, on the other hand, while being a romanticist, was still part of that living tradition, and the texts, both theoretical and practical, that he printed in "The Straggling Astrologer" and "The Familiar Astrologer", reflect that worldview itself.

Part V

Remarks on the Contents of the Present Volume.

The Theosophists.

Smith reprinted a small part of the writings of Dionysius Andreas Freher, Francis Lee, and John Pordage in "Astrologer of the Nineteenth Century", although he may not have realized that he was reprinting Freher's work. This is because the manuscript that contained a version of Freher's commentary on his Three Tables, which illustrated the state of man before the fall, after the fall, and on the way to regeneration, was mislabeled as written by the Dutch artist Peter-Paul Rubens. This "Rubens Manuscript" was sold to Richard Cosway, who was a great admirer of Rubens, and was then bought at auction after his passing. Incidentally, it's possible that the identity of "Philadelphus" might be discovered by looking at the provenance of that manuscript in the present day. The manuscript is part of the Ferguson collection at the University of Glasgow.

Besides the partial commentary on the Three Tables, Smith reprinted a description of the heavenly and angelic worlds by John Pordage, which was reputedly derived from an unpublished manuscript that had come into the hands of "Philadelphus". Pordage was the founder of the mystical group that would later become the "Philadelphian Society" after his death. Pordage was a Behmenist mystic who collaborated with his wife Mary on mystical writings. Mary wrote a treatise herself, "The Mystery of Deity in the Humanity, or the Mystery of God in Man", and appears to have been inclined to mystical trances and visions.

John Pordage was accused of practicing malevolent magic, and wrote a defense against the charges, but nevertheless lost his position within the Church of England. Afterwards, he decided to only write for a Continental audience, made up of German Behmenists and others, with the result being that many of his works were translated into German and sold abroad, with the only later works available in English being those circulated in manuscript form among his immediate followers. Some of these were published posthumously in English. Pordage's son Samuel was also an active writer on mystical topics, writing an epic poem entitled "Mundorum Explicatio: or the Explanation of the Hieroglyphic Figure", which took the reader on a tour of heaven and hell, and which is said to conform in many ways to the elder Pordage's philosophy.

Also represented in Smith's collection was Francis Lee, one of the main theological inheritors of Pordage. Lee, as a young man, befriended the older Jane Leade, the visionary protege of Pordage who was the inheritor of the mantle of both John and Mary Pordage themselves. It was Lee who organized the formal Philadelphian Society around the visions and doctrines of Leade and Pordage. Francis Lee was also immensely educated and well traveled. His writings that were published posthumously as "Apoleipomena: or Dissertations, Theological, Mathematical, and Physical", show Lee to be familiar with Greek and Hebrew theological and mystical writing in their original languaåges, as well as with commentaries in these languages on the Old and New Testaments, on top of Latin.

Lee's contribution to "The Astrologer of the Nineteenth Century" was taken from the publication "Theosophical Transactions", which was a record of writings produced by the Philadelphian Society, and which is now extremely rare. In it, Lee answers several queries about an incident where a man was reported to have been lead into a mountain by a gnome. The answers deal with the nature of elemental spirits in relation to man, as well as their role in guarding treasure. They also highly suggest that Lee was either familiar with or a practitioner of ceremonial magic.

As for Dionysius Andreas Freher, he was part of a younger generation that was centered around Lee, and was also extremely well educated and traveled. Freher fused Behemenist thought with alchemy and hermeticism in a more direct way than Lee, Leade, and Pordage. His Three Tables are representative of this fusion.

Smith, or more likely "Philadelphus", also includes a general introductory essay on Pordage, Lee, and the "Rubens Manuscript", inserted as a very long footnote in the original publication of "The Astrologer of the Nineteenth Century". This essay is illuminating on its own, but a detailed discussion would take us too far afield. In the current edition, it has been taken out of footnote form and presented on its own.

Mention should also be made of the writing of Karl von Eckartshausen included in "The Familiar Astrologer". Eckartshausen, best known for his mystical work "The Cloud Upon the Sanctuary", is represented here by a translation from the German of a section of his work "Magic". Unfortunately, this piece does not have to do with the actual doctrines of magic, but with the use of narcotic plants in magical ceremonies in order to produce visions of people who are absent. Nevertheless, Eckartshausen's "Magic" was not fully published in English until 1991, when Merkur Publishing released a translation, and the inclusion of anything by Eckartshausen in the pages of "The Familiar Astrologer" is in itself extraordinary.

Ritual Magic.

Likewise, the ritual magic material that is reproduced in "The Astrologer of the Nineteenth Century" and in "The Familiar Astrologer" goes far beyond that contained in other collections. "The Familiar Astrologer" included a lengthy two part course on how to evoke and invoke angels and demons entitled "Celestial Science", part of it's "World of Spirits" series. This material presents all the stages of drawing these spirits into crystals and working with them, although it says the instructions can also be adapted for work without crystals. On top of presenting a step by step guide of how to do this, the section also includes the first Angelic Key of "Dr. Rudd", which is a lengthy invocation of the angel Metatron, called "Methattron" in the text. This key has been reprinted in Stephen Skinner's "Keys to the Gateways of Magic", which is a transcription of a document called "Janua Magica Reserata". This was a manuscript collection of theoretical and practical texts on the nature of the magical universe that was often paired with other, more operative, grimoires.

"Astrologer of the Nineteenth Century" also included its own course on how to evoke and invoke spirits, which is substantially different from that included in "The Familiar Astrologer". Likewise, it also includes two ritual evocations from the "Folger Manuscript", which have recently been republished in "The Book of Oberon". The Folger Manuscript is a lengthy compilation of medieval and renaissance grimoires that was owned by Robert Cross Smith himself. The two evocations taken from it are the "Conjuration of Oberion" and "The Conjuration of Egin, King of the North". Oberion is "Oberon", the mythical king of the fairies that Shakespeare includes in "A Midsummer Night's Dream". Egin is one of the four Demon Kings of the directions.

"Astrologer of the Nineteenth Century" also includes a novel section on the "Names of Intelligences and Spirits" which provides an overview of the magical universe, one that isn't a cut and paste job from more easily available sources, but instead a restatement of the nature of the spiritual universe that uses sources in a creative fashion.

After this, more conventional descriptions of the planetary spirits are given, drawn from pseudo-Agrippa's "Fourth Book", as well as names of other planetary, elemental, and demonic spirits.

Both "Astrologer of the Nineteenth Century" and "The Familiar Astrologer" also contain necromantic rituals, some of which are taken from Ebenezer Sibly's "A New and Complete Illustration of the Celestial Science of Astrology", which was later (and somewhat misleading) renamed "A New and Complete Illustration of the Occult Sciences". Some of these rituals, in turn, were taken by Sibly from the anonymous additions to the 1665 edition of Reginald Scot's "Discoverie of Witchcraft", which is the focus of the Topaz House series "The Magitians Discovered". The versions that Robert Cross Smith drew from are available as part of "The Station of Man in the Universe, Ebenezer Sibly on the Spirit World and Magic".

Notably, however, Smith partially rewrote the material which Sibly reproduced, and added his own commentary to it. Sibly, while he essentially took the "Discoverie" material and reworked it to reflect his own philosophy, nevertheless left most of the sections intact, changing the order that they appeared in as opposed to the content itself. Smith also added a new necromantic ritual for calling up the dead that involves using graveyard dirt, which is not found in the material used by Sibly.

Also, Smith includes two different, and rare, instructions on how to construct magical devices. The first one, on how to create a magical bell for evoking spirits, is labeled as coming from "a rare German manuscript", and this appears to be correct. An almost identical set of instructions is contained in the Faustian collection "Der Kloster", created by the bookseller Joseph Scheible, sections of which have recently been translated and printed as "Doctor Johannes Faust's Magia Naturalis and Innaturalis", by Enodia Press. Smith also includes instructions on how to create the "Urim and Thummim", which is essentially a magical mirror for interacting with the world and with spirits. The origin of this device appears to be an appendix added to a book of essays purportedly by Paracelsus that was translated into english in the mid 17th century.

Significant as well is the inclusion of the story of Thomas Perks in "The Familiar Astrologer", and the mention of the story in "The Astrologer of the Nineteenth Century". The story of Thomas Perks is a cautionary tale of a man who experimented with calling up spirits, got more than he bargained for, and was supposedly ruined by the experience. This story is unique in that it was also reproduced by Sibly in "A New and Complete Illustration", as well as by John Beaumont in "A History of Genii and Familiar Spirits", yet Smith synthesizes the various versions and adds new material, which may or may not be derived from unknown sources outside of himself.

The story of Thomas Perks is examined in great detail in Jonathan Barry's "Raising Spirits: how a Conjurer's Tale was transmitted across the Enlightenment". Barry, in tracing the thread of transmission of the story, looks at each of the figures who published it, and in doing so draws on local archives and other material in the UK that are generally inaccessible to people outside of the country. His section on Sibly reveals aspects of his life that, unfortunately, I was not aware of when writing the introduction to "The Station of Man in the Universe", not knowing about the existence of "Raising Spirits" at the time.

Other remarks on the Contents

Because astrology was so much a part of Smith's life, it would be improper to create a collection that did not have at least a representative sample of his thought on the subject. Therefore, besides the collection of Moon lore, we've included Smith's "Historical and Introductory Remarks on the Antiquity, Verity, and Utility of the Science" of astrology, taken Smith's "Manual of Astrology". I would encourage readers not to skip this essay, in that it reveals quite a bit of where Smith was coming from ideologically.

The other additions to the book beyond what's contained in "The Astrologer of the Nineteenth Century" and "The Familiar Astrologer" are the horoscope of Smith written by fellow astrologer Zadkiel, the horoscope of William Blake from "Urania", that was reprinted in Arthur Symons' "William Blake", a large selection of charms from the republication of the "Book of Fate", "A Short Essay on Dreaming" from "The Royal Dream Book", and an essay on the mystical natures of the planets from "A Manual of Astrology".

Zadkiel's horoscope is an obituary, and is the largest biographical writing on Smith produced by a contemporary. The horoscope of William Blake is inherently interesting, both for its insight into Blake as well as into Smith's attitudes towards artistry and the occult. The selection of charms from "The Book of Fate", provides instructions not found in either "The Astrologer of the Nineteenth Century" or "The Familiar Astrologer", and also includes the essay "Witchcraft", which is a look at how malefic magic might operate. Smith's "Short Essay on Dreaming" has been included after the abbreviated version of Smith's geomantic dream oracle. Because Smith devoted an entire book to looking at how geomantic readings can shed light on dreams, it follows that including one of Smith's essays on dreams themselves would help to round out the collection. The "Mystical Signatures" is a manuscript provided by "Philadelphus" to Smith, that was printed outside of the two collections.

There is a bit of terminology that's present in "Astrologer of the Nineteenth Century" that needs explaining. To make the book, Smith took articles from different issues of "The Straggling Astrologer" and "Urania" and arranged them in "Circles", which were common subject matters. Smith occasionally refers to other articles "in this circle", and these refer to other articles in that particular section.

Suggestions for further reading.

In looking at Robert Cross Smith, his time, and his worldview, the best overall book is one that doesn't mention him: "Solomon's Secret Arts" by Paul Kléber Monod. This is a masterful look at magic and the occult in Great Britain from the early 17th century to the early 19th centuries. Although Smith himself is not mentioned, Monod examines the tradition of which he was the last major representative of in depth, as well as devoting a chapter to the shift towards Gothic and Romantic fiction.

The work that has the most information about Smith himself is Joscelyn Godwin's "Theosophical Enlightenment". There, Smith receives a good amount of space in chapter seven, "Artists and Astrologers", and Godwin provides invaluable information on the social occult scene that Smith existed in. The next most important book for information on Smith and his world would be "Urania's Children", by Ellic Howe. Known for his history of the Golden Dawn, Howe's examination of the history and revival of modern astrology also gives essential context to Smith's work.

After "Urania's Children", Jonathan Barry's recent book, "Raising Spirits: How a Conjurer's Tale was transmitted across the Enlightenment" is likely the most important. This book also provides essential biographical details about Smith and his world, ones that are not found in previous studies. Ebenezer Sibly is also treated there, and Barry presents new biographical details derived from primary research in archives in the UK that clarify many ambiguities. Two other works that briefly, though importantly, look at Smith are "Geomancy in Theory and Practice" by Stephen Skinner, formerly "Terrestrial Astrology", which examines Smith's contributions to the geomantic art, as well as "The Flying Sorcerer" by Francis King, which examines the life and social context of Francis Barrett. Barrett's life and social scene intersected with that of Smith's, although Smith was active two decades after the heyday of Barrett's public occult activity.

Finally, I would suggest that interested readers consult my introduction to "The Station of Man in the Universe: Ebenezer Sibly on the Spirit World and Magic." This writing traces the line of occult connections in the United Kingdom from Sibly to the Golden Dawn, and provides insight on the transformations that happened to the doctrines in between.

Notes.

1 Zadkiel, p. xiv.
2 Skinner, p. 159
3. ibid, p. 166
4. ibid, p. 164-165
5. Howe, p. 31
6. ibid, p. 31
7. ibid, p. 32
8. ibid, p. 32
9. ibid, p. 32
10. Skinner, p. 168-169
11. Howe, p.29
12. ibid, p. 30
13. Godwin, p. 144
14. ibid p. 145
15. Davies, p. 198
16. ibid, p. 198
17. Godwin, p. 107
18. King,p. 19
19. ibid, p. 19
20. ibid, p. 19
21. Godwin, p. 143
22. ibid, p. 171
23. Howe, p. 29
24. ibid, p. 29
25. Monod, p. 284
26. Godwin, p. 146
27. Barry, p. 88
28. Godwin, p. 147-148
29. Smith, Raphael's Lady-Witch, p.152
30. Smith, Manual of Astrology, p. 19
31. Smith, Astrologer of the Nineteenth Century, p. 558
32. ibid, p.xiii
33. Smith, Manual of Astrology, p. iii
34. Smith, Astrologer of the Nineteenth Century, p.xiii
35. ibid, p.495
36. Smith, Familiar Astrologer, p. 72

37. Smith, Raphael's-Lady Witch, p. 123
38. Smith, Astrologer of the Nineteenth Century, p. 422-427
39. ibid, p. viii
40. ibid, p. 427
41. ibid, p. 490
42. ibid, p. 73
43. Smith, Manual of Astrology, p. 159-160
44. Smith, The Familiar Astrologer, p. 670
45. Godwin, p. 113
46. Smith, The Familiar Astrologer, p. 7
47. Barry, p. 88
48. Symons, p. 340
49. Smith, Astrologer of the Nineteenth Century, p. 542-543 note 2,
50. ibid, p. 543, note 2
51. ibid, p. 432-433
52. Godwin, p. 147
53. Smith, Astrologer of the Nineteenth Century, p. v-vi

Introduction

Works Cited

Barry, Jonathan, *Raising Spirits, How a Conjurers Tale was Transmitted across the Enlightenment*, New York, NY, Palgrave Macmillan Press, 2013.

Davies, Owen, *Grimoires, a History of Magical Books*, New York, NY, Oxford University Press, 2009.

Godwin, Joscelyn, *The Theosophical Enlightenment*, Albany, NY, State University of New York Press, 1994

Howe, Ellic, *Urania's Children, the Strange World of the Astrologers*, London, UK, William Kimber & Co Ltd., 1967

King, Francis X., *The Flying Sorcerer*, Oxford, UK, Mandrake of Oxford, 1992

Monod, Paul Kléber, *Solomon's Secret Arts*, New Haven, CT, Yale University Press, 2013

Skinner, Stephen, *Geomancy in Theory and Practice*, Singapore, Golden Hoard Press, 2011

Smith, Robert Cross, *The Astrologer of the Nineteenth Century, or The Master Key of Futurity, Being a Complete System of Astrology, Geomancy, and Occult Science*, London, UK, William Charlton Wright, 1825.

ibid. *The Familiar Astrologer, and Easy Guide to Fate, Destiny, & Foreknowledge, as well as to the Secret and Wonderful Properties of Nature*, London, UK, John Bennett, 1831

ibid. *Manual of Astrology, or the Book the Stars, Being the Art of Foretelling Future Events by the Heavenly Bodies*, London, UK, C.S. Arnold, 1828.

Ibid. *Royal Book of Dreams, from an Ancient and Curious Manuscript*, London, UK, Effingham Wilson, 1830.

Ibid. *Book of Fate*, London, UK, W. Foulsham & Co., 1887

Ibid. *Raphael's Lady-Witch*, London, UK, William Charlton Wright, 1831

Symons, Arthur, *William Blake*, London, UK, Archibald Constable and Company Ltd., 1907

Zadkiel, (pseud. Richard James Morrison), horoscope of Raphael, *Royal Book of Fate, Queen Elizabeth's Oracle*, by Robert Cross Smith, London, UK, Sherwood and Co., 1856

Part One:
Introductions and Astrology

NOTICE,

AS the readers of the Royal Book of Fate, while seeking for information as to their own destiny, may feel curious to know something of the history of its Editor, Raphael, the following brief account of the Nativity, and some particulars of the life and last wishes of that extraordinary individual, may not be without interest. His life was spent in endeavouring to stem the current of public opinion, which has long run counter to the belief that mankind are permitted to dive into the secrets of futurity. That he was honest in his professed opinions, those who knew him well can best testify; and it seems not inappropriate, that his own death should give a further stamp to the reality of those opinions. To persons who may have a knowledge of Astrology, the following pages must be particularly pleasing.

Natus Raphael,
9h. 5m. 20s. a.m. 19th March, 1795.
Solar Time.
Lat. 51° 27′ N, Lon. 2 35 29″ W, Bristol.

NATIVITY OF RAPHAEL,
By ZADKIEL THE SEER.*

ALAS, poor Raphael! He was a good man, and possessed a mind of no ordinary calibre. His career was brief, but his name will endure. He was the first man who, during the present century, dared to front the scorn and contempt of an age remarkable for prejudice, "the age of *cant*." Raphael discovered truth in the repudiated and almost forgotten doctrines of the science of the stars, and he dared to proclaim it; for which his name will be honoured when those who ridiculed him will be forgotten. I knew him well; an honest man; who, if he had lived to the ordinary age of man, would have done the cause of truth still more essential service.

---

* *Author of the Grammar of "Astrology" &c. &c.*

The Editor of the *"Royal Book of Fate"* was born of respectable parents, at the village of Abbott's Leigh, near Bristol. He informed me that he begun to study Astrology at an early age, and that he took a few lessons therein at Bristol. Finding but poor success in life while residing in that ancient city, he resolved to remove to London; the sign Gemini, under which he was born, being the ruling sign of London. The result was every way demonstrative of the correctness of his judgment, and of the fact, that individuals thrive best in the towns or places ruled by their own ascendant or meridian sign, &c. He quickly found friends, who enabled him to resign a clerk's place, and at the early age of twenty nine years he became a well-known public professor of that science which has been honoured by Plato and defended by Kepler. If we consider the many difficulties he had to encounter in maintaining a growing family, and the troubles he had to conquer in combating the mistaken pity of friends, who were ignorant of what they pitied, and the open abuse of enemies, alike unacquainted with the grounds on which he founded his faith, we must admit that his success was triumphant. For, although he lived not beyond the age of thirty-seven, and left behind a widow and six children, he had been able to accumulate about £1000, the fruits of his industry as an author and professor.

In 1822 he first became an author, by publishing a tract on Geomancy; and that was also the period of his becoming known to the public as a professed Astrologer. In this character, as a man of some education, he was quite a *rara avis*; for since the days of William Lilly, who flourished during the Commonwealth, most professors of the science have been extremely illiterate, the necessary effect of the study having been placed under the ban of public opinion.

In 1824 he became editor of the "Straggling Astrologer," which he afterwards called "The Astrologer of the 19th Century." By this work Raphael became first extensively known; and he afterwards received the visits of nobles, and even of *the greatest man in the realm*. Its merits need not my praise; but I may observe, that he lived to repent that he had not adhered therein to Astrology alone. The occult sciences have no connexion with Astrology in the bosom of Nature; they have been needlessly mixed up therewith. Many persons who reject the occult sciences as fabulous and absurd, do, at the same time, equally admit the truths of Astrology, from the well-grounded evidence of never-failing experience.

In 1826 Raphael brought forward his "Prophetic Messenger," a work entirely devoted to *Mundane Astrology*, or as he himself terms it, State Astrology. It met a rapid sale, and this increased yearly, owing to the novelty of the subject, and the fulfilment of several important predictions made by the author, such as the Battle of Navarino, the Burmese War the Death of Queen Caroline, on the very day it happened, &c.

In 1830 I published the Herald of Astrology in opposition to it; but though we were "two of a trade," this did not interrupt our former friendly feelings. In proof of this, I possess a letter from Raphael, dated 1831, in which he compliments my work, and expresses his belief that there was room for more than two writers on the subject. Indeed I believe that he was too liberal to entertain a sentiment so despicable as jealousy.

In 1828 he brought out his "Manual of Astrology," decidedly the best work on the science which has appeared for some years, but not without considerable blemishes. There can be no dispute that Raphael thoroughly understood Horary Questions, and that he had a fair knowledge of the mundane branch, though he did not adhere sufficiently to the doctrines of Ptolemy; but it is quite as certain that he did not fully understand some parts of the science of nativities. He failed from the very constitution of his own nativity in the mathematical portion of the work; and in an evil hour he adopted the notice of a *New Measure of time* for equating the arcs of direction, which is neither that of Ptolemy nor of Valentine Naibod, but yet appears to be framed like theirs. By reference to Raphael's table of the measure of time, page 178 of the Manuel of Astrology, it will be seen that he allows for *one degree*, one year and five days; and for *two degrees*, the same amount doubled, or two years ten days. Now as sixty minutes are one degree, they should give one year five days, but the table gives only three hundred and sixty-five days, or six hours short of a year. I can only account for this by supposing, that he did not know that the true principle of the measure of time is the sun's apparent motion in the equator at the time of birth, and not his mean motion. He also published the "Familiar Astrologer," and several minor works, chiefly on Geomancy; such as the Lady Witch, &c.; but these, I believe, were less germane to his feelings than to the interest of his publisher.

The personal appearance of Mr. R. C. Smith was slender and delicate; he was of a pale complexion, and had fine intelligent eyes, such as persons born with the sign Gemini ascending are generally observed to have. His bodily health was by no means good; he had a poor appetite, and showed no symptom of a good constitution. The winter of 1831-2 was fatal to his health; he was extremely weak, and for some weeks previous to his death suffered from a violent cough, and was subject to fits. At length the system broke up, and he expired sitting in his chair by the fire-side, without a struggle. This fatal event took place at a quarter past four o'clock on Sunday afternoon, the 26th February, 1832. His will had been made the day previous.

The time of Raphael's Birth I have taken from the Astrologer of the 19th Century, page 435, seventh edition. He there says, "This horoscope is inserted merely to guard against any future misrepresentation of the envious, who oftentimes, upon the decease of an astrologer, publish some erroneous nativity, and pass it off upon the world as genuine." From this extract it may be assumed that the time is nearly correct, or at least that he thought it so. The time he there gives is March 19th, 1795, nine hours seven min. a. m. From this I conclude that the time noted by the clock was a quarter past nine, as the clock was eight minutes before the Sun. This nativity he published without any calculations to show its correctness; and I find that the true time was one minute and forty seconds earlier, and that the birth took place exactly at nine hours five minutes twenty seconds, a. m. on the 19th March, 1795.

Raphael states, at page 436, that "there is but one evil aspect in the whole nativity (the opposition of the *Moon* to *Herschel*), and that is too weak to have any peculiar effect." Alas! he lived to discover how much he was in error. Not only has the Moon no aspect of the good planets to strengthen the native's constitution, but she was only 6° 34′ from Herschel's opposition *in mundo*, 5° 7′ from Saturn's semiquartile, and lay exactly between the declination of Herschel and Mars, being but 0° 50′ from the latter, 0° 44′ from the former. In short, the Moon was extremely afflicted, and the Ascendant also, by the Sun and Mercury being in semiquartile aspect thereto. The Sun is the giver of life; but it also is weak, by being in aspect to Saturn, and having no assistance but the sextile of Jupiter, whose power to prolong life is lessened by being himself in square aspect to Mars. All this proved, by the true rules of astrological science, that the native would not be of long life.

The good aspect of Jupiter to Mercury gave him considerable ability; and the Moon being near the declination of Mars and Herschel, gave him an independent spirit, and a bent for eccentric and antiquated studies. The position of Venus on the meridian supported him in respectability, and will keep his name before the world for many years to come. The aspect of Saturn to Mercury created a taste for the occult sciences, and a belief in the visions of the dead. The position of *seven* planates above the Earth, and the aspect of Jupiter to the Sun, procured him fame and notoriety: but the close conjunction of Mercury and the Sun diminished his powers of calculation, and rendered him fitter for the business-like calculations of Horary Questions than the mathematical acquirements of the science of nativities. His early marriage and numerous family are denoted by the oriental positions of the Moon and Venus.

THE
FAMILIAR ASTROLOGER

INTRODUCTORY REMARKS RELATIVE TO THE SCOPE AND DESIGN OF THE PRESENT WORK.

SCIENCES the least complex, Arts the most simple and common, appear difficult when in their infancy, as long as they are taught only by words or writings, and before experience and daily practice have rendered them familiar. What numerous dangers and difficulties might be started against all the daily enterprises of men, were it not undeniable that they are performed with facility! How might not the possibility of making a watch, and still more a watch to wear in a ring, or of sailing over the vast ocean, and of numberless other arts and inventions, be disputed, did we not behold them constantly practised! How many arguments, likewise, might be urged against the practice of Physic! And though some of them may be unanswerable, how many are the reverse! How many difficulties are in the way of every project or invention! And yet it is possible to surmount the greater part of these obstacles, which, in a physical way, we have to combat, where these same Arts and Sciences are concerned.

This should teach us, that we ought never to decide precipitately, without carefully examining respecting the possibility, the ease, or difficulty of what we have never tried. The easiest thing imaginable may be difficult to one who has not, by repeated trials, acquired the power of performing it; whereas the greatest difficulties vanish before exertion and perseverance. And why may not Astrology, like every other study, receive improvement, acquire fixed principles, and gradually overthrow the specious reasonings of its opposers, to their utter confusion and disgrace?

All Sciences are, more or less, surrounded with difficulties; and is it, then, any wonder that Astrology, which, above all other arts, claims pre-eminence, on account of its dignified pretensions, should be hedged round with doubts and mists, which are rendered much more gross by the prevailing prejudices of bigotry, and incredulity? Yet it may be fairly said that Astrology, of all other Sciences, is the most sublime, curious, and beautiful!

If we take, a view of the Universe at large, we shall find that there are many mysteries of an important nature, disclosed to the penetrating and curious eye of man, which are less useful than a knowledge of futurity. Has not Science taught him to trace the path of Comets, and to calculate their orbits? Has she not placed the telescope in his hand, and discovered to him, through its tube, the Planetary Laws and Motions? Has she not enabled him to read the names and signatures of each orb in the starry concave? Why, then, should the knowledge of their power and influence over the mind and body of man be neglected?

The human mind is, in a manner, governed by authority. The reaction of a name has more weight with the multitude than reason. Even in things which belong to the province of the understanding, example carries the greatest sway. To awake, therefore, the attention of my Readers, and to furnish, at the same time, the more enlightened with popular arguments, calculated to persuade weaker minds, I shall, in the following pages, produce anecdotes and authorities (relative to the truth of Astrological presages), some more or less important, *of wise and learned men*, in whose company I am under no apprehension of exposing myself to the ridiculous observations of some persons more inclined to laugh than to think.

I have already treated of the more abstruse and difficult part of the Astral Science, in a manner which has *secured* the public attention. The present Work is more calculated for the general (but not leas judicious) reader. It will display those Secrets of Planetary Influence, to which *all* are subject, *in a manner entirely devoid of difficulty,* mingling "instruction with delight," and explaining hidden truths by novel and familiar illustrations; and thus it cannot fail to be an instructive and amusing companion, for all who are fond of tracing the mysterious and wonderful (but no less certain) laws and properties of nature.

The marvellous Properties of Herbs, Stones, and Roots — the curious and occult Influences of certain Constellations — the Interpretations of Dreams — and the Display of ancient Traditions, Legends, and Superstitions, relative to the former belief in Charms, Enchantments, and such like curious Arts, — which are, for the most part, gathered from costly and partly inaccessible sources of information, — the Author flatters himself are too valuable, to need either comment or reflection; and the Reader may rest assured, that *as the Work begins, so shall it be continued, and so concluded,* — the Proprietors being determined to render it the *most* curious and entertaining Work ever published in that grand emporium of Literature — the British Metropolis.

London, 1831.

[The Astrologer of the Nineteenth Century]

INTRODUCTORY REMARKS

TO

THE SEVENTH EDITION.

IN consequence of the rapid sale of the former editions, and the unprecedented inquiries after the " Astrologer of the Nineteenth Century," which, (however envy may rail at the assertion, is nevertheless a fact,) has been honoured by the notice of some of the highest characters in the kingdom, and has, in fact, made converts of many an infidel to the doctrine of the stars, the proprietors have deemed it expedient to present the philosophical world with a new and more compendious edition, wherein the faults, repetitions, and inconsistencies of the former volumes, necessarily attendant upon periodicals, are carefully expunged, and replaced by more valuable matter, both original and select; amongst which may be pointed out, as worthy attention, the complete analysis of astrological science, which will enable the tyro to become, in a short time, capable of learning the astral theory in its most essential parts, and thus proving its truth or falsehood himself; and if there is a possibility (which we contend there is) of reading our fate in the stars of heaven, this volume will afford him a satisfactory clue for doing it.

It is really surprising to what an extent prejudice may be carried, and no less strange, that men of science, literature, and profound learning, men accustomed to logical reasoning and mathematical demonstration, who are in the habit of scrutinizing every theory, whether novel or ancient, that crosses their path, and who are many of them earnestly intent upon unravelling the choicest of nature's secrets, even in her most retired forms, who take nothing upon mere hearsay, but require the test of experience; it is certainly astonishing that *such* characters should yet, in *one* instance, be universally the slaves of custom and the dupes of prejudice—We allude to those men of science and learning who do not scruple unhesitatingly to cry down, and even contemn the science of astrology, without perusing or studying a single principle of its theory; or without any examination by the touchstone of truth, whether those doctrines which have stood the test of ages, and are as old or older than the scriptures, are founded upon truth or fiction—or whether there is any difference between the sublime theory of the *skilful* astrologer, and the chance predictions of a gipsy fortune teller! In former periods, astrology may have been said to have reigned supreme lord of the ascendant, and to have been the star by whose light men guided their paths to riches and power: this is well known to the historical student; neither have later ages been deficient in producing the most firm admirers of the "predictive art." Witness the famous *Roger Bacon*, the monk of science, and founder of our modern chymistry, and his greater namesake, the celebrated and matchless reasoner, *Lord Bacon*. Sir *Christopher Heydon*, whose admirable defence of the art drove the learned *Chambers* from the stage of life;*
the metaphysician *Locke*, the immortal *Newton*, and amongst

---

* It is an unquestionable fact, that *Chambers* was so mortified at Sir Christopher Heydon's defense of judicial astrology, that in a short period he actually died through mere vexation. Why do not the editors of the "*Retrospective Review*" prove or deny this stubborn fact?

many others, *Flamstead*,* the founder of the Royal Observatory at Greenwich; and lastly, the late learned Dr. Tilloch, late editor of that established scientific periodical, "*The Philosophical Magazine*,"† who was a secret admirer and firm advocate of *judicial astrology*, with several others that we could mention, no less distinguished for soaring above the heads of their scientific competitors, and who were an honour to their day and generation.

We are however aware, that the prejudiced enemies of the art will evade the conclusion derived from such premises, and instead of considering them as a *proof* of astrology, will declare such facts to be "weaknesses" of these great men. This sweeping assertion is but too often used as an *argument*, when, at the same time, it is an assertion devoid of *all* argument; yet, as the majority of mankind still follow the slavish trammels of custom, it is difficult to disprove that which is so congenial to the commonly received opinion of our literary compeers. However, in no instance whatever is prejudice respectable, and least of all so, when found in a quarter where it should be entirely out of the question. If, however, astrology be a delusion, and the offspring of superstition as they term it, so is the greater part of astronomical principles, for more than two-thirds of the science depends upon mathematical and astronomical data, and therefore demonstrable; neither is it the offspring of ignorance, as some also term it, since it requires a very able calculator to make use of its theory.

The matter however may, in our opinion, be soon set in a right view, and its truth or falsehood rendered obvious, for in this volume are found the most established rules of the science; and if its opponents, previous to decrying the art as fallacious, would bestow a little study upon the subject, and deign to calculate their own horoscopes thereby, they would soon set the matter entirely at rest. And further, if some one

---

* Vide Hone's excellent Every Day Book, where the history thereof is published

† His horoscope, as given by himself a short time before his death to Mr. John Varley, is in the possession of the Mercurii.

out of those numerous critics who will doubtless pounce most cruelly upon this volume, will condescend to cast their own nativities by the rules therein contained, and will afterwards give the result of *their* calculations to the public, prefixing to their horoscopes a list of the most remarkable events which have befallen them, and will thence undertake to prove that those events were not foreshown by the configurations and aspects of the heavenly bodies at their birth, giving the rules in art for such events and their failure; it will *then* become every sober and judicious admirer of Nature's secrets to endeavour to exterminate the astrological science as a blot on the page of history, and a disgrace to the age in which they live; but *until then*, let them give astrology fair quarter, and allow it as a *science* to be capable of rendering mankind wiser, happier, and better, as it undoubtedly does. And until the science is thus *experimentally* disproved, it will become *every* critic to *remember*, that *no one can prove the truth or falsehood of a science without first learning its theory**; for, as an excellent writer justly observes, "it is equally as ridiculous to listen to any argument against astrology from one who is *ignorant* of its principles, as it would be to listen to the arguments of an illiterate cobbler upon the science of architecture." It is also obvious, that those who may in future inveigh against the science, without having learned to analyse its well-digested theory, will be entitled to just about as much respect in their opinions as an illiterate rustic would deserve

---

* Some short time since, Dr. Woolaston, the celebrated astronomer and philosopher, called, in company with a friend, upon an amateur in astrology, of high renown in the arts, and when the subject was broached, the doctor expressed his surprise at hearing that astrology contained anything like *scientific* development. Nay he had never even seen a single author on the subject, and was astonished to see a thick quarto volume written in defense of its principles, and he even went so far as to confess the subject worthy attention. Yet it must be recollected, that this worthy doctor had previously spoken and inveighed *against* astrology, and declared it a chimera, but with what show of reason we will leave the reader to judge.

were he to attempt a refutation of Newton's Principiæ, and, by a sweeping assertion, affirm the beautiful machinery of the universe to be the effect of mere Chance.

Thus far we have argued negatively, and, on the other hand, what unprejudiced mind can view the nice agreement between celestial cause and terrestrial effect, *detailed* in the second circle of this work, without acknowledging the efficacy and influence of "heaven's beauteous orbs?" *One* instance in particular we would wish to be borne in mind — that of *Saturn* in his progress through the sign *Gemini*. *Thirty* years ago *Saturn* was there, and only let the reader consult the chronology of that period, and compare them with the *present* progress of that infortune through the same sign. *Thirty* years ago the Sister island was filled with discontent, and the Metropolis the scene of riots, and filled with excitement from factious demagogues. The fanaticism of Brothers was in full activity; the Fires in the metropolis were numerous, and other disasters, amongst which were prominent the abridgment of the subjects liberty, through the enactment of severe statutes, and the disastrous marriage of the Prince of Wales, which had some years after well nigh plunged England into a state of civil war. Abroad, also, we find similar events to have happened, such as Copenhagen nearly destroyed by fire, the Archduke Leopold blown up by fire-works, death of the Dauphin, and France torn by domestic factions. Under the *present* transit of Saturn, which began in June 1824, we have seen the rage for Joint stock companies, (which will certainly be the ruin, eventually, of thousands) the excitement caused by the Catholic question; the death of the King of France; the popular commotions caused by the repeal of the combination laws; and innumerable Fires, disasters, and distressing occurrences; amongst which stand conspicuous the great fire in Tichfield Street, when the two infortunes, *Saturn* and *Mars*, were in conjunction; and much more of a similar nature remains *yet to come*. Who is there that, viewing these *facts*, and the peculiar combination of planetary influence acting at the time, but will own the stars to have *influence* over sublunary affairs?

Or who is there that can view the illustrious positions in the Nativity of our most gracious sovereign, the unfortunate propensities so visible in the Horoscope of the unfortunate *Caroline*, the position of *Mercury* in the Horoscope of the calculating youth, the arithmetical calculation of Byron's death, or the authenticated predictions which this volume contains, but must acknowledge the axiom laid down by us that there *is* an astrology in nature, and a *possibility* of foreknowledge, to be sterling truth?

If these facts are not sufficient to excite the attention of the incredulous, we would point out to their notice the obvious effects of that dread celestial messenger, the " blazing comet," which was never more plainly exemplified than in the life and fortunes of the *now* harmless, but late mighty conqueror, NAPOLEON BONAPARTE. Without tracing his career of fame to his forlorn end, be it first of all here remembered, that he was born in August 1769, and, for several months *preceding* his birth, the northern regions of the heavens were visited by one of those blazing messengers; and, without following his steps to the summit of his fame, let us pause a moment to behold him upon it, *surrounded* by majesty *of his own creating, himself* seated on the throne of the world, Spain on his *west,* the allotted portion of one brother, Westphalia of another, on his *eastern* quarter; Holland on his *north,* having the third for her king; and on his *south,* with the crown of Naples, was decked the husband of his sister! At every point were his military dukes and minor relatives posted, and the validity of his solid greatness seemed ratified by his illustrious marriage with the Archduchess of Austria. Could anything human appear more stable than the monarchy of France in 1811? *But at the meridian of his glory a comet of prodigious character came to witness his eminent station. Returning from its perihelion, that magnificent luminary became faintly perceptible, at the beginning of September,* 1811, *at which time it had acquired* 20° *of celestial north latitude, and was then vertical in the latitude of* CORSICA, *and the southern extremity of natural France. Its splendour continued to increase, until it had reached* 48° *of latitude, at which time, blazing with unspeakable splendour, it hovered upon the latitude of Paris! Having traversed the heavens in such a track* as to reign *vertically over every point of latitude from south to north of* France, *let it be strictly noticed, that its highest degree of lustre was at that precise time when it was on the meridian and zenith of* PARIS, *at noon-day. It again retreated towards the south, retracing back again the whole of* FRANCE, *until it vanished over the latitude of* CORSICA. Can any reflecting mind fail to associate the appearance of this illustrious messenger of the skies, with the fate of Napoleon? Let it also be remembered that during the few latter weeks of his life, whilst the spirit of his mortal existence was gradually evaporating, *the same blazing star of Fate again appeared, as though it came, a bark launched on the calm, wide, azure sea of heaven, to meet his soul expiring, and bear it hence to its realm of rest.*

Let its errand be what it might, these *facts* we know—that at his *birth* it ministered—it came again and testified his *fame*—once more it came to *beam upon his bier*!

And who is there that has not noticed the remarkable and intense heat of the present summer (1825)? which has also seen the appearance of two *inferior* comets, which were doubtless the primary causes of the extraordinary weather we have experienced; for one of these was, a short time back, in conjunction with the sun, and the other is still visible at the period we now write.

These facts, certainly, if well weighed by thinking persons, must cause Astrology to be *discussed*; and as discussion is the prelude to truth, we may venture to predict that, like *phrenology*, its sister science, it will eventually triumph over its opponents.

The science of GEOMANCY is an amusing, and in many instances, a correct science, being founded on astrology, yet by no means so certain; it was of old, termed *"The Philosopher's Play"* and as pourtraying the ancient method of "casting lots," is worthy the attention of the curious as an amusement of the most rational kind. In neither of these sciences is there anything either supernatural or diabolical, and they may be practised without fear of evil by the most fastidious.

As to the more *mystical* part of the work, the theory of *magic rites, charms, and incantations*, they are inserted merely to complete the development of the occult studies, formerly pursued by our forefathers, who firmly believed therein; we ourselves, however, advocate them not, but leave them to those who delight in the terrific, and the horribly sublime. At any rate, both this part and the legendary tales which are inserted, may serve to beguile many a weary hour, if they do no other; and those who do not like them, may peruse another part of the work, for which purpose they are inserted in a separate circle, not interfering with the other branches of science. Yet it is possible that even *this* part of the work may not be devoid of utility; but may, by the horrors it portrays, serve to create an enthusiasm that may hereafter serve to enkindle some master spirit, who shall weave therefrom a tale of deep and fearful interest, which may, in reality, *spellbind* its numerous readers.—Those who delight in terrific legends, will find ample room for gratification in the perusal of those mystical pages, many of which are replete with those horrors now so much sought after. We conclude by expressing our grateful remembrances to those *erudite* correspondents who have enriched our pages with their contributions, and in the insertion of which, we have acted with the greatest impartiality; we hope, therefore, upon the whole, that our labours will be well received, as we have executed them in the spirit of men who mean well, which, we hope, will be an excuse for any accidental defect; yet if any critic should upbraid us with insufficiency and slight our pains, we care not, neither shall we seek revenge,

"Nam mihi non datur
Est posse tonare Jovis."

But if he will set his hand to increase the common stock of learning, and become emulous to promote the search after scientific truths, he shall have our sincerest thanks, whether his labours are for or against us. And, in the hope that this volume may be found acceptable to the legitimate students of the celestial science, we conclude our "introductory remarks," and long may ASTROLOGY triumph over its united adversaries.

London, Sept. 1825.

THE MERCURII

NATIVITY OF MR. BLAKE, THE MYSTICAL ARTIST

NOV. 28, 1757. 7.45 P.M., LONDON

The above horoscope is calculated for the *estimate* time of birth, and Mr. Blake, the subject therof, is well known amongst scientific characters, as having a most peculiar and extraordinary turn of genius and vivid imagination. His illustrations of the Book of Job have met with much and desrved praise; indeed, in the line which this artist has adopted, his is perhaps equalled by none of the present day. Mr. Blake is no less peculiar and outre in his ideas, as he seems to have some curious intercourse with the invisible world; and, according to his own account (in which he is certainly, to all appearance, perfectly sincere), he is continually surrounded by the spirits of the deceased of all ages, nations, and countries. He has, so he affirms, held actual conversations with Michael Angelo, Raphael, Milton, Dryden, and the worthies of antiquity. He has now by him a long poem nearly finished, which he affirms was recited to him by the spirit of Milton; and the mystical drawings of this gentleman are no less curious and worthy of notice, by all those whose minds soar above the cloggings of this terrestrial element, to which we are most of us too fastly chained to comprehend the nature and operations of the world of spirits.

Mr. Blake's pictures of the last judgment, his profiles of Wallace, Edward the Sixth, Harold, Cleopatra, and numerous others which we have seen, are really wonderful for the spirit in which they are delineated. We have been in company with this gentleman several times, and have frequently been not only delighted with his conversation, but also filled with feelings of wonder at his extraordinary faculties which, whatever some may say to the contrary, are by no means tinctured with superstition, as he clearly believes what he promulgates. Our limits will not permit us to enlarge upon this geniture, which we merely give as an example worthy to be noticed by the astrological student in his list of remarkable nativities. But it is probable that the extraordinary faculties and eccentricities of ideas which this gentleman possesses, are the effects of the Moon in Cancer in the twelfth house (both sign and house being mystical), in trine to Herschell from the mystical sign Pisces, from the house of science, and from the mundane trine to Saturn in the scientific sign Aquarius, which latter planet is in square to Mercury in Scorpio, and in quintile to the Sun and Jupiter, in the mystical sign Sagittarius. The square of Mars and Mercury, from fixed signs, also, has a remarkable tendency to sharpen the intellects, and lay the foundation of extraordinary ideas. There are also many other reasons for the strange peculiarities above noticed, but these the student will no doubt readily discover.

HISTORICAL AND INTRODUCTORY REMARKS ON THE ANTIQUITY, VERITY, AND UTILITY OF THE SCIENCE.

THE celestial science termed ASTROLOGY, or the doctrine of the stars, may be properly defined the art of *foreknowing* and *predicting* future events, by the motions, positions, configurations, and influences of the planetary orbs, and various celestial phenomena; as eclipses, comets, and peculiar aspects of the most powerful stars: deduced from various experimental observations of the philosophical enquirer, through a series of ages, commencing with the earliest known records; whereon is founded a system that neither the revolutions of empires, the fall of the mightiest monarchies, nor the *physical* changes in the moral and intellectual world, have been able to annihilate: but which, like the fabled phoenix of old, has not unfrequently arisen, splendid and beauteous, even from its own ashes. And while in former times it might be compared to a mighty Colossus that overstrode all other sciences, commanding the submissive homage of kings and princes; or, like "the bright star of the morning," heralding the path of learning, and enlightening the way to knowledge: In modern times, it has not unfrequently, in its etherial circuit, asserted its supremacy above other perishable arts; by some remarkable prediction (or curious coincidence, as the fashion of the day is pleased to term it) that could not have been founded on any natural conjecture, but which like "a meteoric flash" has so enlightened the gloomy atmosphere of incredulity, that the thinking part of mankind, who are not content with judging these mysterious matters upon mere hearsay, have been half inclined to believe in the *possibility* of prescience by the etherial orbs.

> "Knowledge; by favour sent
> Down from the empyrean, to forewarn
> Us timely ———————————
> For which, to the infinitely good, we owe
> Immortal thanks"
>
> MILTON.

The *antiquity* of the Astrological Science, and of Celestial Observations, may be fairly inferred from what was spoken by the all wise CREATOR of the universe; who is said in the sublime language of the sacred scriptures, to have "prepared the light;" to have formed the celestial orbs, and appointed them by the Almighty fiat, *"to be for signs and for seasons, and for days and for years."* Whence it is probable that the human reason never existed, without some portion of this heavenly knowledge being diffused amongst mankind; because, independent of motives of curiosity, which may of themselves excited the wisest of the ancient philosophers, to contemplate the splendors of the celestial canopy—It is easy to perceive that some parts of the science answer such essential purposes to mankind, that they *could not* be dispensed with. Instance, the rising and setting of the planetary orbs and the constellations; peculiar to the *seasons*—whereby the antediluvians, no doubt, were enabled to order their most important transactions; so as to cultivate the auspices of favourable periods; and apply the benevolent influences of the "Starry orbs" to the arts and customs of life. Indeed, the pastoral way of living, the serene unclouded sky and the longevity, not only of the antediluvians, but of the patriarchs of the first ages, were extremely favourable to astronomical observations; and hence we may trace the *causes* of the symbolically terrestrial signs, which mankind have by common consent placed to occupy the heavens. But those were probably not "exalted to the skies," until mankind had made some progress in *poetry*; which also is of great antiquity, having been practised in the very *first* ages of the world, whilst they "tended their flocks." Hence, also poetry and astrology should be combined *together*, as accompanying each other from the earliest ages; even in the antediluvian æra. This will not derogate from the dignity of these sciences, when it is remembered, that the ancient shepherds were not merely the vulgar, or illiterate of mankind, for in those times even *princes* did not think it beneath themselves to act as shepherds, and to "watch their flocks," or attend to pastoral affairs; which can be proved from many instances of the sacred history, of Laban, Jacob, David, Job, &c: nay, we know that several ages afterwards, many of the *chief magistrates* of ancient Rome, had been husbandmen themselves. Thus Lucius Cincinnatus was found at the plough, when he was called to be dictator: and Fabricius Curius and Camillus were no less skilled in the science of husbandry, than in the art of war.

Indeed it appears that husbandmen were in such esteem among the Romans, that they highly resented the least affront offered to any of them, of which Scipio Nasica was an instance, for he being a candidate for the place of *Edile*, meeting a plain countryman, took him by the hand, and jesting with him on "the hardness of his hands," the Romans so resented it that he lost the *Edileship*.

In the unrivalled poems of Virgil, particularly the "Georgics," the poet has enriched his work, in almost every page, with an *astrological* regard to the months, seasons, the ascending and descending *signs* and *constellations*, as though he had himself traced effects to their first cause; and by thus availing himself of the accumulated wisdom of past ages, respecting the extensive sciences on which he wrote, he produced the most beautiful poem on the subject of husbandry that the world has ever beheld. While so just, are the greater part of his observations, and so extensively useful, that the principal part of them are put in practice in many places of the world, even at this very day. Amongst other beautiful references to the magnificent machinery of the heavenly host, the following, Georg. I. 335. beginning "*Hoc metuens coeli menses et sidera serva,* &c." is very appropriate.

> "In fear of this, observe the starry signs,
> Where Saturn's houses and where Hermes join—
> The sovereign of the heav'ns has set on high,
> The moon, to mark the changes of the sky.
> When southern blasts should cease."

It is also reported by the poet LUCAN (observes Dr. Johnson with "historical veracity") that Cæsar, the imperial "Lord of the world" "*noted the revolutions of the stars, in the midst of preparations for battle.*"

According to *Josephus,* the celebrated Jewish historian, "our first father *Adam,* was instructed in Astrology by *divine inspiration.*" Adam taught it to his posterity; for it appears that *Seth* was so excellent a proficient therein, "that foreseeing the flood, and the destruction of the world thereby, he engraved the fundamental principles of his art, in hieroglyphical emblems, for the benefit of after ages, on two pillars of brick and stone." Josephus affirms, that "*he saw himself that of stone to remain in Syria in his own time:*" and in the 3rd chapter of his first book, he says, that "man lived so long before the flood, to learn the arts and sciences, especially naming Astrology and Geometry," and in the same work he states, that Abraham, "having learned the art in Chaldea, when he sojourned into Egypt, he taught the Egyptians the knowledge of Arithmetic and Astrology."

The great sir Isaac Newton has the following remarks in regard to the *origin* of Astrology. "After the study of Astronomy was set on foot for the use of navigation, and the Egyptians, by the heliacal risings and settings of the stars, had determined the length of the solar year, and by other observations had fixed the solstices, and formed the fixed stars into asterisms, all which was done in the reigns of Ammon, Sesac, Orus, and Memnon, *about a thousand years before Christ*! Nicepsos, king of Sais, by the assistance of a priest of Egypt, invented Astrology; *grounding it on the aspects of the planets*, and after the Ethiopians had invaded Egypt, those Egyptians who fled from him to Babylon, carried thither the study of Astronomy and Astrology. And so says Diodorus, "the Chaldeans in Babylon, being colonies of the Egyptians, became famous for Astrology, having learnt it from the priests of Egypt."

The *eastern nations* have ever been famous for their skill in these abstruse sciences, which in those countries have always served as a ruling principle for the public administration of the state. It is true that as Astrology is practised in those *despotic* countries, it is liable to very great abuse; and in too many instances has led the way to fanaticism and imposition. But these considerations should have no real weight with the character of the *science* in general, since the most meritorious of discoveries, the most pure theories of an abstract nature, are liable to the *same* objection; which in fact will always be the case, where the fallibility of human nature is concerned. According to the *oriental records*, the *birth* of Astrology is confounded with the epocha, of the creation of the world. We are informed by their historians, that the son of Misraim, Naorawousch, was the first Egyptian prince, and the first of the magicians who excelled in *Astrology* and (as they never fail to add) enchantment. Retiring into Egypt with his family, consisting of eighty persons, he settled on the banks of the *hill*, built *Essous*, the most ancient of the Egyptian cities, and commenced the first dynasty of the *Missraimian* princes, who were stated to be cabalists, diviners, and eminently skilful in the mystic arts. The most celebrated of these were Naerasch, who according to oriental mythology, was the first who represented in figures and *images*, the twelve signs of the zodiac. Gharnak, who had the folly to publish these mysterious secrets, till then concealed by his family. Khasslim, author of the nilometer. Hersall, who devoted himself to the worship of idols. Sehlouk, who worshipped fire; Sourid, his son, who erected the first pyramids, and who is also considered as the inventor of that wonderful mirror, which the ancient oriental poets have so much celebrated in their verses: and FIRAWNN, or Pharoah, the last prince of that dynasty, whose name was afterwards attributed to the most iniquitous kings of Egypt

Terrified by the predictions and menaces of Noah, this prince endeavoured to destroy that prophet, believing that he should prevent, by his death, the threatened deluge. It, however, destroyed him and his whole family. EFILIMOUN alone, chief Astrologer of his time, had the good fortune to save himself from that general desolation. Admonished in a *dream*, to seek refuge in the ark of Noah, he flew to Babylon, where he acknowledged the divine mission of that prophet, embraced the dogma of the unity of God, and was admitted into the ark with all his family. Forming an alliance with Noah's family, he became the ancestor of twenty-six kings of the *second* dynasty, and built the city of *Memphis*,

MISRAIM, his descendant, was the depositary of all the magical and Astrological secrets of the first ages of the world. All his descendants are said also to have excelled in these sciences, and in others which the *enemies of Astrology* have endeavoured to link *with* the science of the stars. From that prince was descended the celebrated ELBOUD-SCHIR, who surpassed all his ancestors in the great art of *Cabal*; and ADINE, his son, under whose reign the noted magicians HAROUTH and MAROUTH filled the east with their reputation: they were considered "as two demons escaped from hell." Under this reign the celebrated magician NEDOURE, established the worship of the great idol of the sun. This person, to whom *tradition* attributes a thousand astonishing and incredible events, was the author of that *inexhaustible vase*, which is mentioned by all the oriental poets.

Of his successors, they who were most distinguished in these mysterious sciences, were SCHEDAD, whom the orientals consider as the *first* astronomer, and the father of the *signs* and celestial themes, *or houses of heaven*, which he formed from viewing the stars and constellations. MENNCAWOUSCH, the first who published *these* mysteries, and who is said to have circulated throughout Egypt several thousand copies of his work. He was said also to have been the inventor of warm baths; the institutor of the twelve religious feasts, in honor of the twelve signs of the zodiac; and is said, by his own single genius, to have discovered the secrets of the philosopher's stone: whereby the orientals affirm he acquired *"an immense treasure,"* by converting simple metals into gold and silver. MENAWOUSCH, who is said to have made an *ox*, the object of his adoration. When afflicted by a severe malady, he heard a voice announcing his death, except he should have recourse to the benign influence of that animal. Under *his* reign, Egypt was desolated by the *Arabians, who took this opportunity of learning from the Egyptians the Theurgic sciences,* by which they afterwards acquired such distinguished reputation.

To the unfortunate *view* of these sciences, Mythology, attributes much of the cruelties of the Pharoah of Moses. Terrified by the alarming predictions of his Astrologers, who announced his death by the hand of a young Israelite, he commanded, *in the weakness of his mind,* that all the male children of that chosen people should be thrown into the Nile. The hand of omnipotence, which never fails even from the most unexpected and discordant causes, to produce the desired effect, if such be his divine will, ordained that *this* event should operate for the *deliverance* of the Israelites, and the ruin of the tyrant, who with his nobles and his whole army, were overwhelmed in the depths of the Red Sea. Amidst this general desolation, there being no male surviving on whom the widows could bestow the throne, the oriental writers affirm, that they chose DELUKE, the most aged amongst themselves, concerning whom they recount the following *tradition,* which is perhaps as *wild and singular* as any to be found in the oriental records.

"To preserve the state from foreign invasion, this queen had recourse to the enchantments of NEDOURE, the greatest female magician of the country. In the centre of the capital, she erected a superb edifice of stone, *whose four doors fronting the four cardinal points, were decorated with figures and images, representing numerous armies.* Several thousand persons were day and night employed in the most active exertions. "Now" said she to the queen, "you may enjoy tranquillity, your capital and empire are exempt from danger. If an enemy should have the temerity to *approach you, combat him, by attacking the figures, which are on that side of the edifice, to which he directs his march*; cut off their heads, break their arms and legs, heat out their eyes: *the destiny of these figures shall be that of your enemies.*" The virtue of this magic edifice, says the historian, kept in awe all the neighbouring people; *and Egypt continued in prosperity during four centuries, till the epocha of the destruction of that miraculous building,* which began under the reign of Licass, and fell down entirely under that of Cawmess. It is strange, that the event *verified* the *baneful prediction* of the fall and ruin of that monarchy. In consequence of Cawmess having afforded an asylum to the melancholy remnant of the Israelites, who were subjected and led into captivity by Nabuchodonosor; that savage conqueror, irritated by the contemptuous refusal of the Egyptian king, made war against him, and killed him in battle: this was followed by the massacre of one part of the nation, the captivity of the other, and *the entire ruin of Egypt*. This remarkable desolation, *which the Astrologers had predicted*, fortified more strongly the popular opinion of these occult sciences. They were perpetuated in the nation, notwithstanding the political revolutions which it successively experienced under the Babylonians, Macedonians, Romans, Persians, Greeks, and Mahometan Arabs.

    Amidst the "crash of empires," the vicissitudes of ages, and the revolutions of public opinion, (which in no other instance had evinced such firmness) these sciences, but more especially Astrology, were preserved in Egypt from one generation to another; with various degrees of power and enthusiasm; now reigning "*Lord of the ascendant,*" and again suffering a temporary wane, as fanaticism occasionally overshadowed its sublime truths. Hence these sciences were circulated amongst the different *Arabian tribes,* by whom they were as much respected as in Egypt: indeed the respect entertained for them by the Arabians in general, contributed in a great degree to the success of Mohammed. In his life we see the favourable predictions of many very celebrated Astrologers of his time; and among others, that of a priest of EUKEAZ, who told the uncle of the "Prophet" that all circumstances in his infancy conspired to announce that he would be an extraordinary man, and that his life should be guarded with the most vigilant attention. As also the prediction of another, no less famous in the art, who on being presented to him at Bassora, took Mohammed by the hand, and exclaimed with transport, *"Behold the Lord of the World, the Mercy of the Universe,"* &c. These predictions are said to have been corroborated by a remarkable vision, which Mohammed made known at the beginning of his enterprise. He declared, that in a dream he saw the two hemispheres recede in such a manner, as to show him distinctly the utmost extremities of the east and west. This he explained to his disciples, as expressive of the extensive territories and immense dominion which, by the decrees of heaven, were reserved for those, who in obedience to the *Cour'ann*, combated for his religion.

The annals of the *Othoman* empire, and the history of Mohammedanism, are replete with marvellous events, predictions, supernatural warnings, and ominous details; no less wonderful than the foregoing recitals; some few of which shall be related, since they will not only prove interesting to the curious reader, but will serve to give an idea of the spirit of that nation; and the extraordinary events which have sprung from their wild enthusiasm.

Osman I. experienced happy *presages*, respecting the future prosperity of his family. A *Scheykh*, who was an Astrologer, who passed a solitary life in the study of the occult sciences, came to him, and declared with enthusiastic rapture, that the prophet Elijah had appeared to him, and commanded him to announce, by his authority, the successful enterprises of Osman; *that he should be the brightest sun of the east, and that his posterity should reign over seven climates*; that is, over all the habitable regions of our globe. Osman loaded the old man with caresses; he offered him a rich sabre, and a costly vase. He accepted only the latter, and left the young prince with many blessings. The prediction became fulfilled, so far as success and enterprise were concerned; and at the height of his sovereign power, Osman recollected the Scheykh, sent him valuable presents, and ordered an ample convent to be built in the city where he resided, with a considerable fund, which subsists even at present.

The appearance of a *Comet*, determined the intrepid and ferocious TIMOUR, in the midst of his quarrels with BAYEZD I. to decide for war. He was at first impelled by terror, to prepare the means of *avoiding* a rupture with the Othomans, when he consulted ABDULLAH LISSAN, at that time the most skilful Astrologer of the east, and desired his opinion respecting the tendency of the comet. The Astrologer declared that this phenomenon having appeared to the west of his dominions, and of the constellation Aries, could only have an evil influence in regard to his enemies, and that it presaged the utmost disasters to the Othoman empire. Relying on this *prediction*, TIMOUR determined immediately upon war, refused every kind of accommodation, and entered at the head of a powerful army the dominions of the empire. The consequences of this war between the two heroes of the east, are well known; as also the *disasters* which befel the Othoman monarchy, after the fatal battle of *Angora*.

The death of MOURAD II. justified a strange *prediction*. This sultan was hunting in the vicinity of Adrinople; at the close of day, as he entered the city, a *Derwisch* placed himself on the bridge over which Mourad was obliged to pass; as soon as he perceived him, he fixed his eyes upon the sultan, and as he approached, exclaimed in an inspired tone, "You have no time, august monarch, to spare, to impede the progress of that abyss, which is the effect of our sins and prevarications against the divine law; you are just approaching the limit of your reign, *and the last moment of your life!* *The angel of death is already at your door*; open your arms, and receive with entire resignation, this messenger from heaven." These words made a strong impression upon the monarch and his retinue; he immediately expressed his profession of the faith, and performed several acts of contrition. Convinced that this prediction was the decrees of heaven, from hearing that this *Derwisch* was the disciple of a profound Astrologer, he prepared for death, made his will, settled the succession to the throne, *and died on the third day*; notwithstanding (says the annals,) *all the aid of medicine*, and every exertion of his ministers, officers, and courtiers, to prevent the catastrophe.

The most favourable prognostics accompanied the accession of MOHAMMED II. *The Astrologers foretold that his reign should become illustrious by the glories of conquest*: he depended also on the circumstance of his proclamation, which happened on a Thursday, the 5th day of the week; and on his being the *seventh* sultan of his family. The following words of the Cour'ann were quoted: "*God hath blessed the fifth and the seventh .*" These predictions had a powerful effect on the projects of this monarch, who became the conqueror of Constantinople, the destroyer of the Greek empire; *and one of the most illustrious princes of his family* for genius, talents, and taste for learning.

SELIM I. previous to his turning his arms against Egypt, consulted a celebrated Astrologer, who resided at *Damas*, and living like a hermit, had the reputation almost of a saint. He assured the sultan *that victory should attend his steps*; and that the kingdom of Egypt should be subject to his power. In the transports of his joy, SELIM loaded him with kindness and honor; he would not however depart from him, till he had learned the *fate* and duration of his reign. The sage refused for some time to comply with his request, but at length obliged to yield to his earnest solicitation, he informed him "*his reign would conclude before the expiration of nine years; but that from its glorious events, he would hold a distinguished rank in the history of nations.*" At these words, *Selim* observed a melancholy silence, which was only interrupted by deep sighs and accents of grief. After a gloomy pause, he desired to know the *horoscope* of prince SULEYMAN, his son. "He shall be happy," replied the hermit. "He shall reign near half a century, and be equally distinguished by his splendid actions and warlike virtues." The above observation determined the sultan to march against his enemies, and the event having corresponded with the prediction, he from that moment became a prey to fatal melancholy, and died in the *ninth* year of his reign.

As the hermit had *foretold*, his son, SULEYMAN I. ascended the throne, attended by a thousand presages respecting the future splendor of his reign, and the prosperity of his empire. These favourable predictions were chiefly founded on the good fortune which the Arabians attribute to whole numbers, since this sultan was born in the 900th year of the Hegira, and was the *tenth* monarch of his family. Prompted by these circumstances, SULEYMAN undertook those enterprises which rendered his reign so illustrious. He extended the limits of his empire on our continent in three directions, and his reign was indeed the most *prosperous* period of the monarchy.

In the reign of SELIM II. (1572) there appeared a *Comet*, which had the brightness and magnitude of *Venus*. This excited his apprehensions, which were augmented by the predictions of his Astrologers, who declared that this phenomenon announced *the calamities which excessive rain* would inflict upon the empire. Forty days afterwards, says the historian *"they imagined themselves threatened with an universal deluge*: incessant rains overflowed his dominions in Europe and Asia; laid waste three of his chief cities; swept away on all sides, men, cattle, houses, and rendered impassable, during several weeks, the bridges and public roads! This *prediction*, which is well authenticated by historians, affords a striking instance of the singular skill possessed by the Arabian Astrologers, and how astonishingly correct those rules must have been on which their presages were founded.

The death of MOHAMMED III. was likewise extremely singular and remarkable. On entering the seraglio, he met one day a *Derwisch*, who exclaimed in the following terms: "O august monarch! do not slumber over your situation. *I announce to you a melancholy event*, which will happen in *fifty-six days* from the present time. The sultan was agitated by this address. He soon after sickened, and really died on the *fifty-sixth* day.

Some months previous to the death of MOURAD IV. an *Eclipse* of the Sun, alarming this monarch, he wished to consult a mysterious volume, which *Selim I.* the conqueror of Egypt, had brought from that kingdom, with many other curiosities, which are still carefully preserved in the seraglio. It is believed that this volume, written in cyphers and magic characters, mentions the *name and destiny* of every sultan, and of every sovereign, who will reign over Egypt to the end of the world. After long and studied diligence, he fancied that he had discovered *his own name*, and his approaching *death*. In the anguish of grief he shut the volume, and denounced a thousand anathemas against whoever should hereafter presume to open it. His agitation was still further increased, on hearing that a Scheykh from Mecca, who was considered at Constantinople as a most skilful Astrologer, had privately predicted that the month of *Schewal*, in which the sultan was born, would produce in that year (1640) *something unpropitious*, and that alms should be speedily delivered to avert the impending evil. MOURAD IV. ordered these preventives to be profusely used; he even opened the public prisons, and set all at liberty except assassins; but a prey to his fate, he fell sick and *died* the 16th day of the month of *Schewal*.

"The arcana of Astrology," as a judicious writer observes, "constituted a main feature in the doctrines of the Persian magic," to which the following extract from the "Ancient Universal History," is appropriate. "In the reign of Darius Hystaspis, king of Persia, flourished *a celebrated Astrologer*, whose name was Gjamasp, surnamed Alhakim, or "the wise." The most credible writers say that he was the brother of the king, and his confidant or chief minister. He is said, by the most credible historians, *to have predicted the coming of the Messiah*; and some treatises under his name are yet current in the east. Dr. Thomas Hyde, in speaking of this philosopher, cites a passage from a very ancient author, (having before told us that this author asserted there had been among the Persians ten doctors of such consummate wisdom, as the whole world could not boast the like. He then gives the author's words.) Of these the sixth was *Gjamasp*, an *Astrologer* who was counsellor in Hystaspis. He is the author of a book intitled *Judicia Gjmaspis,*in which is contained his judgment on the Planetary Conjunctions: *and therein he predicted that Jesus should appear;* that Mohammed should be born; that the Magian religion should be abolished, &c. Nor did any Astrologer ever come up to him. "But of all the provinces of Persia, *Chorassan* is the most famous for producing great men in that art; and in Chorassan, there is a little town called Genabed, and in that town a certain family, which for six or seven hundred years past, has produced the most famous Astrologers in Persia. And the king's Astrologer is always either a native of that place, or one brought up there."

By the foregoing historical researches into the records of the Oriental Nations, we have given *their* account of the origin and beginning of the Celestial Science; but the ancient *Greek* and *Roman* historians affirm, (particularly Diodorus Siculus) that *Hercules* first brought Astrology into *Greece;* and Plutarch reports, that Hesiod practised the art. But another ancient writer (Philostratus) states, that Palamedes, *before the siege of Troy,* was esteemed skilful in Astrology; and was the first that limited the course of the seasons, and the order of the months by the solar motion. *Anaximander,* and his scholar Anaximenes, were learned in the art of Geometry and Astrology, if we may believe the ancient historians; as the one is said to have discovered Geometrical Astronomy, the other the obliquity of the zodiac. *Thales* and *Democritus* also gained a singular name in the annals of ancient history, by their foreseeing, the one a dearth, the other a plentiful crop, of olives, whereby they not only enriched themselves, but are said to have confounded the despisers of their art. *Hippocrates,* the father of medicine, is said to have foretold the plague, which took place long before it happened; and relying on the verity of his foresight, it is stated by historians, that he sent his scholars abroad into different cities, to be prepared for the dreadful calamity. In consequence of this, it is said that "all Greece looked up to him as a God, and decreed to his name the sacrifices of Hercules." *Anaxagoras* is said to have been so addicted to Astrology, and the contemplation of the heavenly bodies, that he "accounted not the earth, but the heavens to be his country" Affirming himself born for no other purpose than to contemplate and behold the Sun, the Moon, and the rest of the celestial orbs. *Thales* is known also to have predicted that great Eclipse of the Sun, in the time of Astyages, which presaged those mutations in Asia that afterwards took place. *Apollonius Tyaneus* is said to have travelled over the greater part of Egypt, India, Persia, and Chaldea, growing to that admirable perfection in the celestial art, that for his oracular presages, he was by the persons of those times, "reputed almost as a God, in the shape of man." He is said to have written four books of Astrology, which were lost in the confusion of those dark ages. These, with numerous others of the ancient worthies, are on record as delighting in the astral art. The poet *Virgil*, who has been before quoted, and who was a great mathematician, which in the sense of those times, always included *Astrology*, and skill in the Chaldean mysteries, describes his hero *Eneas*, as being born under the favourable influence of *Jupiter*, *Venus*, and the *Sun*. *Horace*, *Persius*, and even *Augustus* himself, thought highly of Astrology. In latter times, we have on record the famous prediction relative to *Picus*, earl of Mirandola, who from his antipathy to the art, was surnamed the *Scourge* of Astrology, who being foretold by three different Astrologers, *that he should not live above the age of thirty-three years*; flattering himself that the art and its predictions were false and groundless, as if he could (as Sir Christopher Heydon observes) "wrangle away death, by writing against Astrology." Lo, while he sought to prove the art vain, *his own death*, concurring *exactly with the time foretold by the Astrologers*, confirmed it to be true; and more actually confuted that which he had written against it, than if all the world besides had conspired to answer him. This is perhaps the most striking instance on record as to the truth of the art.

In the writings of *Nostradamus*, the Gallic Astrologer, are to be found almost every important event, that for centuries past has taken place. A writer in the Gentleman's Magazine (in December 1824) has pointed out to its readers the truth of two remarkable prophecies; one regarding the death of Henry II. of France, who was killed at a tournament, by an unlucky thrust in the eye, through the gilt bars of his royal helmet; which event was prophecied and printed full three years *before it happened*. The other, a more remarkable one still, of the French revolution, wherein Nostradamus predicts "that the Christian religion would be abolished in France, and many of the nobles and clergy put to death." This prophecy was likewise in print so early as the year 1556, or near 242 years before the event, which was certainly an instance of singular skill in this great Astrologer.

No less extraordinary to those who are ignorant of the firm principles on which this art is founded, was the prediction of *Guido Bonatus*, an Italian Astrologer; who being at a city in Italy when it was closely besieged, he elected a *proper time* for the earl of Montserrat to make a sally, *predicting* that the earl would rout his enemies and obtain a complete victory, but not without receiving a slight wound in the knee; and that the earl might be more assured, Bonatus marched out with him, carrying every necessary to dress the wound! The event corresponded accurately and fully with the prediction; for the enemy was vanquished totally, and the earl wounded, punctually as he foretold.

Valentine Naibod, a celebrated Astrologer of Padua, from the rules of Astrology, predicted his own death in the following singular manner. Living at Padua, he spent his time in study, and having considered his own nativity, he found some directions approaching, that gave him ground to fear he should *"be killed or wounded with a sword;"* to prevent which, and to shun the fate he apprehended, he took in all sorts of provisions from abroad, to serve him for some months to come; shut and barred all his gates, doors, and windows: and resolved to continue there to avoid the mischief. In the mean time, it happened that some thieves went by, and seeing the house made so secure, supposed, no doubt, that there must be some great wealth therein; and in the night time, breaking into the house and meeting with the master thereof, they *barbarously murdered him*, as his horoscope foretold.

Michael Scot, a mathematician and Astrologer of the thirteenth century, was much esteemed by the emperor Frederic II. He predicted that the emperor should die at *Florence*; which prediction was answered by the event. He likewise foretold that himself should die *with the fall of a stone*; which happened accordingly; for being in a church at his devotions, *a stone fell from the roof*, which gave him a mortal wound. His singular predictions caused him to be accused by the vulgar for a magician, although his contemporaries report him as a man of learning, and a great divine.

Antiochus Tibertus was one of the most famous Astrologers of the fifteenth century; and although his death was very unhappy, yet his singular predictions render his name immortal.

He was a native of a town in Romagna: a certain officer carried him to Paris, where he studied; and where following the bent of his genius, he applied himself to the occult sciences, or rather to all the branches of that secret and curious art, called *natural magic*.

Considering in his own mind that this science had been decryed from its having been mostly in the hands of bold, ignorant, and profligate persons, he thought to restore it to its former credit and repute, by giving it all the advantages that could possibly be derived from physic, mathematics, natural philosophy, history, and the fine arts; of which he was a perfect master. The pains he took in this respect, were attended with rather more success than he anticipated: so much indeed, that before he quitted France, be had attained a very high reputation, and was considered as the cleverest Astrologer of the day.

Upon his return to his native country, where that sort of knowledge was in the highest repute, he found it *necessary*, for his own security, to ingratiate himself with some of the petty tyrants, or little princes, that were possessed of the several cities and territories in Italy. Nor was it long before

Part One: Introductions & Astrology 35

he gained the confidence of *Pandolfo Malatesta*, at that time sovereign of Remini, with whom he lived in the greatest ease and credit. His reputation was quickly raised to such a height, (as well by the curious books he published, as by the happy verification of many of his predictions) that his house was continually thronged, either with visitors, who were persons of distinction, or clients who came to him for advice; so that in a very short time, he amassed a competent fortune: and as he was esteemed, courted, and beloved by persons of the highest rank, he might, according to appearances, have promised himself a comfortable journey through life, and a peaceable passage out of it, in his old age. But fate, (to whose decrees Antiochus Tibertus was no stranger) had it seems willed otherwise. In a word, he has established his fame to posterity by *three incontestible predictions*; one with respect to his most intimate friend; another in regard to himself; and the third, relating to the prince his patron. Each of them wholly improbable at the time they were delivered; all of them inscrutable, by the rules of human policy or prudence; and yet all exactly accomplished.

This friend of his was *Guido de Bogni*, one of the greatest captains of his time, as well as one of the bravest and boldest men that ever lived. He was very earnest with Tibertus to reveal to him the secret of his destiny. After considerable reluctance, this great master of his art declared that Guido would certainly *lose his life by the hands of one of his best friends*, upon an ill-grounded suspicion. Some time after this, Tiberius calculated his own *nativity*; and made no scruple of declaring that himself was fated *to lose his head* upon the scaffold.

Pandolfo, his patron, would likewise have his horoscope calculated, which Tiberius would willingly have declined; but finding it impossible, he would not hazard the credit of his art by telling a falsity; and therefore, although he was at that time the *richest* person in all Italy, Tibertus ventured to acquaint him, that *after suffering great want*, he would *die in the common hospital* at Bologna.

Not long after this *Guido* was made commander-in-chief of the army of Pandolfo, the aforesaid prince, and patron of Tibertus, upon which the count de Beulivoglio, who was father-in-law to that prince, wrote him a letter, in which he assured him, "that he had made a shepherd of a wolf" and that Guido "was actively intriguing with the pope, and had promised to deliver up the city of Remini whenever he desired it" The tyrants of Italy were never men of much discernment, and therefore the prince Pandolfo, as soon as he had this information, made a great entertainment, to which he invited all his favourites, and among the rest *Guido*, and *Tibertus* the Astrologer. At this supper *Guido was stabbed*, (exactly as the former *predicted*) and as it was suspected that Tibertus, from his great intimacy with him, might have some share in the conspiracy, — *He was thrown into a dungeon*, and loaded with irons.

It may easily be imagined that Tibertus passed his time very unpleasantly in this dismal situation, and therefore it will not be deemed surprising, when it is stated, that he endeavoured to seize the first opportunity of escaping which offered. It seems the gaoler to whose care Tibertus was committed, had a daughter of singularly mild and gentle manners, whom he at length persuaded to furnish him with the means of breaking out of his dungeon into the castle ditch, from whence he might easily escape.

In the interim, count Bentivoglio had discovered that the information he gave his relation was ill-founded; and of this he sent him an account, as soon as it was in his power; at which news Pandolfo was infinitely affected, and grieved at his late rash and cruel measures.

It was however impossible to recall his unfortunate general *Guido*, from the grave; but he gave instant orders that Tibertus should be set at liberty. The persons who brought these orders, came just at the fall of night, and strange to say, precisely at the time that the Astrologer had forced his passage into the ditch, where, after a slight search they found him.

When this was reported to the tyrant, his former suspicions returned upon him with redoubled vigour; and recollecting at the same time, the prediction of Tibertus, that he should be deprived of his patrimony before his death, he concluded that the first information could not be groundless: but that, without doubt, the Astrologer must be concerned in some such pernicious design. To free himself therefore from these apprehensions, he gave orders that the next morning Tibertus *should be beheaded,* before the prison gate: and thus the *second* prediction was verified, in a manner equally strange, and out of the reach of human foresight to penetrate unassisted by the rules of art. Let us now proceed to the *third* prediction, which really took place not long after.

It is to be observed that though the intelligence of the count proved false, with respect to the persons concerned, which very probably was the effects of his own suspicions, yet his information was right enough in the main; for a conspiracy was actually carrying on, to place the city of Remini into the hands of the pope: and it was accordingly seized by the Duc-de-Valentinois, not long after; but in the confusion which this occasioned, Pandolfo made his escape. He fled for some time from place to place, vigorously pursued by his enemies, and meeting (as is generally the case of tyrants) with very few friends; at length, having endeavoured to sow dissension among his own children, he was abandoned by them, and every one else; inasmuch, that falling ill of a languishing disease at *Bologna,* where nobody cared to take him in, he was at last *carried to the hospital, where he dragged out the remainder of his days in penury and pain,* and at last *died there,* as the Astrologer had foretold.

At the birth of Louis XIV. the king of France, the gentlemen of the Royal Academy of Inscriptions, caused a splendid medal to be struck to commemorate the event. Around this medal was placed the twelve signs of the zodiac, forming the twelve houses of heaven. The planets were placed in the same degrees as they then occupied in the heavens. The following was given as the *interpretation* of the celestial theme. "The sun, who gives perfection to the other planets, is in the mid-heaven; Mars, lord of the ascendant, in reception with Jupiter, the protector of life; Saturn, the enemy of nature, is in his dignities, which makes him less malevolent. The moon is in conjunction with Venus; and Mercury, in his house of predilection to the sun, but out of combustion, giving a superiority of genius in the most difficult enterprises; which his being in square to Mars, is not able to abate." Such was the interpretation of this monarch's *horoscope*, which was figured in the midst of this medal, by a rising sun. The king was placed in the chariot of this glorious planet, of which Ovid has given us a description. This chariot was drawn by four horses, guided by victory. The inscription was in these words: "ORTUS SOLIS GALLICI." "The rising of the Gallic Sun," and the exergue thereof, contained this other inscription. "SEPTEMBRIS QUINTO MINUTIS 38 ANTE MERIDIAN, 1638." This curious medal exhibits a remarkable instance of the high reputation in which Astrology was held at the period of its formation. Neither were the *predictions* of the Astrologers, relative to the celebrity of the future "Grand Monarque" unfulfilled, as history is sufficient to prove.

In the reign of the *Stuarts*, we have many striking accounts, of remarkable predictions and celebrated Astrologers; but the chief amongst these (and indeed in the History of England) was the renowned Astrologer *William Lilly*; amongst a series of Astrological Hieroglyphics, relative to the fate of the English nation, and to last for several centuries; Published by him in 1651, were two *immediately succeeding* each other; the *first* of which represented several dead bodies in winding sheets, a church-yard with sextons employed, and cart-loads of dead emptying into the graves. The *second* was a view of London Bridge, on both sides the water, and the city of London in flames. Nothing could have more *unequivocally predicted the Plague and dreadful fire*, (which really succeeded each, other, as did these hieroglyphics) than the above forewarnings. After the *fire*, and when Lilly had for some time retired from business, and lived at Richmond, the House of Commons sent him an order to attend at their bar; when appearing, the speaker informed him, that "as he had fifteen years before *predicted* the Plague and dreadful fire, the House wished to ask him, if he could give any intelligence concerning the causes or authors thereof?" Lilly answered, "that the House might readily believe, that having predicted it, he had spared no pains to investigate the cause, but that all his endeavours had been ineffectual; from whence he was led to attribute the conflagration, to the immediate finger of God." It is singular, that what this profound Astrologer was unable to discover, *every one else has failed in*, even the usual lights which the revolution of ages generally throw on subjects which, at the period of their *transaction*, may be enveloped in casual gloom, in this instance have totally failed to give any real information as to the actual perpetrators of the above calamity.

No less singular was this distinguished Astrologer's presage respecting Charles I. In a volume of "Lilly's Astrology" purchased at the sale of the Duke of Marlborough's library, there is the following curious note. "The immediate use which Charles I. made of one thousand pounds, which was sent to him at Hampton Court, was to Consult Lilly the Astrologer." "*I advised him*," says the sage, "*to travel eastward, whereas he travelled westward, and all the world knows the consequence.*"

The *death* of William, earl of Pembroke, was foretold by lady Davy's, *to happen on his birth day* in the year 1630 (which is mentioned in Rushworth's collections). When evening came, the earl cheerfully took notice "how well he was" saying "he would for lady Davy's sake, never trust a female prophetess again." He was notwithstanding found *dead in his bed* next morning!

In still more recent times, we have the instance of a remarkable prediction relative to the late fallen emperor NAPOLEON, by a celebrated French Astrologer. Observing that in Napoleon's horoscope "the planet Saturn was in the house of honor, he declared, without hesitation, that "at the moment when the *meridian* altitude of his power should be obtained: from *that* period he should meet with a *decline*, as rapid as his elevation and be finally *deserted* by his friends." After the fall of Napoleon, this circumstance was noticed publicly in the French journals. And if Napoleon's horoscope *were* correct, the above configuration of the "evil orb" was quite sufficient to authorise the aforesaid prediction, on the most rational grounds.

Numerous other instances are on record, which we could readily adduce in support of the astonishing verity of this art, in judicious hands , but let those suffice. The *Sacred Scriptures* abound with the most beautiful imagery, derived from the heavenly host; thus we are told by the inspired writers that "they fought from heaven, *the stars in their courses fought against Sisera.*" Again, "so let all thine enemies perish; but let them that love him, *be as the sun, when he goeth forth of his might:*" and according to the most ancient and approved Astrology, "the person who shall have the *sun for his significator,* well dignified, will be invincible in battle." In another place, the sacred writer declares, "the *sun* shall not smite thee *by day,* nor the *moon by night.*" which plainly refers to the office of *Hyleg,* or what is termed by Astrologers, "the Lord of life," which is always chosen from "the sun by day, and the moon by night" Also it is declared, that *"to every thing there is a season, and a time to every purpose under heaven,"* &c. which plainly relates to the doctrine of *"Astrological Elections,"* or the choice of appropriate "times and seasons," for the most important purposes; wherein it is observed, that "there are times so peculiarly propitious to the spirit of enterprise, that if a man were to go out to battle, although assisted by a comparatively small force, yet he shall obtain the victory; while there are other times, when with a mighty army, more completely equipped, instead of laurels, he shall acquire nothing but disappointment and disgrace." The sacred writers also speak of the "sweet influences of the Pleïades," and the "bands of Orion." In short, wherever we search, whether amongst sacred or profane historians, numerous instances are to be found, which set forth the astonishing presages of this formerly resplendent science; which even in the ruins that time and the revolutions of public opinion have brought upon it, is grand and magnificent, and like the starry host, from which its principles are derived, continues wherever its stupendous footsteps are traced, to soar above all other arts, even by the lofty and dignified nature of its pretensions; but when these pretensions are backed by truth, and demonstrated by the light of philosophic research, it may be asserted, without fear of contradiction, that there exists not a science more truly sublime, or more generally interesting, than the *celestial science of the stars.*

The Mystic Signatures.
OF THE SEVEN PLANETS;
AN EXTRACT FROM AN HIGHLY CURIOUS AND ANCIENT ORIGINAL MANUSCRIPT.

Communicated by Philadelphus.

"THE heaven, stars, and planets, cause no evil, neither were we corrupted and tempted by them, but by parents, from whom by a natural induction of blood and inheritance, we all derive a corrupt will, which causeth in us many unlawful desires and their consequences; the fountain and cause whereof is, a corrupt will, for every planet in its own property is good, and communicates nothing to us but what is good, but our will being corrupt, makes a bad use of that which is good in itself; as for example:— *fire* is good, and so necessary, that we cannot live without it; but he who is corrupt in his will, may set his neighbour's house on fire with it, *and so it is of the planets,* as it is manifested in their order."

Saturn.

♄ in his property is contemplative, and conduceth to all *secret wisdom and deep science,* in which respect he is uppermost, like the head over the body, for contemplation always goes before action; wherefore Saturn having the *contemplative* property, is placed above the other planets whose properties are only active. The property of Saturn stirs up the contemplative faculty of man, and kindles in him a desire to know the mysteries of God and nature, and this is done accordingly, if the soul be good; but if the unlawful appetite of the fiery essence prevail, then it seeks not the mysteries from God and nature, for it knoweth that a good life is required, and that wisdom cometh from God, so that it despaireth to obtain the mysteries from God; and being unwilling to forsake sinful appetites, it endeavours to obtain the knowledge of the mysteries by unlawful means, and so makes a bad use of the magical desire which was kindled in him by the saturnial property; for he runs to the devil, studies witchcraft, and all forbidden arts, to gain thereby a familiarity with wicked spirits, and knowing that the devil will not call upon him for amendment of life, but will, as he hopeth, put him in possession of these mysteries, and suffer him to continue in his wicked and vain hopes, flying from God because he is good, seeking after the devil, who in the end will deceive him in his hopes, and destroy his soul.

Jupiter.

♃ among the planets hath *a goodly splendor*, and lively sprightly light; a certain joy, for the contemplative melancholy of Saturn, breaks out in Jupiter into action, which causeth in him flashing rejoicing lights, with a quick brightness and shining. This cannot be better expressed, than by a wise contemplative person, who being desirous of wisdom and secret knowledge, seeks it with a kind of melancholy contemplative look, if we consider only his outward appearance, for so far he is truly saturnine, so as we judge him sad, when indeed he is only serious; and although his countenance be heavy, yet his heart is pleasant inwardly, and this is the right saturnine property. But when the wise man, after much melancholy and contemplation, hath found out the secret he sought for, then he falls with great joy from contemplation to action, and then the pleasure that was only inwardly, appears outwardly on his face; for the color ♃ (tin) is bright and lively, though his outward appearance be dark and cloudy, so that Jupiter is nothing but the centre of ♄ (lead) manifested; for in Jupiter, which is the next planet under Saturn, the contemplative influence begins to be active, which causeth such a bright light, and such a lively stirring brightness in Jupiter, for he is the first active planet wherein the joy of the contemplative faculty is manifested, which it sets forward for action, and descends from Saturn to Jupiter. ♃ then, as we have said, is the first *active* planet, for in him, that which first begins to break out into action was formerly conceived in Saturn, even as the thoughts which are silently concealed in the heart, are actually and audibly manifested in the mouth, where the very thought begins to break out into action, in the voice, in articulate formed sounds and words: not without reason, therefore, did the wise men attribute to *Saturn* all scholars and philosophers, as also all priests and hermits, all melancholy and reserved persons, who love a solitary and retired life, and who are always full of thoughts, and are more disposed to contemplation than to action. On the contrary, to *Jupiter* all statesmen, magistrates, and tradesmen, who use their heads more than their hearts, and who are always busied in outward mechanical actions, and not in the inward profound speculations of the mind; and truly all professed mechanical arts were found out first by the speculation of the mind, for they are but the inventions of contemplative spirits, so that the statesman receives his politics from the philosopher, the one finding, and the other executing, so that contemplation still *precedes* action, as Saturn is before Jupiter in the heavens, even as thoughts are conceived in the mind prior to the action of speech. Again, who can see the leaves and flowers that are in the tree; certainly no man, but when the tree hath put them forth, then they are manifest to all men; even so our thoughts, while they are in the heart, appear to none but God and our own souls; but when manifested by words or actions, they are known to all, *the heart is the forge of the saturnine properties wherein the thoughts rise and are formed*, and such as the thoughts are, such are the actions; therefore if the saturnine properties be good, those of Jupiter must be the same, the saturnine being the source of all. Therefore, a wicked man being of the saturnine or melancholy nature, he is exceedingly wicked and dangerous.

Mars.

♂ signifies the fiery principle. This is worthy of our observation, that among the planets the Sun signifies the pure principle of light, and Mars the principle of fire, whence observe that Mars is exalted above the Sun in the great world, which shows to us the corrupt complexion of nature at present and of man: also, the fire in both being placed *above* the light, the principle of wrath being more predominant than the principle of love; thus hath God portrayed, as we may say, the fall of man, in the great world out of which he was taken, and in which, as in a glass, he may see his present and future state.

Sun.

We are now come to the noblest of all the planets, the ☉; we will begin with the metal attributed to that planet, which is *gold,* the most perfect body under the Sun, for there is no superfluidity in it, nor any inequality of elements, for it consists of most pure elements, equally proportioned by nature, and by a long concoction of many years; it is most perfectly fixed, and digested into the best temperature that can be, in which respect it is *incorruptible,* for neither fire nor water can destroy it, nor can length of days waste or alter it, nor can the earth ever rust it; but amidst all these inferior elements, which corrupt all other bodies, *gold remains invincible for ever*; a wonderful thing indeed, that a body born in a corruptible place in the earth, should be incorruptible, contrary to the nature of the parents. This made the wise men conclude, that there was in the centre of the elements, a certain incorruptible hidden substance or seed, out of which gold was made; and in the search or inquisition after this, they labored much, but they chiefly sought it in gold, because in gold it was most perfectly digested. It has been asked, why and wherefore all the world have unanimously admired gold, and made it the price of all other commodities; how came they to agree in this point, when they disagree in all others, more or less? for my part, the scriptures have given me the amplest satisfaction on this head; and since I have already entered into this discourse, I shall, in as few words as I can, lay down my judgment concerning it. We read, in Genesis, that the use of metals were known to man, even in the days of Adam, long before the flood; and though the scriptures mention no metals but brass and iron, yet may we from thence conclude, that gold and silver were not then known, but rather infer the contrary, for gold and silver are easily melted out of their ore, but iron and brass not without difficulty and labor; wherefore, if they knew that which was most difficult, consequently they were no strangers to that of easy access. Now in the days of Adam and Tubal Cain, there were but few men in the world, so that there was more riches than they could possess; nor need they to have looked for metals to exchange with, for all was in common without purchase. It is plain then, that the first use that man made of gold was not to traffic with; let us then enquire, what it was that made gold so precious, and so much admired. Certainly the world is in the most gross ignorance, inasmuch as there is not one who can tell what gold is good for; did nature make it only to look at, and to pass from one hand to another? Can it only be seen and felt, and is there no other use for it? Moses took more than ordinary notice of it, and knew its nature, and what it was good for; otherwise he had not been so curious, as so particularly to mention and praise it, as he has in Genesis, where speaking of the four rivers that came out of Eden, says "the name of the first is Pison, and is that which encompasses the land of Havilah, where there is gold, and the gold of that land is good." I ask now those ignorant enemies of divine and natural magic, if Moses *was* skilled in metals or not; if he was, and being so great and pious a man, how dare they condemn that which teaches the knowledge of metals: if they say he was *not* skilled, his own writings will condemn them, for in this text, he not only says that gold is there, but that likewise the gold of that land is good; for my own part, I could wish he had said what it was good for, and wherein the goodness consisted; but surely as to the skill of Moses, the scriptures bear him witness, that *he was skilled in all the learning of the Egyptians;* but if we will prove the skill of Moses out of his own practice, we need go no further than the golden calf, which by his skill he calcined and burnt to powder, and sprinkling it with water, gave it the Israelites to drink, and so made an *aurum potabile*. Surely gold is good for health, and was first used for that purpose, which made it so precious, though that use is not known in our days, yet we have been so fortunate as to see gold dissolved in certain water, and that water, together with the gold in a long decoction, congealed into little red stones like rubies, which when re-dissolved, and exalted by several multiplications, will show us what gold is good for, and why the first fathers of the world did so much esteem it, which continues to be highly valued to this day, though the principle cause why it was so esteemed originally, is not now known to the usurers. Gold by Ante-Diluvians was used for physic, and not for traffic; and its use as a medicine made it much desired and sought after, inasmuch, as it was not only necessary for the prolongation, but also preservation of life; for many learned and religious persons are of opinion, *that Adam and the other patriarchs who lived before the flood, did excel in this kind of knowledge, and prolonged their lives many hundred years, with the use of this medicine*, whose virtues all men admire, and place more esteem on it than on any other thing; and though the knowledge of the use and *virtues* of gold was lost in process of time, yet the custom of admiring and valuing it has remained, so that gold came to be accounted the most precious of *all* substances, and at last was appointed to be the price of all commodities, and to pass in exchange for all necessaries whatsoever. I shall not now forbear to lay down the reasons which made Adam seek for a medicine in gold; though we have no books written by Adam out of which we may take these reasons, yet we have still the book of created nature, which was the only book Adam had to use, and therein is as much to be seen now as in the days of Adam, and those reasons which Adam therein saw, the same do we now see. Before the fall of Adam the elements of earth and water were much purer than they are now, and the influences that descended from Heaven were more abundant and more vigorous than they have been since; thus the fruits that were in paradise, and on which Adam fed, were without doubt of an heavenly complexion, there being in them such an abundance of light and brightness that they shone like the Sun and Moon, by whose influence they were produced; yea, even the ancient poets in their allegories tell us of the *golden age*, &c., by which pictures they mean nothing else but the great fertility before the fall, and without doubt the waters and dews *then* were considerably more luxurious and bright than they are now, from having much more of the heavenly influence and light in them, so that the fruits of paradise being nourished with those bright, luxurious, and shining dews, *did glisten and sparkle like the stars of heaven*; for at that time man was not at variance with his God, wherefore God did most lovingly pour down his blessings in a much greater degree than the earth now does or would receive. But when man transgressed, he became *separated* from his god, and immediately the earth wwas cursed, and as the rabbins express it, the upper springs of heavenly fountains were stopped, so that the stars did not so abundantly shed down *the spirit of life* as they did before, for Adam was cast out of God's paradise (the Sun) to dwell (as a banished man) on the cursed earth, and to eat the cursed bitter fruits thereof, and we must naturally conceive that the remembrance of the paradise and the heavenly glittering fruits therein, was most fresh in Adam's memory, even as the remembrance of our country will remain to a banished man. When therefore, he was constrained to make use of the corruptible fruits of the accursed earth, he must needs see the difference between them and the fruits of paradise, for the paradisiacal light and glory was not in them; this recollection we may reasonably conclude made Adam and his posterity, who were instructed by him, to search dilligently; if any amongst the fruits and productions of the earth retained their primitive paradisiacal splendor; but when they had done all they could, none such were to be found in all the vegetable kingdom; colors there were, in flowers and fruits, but fading and corruptible, there was no durable light nor shining lustre in them; at last they came to search the mineral kingdom, but God had removed that from their eyes, it was locked up like a treasure in the bowels of the earth, and they must dig for it, and with much labor they find it. Then saw they a resemblance to the first paradisiacal splendor, and that most durable and incorruptible, having in some measure the primitive glory of paradise; *for in gold the fire of heavenly complextion aboundeth, and in silver the light*, and the like appearance is in all the inferior metals, though not in the same purity. They also saw it sparkling in precious stones, as diamonds, rubies, &c. which made them respect them as certain relics of paradise. But as gold and silver could be neither eat nor drank, they therefore labored much to *extract the light and tincture out of them, that they might feed on them sa on heavenly paradisiacal food or essences*. This transcendant art they received from God, and not by any human industry, God having revealed it to them as a means to prolong life, and by which they lived many hundred years, through the will and providence of God. Therefore in the first and early times, gold was respected by wise men for its *medicinal* qualities (and it is for these ends all *true* alchemystical philosophers labor). I cannot pass by a tradition of Pliny, who mentions that the broth of a hen destroys gold, if it be boiled in it, and some physicians have affirmed the same on their own experience, whereupon they prescribe that decoction as a prime restorative in physic.

The scripture tells us, that God has placed his tabernacle *in the Sun*, [the original paradise of Adam] and truly there is more of the power and majesty of God manifested in the Sun, than in any other created body, if we consider only the parts of the great world; for we see that when the *Sun* withdraws from us in the winter time, the *life* also withdraws with it, and that many living creatures, as well as the herbs, suffer for that time, a kind of death. Not in vain then did the magi affirm, that the *anima mundi*, or soul of the world, was principally resident in the Sun; for if it be true that where there is life, there must be heat, which no man can deny, then the life of the world must needs be from whence the heat arises, and questionless all the heat of this world is derived from the Sun, and communicated to all other parts, especially to the inferior elements; and likewise in the heavens, where we observe the *Moon* suffers her monthly change, agony, and as it were death, by the absence of the Sun from her, for darkness totally possesses her, and she quite loses her light, and so continues until the Sun *again*, who with his excellent brightness and abundance of light illuminates the Moon, *filling her with new light*; for, from conjunction with the Sun, she appears red and not unlike the color of heated iron, the Sun having penetrated her whole substance and infused his tincture into her.

The *Sun* then stirs up the sadness of ♄, and causes an active pleasant complexion, which otherwise, without the mixture of the Sun would be a black melancholy, which is a dangerous complexion; but where Sol and Saturn unite, then there is the true philosophical genius. *Sol* therefore awakens the vital spirits, and *in all his operations resembles God, for as God hath the keys of life and death in his hand, and by his sole power kills and restores: so likewise doth the Sun bear a resemblance*; for the Almighty does, as it were, look into this world through the Sun, [the local residence of the glorified humanity of Jesus Christ and the original Paradise,] and communicates his goodness by the light that is measured and proportioned to our capacities, who are not able to look on his inexhaustible light, for "no man can see him and live."

Venus.

♀ In the heavens is the next beneath the Sun, she is the *day star* and rises with him, and likewise she is the *evening star* and setteth with the Sun. Life is manifested in Sol and is shed into all parts of the world, as the life is diffused into all parts of the body. But the joy and pleasure which ariseth from the life is manifested in ♀, which makes her light more cheerly and quick than any other stars or planets, for there is in her light *such a freshness, and liveliness, as is beyond expression;* hence the Astrologers have acknowledged her the lady of love, and have made her supreme over all our pleasures.

Mercury.

☿ In the heavens representeth the subtile vital spirit, and is therefore seldom separated from the Sun any great distance, keeping always in his beams, *even as the vital spirit accompanieth the soul.*

Luna.

☽ In the heavens *signifies the sensual soul*, for though the Moon puts on the image of the Sun and is full of light, and hath a true heavenly complexion, yet by and by she loses all her light, becomes dark, and puts on the image of the Earth; even so doth the animal soul, for one while she adheres to the image of God and is full of heavenly thoughts and desires, and in an instant she adheres to the flesh and is full of sinful affections; and thus she falls and rises, rises and falls again, in a perpetual course of revolution, so that the most righteous here on earth are subject to these failings, for they wax and wane, in evil and good dispositions; though they are the children of the light, yet have they their spots and eclipses, which makes the Scriptures describe the church triumphant, *as a woman that hath the Moon under her feet*, for, in that glorious church in heaven, we shall be no more subject to such inconstancy; but shall trample the Moon under our feet, and be like the Sun, penetrated through and through with light, splendor, glory, and majesty; and consequently free from every degree of darkness.

FINIS.

Part Two:
Divination

GEOMANCY;

OR, THE ART OF FORETELLING EVENTS BY LOTS OR POINTS.

No. I.

This curious art was formerly in high repute; being a favourite science among the monks and friars of the middle ages; who, immured in the solitary gloom of their abbeys and monasteries, stood in need of some peculiar invention, that combined the then universal desire for unveiling futurity, with a recreation at once pleasant and amusing. Such advantages were speedily discovered in the practice of Geomancy; added to which, *where the inquirer is sincere in his wishes*, the universal sympathy so prevalent throughout all nature, (and which not even the profoundest philosopher of the present day can deny or satisfactorily explain, except by admitting occult principles,) will seldom fail, to procure him a rational and true answer.

The art or science of Geomancy consists of two parts, which, although distinct in a manner from each other, are nevertheless founded on, and produced by, the same sympathetic impulse. The first is termed *Simple* Geomancy; and consists in judging of future events by the nature and properties of the sixteen figures or emblems, without combination, by house, place, or aspect. The other is termed *Compound*; as it teaches the method of judging the correlative contingencies of each question by means of aspects, houses, and emblematical movements. This latter part is far more difficult than the former; and I shall therefore *first* initiate my readers into the practice of the former, or Simple Geomancy; as it cannot fail to afford many an hour's *rational* amusement.

I need scarcely observe, that books on this subject are so extremely rare as seldom to be met with at *any* price.

The method of working the questions in Geomancy consists in marking down with pen, pencil, or any other instrument, upon paper, slate, or any legible material, a certain number of points, or dots, leaving the precise number to chance; and all the time the inquirer is so doing, his thoughts must dwell *earnestly* upon the matter upon which he wishes to be informed, with a fervent wish (devoid of doubting as much as possible) to have a correct and true answer.

The ancients affirmed, that in these cases an invisible spirit, or planetary angel, uniformly directed the hand of the querist, so to form the mystic points as to obtain the desired resolution of his query: but whether or not this may be the case, it is quite certain that the thoughts and earnest desires of the mind have a wonderful control over the nerves, muscles, and pulsations of the body. This is seen plainly in the case of timid, weak, and *nervous* persons, who, when writing letters, or sentences where their *feelings* are more than usually wrought upon, never fail to exhibit *signs* of such mental irritation in their hand-writing. But this fact, which is, I believe, well known to every one, is more clearly demonstrated by the following *simple but curious experiment*, the truth of which I can avouch from my own experience.

Sling a shilling or sixpence at the end of a piece of thread, by means of a loop, or tie a ring thereto; then, resting your elbow upon a table, hold tightly the other end of the thread *between your forefinger and thumb*, taking care that the thread passes across the ball of the thumb (where the pulse lies), and thus suspend the shilling or ring in an *empty* goblet. Observe to keep your hand as steady as possible, or otherwise it is useless to attempt the experiment.

When the shilling or ring is properly suspended, you will find it will for a moment be stationary. It will then, *of its own accord, and without the least agency from the person holding it,* vibrate like the pendulum of a clock, from side to side of the glass; and, after a few seconds, *it will strike the hour nearest to the time of day or night*. For instance, if the time be twenty-five minutes past six o'clock, it will strike six; if thirty-five minutes past, it will strike seven, and so on of any other hour. *It will also strike any number you think of;* which latter property arises solely from the pulsation of the thumb, communicating, by an occult principle, the desires of the mind to the nervous system. But to what cause its striking the precise hour is to be traced, as the author of "Rational Recreations" observes, "remains unexplained; for it is no less astonishing than true, that when it has struck the proper number, its vibration ceases, it acquires a kind of rotary motion, and at last becomes stationary as before."

NAMES OF THE SIXTEEN FIGURES OF GEOMANCY

- Acquisitio
- Amissio
- Rubeus
- Albus
- Letitia
- Tristitia
- Conjunctio
- Carcer
- Caput
- Cauda
- Fortuna Major
- Fortuna Minor
- Puella
- Puer
- Via
- Populus

GEOMANCY.
No. 2.

TO CAST A FIGURE OF THE TRIPLICITIES, ACCORDING TO SIMPLE GEOMANCY.

It has been before observed (page [53]), that the method made use of in working the Schemes of Geomancy, was to mark down a certain number of points or dots, casually, without counting the number, and then joining them by the rules of art into a Scheme, or *Figure*, whence the answers were readily obtained.

Such *is* the process; but a very curious, and, indeed, *ancient*, manuscript now before me gives the following formula for divining, which will probably be read with interest, as affording a partial view of the singular hold which superstition had upon the customs, and even amusements, of former times.

Extract from an ancient Manuscript of the Eleventh Century.

"The Seven Planets are called *the Kings of the World*; and every one of these may do in his hemisphere as an emperor in his empire, or a prince in his kingdom. They are termed by some of the wisest of men, Seven Candlesticks of Light and of life, and are as seven quick spirits, whereunto all living things and all terrestrial affairs are subject.

"Now to *divine* by their influences is the scope of our doctrine, even by the art called Geomancy, which is none other but the cogitation of the heart of the asker, joined to the earnest desire of *the will to know* the thing or matter uncertain and dark, which nevertheless is contained in the arcanum, or hidden cabinet of nature, and governed by the secrets of fortune.

"This art, curious in its method, and of diverse efficacy, is attainable by him alone who will, amidst thorny paths and rugged journeys, guide his footsteps aright; for doubtless divers ways lead to the selfsame end. But know, O man!

whoever thou art, that shall inquire into these hidden mysteries, that thou must forbear to consult the heavenly oracles, or to cast thy divining points, in a cloudy, windy, or rainy season; or when the heavens above thee are stricken with thunder; or when the lightnings glare amidst thy path; for thou art governed by an invisible demon who wills thy answer, and will guide thy trembling fingers to cast thy figure rightly. So that what to thee may seem the sport and pastime of very chance, is the work of an unseen power. Therefore, mark well, else the mighty spirits of the earth, who rule thy destiny, will be to thee as deceivers, and even as the false and lying spirits recorded in holy writ.

"Thou shalt therefore cast thy divining points in earth (thy fellow clay) tempered according to the high and hidden mysteries of the seven wandering fires of heaven, which the vulgar call planets, or stars. Thou shalt take clean earth, in the manner of sand, *mingled with the dews of the night, and the rain of the clouds that shall fall during the full of the moon, commixed in equal portions for the space of seven days,* under the celestial signs or reigning constellations, or otherwise in the lordship of the hours of the presiding planets; and then shalt thou mingle the whole mass together, to the intent that by their commixion the universal effect may be the better known, and the end thereof prophesied.

"Choose, therefore, a clear and goodly season, bright and fair, and neither dark, windy, nor rainy—and fear not, but rest assured thou shalt be satisfied.

"Moreover, shouldest thou make use of the magical suffumigations of the heavenly orbs, thou shalt make glad (by sympathy) the spirits of the air. They are these;—viz. mastic, cinnamon, frankincense, musk, the wood of aloes, coriandrum, violets, saunders, and saffron. Commix and ignite these in due and just proportions; and then mayest thou proceed to consult thy future lot. Therefore, cast aside all unbelief and all vain scoffing, for the Fathers of the

Church, and the wise and holy men of all ages, have exercised these matters, —and truth is in them, *if thou searchest rightly.*"

Happily for the reader, there is not the least occasion for the superstitious observance contained in the foregoing ceremonial, or he might grope on in darkness and mystery, till utterly bewildered in the labyrinth of error. It is quite sufficient, and has equally the same effect, to cast the points upon slate or paper, or with pen or pencil, as on the earth.

The following are therefore

The First Steps of the Figure.

When the asker or inquirer has thought earnestly upon the subject or matter of which he inquires, let him mark down *sixteen* lines of dots, marks, or points, without counting them, so that at the least there be not less than twelve points in each line, —which done, let him join the points or marks in each line together, two and two; and if the number of points in the line be even, which is if they will all join together, let him mark down at the end of the line two dots, ciphers, or marks; but if the number of points in the line be odd, which is when one remains, after they are joined by two and two, then let him write down but one point. Every four lines form one Geomantic figure, as follows:—

```
|—| |—| |—| |—| |—| |—| |—| |—| |—|   First Figure.
|—| |—| |—| |—| |—| |—| |                ● ●
|—| |—| |—| |—| |—| |—| |—| |—|           ●
|—| |—| |—| |—| |—| |—| |                ● ●
                                            ●

|—| |—| |—| |—| |—| |—| |—| |—| |—|   Second Figure.
|—| |—| |—| |—| |—| |—| |—| |             ● ●
|—| |—| |—| |—| |—| |—| |—| |—| |         ●
|—| |—| |—| |—| |—| |—| |                  ●
                                            ●
```

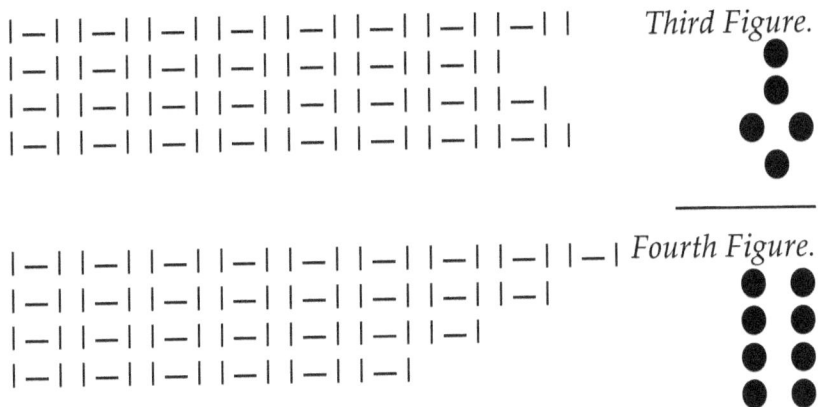

To exemplify and explain the *first steps*, it will be seen, by counting the points in line the first, that the number of points are twenty, and *even*, consequently they admit of being joined together two and two; but in the second line the number of points are but thirteen, and consequently being *odd*, cannot be all joined but by leaving one point unjoined to the rest. The same rules are observed in the other lines, which produces the four first steps of the figure; and in placing them they must be read from right to left, as underneath.

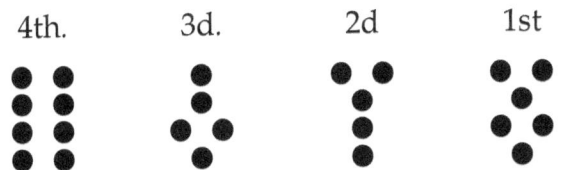

In all cases they are placed in the same manner.

The next process is to form *four* other figures from out of the first four, which is done by taking the number of points in the separate lines of each figure; thus, in the figure

Figure 5.

No. 1, the points in the first line are *two*, placed thus
In No. 2, the points in the first line are also *two*, placed thus
In No. 3 there is but *one* point, thus
In No. 4 there are again *two*, thus

Giving this figure, No. 5.

Figure the 6th is found the same way, by taking the odd or even points in the *second* line of the figures, thus:—

Figure 6.

In the second line of No. 1 is an odd point, thus
In the second line of No. 2 is also an odd point
In the second line of No. 3 is also an odd point
In the second line of No. 4 are two points, thus

Giving this figure, No. 6.

Figure the 7th is also found the same way; thus

Figure 7.

In the *third* line of No. 1, there are two points, thus
In the third line of No. 2, one point, thus
In the third line of No. 3, two points, thus
In the third line of No. 4, also two points, thus

Part Two: Divination

Giving this figure, No. 7.

Figure the 8th is formed thus, the same way. *Figure 8.*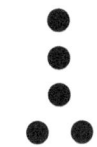

In the fourth line of No. 1, one point
In the fourth line of No. 2, one point
In the fourth line of No. 3, one point
In the fourth line of No. 4, two points

Giving this figure, No. 8.

The next step is to place the whole in order from right to left, as under.

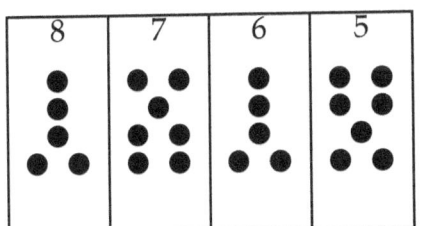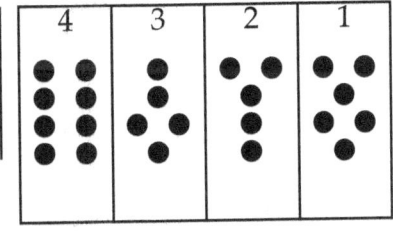

Next, a triangle is formed out of each, by joining together the 1st and 2d, the 3d and 4th, the 5th and 6th, and the 7th and 8th figures thus, according as the points in each are odd or even.

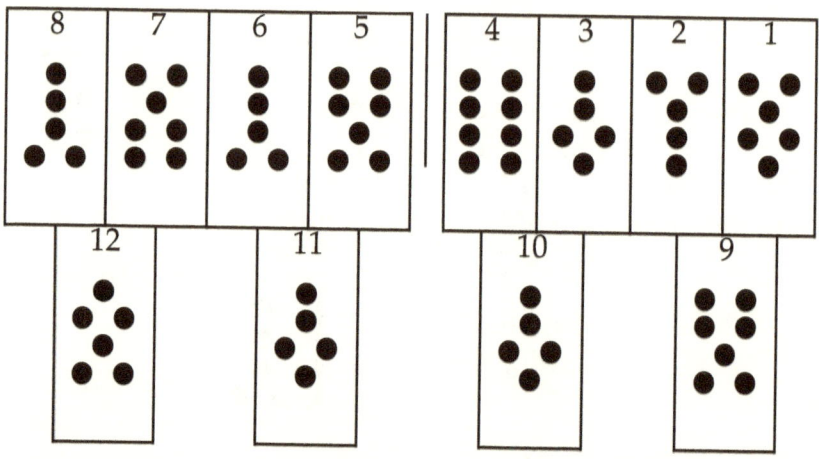

By this means, an additional four figures. Nos. 9, 10, 11, and 12, are gained, after which they are again to be joined together triangularly, as 9 and 10, and 11 and 12, thus:

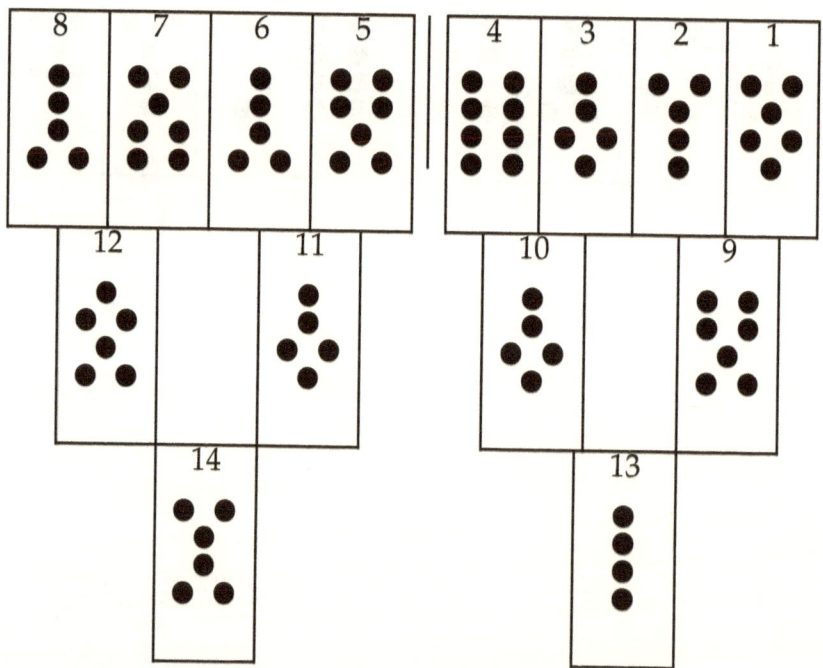

And lastly. No. 13 and 14 are joined in like manner together thus; No. 13 has one mark and odd in the first line, and No. 14 two.

Figure 15.

The number *three* is *odd*, marked thus
In the second line of each, *two* points, *even*
In the third line of each, *two*, also even
In the fourth line of each, *three*, odd

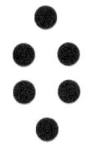

The whole process is exemplified in the complete figure, which is here given

Example 1.

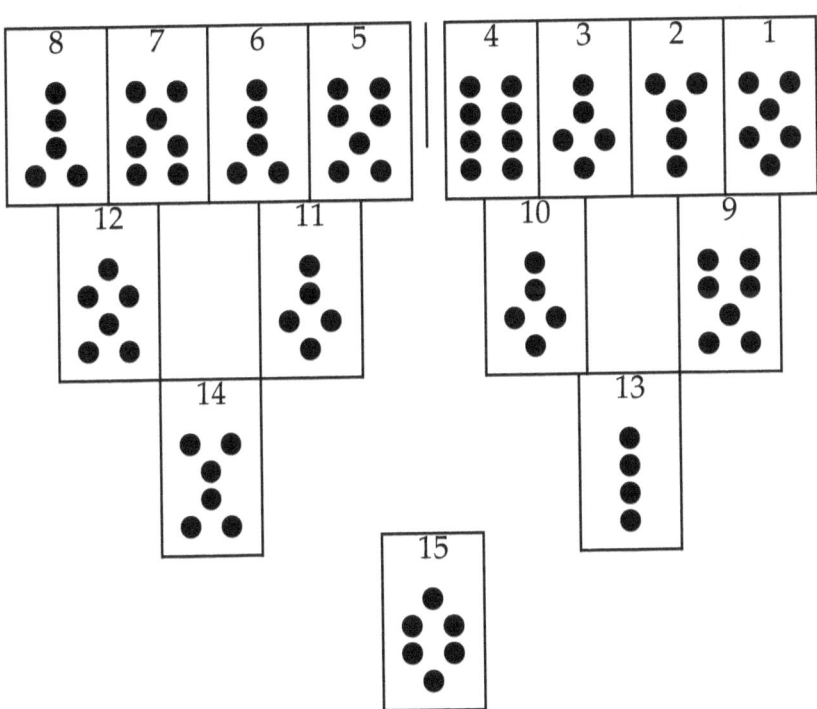

In order, however, to render the reader *perfect* in casting his figures, I shall subjoin one more example at large.

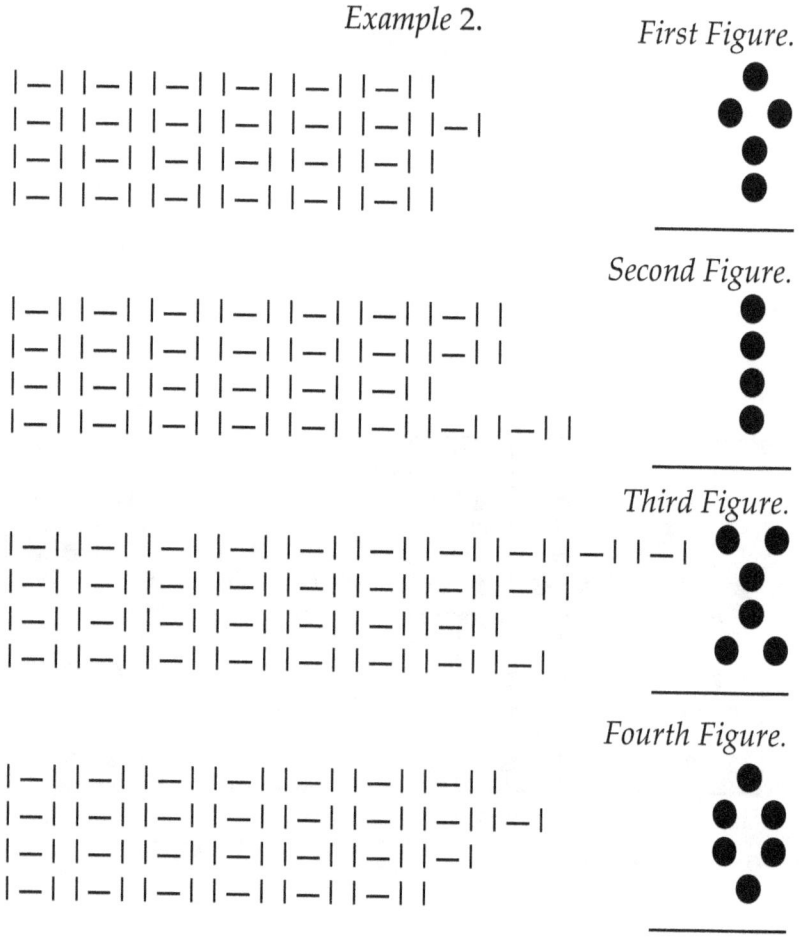

Part Two: Divination

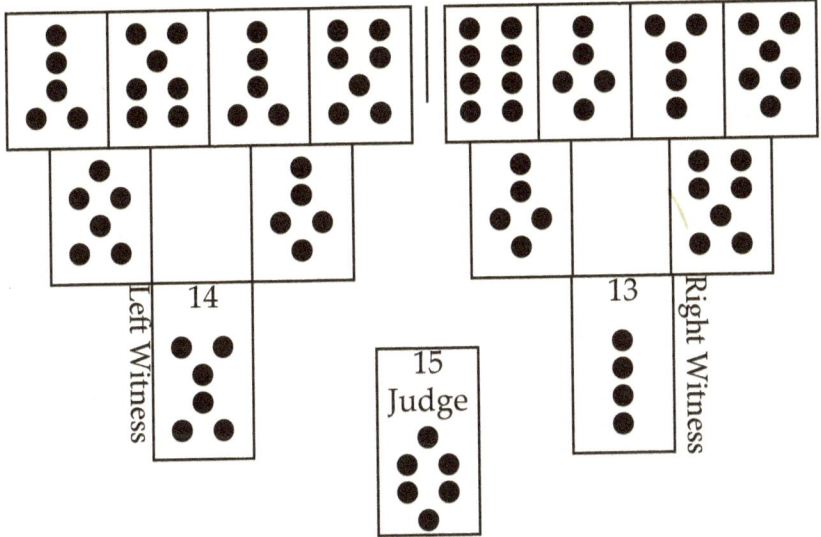

In resolving questions by *simple* Geomancy, it is the *three last figures alone*, No. 13, 14, and 15, which are used in giving the answers. These are termed

A FIGURE OF TRIPLICITY.

Of these three figures, No. 13 is termed the *Right Witness*, and No. 14 the *Left Witness*; out of these two is drawn the JUDGE of the whole figure, to whom the sentence or answer of the whole question belongs, as will be hereafter shown.

There is a striking peculiarity, or *arithmetical* property, in a scheme of Geomancy thus cast; which is, that only eight out of the sixteen figures can ever be found in the place of the Judge; the latter, therefore, is always formed of *even* points. For it must be observed, that to the first four figures belong the ground-work of the whole; and these must be either odd or even:—if odd, the next four figures will be also odd; and, according to a geometrical axiom, out of two negative qualities comes an affirmative; and, therefore, the *Judge* will be even. Again, if the first four figures are even, the next four figures will be even also, and of course *the Judge will always be even*. Thus, the figures

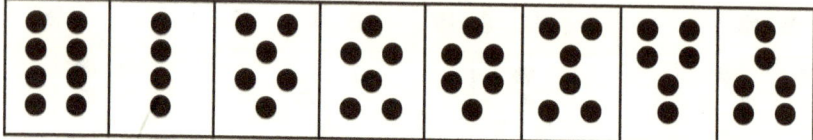

are the only figures which can ever be the Judge, being all of an even number of points; and the figures

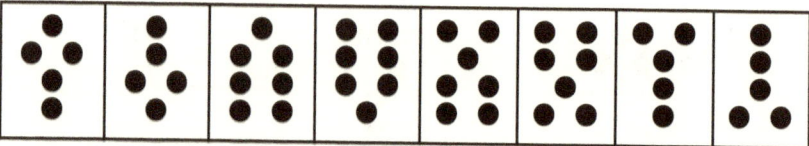

never can be judges, for the reasons before shown.

At first sight, the reader may probably feel inclined to discover many difficulties in the way of casting a figure; but a little practice will render the system familiar, plain, and easy, therefore let him not reject it without a trial. The next paper (No. III) will explain the method of obtaining the answers, in which the reader will at once see the easiness of the method propounded.

GEOMANCY

No. 3.

The method of casting or forming a figure of Geomancy, has been already shown; as also, what is termed, the "Figure of the Triplicities" for the better judging of which, the old authors have left on record certain Tables, which contain the "*Sentence*" of the witnesses and judge; by which, without further trouble, the answer, so far as a negative or affirmative is concerned, may be found without trouble.

It has been also observed, that only eight out of the sixteen figures can ever be judge; yet, as there are two witnesses also to be taken into account, the variations to the answers are 8x16, and therefore equal to 128 in number. In these cases, however, it is of consequence to notice on which side the good or evil figures fall, as *that* gives the variations in the result. Thus, for instance, the Triplicities—

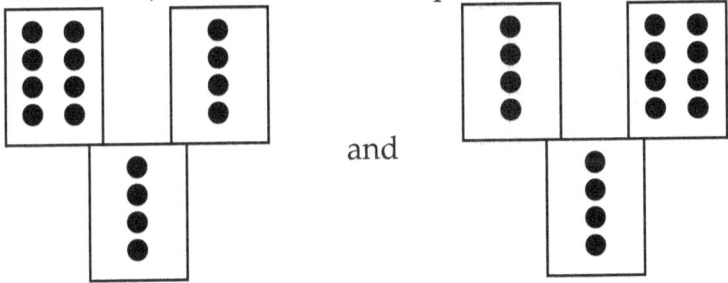

although the judge is the same in each, yet the answers corresponding are different; and so in all other cases whatever.

In order to work by the following Tables, the reader must cut the figure, and refer to the page for the answer to his question: thus, for instance, in the following figure:—

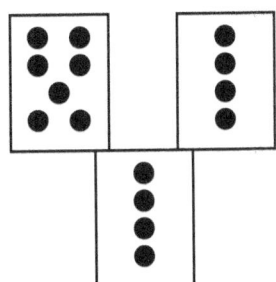

If the question were "of the Length of Life," the answer would be, "*Short Life.*"

If it were of an affair connected with "Money," the answer would be, "*Unfortunate.*"

If it were of "Sickness," it would denote "*Death*" to the Patient, and so on in all other cases; referring to that page of the work which has the required Triplicities. I have only to observe that the following Tables are compiled from an old and curious author, now out of print: the answers are concise, and the explanation simple; which is as much as can be wished.

Verbum sapientis satis. (Bur.)

Example at large of the whole Figure whereby the Judge is obtained.

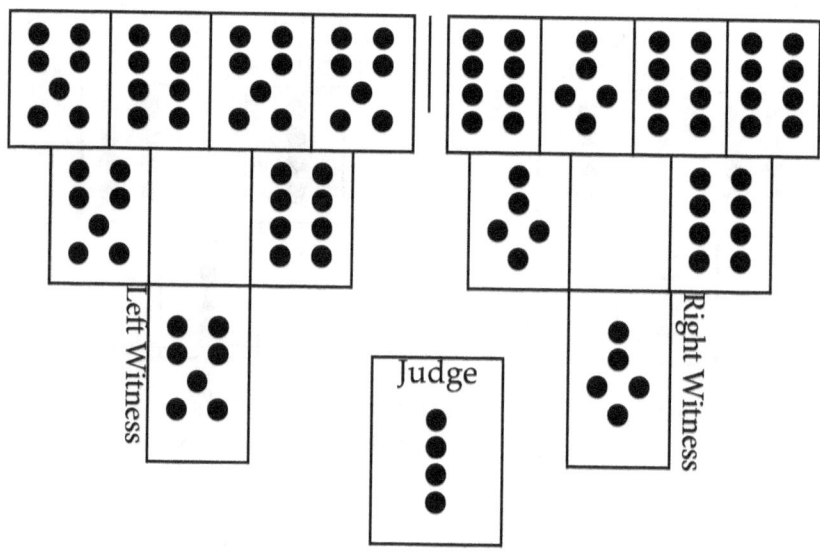

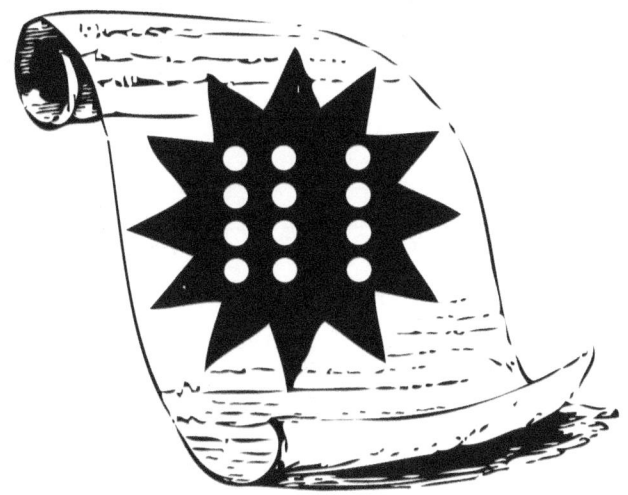

THE SENTENCE
OF
Populus
AND
Via,
AS THE
JUDGE

IN THE QUESTIONS RELATING TO

1. Length of Life,
2. Money or Gain,
3. Honour or Credit,
4. Business,
5. Marriage,
6. Pregnancy,
7. Sickness,
8. Imprisonment,
9. Journeys and
10. Things Lost

Questions.	Answers.	Questions.	Answers.
Life............	*Moderately long.*	Life............	*Moderate.*
Money.........	*Meanly good.*	Money.........	*Evil.*
Honour......	*Meanly good*	Honour......	*Mean.*
Business......	*Fortunate.*	Business......	*Unfortunate.*
Marriage.......	*Good.*	Marriage.......	*Good.*
Pregnancy...	*A Daughter.*	Pregnancy...	*A Son.*
Sickness........	*Dangerous.*	Sickness........	*Health.*
Imprisonment.	*Delivery.*	Imprisonment.	*Quick Release.*
Journey......	*Good by Water.*	Journey......	*Good and quick*
Thing Lost...	*Found.*	Thing Lost...	*Not found.*

Questions.	Answers.	Questions.	Answers.
Life............	*Evil.*	Life............	*Good and Long*
Money.........	*Evil.*	Money.........	*An increase.*
Honour......	*Good.*	Honour......	*Good.*
Business......	*Fortunate.*	Business......	*Good.*
Marriage.......	*Good.*	Marriage.......	*Good.*
Pregnancy...	*A Daughter.*	Pregnancy...	*A Son.*
Sickness........	*Dangerous.*	Sickness........	*Health.*
Imprisonment.	*Long.*	Imprisonment.	*Late out.*
Journey......	*Good by Sea.*	Journey......	*Ends good.*
Thing Lost...	*Not found.*	Thing Lost...	*Found.*

Part Two: Divination

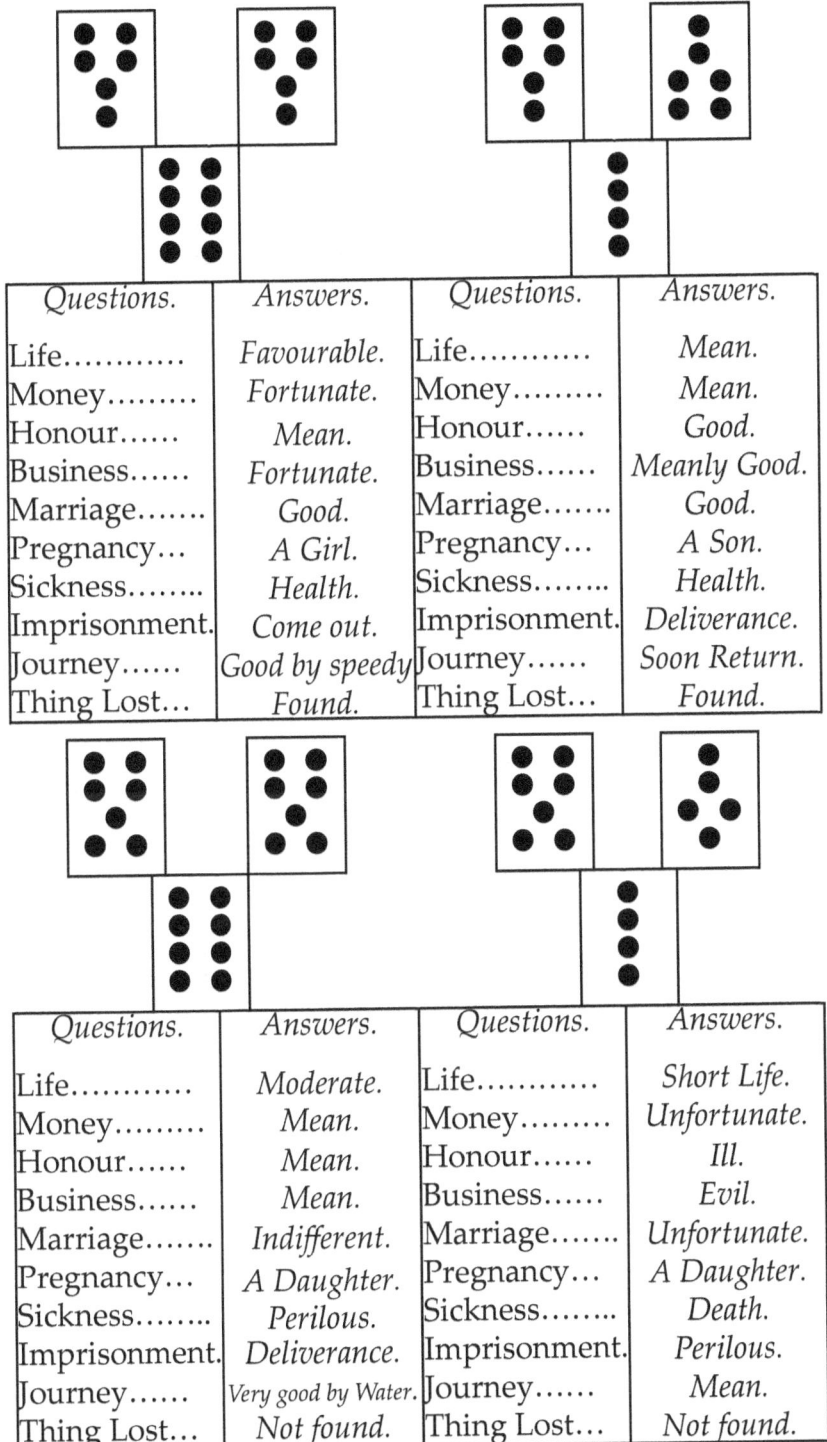

Questions.	Answers.	Questions.	Answers.
Life............	Favourable.	Life............	Mean.
Money.........	Fortunate.	Money.........	Mean.
Honour......	Mean.	Honour......	Good.
Business......	Fortunate.	Business......	Meanly Good.
Marriage.......	Good.	Marriage.......	Good.
Pregnancy...	A Girl.	Pregnancy...	A Son.
Sickness........	Health.	Sickness........	Health.
Imprisonment.	Come out.	Imprisonment.	Deliverance.
Journey......	Good by speedy	Journey......	Soon Return.
Thing Lost...	Found.	Thing Lost...	Found.

Questions.	Answers.	Questions.	Answers.
Life............	Moderate.	Life............	Short Life.
Money.........	Mean.	Money.........	Unfortunate.
Honour......	Mean.	Honour......	Ill.
Business......	Mean.	Business......	Evil.
Marriage.......	Indifferent.	Marriage.......	Unfortunate.
Pregnancy...	A Daughter.	Pregnancy...	A Daughter.
Sickness........	Perilous.	Sickness........	Death.
Imprisonment.	Deliverance.	Imprisonment.	Perilous.
Journey......	Very good by Water.	Journey......	Mean.
Thing Lost...	Not found.	Thing Lost...	Not found.

Questions.	Answers.	Questions.	Answers.
Life............	Very evil.	Life............	Moderate.
Money.........	Unlucky.	Money.........	Meanly Good.
Honour......	Very ill.	Honour......	Mean.
Business......	Unfortunate.	Business......	Indifferent.
Marriage.......	A bad one.	Marriage.......	Prosperous.
Pregnancy...	A Girl.	Pregnancy...	A Daughter.
Sickness........	Perilous.	Sickness........	Long Sick.
Imprisonment.	Death.	Imprisonment.	Soon out.
Journey......	Robbed.	Journey......	Slow.
Thing Lost...	Not found.	Thing Lost...	Found.

Questions.	Answers.	Questions.	Answers.
Life............	Short.	Life............	Very evil
Money.........	Unlucky.	Money.........	Very ill.
Honour......	Evil.	Honour......	Ill.
Business......	Evil.	Business......	Unlucky.
Marriage.......	Jarring.	Marriage.......	Evil.
Pregnancy...	Abortion.	Pregnancy...	Abortion.
Sickness........	Death.	Sickness........	Perilous.
Imprisonment.	Dangerous.	Imprisonment.	Long.
Journey......	Unlucky.	Journey......	Unlucky.
Thing Lost...	Not found.	Thing Lost...	Not found.

Part Two: Divination

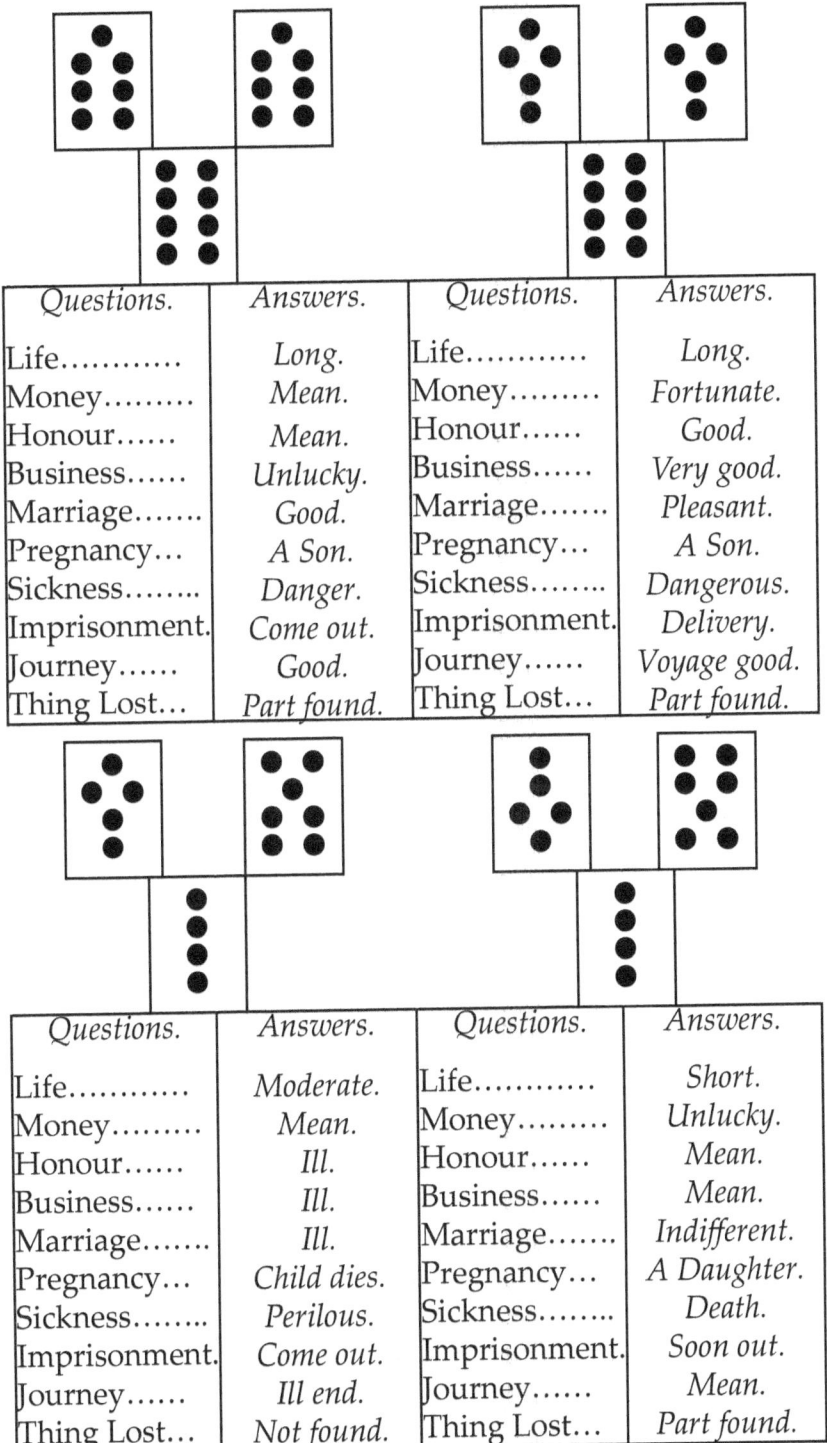

Questions.	Answers.	Questions.	Answers.
Life............	Long.	Life............	Long.
Money.........	Mean.	Money.........	Fortunate.
Honour......	Mean.	Honour......	Good.
Business......	Unlucky.	Business......	Very good.
Marriage.......	Good.	Marriage.......	Pleasant.
Pregnancy...	A Son.	Pregnancy...	A Son.
Sickness........	Danger.	Sickness........	Dangerous.
Imprisonment.	Come out.	Imprisonment.	Delivery.
Journey......	Good.	Journey......	Voyage good.
Thing Lost...	Part found.	Thing Lost...	Part found.

Questions.	Answers.	Questions.	Answers.
Life............	Moderate.	Life............	Short.
Money.........	Mean.	Money.........	Unlucky.
Honour......	Ill.	Honour......	Mean.
Business......	Ill.	Business......	Mean.
Marriage.......	Ill.	Marriage.......	Indifferent.
Pregnancy...	Child dies.	Pregnancy...	A Daughter.
Sickness........	Perilous.	Sickness........	Death.
Imprisonment.	Come out.	Imprisonment.	Soon out.
Journey......	Ill end.	Journey......	Mean.
Thing Lost...	Not found.	Thing Lost...	Part found.

Questions.	Answers.	Questions.	Answers.
Life............	Short.	Life............	Long.
Money.........	Unlucky.	Money.........	Great Riches.
Honour......	Evil.	Honour......	Excellent.
Business......	Evil.	Business......	Very good.
Marriage.......	Unlucky.	Marriage.......	Good.
Pregnancy...	Daughter.	Pregnancy...	A Son.
Sickness........	Soon die.	Sickness........	Dangerous.
Imprisonment.	Soon out.	Imprisonment.	Come out.
Journey......	Vexatious.	Journey......	Voyage good.
Thing Lost...	Not found.	Thing Lost...	Found.

Questions.	Answers.	Questions.	Answers.
Life............	Long.	Life............	Short.
Money.........	Very Good.	Money.........	Ill.
Honour......	Good.	Honour......	Ill.
Business......	Good.	Business......	Mean.
Marriage.......	Mean.	Marriage.......	Very bad.
Pregnancy...	A Son.	Pregnancy...	A Daughter.
Sickness........	Health.	Sickness........	Death.
Imprisonment.	Come out.	Imprisonment.	Dangerous.
Journey......	Good.	Journey......	Unlucky.
Thing Lost...	Found.	Thing Lost...	Not found.

Part Two: Divination

Questions.	Answers.	Questions.	Answers.
Life............	Short.	Life............	Long.
Money.........	Unlucky.	Money.........	Very fortunate.
Honour......	Evil.	Honour......	Good.
Business......	Ill.	Business......	Fortunate.
Marriage.......	Unlucky.	Marriage.......	Fortunate.
Pregnancy...	Daughter.	Pregnancy...	Daughter.
Sickness........	Death.	Sickness........	Health.
Imprisonment.	Dangerous.	Imprisonment.	Delivery.
Journey......	Loss.	Journey......	Good.
Thing Lost...	Not found.	Thing Lost...	Found.

Questions.	Answers.	Questions.	Answers.
Life............	Mean.	Life............	Good.
Money.........	Bad.	Money.........	Good.
Honour......	Ill.	Honour......	Mean.
Business......	Ill.	Business......	Mean.
Marriage.......	Ill.	Marriage.......	Mean.
Pregnancy...	A Daughter.	Pregnancy...	Abortion
Sickness........	Health.	Sickness........	End, health.
Imprisonment.	Come out.	Imprisonment.	Long.
Journey......	Mean.	Journey......	Good.
Thing Lost...	Not found.	Thing Lost...	Not found.

Questions.	Answers.	Questions.	Answers.
Life............	Short.	Life............	Mean.
Money.........	Unlucky.	Money.........	Mean.
Honour......	Ill.	Honour......	Indifferent.
Business......	Evil.	Business......	Mean.
Marriage.......	Evil.	Marriage.......	Mean.
Pregnancy...	Doubtful.	Pregnancy...	A Son.
Sickness........	Perilous.	Sickness........	Death.
Imprisonment.	Difficult.	Imprisonment.	Perilous.
Journey......	Unlucky.	Journey......	Good by water.
Thing Lost...	Not found.	Thing Lost...	Not found.

Questions.	Answers.	Questions.	Answers.
Life............	Moderate.	Life............	Mean.
Money.........	Mean.	Money.........	Mean.
Honour......	Bad.	Honour......	Mean.
Business......	Indifferent.	Business......	Good.
Marriage.......	Mean.	Marriage.......	Good.
Pregnancy...	A Daughter.	Pregnancy...	A Daughter.
Sickness........	Dangerous.	Sickness........	Dangerous.
Imprisonment.	Long.	Imprisonment.	Late out.
Journey......	Bad.	Journey......	Ill.
Thing Lost...	Found.	Thing Lost...	Found.

Part Two: Divination

Questions.	Answers.	Questions.	Answers.
Life............	Ill.	Life............	Moderate.
Money.........	Evil.	Money.........	Indifferent.
Honour......	Vexatious.	Honour......	Good.
Business......	Unlucky.	Business......	Mean.
Marriage.......	Ill.	Marriage.......	Mean.
Pregnancy...	A Daughter.	Pregnancy...	A Son.
Sickness........	Perilous.	Sickness........	Health.
Imprisonment.	Long.	Imprisonment.	Dangerous.
Journey......	Difficult.	Journey......	Good.
Thing Lost...	Not found.	Thing Lost...	Part found.

Questions.	Answers.	Questions.	Answers.
Life............	Good.	Life............	Moderate.
Money.........	Lucky.	Money.........	Ill.
Honour......	Powerful.	Honour......	Mean.
Business......	Good.	Business......	Ill.
Marriage.......	Good.	Marriage.......	Good.
Pregnancy...	A Son.	Pregnancy...	A Son.
Sickness........	Health.	Sickness........	Health.
Imprisonment.	Come out.	Imprisonment.	Soon out.
Journey......	Good.	Journey......	Voyage Good.
Thing Lost...	Found.	Thing Lost...	Not found.

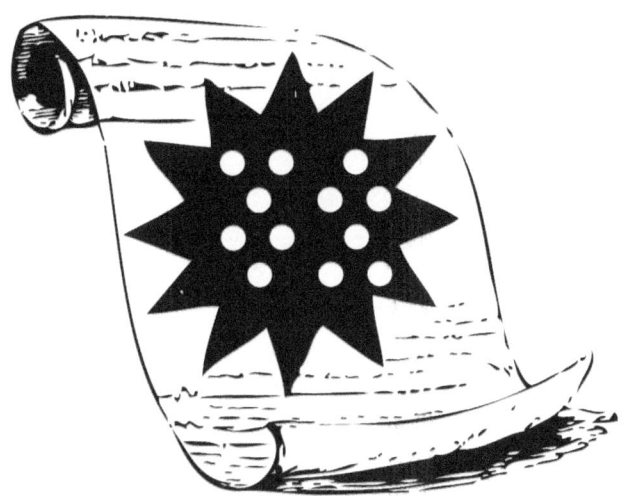

THE SENTENCE

OF

Aquisitio

AND

Amissio

AS THE

JUDGE.

IN THE QUESTIONS RELATING TO

1. Length of Life,
2. Money or Gain,
3. Honour or Credit,
4. Business,
5. Marriage,
6. Pregnancy,
7. Sickness,
8. Imprisonment,
9. Journeys and
10. Things Lost.

Questions.	Answers.	Questions.	Answers.
Life............	Long.	Life............	Long.
Money.........	Moderate.	Money.........	Fortunate.
Honour......	Mean.	Honour......	Good.
Business......	Mean.	Business......	Fortunate.
Marriage.......	Lucky.	Marriage.......	Good.
Pregnancy...	A son.	Pregnancy...	A son.
Sickness........	Health.	Sickness........	Health.
Imprisonment.	Doubtful.	Imprisonment.	Death.
Journey......	Good.	Journey......	Mean.
Thing Lost...	Found.	Thing Lost...	Found.

Questions.	Answers.	Questions.	Answers.
Life............	Meanly long.	Life............	Meanly long.
Money.........	Evil.	Money.........	Mean.
Honour......	Ill.	Honour......	Mean.
Business......	Ill.	Business......	Indifferent.
Marriage.......	Ill.	Marriage.......	Indifferent.
Pregnancy...	A son.	Pregnancy...	A son.
Sickness........	Health.	Sickness........	Health.
Imprisonment.	Escapes.	Imprisonment.	Come out.
Journey......	Evil.	Journey......	Mean.
Thing Lost...	Part found.	Thing Lost...	Found.

Part Two: Divination

Questions.	Answers.	Questions.	Answers.
Life............	Mean.	Life............	Short.
Money.........	Good.	Money.........	Unlucky.
Honour......	Ill.	Honour......	Evil.
Business......	Evil.	Business......	Unfortunate.
Marriage.......	Unlucky.	Marriage.......	Unlucky.
Pregnancy...	A daughter.	Pregnancy...	A daughter.
Sickness........	Recovery.	Sickness........	Health.
Imprisonment.	Die therein.	Imprisonment.	Come out.
Journey......	Evil.	Journey......	Mean.
Thing Lost...	Part found.	Thing Lost...	Not found.

Questions.	Answers.	Questions.	Answers.
Life............	Short.	Life............	Rather long.
Money.........	Mean.	Money.........	Good.
Honour......	Mean.	Honour......	Good.
Business......	Indifferent.	Business......	Fortunate.
Marriage.......	Not good.	Marriage.......	Fortunate.
Pregnancy...	Daughter.	Pregnancy...	A son.
Sickness........	Perilous.	Sickness........	Health.
Imprisonment.	Come out.	Imprisonment.	Come out.
Journey......	Unlucky.	Journey......	Take it.
Thing Lost...	Part found.	Thing Lost...	Part found.

Questions.	Answers.	Questions.	Answers.
Life............	Meanly long.	Life............	Moderate.
Money.........	Indifferent.	Money.........	Unlucky.
Honour......	Mean.	Honour......	Evil.
Business......	Mean.	Business......	Unlucky.
Marriage.......	Moderate.	Marriage.......	Evil.
Pregnancy...	A son.	Pregnancy...	A son.
Sickness........	Health.	Sickness........	Health.
Imprisonment.	Come out.	Imprisonment.	Come out.
Journey......	Good.	Journey......	Indifferent.
Thing Lost...	Not found.	Thing Lost...	Not found.

Questions.	Answers.	Questions.	Answers.
Life............	Moderately Long.	Life............	Short.
Money.........	Indifferent.	Money.........	Little.
Honour......	Mean.	Honour......	Mean.
Business......	Moderate.	Business......	Evil.
Marriage.......	Rather good.	Marriage.......	Unlucky.
Pregnancy...	Daughter.	Pregnancy...	A son.
Sickness........	Health.	Sickness........	Health.
Imprisonment.	Come out.	Imprisonment.	Come out.
Journey......	Late.	Journey......	Good.
Thing Lost...	Little found.	Thing Lost...	Not found.

Part Two: Divination

Questions.	Answers.	Questions.	Answers.
Life............	Meanly long.	Life............	Long.
Money.........	Mean.	Money.........	Good luck.
Honour......	Famous.	Honour......	Excellent.
Business......	Good.	Business......	Fortunate.
Marriage.......	Fortunate.	Marriage.......	Lucky.
Pregnancy...	A female.	Pregnancy...	A son.
Sickness........	Health.	Sickness........	Health.
Imprisonment.	Death.	Imprisonment.	Come out.
Journey......	Mean.	Journey......	Excellent.
Thing Lost...	Found.	Thing Lost...	Found.

Questions.	Answers.	Questions.	Answers.
Life............	Short.	Life............	Short.
Money.........	Rather evil.	Money.........	Not good.
Honour......	Not good.	Honour......	Evil.
Business......	Not lucky.	Business......	Evil.
Marriage.......	Unfortunate.	Marriage.......	Ill-fated.
Pregnancy...	Daughter.	Pregnancy...	A son.
Sickness........	Perilous.	Sickness........	Health.
Imprisonment.	Dangerous.	Imprisonment.	Come out.
Journey......	Late.	Journey......	Slow.
Thing Lost...	Part found.	Thing Lost...	Part found.

Questions.	Answers.	Questions.	Answers.
Life............	Long.	Life............	Long life.
Money.........	Fortunate.	Money.........	Great wealth.
Honour......	Excellent.	Honour......	Good.
Business......	Prosperous.	Business......	Fortunate.
Marriage.......	Prosperous.	Marriage.......	Excellent.
Pregnancy...	A son.	Pregnancy...	A daughter.
Sickness........	Health.	Sickness........	Health.
Imprisonment.	Run away.	Imprisonment.	Perilous.
Journey......	Slow.	Journey......	Mean.
Thing Lost...	Found.	Thing Lost...	Found.

Questions.	Answers.	Questions.	Answers.
Life............	Short.	Life............	Short.
Money.........	Ill-luck.	Money.........	Loss.
Honour......	Evil.	Honour......	Disgrace.
Business......	Vexatious.	Business......	Evil.
Marriage.......	Tedious.	Marriage.......	Unlucky.
Pregnancy...	A daughter.	Pregnancy...	A son.
Sickness........	Wealth.	Sickness........	Health.
Imprisonment.	Come out.	Imprisonment.	Come out.
Journey......	Ill.	Journey......	Good.
Thing Lost...	Not found.	Thing Lost...	Not found.

Part Two: Divination

Questions.	Answers.	Questions.	Answers.
Life............	Meanly long.	Life............	Short.
Money.........	Indifferent.	Money.........	Unlucky.
Honour......	Mean.	Honour......	Evil.
Business......	Mean.	Business......	Unfortunate.
Marriage.......	Evil.	Marriage.......	Evil.
Pregnancy...	Daughter.	Pregnancy...	A son.
Sickness........	Health.	Sickness........	Danger.
Imprisonment.	Difficulty.	Imprisonment.	Perilous.
Journey......	Evil.	Journey......	Unlucky.
Thing Lost...	Part found.	Thing Lost...	Not found.

Questions.	Answers.	Questions.	Answers.
Life............	Meanly long.	Life............	Mean.
Money.........	Evil.	Money.........	Mean.
Honour......	Evil.	Honour......	Mean.
Business......	Bad.	Business......	Indifferent.
Marriage.......	Bad.	Marriage.......	Evil.
Pregnancy...	A girl.	Pregnancy...	A maid.
Sickness........	Health.	Sickness........	Health.
Imprisonment.	Come out.	Imprisonment.	Come out.
Journey......	Very late.	Journey......	Slow.
Thing Lost...	Not found.	Thing Lost...	Not found.

Questions.	Answers.	Questions.	Answers.
Life............	Short.	Life............	Meanly long.
Money.........	Unfortunate.	Money.........	Mean.
Honour......	Disgrace.	Honour......	Indifferent.
Business......	Loss.	Business......	Not good.
Marriage.......	Separation.	Marriage.......	Evil.
Pregnancy...	A son.	Pregnancy...	A daughter.
Sickness........	Danger.	Sickness........	Health.
Imprisonment.	Danger.	Imprisonment.	Difficulty.
Journey......	Ill end.	Journey......	Ill end.
Thing Lost...	Not found.	Thing Lost...	Part found.

Questions.	Answers.	Questions.	Answers.
Life............	Moderate.	Life............	Short.
Money.........	Unlucky.	Money.........	Bad luck.
Honour......	Evil.	Honour......	Evil.
Business......	Bad.	Business......	Evil.
Marriage.......	Moderate.	Marriage.......	Unfortunate.
Pregnancy...	A son.	Pregnancy...	A daughter.
Sickness........	Health.	Sickness........	Health.
Imprisonment.	Escape.	Imprisonment.	Come out.
Journey......	Mean.	Journey......	Evil.
Thing Lost...	Found.	Thing Lost...	Not found.

Part Two: Divination

Questions.	Answers.	Questions.	Answers.
Life............	Sufficient.	Life............	Meanly long.
Money.........	Sufficient.	Money.........	Indifferent.
Honour......	Mean.	Honour......	Evil.
Business......	Moderate.	Business......	Mean.
Marriage.......	Partly good.	Marriage.......	Mean.
Pregnancy...	A son.	Pregnancy...	A maid.
Sickness........	Health.	Sickness........	Perilous.
Imprisonment.	Come out.	Imprisonment.	Dangerous.
Journey......	Slow.	Journey......	Evil.
Thing Lost...	Not found.	Thing Lost...	Found.

Questions.	Answers.	Questions.	Answers.
Life............	Mean.	Life............	Mean.
Money.........	Mean.	Money.........	Mean.
Honour......	Mean.	Honour......	Indifferent.
Business......	Moderate.	Business......	Indifferent.
Marriage.......	Good.	Marriage.......	Moderate.
Pregnancy...	A daughter.	Pregnancy...	A maid.
Sickness........	Perilous.	Sickness........	Death.
Imprisonment.	Come out.	Imprisonment.	Come out.
Journey......	Slow.	Journey......	Mean.
Thing Lost...	Not found.	Thing Lost...	Found.

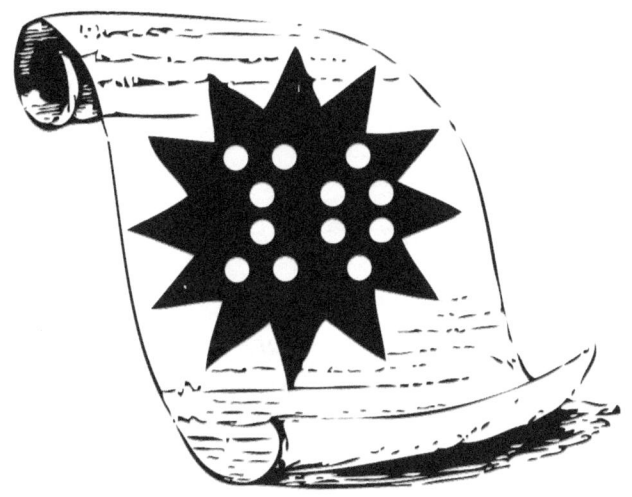

THE SENTENCE

OF

Conjunctio

AND

Carcer

AS THE

JUDGE.
IN THE QUESTIONS RELATING TO

1. Length of Life,
2. Money or Gain,
3. Honour or Credit,
4. Business,
5. Marriage,
6. Pregnancy,
7. Sickness,
8. Imprisonment,
9. Journeys and
10. Things Lost.

Questions.	Answers.	Questions.	Answers.
Life............	Moderate.	Life............	Long.
Money.........	Moderate.	Money.........	Fortunate.
Honour......	Good.	Honour......	Very good.
Business......	Good.	Business......	Excellent.
Marriage.......	Fortunate.	Marriage.......	Fortunate.
Pregnancy...	A daughter.	Pregnancy...	A daughter.
Sickness........	Perilous.	Sickness........	Doubtful.
Imprisonment.	Long.	Imprisonment.	Long.
Journey......	Evil.	Journey......	Safe.
Thing Lost...	Found.	Thing Lost...	Found.

Questions.	Answers.	Questions.	Answers.
Life............	Mean length.	Life............	Long.
Money.........	Evil.	Money.........	Good.
Honour......	Moderate.	Honour......	Favourable.
Business......	Moderate.	Business......	Good.
Marriage.......	Indifferent.	Marriage.......	Indifferent.
Pregnancy...	Female.	Pregnancy...	A male.
Sickness........	Dubious.	Sickness........	Health.
Imprisonment.	Come out.	Imprisonment.	Deliverance.
Journey......	Hurtful.	Journey......	Good.
Thing Lost...	Found.	Thing Lost...	Found.

Part Two: Divination

Questions.	Answers.	Questions.	Answers.
Life…………	Short.	Life…………	Moderate.
Money………	Indifferent.	Money………	Evil.
Honour……	Evil.	Honour……	Mean.
Business……	Good.	Business……	Unfortunate.
Marriage……	Unlucky.	Marriage……	Indifferent.
Pregnancy…	Female.	Pregnancy…	Male.
Sickness……	Death.	Sickness……	Health.
Imprisonment.	No release.	Imprisonment.	Soon released.
Journey……	Late.	Journey……	Good.
Thing Lost…	Part found.	Thing Lost…	Little found.

Questions.	Answers.	Questions.	Answers.
Life…………	Long.	Life…………	Long.
Money………	Excellent.	Money………	Fortunate.
Honour……	Good.	Honour……	Good.
Business……	Excellent.	Business……	Excellent.
Marriage……	Fortunate.	Marriage……	Fortunate.
Pregnancy…	A son.	Pregnancy…	A son.
Sickness……	Health.	Sickness……	Health.
Imprisonment.	Come out.	Imprisonment.	Long.
Journey……	Difficult.	Journey……	Soon return.
Thing Lost…	Found.	Thing Lost…	Found.

Questions.	Answers.	Questions.	Answers.
Life............	Ill.	Life............	Mean.
Money.........	Mean.	Money.........	Mean.
Honour......	Evil.	Honour......	Mean.
Business......	Evil.	Business......	Mean.
Marriage.......	Indifferent.	Marriage.......	Good.
Pregnancy...	Female.	Pregnancy...	A daughter.
Sickness........	Death.	Sickness........	Death.
Imprisonment.	Not out.	Imprisonment.	Ill.
Journey......	Unfortunate.	Journey......	Ill.
Thing Lost...	Not found.	Thing Lost...	Not found.

Questions.	Answers.	Questions.	Answers.
Life............	Long.	Life............	Short.
Money.........	Excellent.	Money.........	Sufficient.
Honour......	Good.	Honour......	Ill.
Business......	Good.	Business......	Mean.
Marriage.......	Fortunate.	Marriage.......	Evil.
Pregnancy...	A girl.	Pregnancy...	A daughter
Sickness........	Health.	Sickness........	Health.
Imprisonment.	Long.	Imprisonment.	Protracted.
Journey......	Late.	Journey......	Ill.
Thing Lost...	Found.	Thing Lost...	Found.

Part Two: Divination 93

Questions.	Answers.	Questions.	Answers.
Life............	Short.	Life............	Long.
Money.........	Indifferent.	Money.........	Riches.
Honour......	Evil.	Honour......	Great.
Business......	Evil.	Business......	Mean.
Marriage.......	Mean.	Marriage.......	Favourable.
Pregnancy...	A daughter.	Pregnancy...	A son.
Sickness........	Dubious.	Sickness........	Health.
Imprisonment.	Out by ill.	Imprisonment.	Well out.
Journey......	Perilous.	Journey......	Return.
Thing Lost...	Part found.	Thing Lost...	Found.

Questions.	Answers.	Questions.	Answers.
Life............	Mean.	Life............	Evil.
Money.........	Indifferent.	Money.........	Evil.
Honour......	Good.	Honour......	Evil.
Business......	Mean.	Business......	Evil.
Marriage.......	Mean.	Marriage.......	Unfortunate.
Pregnancy...	Doubtful.	Pregnancy...	A maid.
Sickness........	Health.	Sickness........	Dubious.
Imprisonment.	Soon out.	Imprisonment.	Come forth.
Journey......	Good.	Journey......	Good.
Thing Lost...	Not found.	Thing Lost...	Not found.

Questions.	Answers.	Questions.	Answers.
Life............	Short.	Life............	Long.
Money.........	Evil.	Money.........	Good.
Honour......	Evil.	Honour......	Evil.
Business......	Unfortunate.	Business......	Mean.
Marriage.......	Evil.	Marriage.......	Unfortunate.
Pregnancy...	A daughter.	Pregnancy...	Female
Sickness........	Health.	Sickness........	Health.
Imprisonment.	Come out.	Imprisonment.	A good end.
Journey......	Mean.	Journey......	Slow.
Thing Lost...	Not found.	Thing Lost...	Found.

Questions.	Answers.	Questions.	Answers.
Life............	Mean.	Life............	Mean.
Money.........	Indifferent.	Money.........	Mean.
Honour......	Mean.	Honour......	Evil.
Business......	Moderate.	Business......	Unlucky.
Marriage.......	Mean.	Marriage.......	Unlucky.
Pregnancy...	A son.	Pregnancy...	Daughter.
Sickness........	Health.	Sickness........	Evil.
Imprisonment.	Slow.	Imprisonment.	Perilous.
Journey......	Return.	Journey......	Dangerous.
Thing Lost...	Found.	Thing Lost...	Not to found.

Part Two: Divination

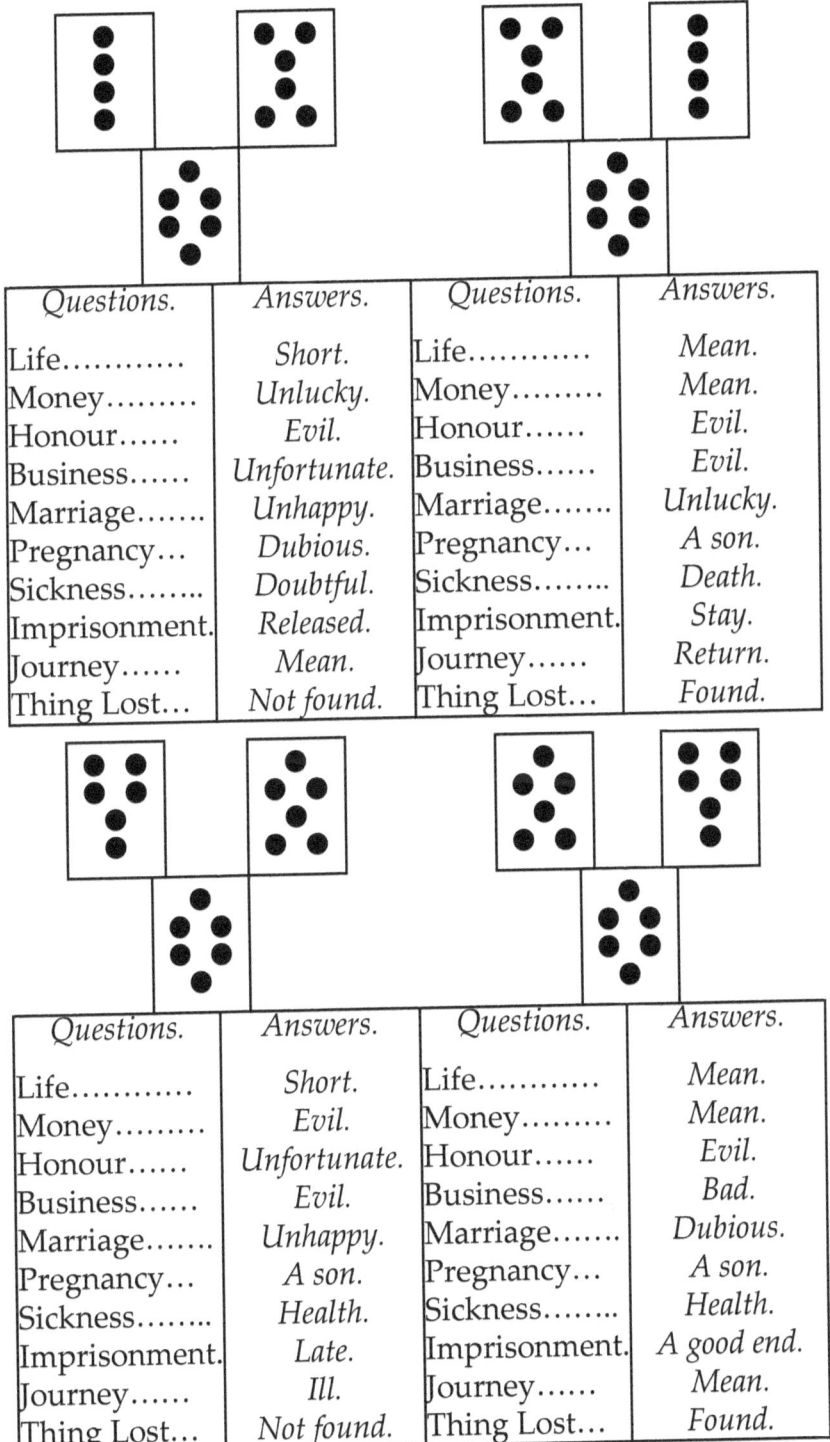

Questions.	Answers.	Questions.	Answers.
Life............	Short.	Life............	Mean.
Money.........	Unlucky.	Money.........	Mean.
Honour......	Evil.	Honour......	Evil.
Business......	Unfortunate.	Business......	Evil.
Marriage.......	Unhappy.	Marriage.......	Unlucky.
Pregnancy...	Dubious.	Pregnancy...	A son.
Sickness........	Doubtful.	Sickness........	Death.
Imprisonment.	Released.	Imprisonment.	Stay.
Journey......	Mean.	Journey......	Return.
Thing Lost...	Not found.	Thing Lost...	Found.

Questions.	Answers.	Questions.	Answers.
Life............	Short.	Life............	Mean.
Money.........	Evil.	Money.........	Mean.
Honour......	Unfortunate.	Honour......	Evil.
Business......	Evil.	Business......	Bad.
Marriage.......	Unhappy.	Marriage.......	Dubious.
Pregnancy...	A son.	Pregnancy...	A son.
Sickness........	Health.	Sickness........	Health.
Imprisonment.	Late.	Imprisonment.	A good end.
Journey......	Ill.	Journey......	Mean.
Thing Lost...	Not found.	Thing Lost...	Found.

Questions.	Answers.	Questions.	Answers.
Life............	Long.	Life............	Long.
Money.........	Good.	Money.........	Good.
Honour......	Good.	Honour......	Favourable.
Business......	Good.	Business......	Good.
Marriage.......	Evil.	Marriage.......	Good.
Pregnancy...	A male.	Pregnancy...	A female.
Sickness........	Health.	Sickness........	Dubious.
Imprisonment.	Late.	Imprisonment.	Good end.
Journey......	Good.	Journey......	Good.
Thing Lost...	Not found.	Thing Lost...	Found.

Questions.	Answers.	Questions.	Answers.
Life............	Short.	Life............	Evil.
Money.........	Unlucky.	Money.........	Evil.
Honour......	Evil.	Honour......	Evil.
Business......	Evil.	Business......	Unlucky.
Marriage.......	Unfortunate.	Marriage.......	Evil.
Pregnancy...	Look to the 1st.	Pregnancy...	Daughter.
Sickness........	Doubtful.	Sickness........	Evil.
Imprisonment.	Dubious.	Imprisonment.	Perilous.
Journey......	Evil.	Journey......	Good.
Thing Lost...	Not found.	Thing Lost...	Not found.

Part Two: Divination

Questions.	Answers.	Questions.	Answers.
Life............	Evil.	Life............	Mean.
Money.........	Unlucky.	Money.........	Fortunate.
Honour......	Evil.	Honour......	Mean.
Business......	Bad.	Business......	Good.
Marriage.......	Unlucky.	Marriage.......	Mean.
Pregnancy...	A daughter.	Pregnancy...	A son.
Sickness........	Dubious.	Sickness........	Health.
Imprisonment.	Long.	Imprisonment.	Good end.
Journey......	Ill.	Journey......	Ill.
Thing Lost...	Not found.	Thing Lost...	Found.

Questions.	Answers.	Questions.	Answers.
Life............	Good.	Life............	Long.
Money.........	Fortunate.	Money.........	Good.
Honour......	Good.	Honour......	Good.
Business......	Lucky.	Business......	Lucky.
Marriage.......	Good.	Marriage.......	Happy.
Pregnancy...	A son.	Pregnancy...	A son.
Sickness........	Dangerous.	Sickness........	Health.
Imprisonment.	Not out.	Imprisonment.	Long.
Journey......	Slow.	Journey......	Tedious.
Thing Lost...	Found.	Thing Lost...	Found.

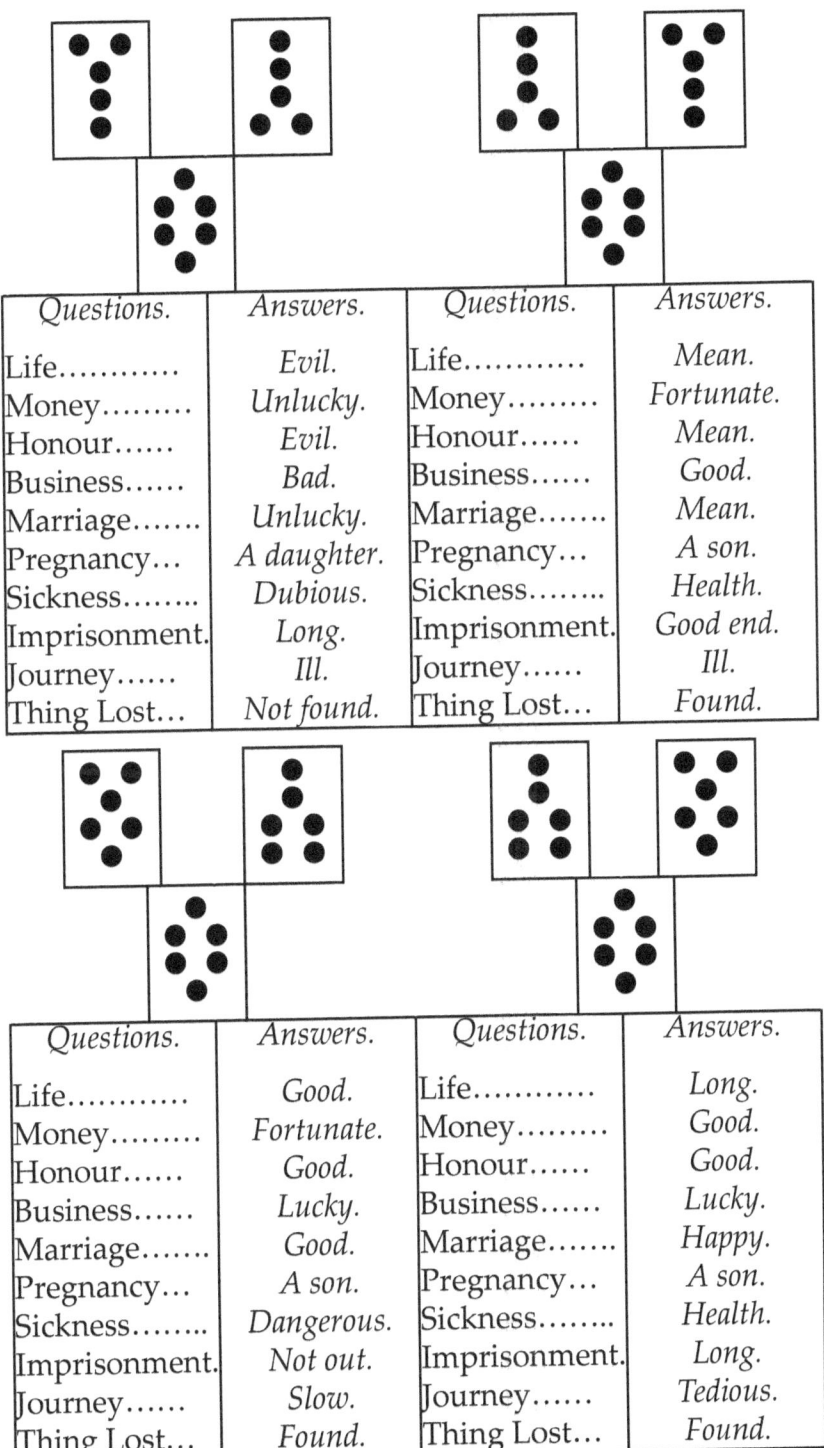

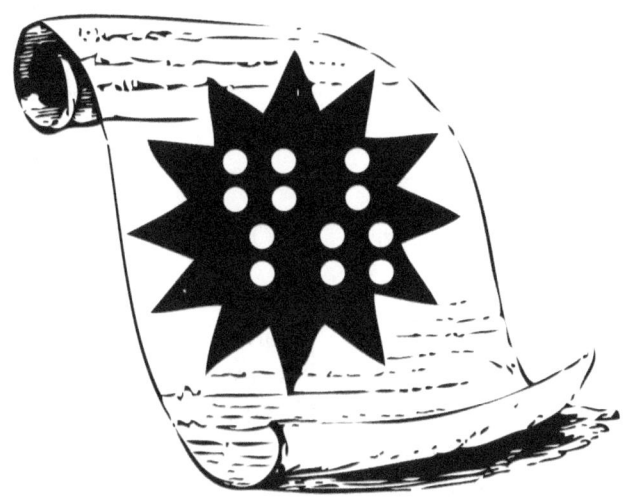

THE SENTENCE
OF
𝔉ortuna 𝔐ajor
AND
𝔐inor
AS THE
JUDGE
IN THE QUESTIONS RELATING TO
1. Length of Life,
2. Money or Gain,
3. Honour or Credit,
4. Business,
5. Marriage,
6. Pregnancy,
7. Sickness,
8. Imprisonment,
9. Journeys and
10. Things Lost.

Questions.	Answers.	Questions.	Answers.
Life............	*Long.*	Life............	*Long.*
Money.........	*Fortunate.*	Money.........	*Excellent.*
Honour......	*Good.*	Honour......	*Great.*
Business......	*Favourable.*	Business......	*Lucky.*
Marriage.......	*Lucky.*	Marriage.......	*Fortunate.*
Pregnancy...	*Hazardous.*	Pregnancy...	*Doubtful.*
Sickness........	*Health.*	Sickness........	*Health.*
Imprisonment.	*Deliverance.*	Imprisonment.	*Come out.*
Journey......	*Slow.*	Journey......	*Good.*
Thing Lost...	*Found.*	Thing Lost...	*Found.*

Questions.	Answers.	Questions.	Answers.
Life............	*Long.*	Life............	*Long.*
Money.........	*Good.*	Money.........	*Good.*
Honour......	*Good.*	Honour......	*Excellent.*
Business......	*Good.*	Business......	*Evil.*
Marriage.......	*Evil.*	Marriage.......	*Ill luck.*
Pregnancy...	*Female.*	Pregnancy...	*A maid.*
Sickness........	*Health.*	Sickness........	*Quick health.*
Imprisonment.	*Soon out.*	Imprisonment.	*Deliverance.*
Journey......	*Mean.*	Journey......	*Mean.*
Thing Lost...	*Part found.*	Thing Lost...	*Not found.*

Part Two: Divination 101

Questions.	Answers.	Questions.	Answers.
Life............	Indifferent.	Life............	Moderate.
Money.........	Fortunate.	Money.........	Lucky.
Honour......	Favourable.	Honour......	Good.
Business......	Excellent.	Business......	Good.
Marriage.......	Fortunate.	Marriage.......	Fortunate.
Pregnancy...	A son.	Pregnancy...	A son.
Sickness........	Health.	Sickness........	Health.
Imprisonment.	Come out.	Imprisonment.	Soon out.
Journey......	Lucky.	Journey......	Good.
Thing Lost...	Part found.	Thing Lost...	Found.

Questions.	Answers.	Questions.	Answers.
Life............	Short.	Life............	Long.
Money.........	Mean.	Money.........	Lucky.
Honour......	Good.	Honour......	Propitious.
Business......	Lucky.	Business......	Prosperous.
Marriage.......	Cross.	Marriage.......	Good.
Pregnancy...	Doubtful.	Pregnancy...	A son.
Sickness........	Dangerous.	Sickness........	Health.
Imprisonment.	Come out.	Imprisonment.	Come out.
Journey......	Ill.	Journey......	Difficult.
Thing Lost...	Part found.	Thing Lost...	Part found.

Questions.	Answers.	Questions.	Answers.
Life............	Moderate.	Life............	Meanly long.
Money.........	Mean.	Money.........	Unlucky.
Honour......	Indifferent.	Honour......	Indifferent.
Business......	Dubious.	Business......	Commix't.
Marriage.......	Ill.	Marriage.......	Mean.
Pregnancy...	Female.	Pregnancy...	A son.
Sickness........	Dangerous.	Sickness........	Health.
Imprisonment.	Not out.	Imprisonment.	Deliverance.
Journey......	Return.	Journey......	Doubtful.
Thing Lost...	Found.	Thing Lost...	Not found.

Questions.	Answers.	Questions.	Answers.
Life............	Moderate.	Life............	Meanly long.
Money.........	Partly good.	Money.........	Indifferent.
Honour......	Mean.	Honour......	Lucky.
Business......	Indifferent.	Business......	Evil.
Marriage.......	Indifferent.	Marriage.......	Cross.
Pregnancy...	Female.	Pregnancy...	A female.
Sickness........	Health.	Sickness........	Health.
Imprisonment.	Come out.	Imprisonment.	Soon out.
Journey......	Quick.	Journey......	Lucky.
Thing Lost...	Part found.	Thing Lost...	Not found.

Part Two: Divination

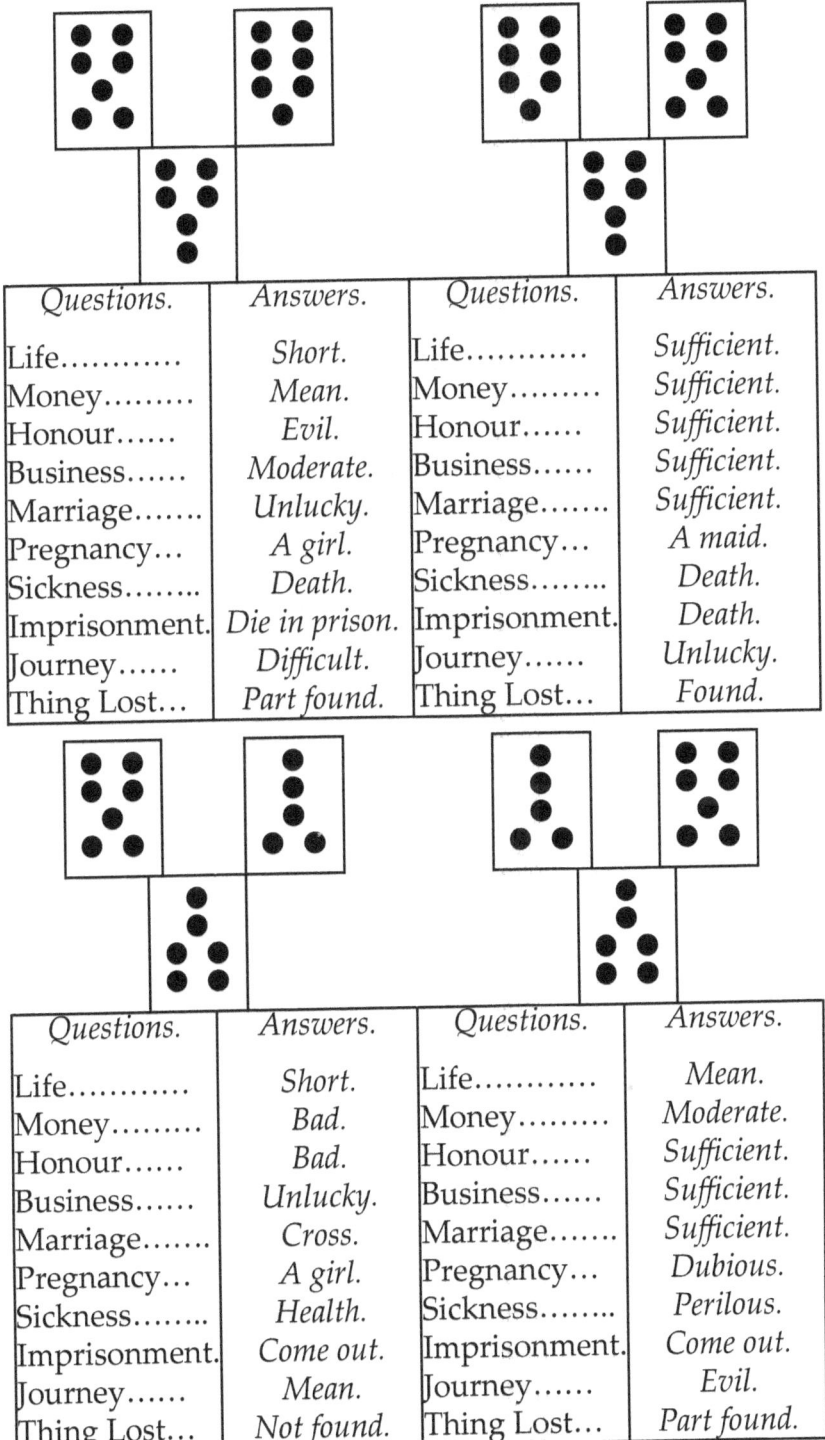

Questions.	Answers.	Questions.	Answers.
Life............	Short.	Life............	Sufficient.
Money.........	Mean.	Money.........	Sufficient.
Honour......	Evil.	Honour......	Sufficient.
Business......	Moderate.	Business......	Sufficient.
Marriage.......	Unlucky.	Marriage.......	Sufficient.
Pregnancy...	A girl.	Pregnancy...	A maid.
Sickness........	Death.	Sickness........	Death.
Imprisonment.	Die in prison.	Imprisonment.	Death.
Journey......	Difficult.	Journey......	Unlucky.
Thing Lost...	Part found.	Thing Lost...	Found.

Questions.	Answers.	Questions.	Answers.
Life............	Short.	Life............	Mean.
Money.........	Bad.	Money.........	Moderate.
Honour......	Bad.	Honour......	Sufficient.
Business......	Unlucky.	Business......	Sufficient.
Marriage.......	Cross.	Marriage.......	Sufficient.
Pregnancy...	A girl.	Pregnancy...	Dubious.
Sickness........	Health.	Sickness........	Perilous.
Imprisonment.	Come out.	Imprisonment.	Come out.
Journey......	Mean.	Journey......	Evil.
Thing Lost...	Not found.	Thing Lost...	Part found.

Questions.	Answers.	Questions.	Answers.
Life............	*Long.*	Life............	*Short.*
Money.........	*Good.*	Money.........	*Mean.*
Honour......	*Mean.*	Honour......	*Good.*
Business......	*Lucky.*	Business......	*Sufficient.*
Marriage.......	*Mean.*	Marriage.......	*Moderate.*
Pregnancy...	*A son.*	Pregnancy...	*A son.*
Sickness........	*Health.*	Sickness........	*A relief.*
Imprisonment.	*Evil.*	Imprisonment.	*Dubious.*
Journey......	*Cross.*	Journey......	*Evil.*
Thing Lost...	*Found.*	Thing Lost...	*Part found.*

Questions.	Answers.	Questions.	Answers.
Life............	*Short.*	Life............	*Evil.*
Money.........	*Unlucky.*	Money.........	*Ill.*
Honour......	*Evil.*	Honour......	*Ill.*
Business......	*Cross.*	Business......	*Bad.*
Marriage.......	*Cross.*	Marriage.......	*Bad.*
Pregnancy...	*Male.*	Pregnancy...	*Female.*
Sickness........	*Ill.*	Sickness........	*Evil.*
Imprisonment.	*Ill.*	Imprisonment.	*Long.*
Journey......	*Evil.*	Journey......	*Unfortunate.*
Thing Lost...	*Not found.*	Thing Lost...	*Not found.*

Part Two: Divination

Questions.	Answers.	Questions.	Answers.
Life............	Short.	Life............	Bad.
Money.........	Bad.	Money.........	Bad.
Honour......	Evil.	Honour......	Evil.
Business......	Ill.	Business......	Evil.
Marriage.......	Cross.	Marriage.......	Cross.
Pregnancy...	Female.	Pregnancy...	Dubious.
Sickness........	Perilous.	Sickness........	Perilous.
Imprisonment.	Perilous.	Imprisonment.	Out in pain.
Journey......	Unlucky.	Journey......	Evil.
Thing Lost...	Not found.	Thing Lost...	Not found.

Questions.	Answers.	Questions.	Answers.
Life............	Long.	Life............	Long.
Money.........	Very Good.	Money.........	Good.
Honour......	Good.	Honour......	Good.
Business......	Lucky.	Business......	Lucky.
Marriage.......	Lucky.	Marriage.......	Lucky.
Pregnancy...	A son.	Pregnancy...	Daughter.
Sickness........	Health.	Sickness........	Long.
Imprisonment.	Out late.	Imprisonment.	Long.
Journey......	Very good.	Journey......	Tedious.
Thing Lost...	Found.	Thing Lost...	Found.

Questions.	Answers.	Questions.	Answers.
Life............	Mean.	Life............	Long.
Money.........	Mean.	Money.........	Lucky.
Honour......	Indifferent.	Honour......	Great.
Business......	Mean.	Business......	Lucky.
Marriage.......	Moderate.	Marriage.......	Fortunate.
Pregnancy...	A girl.	Pregnancy...	A son.
Sickness........	Dubious.	Sickness........	Long pining.
Imprisonment.	Late out.	Imprisonment.	Long about.
Journey......	Ill.	Journey......	Slow.
Thing Lost...	Found.	Thing Lost...	Found.

Questions.	Answers.	Questions.	Answers.
Life............	Short.	Life............	Short.
Money.........	Evil.	Money.........	Evil.
Honour......	Ill.	Honour......	Ill.
Business......	Mean.	Business......	Bad.
Marriage.......	Evil.	Marriage.......	Cross.
Pregnancy...	Dubious.	Pregnancy...	A girl.
Sickness........	Death.	Sickness........	Death.
Imprisonment.	Out with fear.	Imprisonment.	Late.
Journey......	Mean.	Journey......	Ill.
Thing Lost...	Found.	Thing Lost...	Part found.

Questions.	Answers.	Questions.	Answers.
Life............	Long.	Life............	Short.
Money.........	Mean.	Money.........	Mean.
Honour......	Good.	Honour......	Evil.
Business......	Good.	Business......	Mean.
Marriage.......	Lucky.	Marriage.......	Cross.
Pregnancy...	Female.	Pregnancy...	A son.
Sickness……..	Health.	Sickness……..	Health.
Imprisonment.	Come out.	Imprisonment.	Die there.
Journey......	Slow.	Journey......	Not be.
Thing Lost...	Part found.	Thing Lost...	Part found.

Questions.	Answers.	Questions.	Answers.
Life............	Long.	Life............	Moderate.
Money.........	Lucky.	Money.........	Good.
Honour......	Good.	Honour......	Good.
Business......	Fortunate.	Business......	Lucky.
Marriage.......	Fortunate.	Marriage.......	Lucky.
Pregnancy...	A son.	Pregnancy...	A son
Sickness……..	Health.	Sickness……..	Long.
Imprisonment.	Late out.	Imprisonment.	Long.
Journey......	Slow.	Journey......	Doubtful.
Thing Lost...	Found.	Thing Lost...	Found.

Part Two: Divination

𝔄 Synopsis of Geomancy;

OR,

THE SCIENCE OF CASTING CELESTIAL LOTS,

As practiced in former Times by the Chaldean, Arabian, and Rosycrucian Philosophers.

"And as touching the first, it is written in the beginning of the epistle made to Pope Clement, from the beginning all others using, Abraham being an *Astrologian*, by the resone and ordre of the stars, he knew the maker of all, the which by his providence, ruleth and can temper all things — And an angel being assistant unto him, plainly taught him that which by nature he desired to lerne; and the very prophet that oonly knoweth the hert and purposes of men, seeing him so desirous to know the vauses and ye effect of kinde, he appeared to him, and gave him his desire.

"Soothely, *Geomancy* is a science out of *Astrology*, teaching to judge by figures of lynes of points, or whether in earth or by earth, casually is made projection. And the projection of points is formed of an hand, ruled by a reasonable soul, moved in ye hour of ye question, of the form of the thing a coming, the which is had in the mynde of the projector, the succession of which is open, by the signification of the figures ye which he intendeth to exploit. And as the erthe is the modre of all generable and corruptible things, of the heavenly bodies there abideth some impression, and so ancient doctors, making projection of points, found the figures set in the heaven, by the ordre of fixt stars, as shall be plainly shewed."

— Ancient Manuscript.

"*Roderick.* Verily I think thou wert born under Rubeus, and moreover thou hast a scar in thy face.

"*Walter.*—If I am, as thou sayest, under that self-willed sign, I shall not fail to make thee as vile, for though art under *Carcer*, the *six-dotted* figure of prisonment *q. e. d.* a truce to thy councelling—for thy divining is full unfortunate. See, *soyez assuré*, I have the golden *acquisitio*, in my *hand*. What care I for *sand* or *pointel*, or thy *doctrine*."—Old Play;

This curious science termed *Geomancy* is of high antiquity, and was in great repute amongst the ancient Chaldeans, Babylonians, Hebrews, Arabians, and other orientalists. It was a favorite study amongst the Druids, and constitutes a singular feature at the present day in freemasonry, it being the chief study of the *Rosie Crucians*, and was much practised by that singular race of beings whose secrets are now in the care of that society. In the Holy Scriptures we have frequent mention made of "*casting lots*" which was, no doubt, a species of geomantic divination, and was allowed as a final decision amongst the early Christians. In remote ages, the answers given by the seers as recorded in holy writ, was no doubt given by this species of curious knowledge. And in later years, we have had many professors thereof, although not since the seventeenth century: yet few have given the subject the consideration it merited; for there is little doubt but it might in proper hands be brought to such perfection, as to become almost an universal knowledge; and as it does not require so much attention to arithmetical data, as astrology, it becomes far more facile and pleasing, on that account, The best writers on the subject* are *Cattan*, who wrote in the sixteenth century, and after him *Heydon* and *Case*, although each of these works are very scarce and difficult to be

---

* The members of the Mercurii have in their possession a rare old illuminated folio manuscript of the fourteenth century, (part of which may be still more ancient) which treats of geomancy in a stile the most extraordinary, and gives a complete analysis and system thereof. This inestimable relic of antiquity, is invaluable, and has been traced to the successive possessions of *Chaucer*, the ancient poet (and father of English verse), the unfortunate *Earl of Essex*, in Queen Elizabeth's time, *Percy* the gallant Earl of Northumberland, and other ancient worthies. It is in excellent preservation, in the English language, and affords a singular proof of the indefatigable attention bestowed on the sciences by our forefathers. Extracts therefrom will be given in the following pages.

obtained, and which are only useful as books of reference, although neither of them are competent to teach the art correctly. We will trespass no farther by way of preface, but proceed to give a synopsis of the science, as collated from the best sources of information, which we could procure.

A Table of the Sixteen Geomantic Figures.

Acquisitio	Fortuna Major	Letitia	Via
Amissio	Fortuna Minor	Tristitia	Caput
Populus	Puella	Carcer	Cauda
Rubeus	Puer	Conjunctio	Albus

These figures, in number *sixteen*, are attributed to the *four* elements, which the ancients asserted were the basis of all sublunary things:—

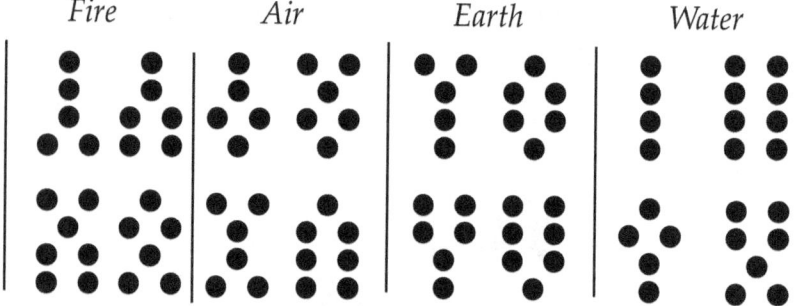

"The *Fiery* this, and the *Terene* compose,
This with the *watery* and the *airy* glows,
Hence the prevailing humours, hence we scan
The never failing character of man."—*Mentor Stellarum*.

The Method of Casting the Celestial Lots.*

"And they gave forth their *lots*, and the *lot* fell upon Matthias, and he was numbered with the eleven apostles."
—Acts 2, 26.

ACCORDING to the system of the ancients, as the manuscript which we have consulted exemplifies, the diviner, or seer, who wishes to predict by these lots, should procure a quantity of clean *earth* or clean sand, either of which should be mixed with water, for *seven* days, in equal portions; which should be done either under the arising of the fortunate *constellations*, or in the hours of the seven *planets*; and when this is done, the earth so formed into portions should be mixed together, in a fortunate day and hour, whereby they affirm that *"the universal effect may be more plainly and easily known and declared."* Others made their figure in wax tables, but they all declare that the projection on *earth*, is the surest and most conducive to the discovery of truth; and that the figure should not be made or *cast* at *any* time, but that divination

---

* In the new edition of the Arabian Nights, edited by Dr. Scott, mention is made of geomancy—vide the tale of Aladdin.

should only be made *"when the weather is bright and clear, and neither dark nor windy, for distemperance in the elements, may cause changes in the passions of the soul."* They also affirm, that when a figure is made, or judged, *"the moon should be free from all impediment,* for if the moon apply to Saturn or Mars, the soul thereby is inclined to lie, and also, that the figure should be made with the most sincere desire to ascertain the truth thereof.

THE MODERN METHOD.

The modern method of casting these celestial *lots*, is by making the points either upon *paper* or a *slate*, with any convenient instrument, either *pen, crayon, chalk, pencil,* or *pointer*, whichever may be the nearest at hand; and the modern *Geomancers* affirm that great verity may be found in the art, when *thus* practised, although they allow that the ancient method is the more exact.

This being seriously thought of, and the *mode* thereof selected, the diviner must proceed to make sixteen lines of points, which points must be made from *right* to *left*, contrary to the usual mode of writing; and in so doing he must not count the *number* of points he makes, but leave that entirely to chance, or to the sympathetic impulse which will guide the hand, so as to produce a figure corresponding to the true *answer* of the event sought after.

The following example will suffice to set this doctrine in an easy light:—[...]

This being done, you have the whole of the figures, which occupy the twelve geomantic houses,* and which constitute the chief part of the scheme. But there yet remain four other accidental figures, namely, the two witnesses, the judge, and the sixteenth figure.

[Unfortunately Smith omits essential information necessary for a Geomantic reading. The first four figures correspond to the first four houses, the next four figures correspond to the next four houses, and the last four figures correspond to

---

* According to the Persians, the planets in their own houses, are in their towers, or citadels of strength

the last four houses. The first house is determined by the first figure. If the figure was Fortuna Major, the first house would be Aquarius, and the 2nd house would be Pisces, etc. Also, the twelve figures correspond to planets, and you place their planetary correspondences in the houses. If, for example, you had Fortuna Major in the first figure, and Via in the second, the first house would be Aquarius, while the second house would be Pisces, and the second house would also contain the Moon, which corresponds to Via. The first house would also contain the Sun, which is the planetary correspondence to Fortuna Major. There can be an unlimited number of duplicate planets in a figure. —Ed]

[...]

The formation of the *sixteenth* figure, has been hitherto unknown, but it is of the utmost consequence in the formation of the judgment, especially where the answer seems ambiguous, and we will therefore give the secret of finding it, which is done by joining together the 1st and 15th figures (the judge), and out of these extracting the figure in question. "This *sixteenth* figure signifieth the cause of the question, and confirmation of the judgment made by the 15th, and thereby we may know what shall fall of ye thing asked after the accomplishing of ye judgment of ye question."

Chaucer's mss,

THE MANNER OF DIVINING BY A FIGURE OF GEOMANCY.

In order to be perfect in the use of Geomancy, it is absolutely necessary that the student should be well acquainted with the science of *astrology*, as illustrated in the *fourth* circle of this work, and to which we refer the reader for information, as it regards the *houses* and quality of the *seven planets*; which are made use of in Geomancy, in the same manner, except as far as the symbolical nature of the figures themselves are concerned;

THE NATURE OF THE SIXTEEN FIGURES OF GEOMANCY.

Acquisitio—Is the best of the whole sixteen figures, and is a sign of riches, joy, gain, acquisition, profit, and a good end of all enterprizes; it is the symbol of good fortune, of honour, renown, and happiness; it denotes long life, fortunate marriages, and success in every undertaking. It is a figure of *Jupiter*, and under the sign *Aries*, it is exalted in the *first* house, and has its *fall* in the *seventh*, which is to be judged the same as in astrology.

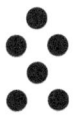

Amissio—As an evil figure, being the symbol of loss, and small profit; it also is found to be generally evil in most undertakings, and is an *issuing* figure. It is under *Venus*, and the sign *Scorpio*, its *exaltation* is in the 8th, and its *fall* in the 2nd house;

Fortuna Major—Is the symbol of wealth and rank, of power, honour, and dignity, and of an exceeding great name. It is singularly good in all matters of gain, and to be preferred to none but acquisitio. It is ruled by the *sun*, and is under the sign *Aquarius*; its exaltation is in the 11th house, and its fall in the 5th.

Fortuna Minor—Is the *lesser* fortune, it betokens disappointments and but small gain, being an issuing and wasteful figure; yet is good for dignities, although evil in matters of profit. It is ruled by the *sun*, and is partially under *Taurus*; its exaltation is in the first house, and its fall in the 7th, or western angle.

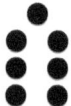

Letitia—Is the figure emblematical of joy, gladness, fullness of pleasure, and gay delights; endearments, profit, gain, and all favourable things, which it signifies similar to acquisitio. It is a very fortunate symbol wherever found, and productive of success.

It is under *Jupiter*, and the sign *Taurus*; it is exalted in the second house, and its fall is in the 8th opposite.

Tristitia—Is the origin or source of sorrow, melancholy, heaviness of heart, lowness of spirits, dolor, grief, malice, and mischief, and is extremely unfortunate in all the affairs she may signify. She is also the cause of loss, disgrace, and trouble. It is under the evil planet *Saturn*, and the sign *Scorpio*, it has its exaltation in the 8th, and its fall in the 2nd house.

Part Two: Divination

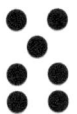

Rubeus—Is another no less vicious and wretched figure, it is the source of war and bloodshed, signifying guile, deceit, and perversion of truth; and intestine quarrels, animosities, and discord. It is highly unfortunate in every undertaking; when it is found in the ascendant, geomancers frequently destroy the figure. It is under *Mars*, in the sign *Gemini*; it is exalted in the 3rd house, and has its fall in the 9th.

Albus—Is a figure termed meanly good, and oftentimes conduces to gain; especially in affairs of science and learning. It is under *Mercury*, and the sign *Cancer*. It is exalted in the 6th house, and its fall in the 12th house, which is opposite thereto.

Conjunctio—Is a figure of gathering or conjoining; it is a controvertible figure, good with good, and evil with evil; it is a symbol of a funeral, "for it representeth the bier on which dead men are borne." The points being 2 before, 2 behind, and 2 in the centre;* it is under *Mercury*, retrograde in *Virgo*.

---

* Ancient manuscript.

It is a bicorporeal figure, exalted in the 6th house, and has its fall in the 12 house.

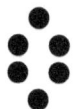

Carcer—Is the emblem of a prison, imprisonment, close shut-up places, close vessels, and is amazingly evil, as its name imports. It gives loss in all things, poverty and wretchedness, it is also unlucky in every undertaking; it is under *Saturn*, and the sign *Pisces*; it is exalted in the 12th house, and has its fall in the 6th house, or house of evil fortune.

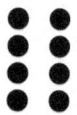

Populus—Is the symbol of a multitude, a congregation, an assembly, a confused retinue. It is generally accounted evil and unpropitious; and generally signifies moving or journeys.

It is under the *full moon*, in the sign *Capricorn*, and is exalted in the 2nd house, having the fall in the 8th.

Via—Is the figure of quickness and facility; of travelling, removals, journeys, and voyages. It is a wasting and dissipating figure, and unlucky in all matters of gain or profit. It denotes hasty news and short visits, when found in the scheme.

It is under the *new moon* in *Leo*, and is *exalted* in the 5th house, having its *fall* in the 11th.

Caput—Is the symbol of the *dragon's head*, and is generally accounted as fortunate and propitious in the undertakings. It is good for matters of gain, and in money-affairs is well. It signifies something quickly coming on, being an entering figure.

It is the *Dragon's Head* in *Virgo*, and is a commixture of *Jupiter* and *Venus* conjoined.

Cauda—Is the symbol of evil and misfortune, disgrace, scandal, slander, poverty, and ruin. It wastes the substance, annoys the asker, and hinders the undertaking. It is always and at all times evil.

This is the *Dragon's Tail* in *Sagittarius*, formed out of a mixture of *Saturn* and *Mars*.

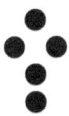

Puella—Is a pleasant and favourable symbol; it signifies fulfilment of wishes, joy and contentment, success in love, and many equally propitious events; it is favourable also in money affairs; it is the sacred emblem of the cross; and is ever found to be a sign of equality, justice, and devotion. It is under the planet *Venus* and the sign *Libra*. It is *exalted* in the *seventh* house, and has its *fall* in the ascendant.

Puer—Is the emblem of a drawn sword, and of war, battle, hostility, quarrels, contentions, and civil discords. It conduces but poorly to gain or profit, being naturally evil and malignant; consequently no success can attend the question, where it is a significator. It is under *Mars*, and the warlike sign *Aries*, the ascendant of England. It is *exalted* in the first house, and has its *fall* in the angle opposite.

In order to judge from the figures,* as before observed, the student must learn to be well acquainted with the essential and accidental dignities, stations, aspects, and positions of the geomantic emblems, and be ready in his reference to the twelve celestial houses, by which means, if he be sincere in his wishes, the most astonishing answers may be obtained.

---

* "The editor scarcely need make any remark to impress upon the minds of his readers the necessity of being *serious* in their trials, and with a full desire to attain a correct answer, as they will find from experience, that the hidden mysteries of nature are only to be obtained by an earnest and serious desire to come at the truth; but if *triflers* try them, they try only to be *trifled* with"
Vide PHILOSOPHICAL MERLIN.

EXAMPLES IN GEOMANCY.

In order to perfect the reader in this amusing knowledge, we shall subjoin a few interesting examples.

EXAMPLE I.

A Figure, or Geomantic Scheme, set for the Spilalfields Silk-Weavers.

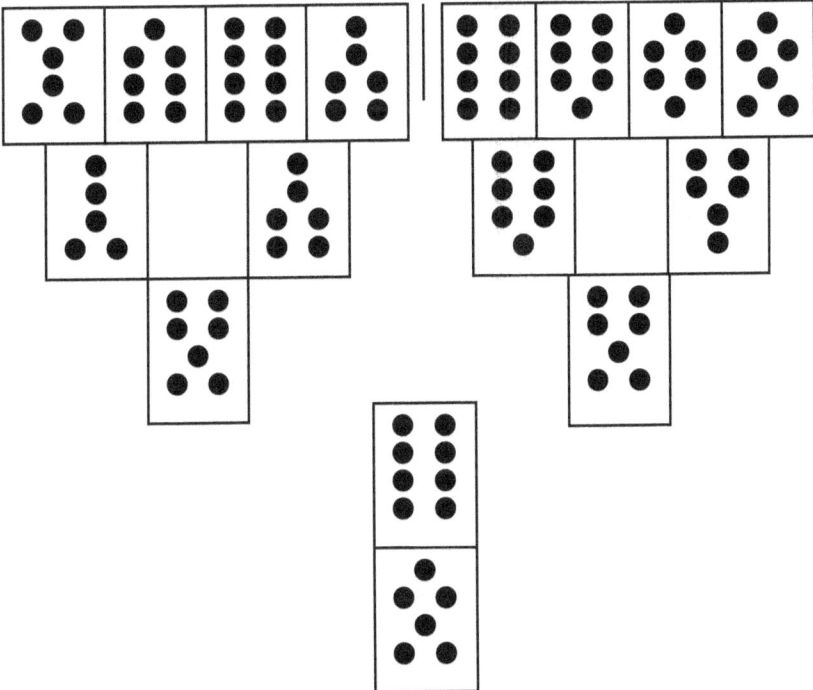

This figure of geomancy was cast for the purpose of ascertaining the result of the bill then pending in Parliament, respecting the Spitalfields silk-weavers, viz. whether they or their opponents would obtain the victory, at the time they were petitioning against the bill.

By examination of the scheme, it will be found that *Amissio* and *Venus* rule the first house, or ascendant of the silk-weavers, and admirably represent this business in hand, while *Tristitia*, a figure of *Saturn* in the 10th house, is symbolical of a decline and falling-off in this trade; and *Carcer* in the house of wealth and gain, a most evil figure, likewise governed by *Saturn* in his most malevolent debilities, sufficiently indicates great loss both to the workmen and their masters. Part of this evil has already taken place, but much more, unfortunately, remains to come.

As we were required by several scientific gentlemen to give our opinion whether the bill, then pending, would be passed, or thrown out altogether; we gave it as our decided opinion, that the opponents of this industrious and numerous class of manufacturers would be the likeliest to gain the victory; but, as the two witnesses are ruled by *Mercury*, and *Populus* the judge, controvertible in nature, while the 16th figure moves in the ascendant, we expected that the bill would receive a partial alteration favourable to the petitioners against it.

It is scarcely necessary to hint, how truly every part of the above prediction has been verified, to the credit and advancement of the science.*

There are several other topics relative to the above class of persons, which may be gathered from the figure,—as, for instance, *Fortuna Major* in the 9th house, showing success in this manufacture to foreigners. *Cauda Draconis* in the 12th house, denoting coolness in the petitioners' friends, and many secret enemies; and *Populus*, in the 4th house, denoting the depreciation of the article in question; while the fixed nature of several significators are likely to cause the whole of these evils to be of long duration, and upon the increase. *Conjunctio* in the 8th house is also typical of short life to the principal agitators of the bill and its supporters, which is yet to be fulfilled, although not many seasons will elapse before this will be verified!

H. W.

---

* "Neither do the terminate. But evil succeeds to evil, and many moons shall pass by ere the train which is now fixed shall have spent its forces."

URANIA, OR THE ASTROLOGER'S CHRONICLE, p. 61.

EXAMPLE II.

Figure cast for the Year in which the late Queen Caroline died, and which most remarkably prefigured her Dissolution.

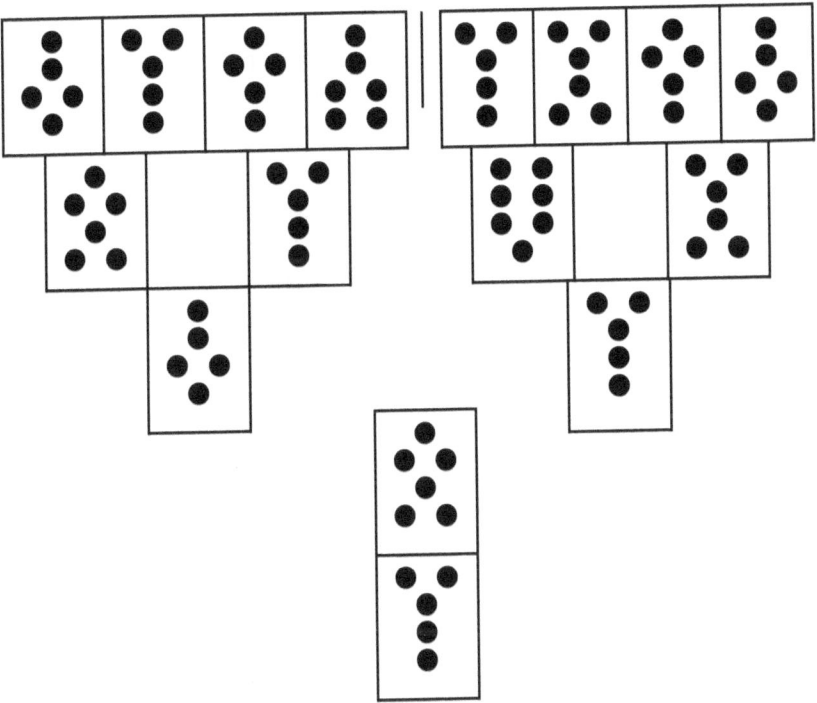

"Ambrose Merlin, the Welsh prophet, declares that the chariot of the moon shall disturb the *zodiac*, and the *Pleiades* shall break forth into lamentations. Which *Lilly* interprets to mean great commotions amongst the common people and contempt of their superiors." —*Vide Lilly's Tracts.*

This figure of geomancy was erected in the month of May, 1821, for the purpose of foreknowing what the fate of that year would be to Queen Caroline, as the affairs of that unfortunate princess were then the general topic of public conversation.

In the first house is found the figure *Puer*, a masculine and martial figure, and well expressing the determination and intrepidity of this illustrious lady, which seemed to have carried her at times beyond her sex.

In the second house, *Puella*, a figure of *Venus*, is favourable for pecuniary resources, and *Caput Draconis*, or the *Dragon's Head*, in the 4th house, symbolically predicts a name and reputation, which should survive the lapse of ages in the page of history. The masculine figure *Fortuna Minor*, in the 5th house, or house of pleasure and enjoyment, signifies that which the attentive student is aware we must not fully express.

But the most remarkable position is the movement of the first figure (which signified the queen personally) into the house of *death*! And this figure being noted by *Mars*, not only showed, beforehand, that she would die that year, but that the death should be in a manner sudden and unexpected.

Tristitia, a figure of *Saturn* (the evil fortune), in the house of honour, and the figure in the house of enemies, significator of the husband also, ruling the house of friends, clearly showed the heavy disappointment and fatality which followed the whole of the actions of this royal native, from the time of setting this figure to that of her death—all which happened precisely as we predicted.

ALFRED.

EXAMPLE III

Figure of the World for the Year of the Coronation; cast March 16, 1821.

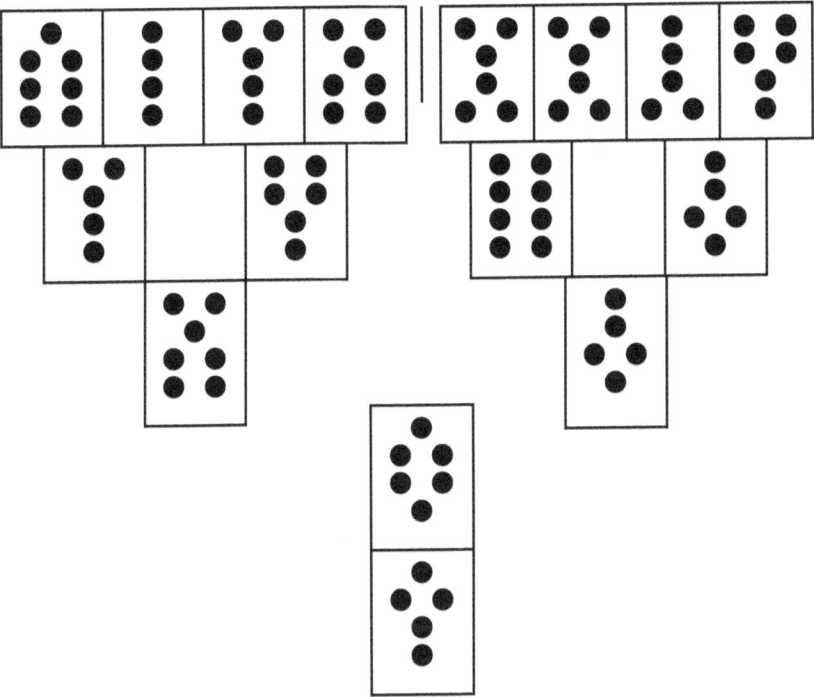

This figure is a striking example that, by geomancy, we may not only judge the fate of private individuals, but also of kingdoms, states and empires; for 𝔉𝔬𝔯𝔱𝔲𝔫𝔞 𝔐𝔞𝔧𝔬𝔯 in the ascendant and eleventh house, and 𝔓𝔬𝔭𝔲𝔩𝔲𝔰 in the mid-heaven, plainly showed the august ceremonies for which the year 1821 was distinguished. 𝔉𝔬𝔯𝔱𝔲𝔫𝔞 𝔐𝔞𝔧𝔬𝔯 being the significator of honour, power, and greatness; and 𝔓𝔬𝔭𝔲𝔩𝔲𝔰 the significator of immense congregations and multitudes of people, both of which were typical of these events; neither were the evils that followed less plainly shown by 𝔘𝔲𝔟𝔢𝔲𝔰, the evil witness, and ℭ𝔞𝔯𝔠𝔢𝔯, the malevolent judge, and final significator of the whole figure.

> "Thus do the planets bear the sovereign rule
> Away from mortals, who, short-sighted as
> The mole or bat, who only see in darkness.

Despise the science of our heav'nly lore.
But we revere the stars." —ANCIENT RHYME.

EXAMPLE IV.

Figure for the End of the Year 1824.

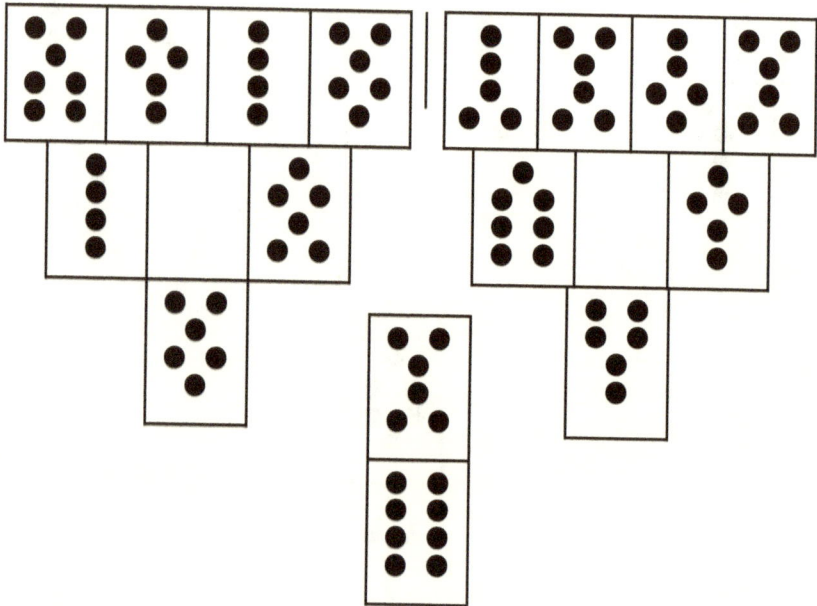

Conjunctio ascending, denotes the time will be busy, active, and remarkable. Much news and rumours, both true and false; and the evil positions of CAUDA in the 4th house, and **Rubeus** in the house of death, are symbolical of heavy calamities, sudden deaths, murders, suicides, robberies, duels, quarrels, and many fatalities. These figures foreshow the ruin of many an upstart, and will pull down the pride of many pretenders. A clergyman, a religious votary, seems ensnared in the wiles of a fair devotee, devoted to love as well as holiness; whispers are abroad concerning it, but Plutus opens his coffers, and all for a time goes on well. The heartless **Amissio**, in the 11th house, will deceive many in their fondest expectations. But yet there are some who, born under more genial influence, will be amazingly prosperous.

"Full many a coward frowns in impotence,
Full many a needless boast is utter'd; but
The planets show the mischief." —Angelus.

EXAMPLE V.

The Geomantic Destiny of Charles X., King of France.

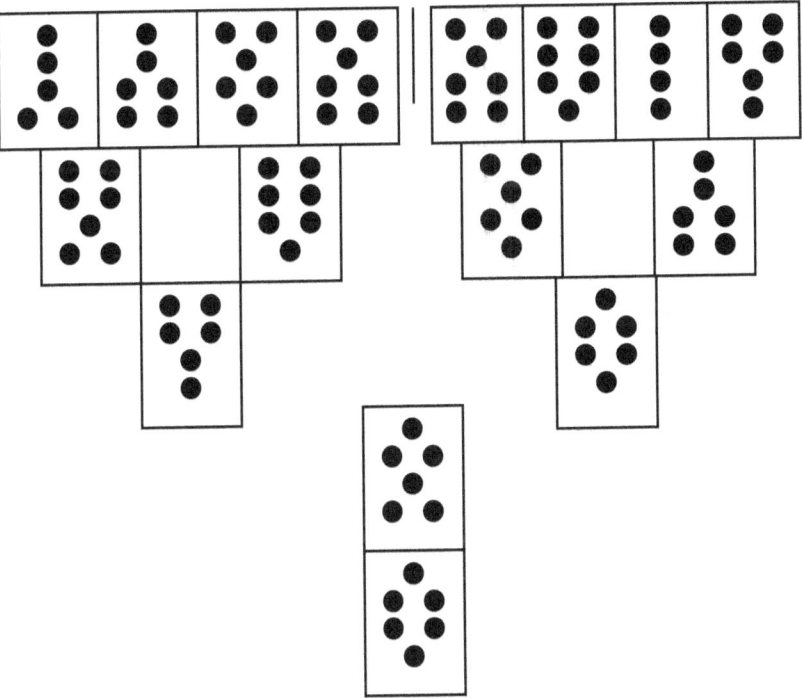

"Bold Arthur drew his line from hence,
And *Jove*, in his best mood, bequeath'd
His lineal succession;—hence the star
Of knighthood reigns.
But yet this figure warns thee to beware;
For whoso *Carcer* threatens seldom yet
Has conquer'd death and liv'd to hoary age.
The points of this said scheme, even as
The sand in which they're made, are fleeting."
Ancient Legend.

Geomancy may well be termed extraordinary knowledge, for by its practice we may discover the principal event of every undertaking, without inquiring as to time or place, so necessary in astrology; and thus does geomancy afford a fund of rational amusement, not to be exceeded by any other science, when rightly practised: but that there are few who understand its practice is certain.

Now, here we have *Fortuna Major* ascending, which leads us to suppose the illustrious native is under the sign *Aquarius*, and under the *solar* reign. *Rubeus*, in the 4th and 5th, argue no issue, and the 7th, going to the 9th, confounds marriage through priestcraft, while the *lord* of the *ascendant*, ruling this figure in the *9th house*, shows his infatuation as it relates to religious ceremonials. But *Cauda* in the 8th and *house of death*, with *Rubeus* in the 4th, or *north angle*, are no very flattering testimonies; they evidently import *danger by falls, bruises, or animals; and one of the family will suffer by fire*. Yet it is probable the native may live to acquire honour enough, for *Acquisitio* in the 10th is a good figure. But what sort of a name will *Rubeus*, in the 4th, give *after* death? This should be looked to by his panegyrists. I have sent this horoscope to the famous astrologer, *M. le Normand*, of Paris, in order that she might give the illustrious native notice of what will befal him—if his courtiers will permit the friendly warning of danger.

Looking at the figure impartially, it seems to denote much celebrity, esteem, and notoriety, were this all—but there is a scourge prepared for the Gallic nation in no very distant quarter, and another more distant—but of which we shall forbear to speak; yet *the reign of this monarch shall not go by without wars and rumours of wars*, and the *north* shall give cause of *terror*.

August, 1825.   ALFRED.

Part Two: Divination

EXAMPLE VI.

A Figure for the Lion Fight at Warwick, cast on the Morning of the Combat.
(Communicated by a Correspondent).

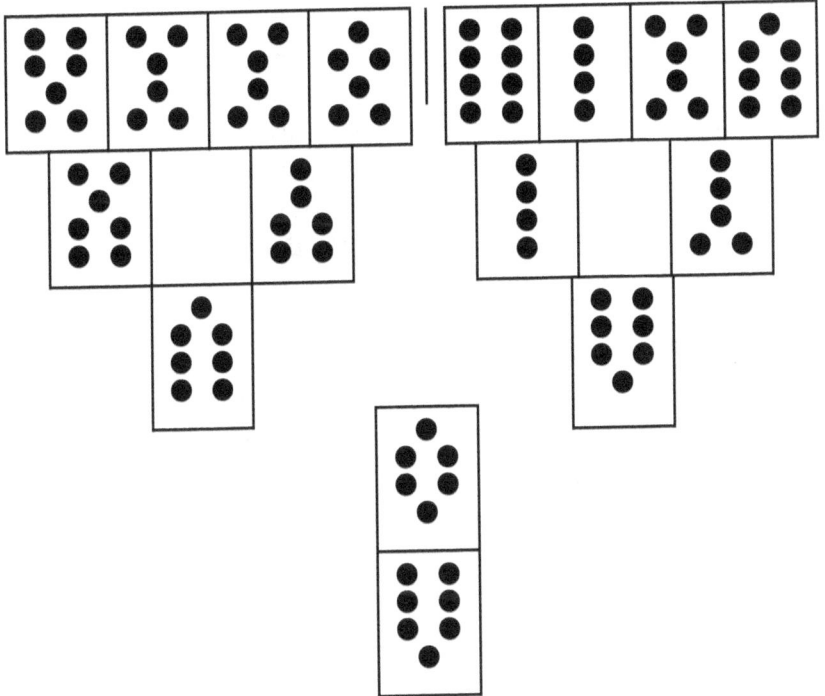

Letitia, which answers to *Jupiter* in *Taurus*, being in the ascendant plainly denoted the generosity and magnanimity of that noble animal, it being the *house of life of the lion*, and *Rubeus* in the 12th denoted the ferocity of his opponents. But the *Judge* being evil, and amissive, denoted that the lion stood no chance of gaining the combat, as it proved.

V.

EXAMPLE VII.

(Communicated by a Correspondent *).

FIGURE FOR THE AUTUMNAL QUARTER, 1825.

"Here *Carcer* wages war with *Populus*,
  And tyranny does lord it. Hence, begone;
For dead men tell not tales. And much I fear,
That malice, lynx-eyed, silent, waits her prey;
Sir Geoffrey." "Ha! say'st so; by my loyalty,
This arm shall wield the lance, the falchion
Temper'd so keenly; and my own stout heart,
Better than sevenfold shield, shall spurn submission.
Sage, I thank thee." — *Old Play.*

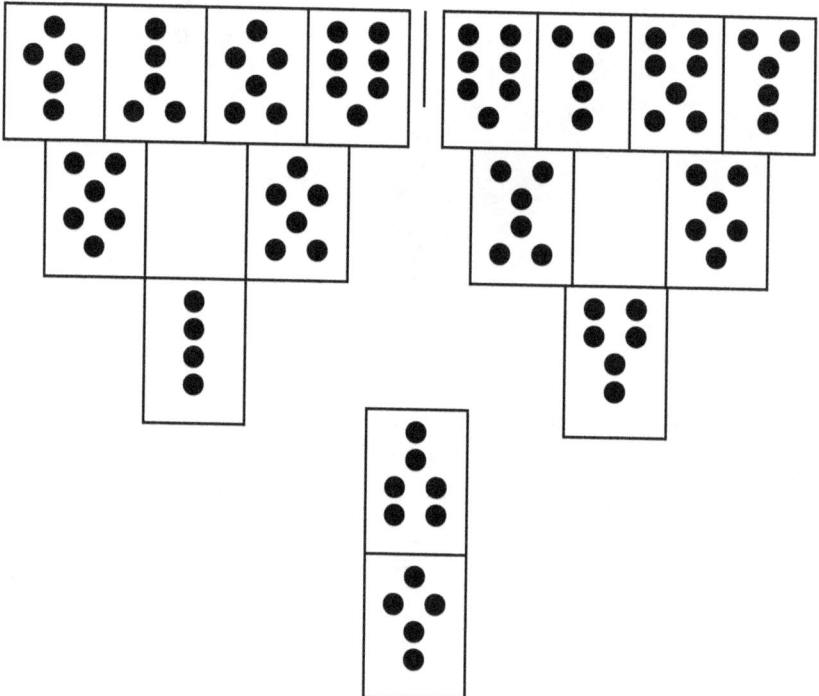

CAPUT in the *first*, and CAUDA in the *eighth* house, are evil and good together remarkably blended; but TRISTITIA in the 4th house, and the first figure opposed by the 7th, and in

---

* See also "Urania, or the Astrologer's Chronicle," page 59; where many curious predictions are made from geomancy.

square to figures of SATURN and MERCURY, denotes immense losses by fire, theft, piracy, and convulsions of nature, most of which will take place here in England, and the metropolis will not be free from its share thereof; but in our eastern possessions, rapine and hostility are more than generally predominant: commerce, however, will flourish. *But a great one dies*; and ere the holy festival is commenced to commemorate the birth of Christians' hope, Rome or Italy shall have suffered a shock which may be long felt in that and other parts of the continent.

MERCURIUS.

EXAMPLES FROM CHAUCERS ILLUMINATED MANUSCRIPT.

EXAMPLE VIII.

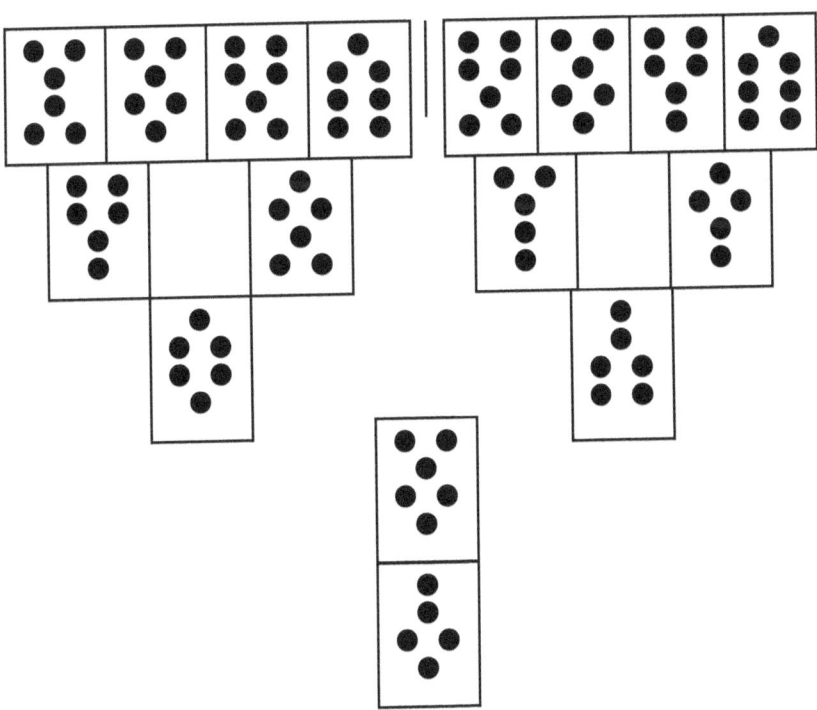

"Our extracts, it will be seen, consist rather of facts than arguments, though they are pretty conclusive as to the latter."—*Literary Chronicle.*

"One, being in the age of judgment, doubted whether he shall have any substance or possession of his father, that was a rich man; and he made his question to a geomancian, and asked whether he should have abundance of goods, and what goods they shall be, and by what means he should gete them, and what tyme. And such projection as above happened.

Now, I beheld the 2nd house, and found therein *Fortuna Major*, that is a laudable figure, acquisitive and *entrant*, that signifieth him to have *good*; and because he was joined* to good and laudable figures, that affirmeth it the more stedfast. But for the 2nd, is *light* in point, it seemeth that goods shall come to him lightly; and in the beginning of that time that he made ye question in, and as the 15th was good, it signifieth finally lucre, substance, and possession, to the asker, and as the 15th is found in the 3rd and 7th houses, *received*, but not *located* (for he was in his *fall*, where he sorroweth). Natheless, as me seemeth, he is joined with good, it signifieth ye in the end of his lyfe, and in the beginning of ye age y^t he is in, he shall wynne by the meens of his brethren, wyfe, and felowes. And because *Acquisitio*, that is figured in *Aries*, is not *located* in the 7th, for it is there opposed to ye house of his formation; that signifieth that the asker hath no great hope to gete his goods, by the aforesaid meens, but because the figure is laudable and good, and a figure of *Jupiter*, signifying science and wisdom, it signifieth the asker, by his prudence, to come to riches. Therefore, the asker is well disposed to have grete riches, as the question supposeth he shall have *pounds*, and *Fortuna Major* representeth 8 in number, and, therefore, he shall have £8000 in money, or near that amount."

Chaucer's mss.

---

* The conjunction is of great force in all questions of geomancy. For, as in astrology, the light planets partake of the nature of those with whom they are *joined*. So in this science, the figures are supposed thereby to change either to good or evil.

EXAMPLE IX.
If the Castle besieged shall be taken?

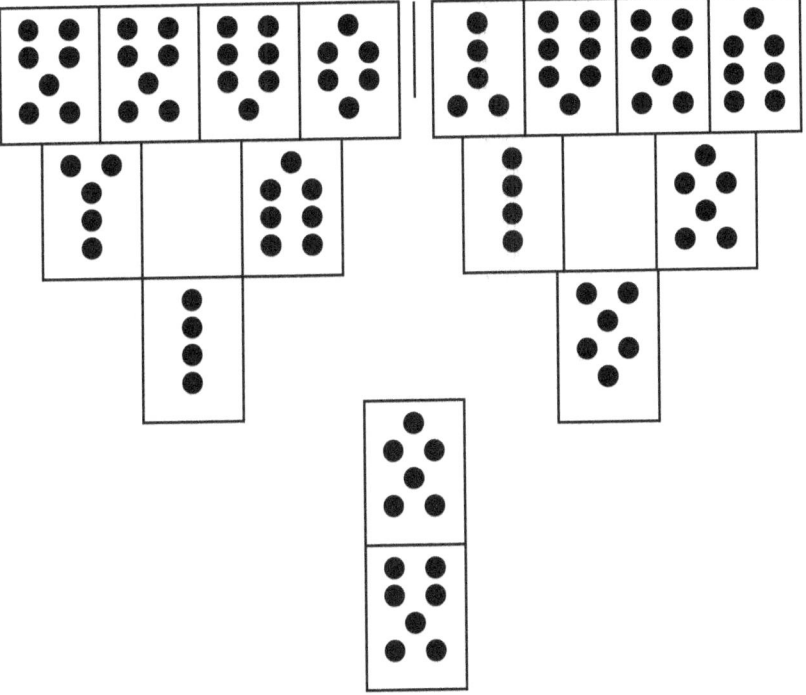

"A lord once yᵉ beseged a castell, desired to wete, yf he shold wynne or no, or destroye it, or in what wyse, &c. And projection was such as aboue. *Letitia*, that is signifier of the asker, is a sign of Saipence and of engyne (ingenuity), yᵗ sheweth him with great skille and prudence to labor for the getyng of yᵗ place and not to profit, for by cause *Letitia* is not *receyved*, and for *Letitia* is agene located in the house of fortune, yᵗ sheweth him to labor the askyng of it for help of his frendes, and to have ayde from them, they thinking to have division thereof, and for all yl he shall not avayle, nor profit, because of the *prohibition* of *Carcer*, and her constitution. And as *Carcer* is a sign of solicitude, yᵗ sheweth that the asker shall haste to gete the Castell. And as *Carcer* is lord of the *fifth*, it is like that his besynes and intentions are in behalfe of a son, or one to him full leef (dear); and for that *Tristitia* is in the house of help, and afterwards goeth to the 6th that sheweth them that he desireth help of, to be slaw, and unlusty, and by happ they be secke (sick) and for povertye and fayntnesse unable to help him. And *Amissio* in the 9th joined with the *first*, it sheweth him to spend moche for to assay to gete ye Castell. And *Acquisitio* in the 13th sheweth that he was a myghty man of good. The signifier of y^m biseged, is *entrant*, and sheweth them to be stable and trew; and *Caput Draconis*, that is in their conjunction, augmenteth their strength, and y^t sheweth ye bisegers to be feebler than ye biseged, but because the signifier of ye biseged is in ye part of ye bisegers, unfortunate by ill *translation*, and is coupled to two ills, to *Via* and *Amissio* that are signs of falseness, y^t sheweth the biseged to faynt, and to make guileful speech to the bisegers; for to yield the Castell, ye which they will not do, for the *first* is not in the *fourth*, neyther in any other places joined, but because *Albus* y^t signifies the asker's purse, maketh translation into the 8th house, which is ye substance of ye biseged, it signifieth the bisegers hath sent money to them biseged for to yield ye Castell, but for by cause *Albus* is *receyved* y^t signifieth y^t they biseged have taken the money, by reason of which money, from strength and consistency, they are become weak and mobile (moveable). And as *Cauda* is in the 4th house, y^t signifyeth the taking and destroying, or breaking up of the Castell, and the destruction of ye biseged."

EXAMPLE X.

Predictions relative to the Arctic Expedition, and whether the North West Passage will be ever discovered.

"Then drew the seer the lines in sand;
And breathing forth in words of skill.
Quoth he, 'The omens here are vile,
For *Reubeus* in thy house of life,
And *Puer*, stimulate to strife.
Beware the blow, beware the brand,
And let not slaughter stain thy hand,
For little good this scheme portends,
And false and guileful are thy friends.—OLD PLAY.

"*Truths* of themselves are to be desired, for science itself is a certain good, now the expectation of *future* good very much delights us, and, on the contrary when future evils are *foreseen*, we may either mitigate them, or at least bear them more contentedly." —GUIDO BONATUS.

CELESTIAL LOTS.

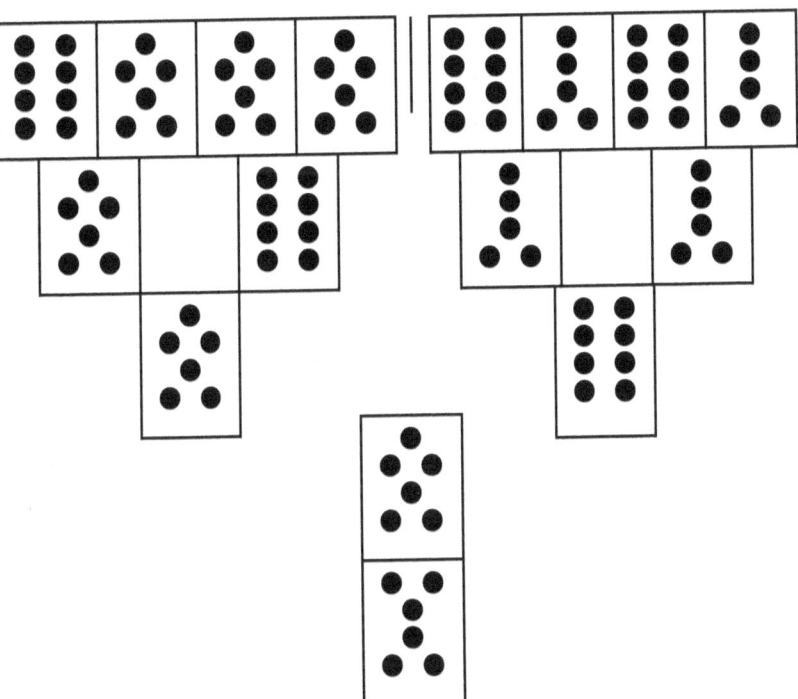

In compliance with the wishes of several friends to this art, I have cast a figure of celestial lots, in order to ascertain whether there is any probability that the north-west passage will ever be discovered: and, by referring to the question, it must be first noticed, that *Cauda*, or the Tail of the Dragon, is found in the *house of life*, the *house of journeys*, and the *house of honour*! This imports great danger to the commander of the expedition, and if the figure speak truth, *Captain Parry will not succeed in his enterprise*; but, it is to be feared, will be in extreme danger during the ensuing year, if not returned previous to that period. And the crew of the vessels, represented by the figure *Populus*, are likewise afflicted.

* * * * * * *

The prevalence of the figures of *Saturn* are worthy of notice; here they recur four times, and at each time become more malignant. Hence the chief failures will be owing to the physical causes and excess of cold, but the figure in the *house of wealth* denotes a want or scarcity of provisions, money, and necessaries.

* * * * * * *

The prospect is gloomy, and some will inevitably suffer. It may happen that the commander is not born under *fortunate stars*; I have not seen his nativity, but would advise him to avoid the *perils* of the *ocean,* and the *dangers* of the elements until his 38th year is past, for the *first* part of his life is represented from this figure to be wild and perilous, but not devoid of hope; and it may be that he may contemn the occult sciences.

* * * * * * *

To proceed;—the *watery* and *fiery* elements predominate, hence one cause of evil and *elementary* strife; while *Populus,* the multitudinous *Populus,* combining the influence of the *full moon,* swift, in *Capricorn;* and after having entered the *house of death,* emerging from thence almost to the very *zenith* of the figure, but stopping short in the house of *hopes* and *wishes,* with the gentle *Amissio* for judicial umpire, bids us look forward to the faint glimmering of *hope,* amidst the chaotic display of dreary benighted obstacles; and hence I conclude, *that the north-west passage will be finally discovered, but by* LAND; *the discovery is most likely, although aquatic excursions constitute partial hopes of success; but neither by the present expeditions nor by the next, nor until England's star shall ascend the horizon, replete with beams of superior influence, from the 11th house of her horoscope, shall the discovery he achieved; but courage and science shall meet their reward.*

August, 1825.

RAPHAEL:

"The more I behold the heavens, the greater mischief do I fear; but knowing God can in a moment reconcile us, I am more sparing in art, yet let none take it ill I predict what I do, from positive rules of art itself." —LILLY.

EXAMPLE XII.

A Figure set for an Accident.

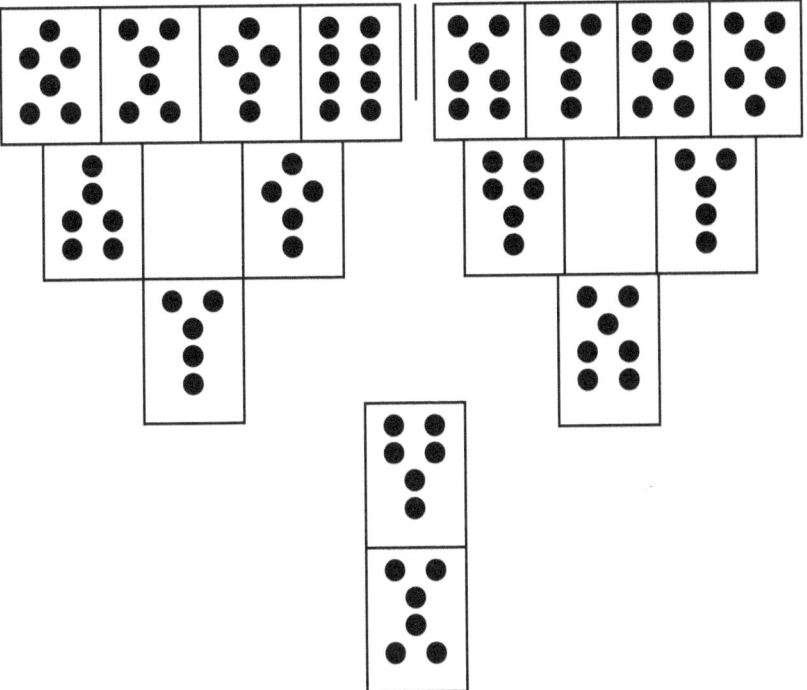

This figure was set upon the following occasion:—M r.L—, a wealthy corn-factor, residing at Whitechapel, met with a fall from his chaise, in consequence of the vehicle being overturned through coming in contact with a waggon. By this accident he suffered such severe bruizes that his life was despaired of; but being requested to give our opinion on the subject, we plainly saw his recovery denoted, for a figure of *Jupiter* is in the *ascendant*, and a figure of *Venus* in the 8th house, which rendered it impossible that he could fall a victim thereto. He recovered within a month of the accident.

EXAMPLE XII.

A figure for Thurtell the Murderer.

"If the house of life be afflicted, there can be no worse harm, especially if the evil figures of *Saturn* be there."

—Albumazar.

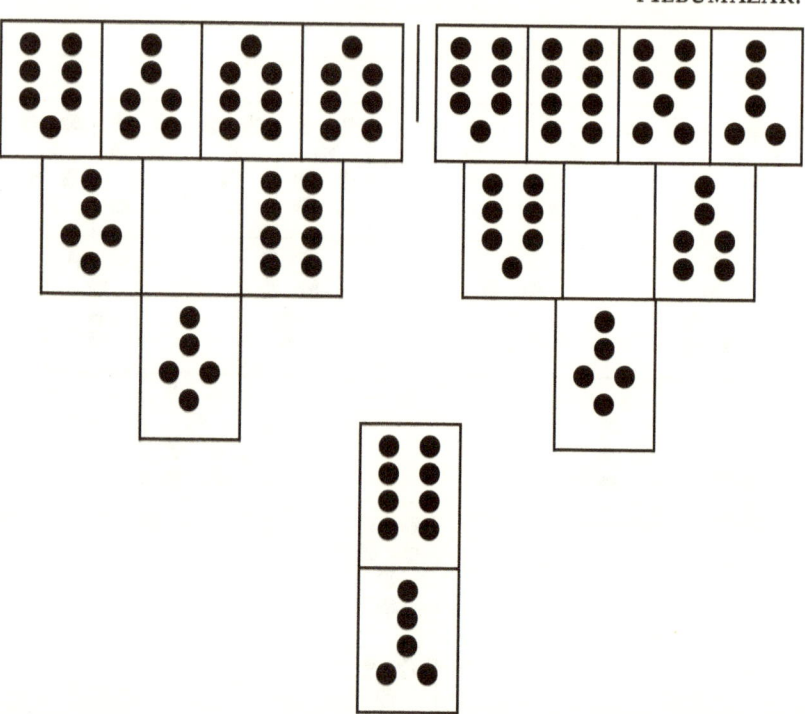

This figure, as could be proved on oath, if requisite, was cast nearly a month previous to the untimely end of this malefactor.— The combinations are remarkable, for the *dragon's tail* in the *house of life*, and a figure of *Saturn*, the anareta, in the *house of death*, coming from the fourth house with the evil figure *Cauda* in the 16th, are each of them particularly typical of that unfortunate end which we predicted, would certainly take place.

Secrets in Geomancy.
TRANSLATED FROM PERUCHIO,
A RARE FRENCH AUTHOR;

by J. PALMER, Esq., Student of Occult Philosophy.

An extraordinary Method of discovering any one's Proper Name, by Geomancy.

It is here that we will give a curious method, to know the **Name of a person, of a city, or of any other thing,** be it what it may; so that if you would discover the name of a thief, or of a worthy man, of a traitor who is in a state, or the natural father of a foundling, of a murderer who has committed homicide, &c., you will follow these rules.

B	C	D	F	G	H	K	L
M	N	P	Q	R	S or Z	T	X

The figure being cast, you will see the 𝔫𝔞𝔪𝔢 of the unknown; but before you make the distinction, you must know the number of syllables it ought to have. That is why you must note that if the judge is a fixed figure, and the two witnesses moveable, it will only be of one syllable. If the judge and one of the witnesses are fixed, it will be of two; and of three, if the two witnesses and the judge are fixed. But if the judge only is moveable, you will only pay attention to the two witnesses, who will denote, as we have already said, two syllables. Lastly, if the judge and one of the witnesses are moveable, the name will be of four syllables; and of five, if these three figures are moveable.

This being understood, you will only take the figures of the first, second, and third, if the name is of one syllable; and if it is of two, you will add the four, five, six, and the others in the same way. But, or as much as the figures in particulars denote only the sixteen consonants, you must have recourse to other places to find the vowels. For that effect, you will place A upon the first three figures, E on the three following, I on the three others, O on the three last, V on the witnesses and judge; and you will remark, that the angular figure which has the least points, will place its vowel in the first syllable, even at the beginning, if it is fixed and masculine; but those which have the most points, will place the vowel at the end of the name; and if they are equal in points, you will place them in their natural rank, that is, where you find them.

As for the consonants, the four angles, and the first witness, give the five consonants which ought to begin the five syllables of the name, if it happens that there are so many. Note, that if the figures of the angles are fixed, the syllable will be but of two letters; it will be of three, if they are moveable; and of four, if a moveable figure follow them; and that is all we have to observe, to find any name soever.

TO DISCOVER NUMBERS BY GEOMANCY.

Those who have put this art in practice, have produced the Table of **numbers** in this form.

6, 8, 12 • • 16, 31, • 400	16 • • 6 • • • 8 • •	6 • • 20, 12 • • • 60 • 500	50 • 6, 3, 5 • • 7
1, 5, 6, 12 • • 50, 60, • 90	16 • 1, 100 • • 1, 1500 • 6	• • 2, • 25, • 14, 4	14, 24 • 1, 1, 12, 50 • • 25
2, 3, 8 • 14, • 21, • 100	7 • • 31, • • 12 • 14	4, 7 • • 14, • • 18, 10 • • 60	22 • • 23, 60 • • 71 • • 70
4, 6, 8, 9 • 10, 24, 40, 90	16 • • 2, 50 • • 3, • • 8, 69 • • 9	6 • • 41, 15, 29 • 9 • • 12	24, 6 • 2, • • 64, 3000 • 10

There are no rules to put this table into practice; nevertheless, as there are but four parts to the figure, namely, the head, the heart, the thighs, and feet. I think that each number, which attaches itself in the figure to either of those parts, can be taken in its value according to its situation, where you find the figure; so that if it is in the angles, you will look at the head, in the succeedents, to the heart, and cadents, to the thighs, and in the houses of the judge and witnesses, you will pay attention to the feet; and by this means you will make a **total number**, by the collection of all these little numbers. This can be practised to know how much money is hid, how much the merchant will gain in traffic, &c.; the numbers to the right signify the gain, and those to the left are the numbers of loss.

TO DISCOVER COLOURS
BY GEOMANCY.

THE third curious observation that we will make here, will be concerning **colours**; that we will discover by the means of figures; for it is necessary to pay attention only to the house of the question, and the figure which is found there denotes the colour. But if you doubt the proper house, you will observe where the ⊕ is placed. To render this curious research easy, here is the table of **figures and colours**; and we will see in the end, the fit place for ⊕, and the point of instruction.

White	Pale	Vermillion Ruddy	Red
Colour of Fire	Citron Orange	Yellow	Green
Violet	Blue	Azure	Flaxen Grey
Grey	Blackish	Black	Changeable Colour

The Part of Fortune

The **Part of Fortune** is very considerable in Geomancy, not only to know the figure of the colour which we wish to know, or the precise number that we are looking for, but also to decide every other case of which a demand can be made; for the said ⊕, following in a bad figure, promises nothing advantageous; on the contrary, you ought to look for every good, when it arrives in a good figure. Here is the manner to find the Part of Fortune:—you must count all the points which occupy the twelve houses, and divide that number by twelve, and the number which remains denotes the ⊕; for instance, if you have seventy-six points, you divide by twelve, there will remain four, which denotes the fourth house, where you ought to put **the Part of Fortune**, &c.; the numbers to the right signify the gain, and those to the left are the numbers of loss.

As for the point of instruction, it serves to denote the subject of the question; for that effect, you must observe what figure passes from the first to another house, and the house where it passes to, indicates the subject of the demand.

The Oracle of Dreams.

According to the Earl of Essex's Manuscript.

In one part of the Manuscript from which the Royal Book of Fate was compiled, the method of "foretelling by the cogitayciones of the nyghte," or, in other words, the Interpretations of Dreams by *Geomancy*, is set forth; from which the following Oracle is extracted.

In using this Oracle, the reader will observe, that it is the figure in *the 9th house of the scheme, from whence the judgment is derived*. Therefore, when any Dream is resolved, let the Student cast the figure of Geomancy, and look to the emblem which is in the 9th house, and the following pages will give the interpretation. In this manner of judgment, neither the judge nor the witnesses are deemed of any power, to alter or nullify the figure in the 9th. The reasons for this mode of judgment are given at full length in the Manuscript, but are useless here to recapitulate.

Oracle 1.

When is in the 9th house

 This is a sign of money, friends, and merry fortune.

Oracle 2.

When is in the 9th house

 The vision is right fortunate: but in gold, silver, and goods, it is best. It predicts also, joy in some unexpected gift, or a friend.

Oracle 3.

When is in the 9th house

 The dream tells chiefly of news. The *absent* will return: the signs also read moderately in good and lucky fortune; and oft-times the dreamer dwells (on voyages) near waters.

Oracle 4.

When is in the 9th house

 The interpretation of the dream is chiefly of some impending misfortune, hard to be eschewed; and it speaks also of private enemies, perchance also of a rival.

Oracle 5.

When is in the 9th house

Read this, to speak of dealings in papers, charts, books, and writings, and moreover of singular or divers employments.

Oracle 6.

When is in the 9th house

Interpret this to be a fortunate sign; the dreamer will have his cogitations granted; but oft-times he buries a friend.

Oracle 7.

When is in the 9th house

Take care an enemy does not injure thee. Perchance something may happen wherein a prison is uppermost. The sign tells also of some cause of a sorrowful kind.

Oracle 8.

When is in the 9th house

This dream is a sign of anger, tumults, ill-blood, and deceitful advisers. Be on they guard—evil is at hand.

Oracle 9.

When is in the 9th house

 This is a right merry and pleasant dream: it tells of carousals, jovial meetings, friends, and banquets; and of good news at hand.

Oracle 10.

When is in the 9th house

 Oft-times when the dreamer casts up this sign, he is unlucky, liable to sorrow, prone to some restraint, and some friend may die.

Oracle 11.

When is in the 9th house

 The dream is felicitous: invitations and various signs of presents or gifts follow. The dreamer is assuredly about to change his present estate to advantage.

Oracle 12.

When is in the 9th house

 The dreamer may well look out for some deceitful person near his habitation. And this may also, perchance, forebode *a loss.*

Oracle 13.

When is in the 9th house

The dream foretold to be prosperous and lucky; fortune has some advantage in store for him who asks, and there will be a journey follow.

Oracle 14.

When is in the 9th house

Either this vision has no meaning, or it forewarns too truly of *misadventures*.

Oracle 15.

When is in the 9th house

This is usually a sign of wedlock to the single, and of offspring to the already united in matrimony. And moreover it is various ways propitious enough.

Oracle 16.

When is in the 9th house

Usually this forebodes angry and vehement words, quarrels and irksome passages in the dreamer's life and fortunes.

Many similar Oracles to the above, are to be found in the Earl of Essex's MSS., which will be inserted in the New Series of *The Astrologer of the 19th Century*, which the author is preparing for the Press.

A SHORT ESSAY ON DREAMING;
WITH A SUCCINCT ACCOUNT OF SEVERAL FAMOUS DREAMS OF THE ANCIENTS AND MODERNS.

The phenomena of dreaming has exercised the ingenuity of mankind in all ages, and various have been the theories invented to account for it. Epicurus fancied that "an infinite number of subtle images, some flowing *from* bodies, some formed *of* their own accord, and others made up of different things variously combined, were continually moving up and down in the air about us; and that those images, being of extreme fineness, penetrate our bodies, and, striking upon the mind, give rise to that mode of perception which we call *Imagination*, and *to which* he refers the origin, both of our waking thoughts and of our dreams.

Aristotle seems to think "that every object of *outward* sense makes, upon the human soul, or upon some other part of our frame, a certain impression, which remains for some time *after* the object that made it is gone; and which, being afterwards recognised by the mind in sleep, gives rise to those visions that then present themselves"

Locke says, "The dreams of *sleeping* men are all made up of the *waking* man's ideas;" but that this is *not the case* the experience of hundreds will prove, for there is scarcely a person now in existence, who, if appealed to whether they have not dreamed of places and persons they have never even thought of, and of events of which they have had no manner or kind of apprehension, but would answer in the affirmative. To say nothing of the vast multitude of *ominous* and prophetic dreams that the history of almost every family, and certainly of every generation, both in past and present times, will furnish.

Other persons adduce the phenomena of dreaming as a proof of the immortality of the soul, grounding their opinions upon the numerous instances recorded in "Holy Writ;" where prophetic inspirations and forewarnings were derived from these nocturnal visions. Mr. Baxter, the celebrated divine, goes so far in this subject as to ascribe "all our dreams to separate spirits, having access to our minds and furnishing us with ideas while we sleep."

The celebrated Dr. YOUNG hath poetically summed up the cases of common dreams, in his usual sprightly, yet solemn manner, thus:

> "'Tis past conjecture; all things rise in proof:
> While o'er my limbs sleep's soft dominion spreads.
> What though my soul fantastic measures trod
> O'er fairy fields; or mourn'd along the gloom
> Of pathless woods; or, down the craggy steep
> Hurl'd headlong, swam with pain the mantled pool;
> Or scaled the cliff; or danc'd on hollow winds
> With antic shapes, wild natives of the brain;
> Her ceaseless flight, though devious, *speaks her nature*
> *Of subtler essence than the trodden clod;*
> Active, aërial, tow'ring unconfin'd,
> Unfetter'd with her gross companions' fall.
> E'en silent night proclaims my soul immortal!
> E'en silent night proclaims eternal day!
> For human weal. Heaven husbands all events;
> Dull sleep instructs, *nor sport vain dreams in vain!*"

The accomplished ADDISON, in one of his Spectators, considers our common dreams as giving us some idea of the great excellency of a human soul, and some intimation of its *independencies on matter*. The heads of what he observes upon them, are as follows:—First, "our dreams are great instances of that activity which is natural to the human soul, and which it is not in the power of sleep to deaden or abate. Secondly, "Dreams are an instance of that agility and perfection which are natural to the faculties of the mind, when they are disengaged from the body." Thirdly, "the passions affect the mind with greater strength when we are asleep, than when we are awake." Fourthly, what gives us a very high idea of the nature of the soul, in regard to what passes in dreams, is that innumerable multitude and variety of ideas which then arise in her." Fifthly, "the next property of the soul is, that wonderful power of producing her own company on these occasions." Sixthly, "the last property of the soul I would mention, is ITS POWER OF DIVINING IN DREAMS." See Spectator, 487, where all these heads are enlarged upon.

The excellent Bishop BULL delivers the following sentiments relative to dreams, in his discourse on the office of the holy angels. "It is true, indeed," says this pious man, "the good angels do not now ordinarily appear in visible forms, or speak by audible voices to men, as in ancient times they did. After God had once spoken unto men by his own son, manifested in the flesh, and by him fully revealed his will to the world, and confirmed that revelation by a long succession of unquestionable miracles, there was no such need of angelic appearances, for the instruction, confirmation, and consolation of the faithful. The succeeding ages do indeed afford us very credible relations of some such apparitions now and then; but ordinarily, I say, the government of angels over us is now administered in a secret and invisible manner. Hence too, too many have been inclined either flatly to deny, or at least to call in question, the truth of the doctrine we are now upon. But they have souls very much immersed in flesh, who can apprehend nothing but what touches and affects their senses; and they that follow this gross and sensual way of procedure, must at last necessarily fall into downright Epicurism, to deny all particular providence of God over the sons of men, and to ascribe all events to those causes that are next to them.

"But, besides, although the ministry of angels be now for the most part invisible, yet to the observant it is not altogether indiscernible.

"We may trace the footsteps of this secret providence over us in many instances, of which I shall note a few. How often may we have observed strong, lasting, and irresistible impulses upon our minds, to do certain things, we can scarce for the present tell why or wherefore; the reason and good success of which we afterwards plainly see. So, on the contrary, there are oftentimes sudden and unexpected accidents, as we call them, cast in our way to divert us from certain enterprises we are just ready to engage in, the ill consequences whereof we do afterwards, but not till then, apprehend. Again, *quantum est in subitis casibus ingenium!* How strange many times are our present thoughts and suggestions in sudden and surprising dangers! We then, upon the spot, resolve and determine as well as if we had a long time deliberated, and taken the best advice and counsel; and we ourselves afterwards wonder how such thoughts came into our minds. Hither, also, we may refer that lucky conspiracy of circumstances which we sometimes experience in our affairs and business, otherwise of great difficulty; when we light upon the nick of opportunity; when the persons whose counsel or assistance we most need strangely occur, and all things fall out according to our desire, but beyond our expectation. What strange ominous forebodings and fears do many times on a sudden seize upon men of certain approaching evils, whereof at present there is no visible appearance! And have we not had some unquestionable instances of men not inclined to melancholy, strongly and unalterably persuaded of the near approach of their death, so as to be able punctually to tell the very day of it, when they have been in good health, and neither themselves nor their friends could discern any present natural cause for such a persuasion, and yet the event hath proved that they were not mistaken. And, although I am no doter on dreams, yet, I verily believe, that some dreams are monitory above the power of fancy, and impressed on us by some superior influence; for of such dreams we have plain and undeniable instances in history, both sacred and profane, and in our own age and observation. Nor shall I so value the laughter of sceptics, and the scoffs of the epicureans, as to be ashamed to profess that I myself have had some convincing experiments of such impressions. Now, it is no enthusiasm, but the best account that can be given of them, to ascribe these things to the ministry of those invisible instruments of God's providence, that guide and govern our affairs and concerns, —namely, the angels of God."

I may here observe, that it has been the opinion of all ranks and denominations of men, in all ages and nations, among

Heathens, Jews, Mahometans, and Christians, that the Divine Being doth make known his will upon some occasions in this manner. The holy scriptures always take it for granted, and indeed give us abundance of instances of such manifestations. Neither are other writings, whether ancient or modern, wanting in similar well-attested relations. The following are a few instances out of the Sacred Scriptures.

1. The first we meet with in the Bible, is in the fifteenth chapter of Genesis, where we are told God appeared unto Abraham, and acquainted him with the captivity and deliverance of his posterity.

2. In the twentieth chapter we are also informed, that Abimelech, king of Gerar, had a dream, wherein God made known unto him that Sarah was the wife of Abraham.

3. In the twenty-sixth chapter it is said, the Lord appeared unto Isaac by night, and blessed him.

4. In the twenty-eighth chapter is recorded a very remarkable mysterious dream that Jacob had of a ladder, and the angels of God ascending and descending upon it.

5. In the thirty-first chapter we find the angel of the Lord spake unto Jacob in a dream, and showed him the reason of Laban's cattle bearing ring-straked, speckled, and grisled young.

6. In the same chapter it is related, that God spake unto Laban by night in a dream.

7. In the thirty-seventh chapter, we have two other prophetic dreams of Joseph; the one about the sheaves making obeisance to his sheaf, and the other about the sun, moon, and eleven stars doing him honour.

8. In the fortieth chapter we have two other significant and prophetic dreams; the one by the chief butler, and the other by the chief baker of Pharoah.

9. In the next chapter of the same book it is related that king Pharoah himself had two expressive and prophetic dreams, both which, as well as the two former, Joseph truly interpreted.

10. There is another singular one recorded in the seventh chapter of the book of Judges, about a cake of barley bread

which tumbled into the host of Midian, and which was interpreted to be the sword of Gideon. After this interpretation Gideon was encouraged to attack the enemy, and obtained a complete victory.

11. In the third chapter of the First Book of Kings, it is said, that the Lord appeared to Solomon in a dream, and held a conversation with him. It is a very instructive one, and therefore I will produce it at length:—In Gibeon the Lord appeared to Solomon in a dream by night; and God said, Ask what I shall give thee. And Solomon said, thou hast showed unto thy servant David, my father, great mercy, according as he walked before thee in truth and righteousness, and in uprightness of heart with thee, and thou hast kept for him this great kindness that thou hast given him a son to sit on his throne, as it is this day. And now, O Lord, my God, thou hast made thy servant king instead of David my father, and I am but a little child; I know not how to go out or come in. And thy servant is in the midst of thy people which thou hast chosen, a great people, that cannot be numbered nor counted for multitude. Give, therefore, thy servant an understanding heart to judge thy people, that I may discern between good and bad: for who is able to judge this thy so great a people? And the speech pleased the Lord, that Solomon had asked this thing. And God said unto him, because thou hast asked this thing, and hast not asked for thyself long life, neither hast asked riches for thyself, nor hast asked the life of thine enemies, but hast asked for thyself understanding to discern judgment; behold, I have done according to thy words; lo, I have given thee a wise and an understanding heart, so that there was none like thee before thee, neither after thee shall any arise like unto thee. And I have also given thee that which thou hast not asked, both riches and honour; so that there shall not be any among the kings like unto thee all thy days. And if thou wilt walk in my ways to keep my statutes and my commandments, as thy father did walk, then I will lengthen thy days. And Solomon awoke, and behold, it was a dream; and he came to Jerusalem, and stood before the ark

of the covenant of the Lord, and offered up burnt-offerings, and peace-offerings, and made a feast to all his servants.

12. The dreams of Nebuchadnezzar, king of Babylon, are very remarkable, and involve the history of the world. Those of Daniel, too, are much of the same kind, and contain a figurative view of the state of mankind to the end of time, and the dissolution of all things.

Several other dreams and night-visions are recorded, both in the Old Testament and in the Apocryphal books, highly worthy the attention of the curious; but as the volume in which they are contained is in every person's hand, and lest I should appear too tedious in multiplying quotations, we will pass on to those in the New Testament.

13. When our Saviour was about to be born, there were several notices conveyed to the mind of Joseph, his reputed father, in the same supernatural manner. Yea, in the two first chapters of St. Matthew's gospel there are no less than five admonitory dreams recorded.

14. I do not know if our Saviour's temptation in the wilderness was not of the dream or vision kind; for, if we read it considerately, we shall see that there are some circumstances in it that cannot easily be accounted for on any other principle.

15. The dream of Pilate's wife appears evidently to have been supernatural and admonitory.

16. In the eighteenth chapter of Acts we have a relation of a vision that St. Paul had, saying, be not afraid, but speak, and hold not thy peace: for I am with thee, and no man shall set on thee, to hurt thee; for I have much people in this city.

17. And again, in the twenty-seventh chapter, there is one similar: there stood by me this night the angel of God, whose I am, and whom I serve, saying, "Fear not, Paul, thou must be brought before Caesar; and lo, God hath given thee all them that sail with thee."

These relations are also recorded in the holy scriptures. Several of them have been attended with the most important consequences in the history of mankind; and they are also so interwoven with the sacred story, that they cannot be rejected without shaking the credit of the whole book wherein they are found. *But the truth of holy scripture is established upon such an immoveable foundation, that it can never be subverted, but upon principles that would overturn the faith of all history.* Before we can commence infidels, therefore, with respect to these parts of the Bible which record the divine interpositions by dreams and night-visions, we must be prepared to reject the whole system of revelation; for the credit of the former stands or falls with that of the latter.

Among the ancients, we know that those famous philosophers, SOCRATES, PLATO, XENOPHON, ARISTOTLE, CICERO, and PLINY, and several more of the great men of antiquity, believed the doctrine of dreams and night visions, as also the ancient poets. HOMER, in particular, expressly tells us, in the beginning of his immortal Poem, the *Iliad*, that *"dreams descend from Jove."* And he gives us a fine example of one, in the beginning of the second book, thus translated by POPE:

> "Now, pleasing sleep had seal'd each mortal eye,
> Stretch'd in the tents the Grecian leaders lie, —
> Th' immortals slumber'd on their thrones above;
> All, but the ever watchful eyes of Jove.
> To honour Thetis' son, he bent his care,
> And plunge the Greeks in all the woes of war;
> Then bids an empty Phantom rise to sight,
> And thus commands the visions of the night:
> 'Fly hence, deluding dream! and, light as air.
> To Agamemnon's ample tent repair.
> Bid him in arms draw forth the embattled train,
> Lead all his Grecians to the dusty plain.
> Declare e'en now, 'tis given him to destroy
> The lofty towers of wide-extended Troy!
> For now no more the gods with fate contend, —
> At Juno's suit the heavenly factions end.
> Destruction hangs o'er yon devoted wall,
> And nodding Ilion waits the impending fall.'
> Swift as the word *the vain illusion fled,*
> *Descends, and hovers o'er Atrides' head!*

Cloth'd in the figure of the Pylian sage,
Renown'd for wisdom, and rever'd for age,
Around his temples spreads his golden wing.
And thus the flattering dream deceives the king.
'Canst thou, with all a monarch's care opprest.
Oh, Atreus' son! canst thou indulge thy rest?
Ill fits a chief who mighty nations guides,
Directs in council, and in war presides—
To whom its safety a whole people owes,
To waste long nights in indolent repose.
Monarch, awake! 'tis Jove's command I bear,—
Thou, and thy glory, claims his heavenly care.
In just array draw forth the embattled train,
Lead all thy Grecians to the dusky plain:
E'en now, O King! 'tis given thee to destroy
The lofty towers of wide-extended Troy.
For now, no more the Gods with fate contend,—
At Juno's suit the heavenly factions end.
Destruction hangs o'er yon deserted wall.
And nodding Ilion waits the impending fall!
Awake, but waking this advice approve,
And trust the vision that descends from Jove.'
The Phantom said; then, vanish'd from his sight,
Resolves to air, and mixes with the night."

HIPPOCRATES, the ancient renowned physician, has some curious observations relative to dreams. "To dream of fire," says he, "indicates a redundance of yellow bile; to dream of fogs, or snow, indicates a predominancy of black bile; to dream of seeing a fall of rain, or snow, or a great quantity of ice, shows that there is a redundancy of phlegm in the body; he who fancies himself among bad smells, may be assured that he harbours some putrid matter in his body; to have red things represented before you in sleep, denotes a redundancy of blood. If the patient dreams of seeing the sun, moon, and stars, hurry on with prodigious swiftness, it indicates an approaching delirium; to dream of seeing the earth overflowed with water, or of being immersed in a pond or river, indicates a redundance of watery humours in the body;

to dream of a turbid sea, indicates abdominal disorders; to dream of seeing the earth burnt up, or parched, is a sign of great heat and dryness; the appearance of monsters and frightful enemies, indicates deliriums in diseases; and to dream of being thrown down from some very high place, threatens an approaching vertigo, or some other disorder of the head, as an epilepsy, apoplexy, or the like."

The poet HESIOD, who, it is supposed, lived nearly a thousand years before our Saviour, imagined our nightly impressions to be *supernatural,* and derived from guardian genii; he writes thus:

> "Exactly mark, ye rulers of mankind,
> The ways of Truth, nor be to justice blind.
> Consider, all ye do, and all ye say,
> The holy demons to their god convey;
> *Aerial spirits,* by great Jove design'd
> To be on earth the guardians of mankind.
> Invisible to mortal eyes they go,
> And mark our actions, good or bad, below.
> The immortal spies with watchful care preside,
> And thrice ten thousand round their charges glide:
> They can reward with glory or with gold,
> A power they by divine permission hold,"

HELIOGABALUS, the Roman emperor, is said by historians to have had such a dread of dreams and visions, that "he watched in the nights, and slept in the day," which custom was reprehended by Seneca, the philosopher, as "discommendatory and unfit for practice."

SOCRATES, the night immediately preceding the day he saw Plato, dreamed that a swan, being presented to him, rested in his lap, and thence flying, pitched upon that gate of *Athens* which was called Academicae, where it so stretched out its neck, that it reached and pierced the heaven: the next day, while Socrates related his dream to his scholars, Plato's father presented his son to Socrates to be instructed, whereupon Socrates cries out,—Behold! this is the swan that shall soar up to the celestial secrets, and discover hidden things.

Part Two: Divination

There is an ancient tradition, that while Plato was an infant, sleeping in his cradle, a cluster or swarm of bees pitched themselves on his lips, and afterwards dispersed themselves in the air. The ancients prophesied, from thence, that the child would be a great philosopher, as it indeed proved.

It is related by historians, that *Nero's* mother, while pregnant with that afterwards inhuman monster, dreamed that she gave birth to "a cruel great dragon," which, rising up against the mother, tore her to pieces. This dream being related to the soothsayers, they prophesied that she should "bring forth a wicked man, one who would be the cause of her own death:" it happened accordingly.

Suetonius relates of Calphurnia, *Julius Caesar's* wife, that the night before the assassination she dreamed that the roof of the house fell, that her husband was stabbed, and that the Chamber door of itself flew open. Julius himself also had a vision, that he flew above the clouds; another time, that he shook hands with Jupiter; and, another time, that he was cast down headlong, all which were ominous of his tragic end and disastrous exit.

The Emperor DARIUS, before the last battle with Alexander the Great, dreamed that he saw a burning army marching through Asia, coming even to Babylon, where he saw Alexander clad in a Persian robe, entering the temple, and presently vanishing. By which dream Darius was persuaded, that by the flames destruction was meant to the Macedonian army; and that Alexander being clad in a Persian habit, signified he should be brought under the power of the Persians, But the event made it appear, that by the flames was portended the swift and victorious progress of Alexander, like that of fire, devouring all things: by the Persian habit, the Persian empire was foresignified to Alexander.

CAMBYSES dreamed that his crown touched the heaven, and that he sat in his brother Smeidis's royal seat, which was an omen of his death.

The favourite of *Ptolomie Alexander*, being hurt with a poisoned dart, through the grievousness of the pain, was in bodily tortures. Alexander, it is said, sitting by him, fell asleep, and in his dream saw a dragon, which his mother Olympias kept, carrying a little root in his mouth, and showing the place where it grew, declared by signs it was of such virtue, that it would cure his friend. Alexander, upon awaking, told his dream, and sent to seek that root (for the place was not far off), which having found, it cured not only Ptolomie, but many of the soldiers that were hurt with those kinds of darts.—Such verifications, also, befell the ominous dream of PHILIP, the father of Alexander the Great, at the nativity of his son, of an eagle being on his palace; with numerous other instances that might be here adduced from the ancient historians.

WHEN Socrates was in prison, Crito went to pay him an early visit, and told him, he was informed by persons come from sea, that the ship from Delos would return that day; the consequence of which was, that Socrates should be put to death on the morrow. Be it so, said Socrates, if it please the gods; yet, I think, the ship will not be here to-day, but to-morrow. Why so, dear friend? said Crito. Because this night, replied Socrates, a woman of a beautiful form, clothed in a white robe, appeared to me in a dream, and, calling me by name, said, "*The third day* shall land thee safe at fruitful Phtia." They are the words of Achilles in Homer, when he proposed to return to his home. Socrates took it for a prediction of his death, because he judged that to die was to go home to his own country. And his dream was accomplished.

Before the martyrdom of POLYCARP, he had a vision: the pillow under his head seemed to him on fire, upon which he said prophetically, that he should be burned alive, which accordingly took place, three days afterwards.

The Emperor MARCUS ANTONINUS, in the first chapter of his Commentaries, professeth, "that he owed it to the gods that certain *remedies were suggested to him in dreams*, and among the rest, that against spitting of blood and giddiness of the head, as happened to him at Gaeta."

Soranus tells us, that HIPPOCRATES, the father of physic and prince of physicians, was divinely admonished in a dream to go and settle in Thessaly.

GALEN, after Hippocrates, prince of the physicians, *chose physic for his profession from a dream* which his father had a little before his death; and Pliny writes that "the cures of many diseases, unknown before, had been discovered in dreams."

When Cicero was forced into exile by an opposite faction, while he abode at a village in the fields of Atinas, in his sleep he thought, that while he wandered through desert places and unknown countries, he met with C. Marius, in all his consular ornaments, and that he asked him, wherefore his countenance was so sad, and whither he intended that uncertain journey of his? And when he had told him of his misfortune, he took him by the right hand, and gave him to the next Lictor, with command to lead him into his monument, insomuch as there was reserved for him a more happy fortune, and change of his condition. And it came to pass accordingly; for in the temple of Jupiter, erected by Marius, there it was that the senate passed the decree for the return of Cicero from his exile.

A rich vessel of gold being stolen out of the temple of Hercules, Sophocles was showed the resemblance and name of the thief in his sleep, which, for the first and second time, he neglected; but, being troubled the third night, he went to the Areopagi, to whom he made known what had passed. They, upon no other evidence, summoned the party before them, who, after strict examination, confessed the fact, and made restitution of the vessel.

Croesus, king of Lydia, had two sons: one of which being dumb, was a perpetual subject of affliction to him; the other, named Atys, distinguished himself by all kinds of good qualities, and was his great consolation and delight. The father dreamed one night, which made a great impression upon his mind, that this beloved son of his was to perish by iron. Upon this, care was taken to remove out of the young prince's way every thing made of iron. No mention was made of armies, wars, or sieges, before him. But one day there was to be an extraordinary hunting-match, for the killing of a wild boar, which had committed great ravage in the neighbourhood. All the young lords of the court were to be at this hunting. Atys very earnestly importuned his father, that he would give him leave to be present, at least as a spectator. The king could not refuse him that request, but let him go, under the care of a discreet young prince, who had taken refuge in his court, and was named Adrastus. And this very Adrastus, as he was aiming to fling his javelin at the boar, unfortunately killed Atys. And so the dream of his father was accomplished, notwithstanding all his precaution.

The next is singularly remarkable, and as well authenticated as any thing of the kind is well capable of being. I will give it in the words of Rollin.

When Alexander laid siege to Tyre, the Samaritans sent him a considerable body of troops; whereas the Jews thought they could not submit themselves to him, so long as Darius, to whom they had taken an oath of allegiance, should be living.

Alexander, being little used to such an answer, particularly since he had obtained so many victories, and thinking that all things ought to bow to him, resolved, the instant he had conquered Tyre, to march against the Jews, and punish their disobedience as rigorously as he had done that of the Tyrians.

In this imminent danger, Jaddus, the high-priest, who governed under the Persians, seeing himself exposed, with all the inhabitants, to the wrath of the conqueror, had recourse to the protection of the Almighty, and gave orders for the offering up public prayers to implore his assistance, and made sacrifices. The night after, God appeared to him in a dream, and bade him to cause flowers to be scattered up and down the city; to set open all the gates, and go, clothed in his pontifical robes, with all the priests dressed also in their vestments, and all the rest clothed in white, and meet Alexander, and not fear any evil from the king, inasmuch as he would protect them. This command was punctually obeyed; and accordingly this august procession, the very day after, marched out of the city to an eminence called Shapha, whence there was a view of all the plain, as well as of the

Part Two: Divination

temple and city of Jerusalem. Here the whole procession waited "the arrival of Alexander.

The Syrians and Phoenicians who were in his army, were persuaded that the wrath of this prince was so great, that he would certainly punish the high priest after an exemplary manner, and destroy that city in the same manner as he had done Tyre; and, flushed with joy upon that account, they waited in expectation of glutting their eyes with the calamities of a people to whom they bore a mortal hatred.

As soon as the Jews heard of the king's approach, they set out to meet him with all the pomp before described. Alexander was struck at the sight of the high-priest, in whose mitre and forehead a golden plate was fixed, on which the name of God was written. The moment the king perceived the high-priest, he advanced towards him with an air of the most profound respect; bowed his body, adored the august name above mentioned, and saluted him who wore it with a religious veneration. Then the Jews, surrounding Alexander, raised their voices to wish him every kind of prosperity. All the spectators were seized with inexpressible surprise; they could scarce believe their eyes; and did not know how to account for a sight, so contrary to their expectation, and so vastly improbable.

Parmenio, who could not yet recover from his astonishment, asked the king how it came to pass that he, who was adored by every one, adored the high-priest. "I do not," replied Alexander, "adore the high-priest, but the God whose minister he is: whilst I was at Dius, in Macedonia (my mind wholly fixed on the great design of the Persian war,) as I was revolving the methods how to conquer Asia, this very man, dressed in the same robes, appeared to me in a dream; exhorted me to banish every fear; bade me cross the Hellespont boldly; and assured me, that God would march at the head of my army, and give me victory over that of the Persians."

Alexander added, that the instant he saw this priest, he knew him, by his habit, his stature, his air, and his face, to be the same person whom he had seen at Dius; that he was firmly persuaded, it was by the command, and under the immediate conduct of Heaven, that he had undertaken this war; that he was sure he should overcome Darius hereafter, and destroy the empire of the Persians; and that this was the reason why he adored this God in the person of his priest. Alexander, after having thus answered Parmenio, embraced the high- priest, and all his brethren; then walking in the midst of them, he arrived at Jerusalem, where he offered sacrifices to God, in the temple, after the manner prescribed to him by the high priest.

Amongst the Orientals, the presages made from dreams are held sacred; traditional historians relate many instances thereof. It is said that the father of OSMAN I., who laid the foundation of the Ottoman empire, was instigated thereto by the denouncements of a dream. A few weeks before the birth of *Osman*, he saw, in a dream, a spring of water break forth from his own house, with such abundance and rapidity as to form immediately an immense torrent, which in its impetuous course almost entirely overflowed the globe. When he arose from his sleep he addressed with terror an aged Scheykh, an interpreter of dreams: "Take confidence," said the old man: "thy family has the blessing of God; thou shalt soon have a son, whom thou shalt behold the founder of a monarchy which shall embrace all the countries of the world."

The same annals ascribe equally to a dream the civil and military virtues of this first of the Othoman monarchs: he was persuaded, they say, one night, that he heard a voice which *warned* him "to be faithful to the duties of the throne, and to all the laws of the prophet;" hence, in 1304, immediately after the conquest of *Nice*, he shared the plunder with his soldiers, and distributed among them the territories of that city, under the title of timar, or military fiefs.

In 1365, a vision also caused the seat of the empire to be established at Adrianople, by Mourad I. This prince declared that he was commanded by a celestial spirit, who pointed out to him in a dream the place where he should erect his palace.

Some years afterwards, Mohammed II. carried on a war against Ouzounn Hassan, and marched himself into Persia, at the head of a powerful army. He dreamed that Ouzounn Hassan, in the habit of a wrestler, appeared on an immense plain, challenging all the heroes of his time to enter the lists with him; that, inflamed with uncommon ardour, he had instantly thrown off his clothes and assumed those of a wrestler; that he engaged his antagonist, and that the victory was disputed with the most furious intrepidity; that fortune appeared at first to declare against him; that, yielding to the first effort of his antagonist, he had bent his knee to the earth; but that, exerting his whole strength, he instantly recovered, and by a skilful and vigorous blow threw his rival on the ground; that he then opened his side, and cast part of his entrails on the plain; and that Ouzounn Hassan, covered with dust and infamy, and weltering in his blood, vanished from his sight, filling the air with cries and lamentations. When he awoke, Mohammed II. mentioned this vision to his courtiers, ministers, and principal officers: they considered it as prophetic of the most signal fortunes. The report was circulated through the camp, and had a powerful influence on the soldiers: they marched with confidence against the enemy, and every event of the war testified the favourable opinion which had been entertained of this mysterious dream.

In the second year of the reign of Osman II., a dream is said to have had a wonderful effect upon the destinies of the empire. He dreamed that he was clad in armour, seated on his throne and reading the Courann, when Mohammed appeared, and with an angry aspect dashed the book from his hand, despoiled him of his armour, smote him on the face, and threw him to the ground, from whence he was unable to rise, to embrace the knees of the prophet. To relieve his perplexity, Osman went *incognito* the same day to consult a celebrated Scheykh, who was respected as a saint, and considered as the most skilful of all interpreters of dreams. This sage told him in general terms that his vision was a celestial warning to repent of his prevarications, and to become, during his future life, attentive to the duties of the throne, and to the precepts and practice of religion. Osman now no longer hesitated to consider his vision as a heavenly oracle: he determined to depart, hastened the preparations for a pilgrimage, and rejected, with unshaken firmness, all the remonstrances of the divan. Mankind are acquainted with the melancholy fate of this young monarch, and with the destructive consequences of his death, which, during many years, distressed and desolated the empire.

Numerous *modern* instances of prophetic dreams might be here recited, and those too well testified by creditable witnesses. *Monsieur Calignan,* Chancellor of Navarre, was esteemed a man of singular virtue: being at Berne, one night as he lay asleep, he heard a voice which called him by his name, *Calignan!!* Awaking and hearing no more of it, he imagined it only a dream, and fell asleep again. A little afterwards he heard the same voice calling him in the same manner: this made a greater impression on him than the former, so that, being awakened, he called his wife, who was with him, and told her what had happened. They both lay waking for some time, expecting to hear it a third time; at length, they went to sleep together, *when the voice awaked him again,* calling him by his name, and advising him to retire immediately out of the town, and to remove his family, for that the plague would rage horribly in that place in a few days. He followed the direction, and within a few days after the plague began in the town and destroyed a great number of people.

When the celebrated Dr. Harvey, being a young man, went to travel towards Padua, he went to Dover with several others, and showed his pass, as the others did, to the governor. The governor told him that *"he must not go,* but he must keep him prisoner." The doctor desired to know the reason, and what he had done amiss; he said, "it was his will to have it so." The packet-boat hoisted sail in the evening, which was very clear, and the doctor's companions in it—a terrible storm ensued, and the packet-boat, with all the passengers, was cast away: the next day the melancholy news was brought to Dover. The governor was a total stranger to Dr. Harvey, but by name and by face: only the night before he had a perfect vision, in a dream, of Dr. Harvey, who came to pass over to Calais, and an order to stop him! This the doctor was told by the governor the next day, and he told the story again to his friends in London.

THOMAS WOTTON, Esq., a little before his death, dreamed that the University of Oxford was robbed by five men. He wrote to his son, who was then in Oxford, and told him the particulars of his dream. The university was robbed accordingly, *the very night before the letter came to his son's hand!* As soon as morning arrived, there was a great noise concerning the robbery; whereupon the young man showed his letter to the persons concerned, and all the five men were taken up and found guilty.

WILLIAM NESSENUS, on a certain day at dinner, in a gentle sleep he had, dreamed that he was passing a river in a fisher's boat, as he frequently did for his diversion, and that the boat, striking on the trunk of a tree, was overturned, and he was drowned. This dream he told to Philip *Melancthon*, who then accidentally came to see him, at the same time deriding the vanity of dreams. But, however, *that very evening* his dream had its accomplishment.

JOHANNES MARIA MAUROSENUS, a senator of Venice, while he was praetor in Dalmatia, saw in his dream one of his brothers, whom he much loved, come to embrace him, and bid him farewell, because he was going to the other world. And having, as he thought, followed him a little way weeping, he awaked all in tears, and was in great fear for his brother at Venice. On the third day letters were brought him from home, acquainting him that his brother died on that night and about the hour he had dreamed of. This he frequently told with tears in his eyes.

In the year 1695, one JOHN STOCKDEN, of the parish of St. Giles's, Cripplegate, was robbed and murdered; soon after which the said Stockden appeared several times to one of his old neighbours, named Elizabeth Greenwood, in her dreams, and laid open to her the whole business, in consequence of which the murderers were taken, confessed the fact, and were executed. And again, after the murderers were taken, Mrs. Greenwood dreamed that Stockden came to her in the street, and said, "Elizabeth, I thank thee; the God of heaven reward thee for what thou hast done." This affair made a great noise at the time, and is attested by the Bishop of Gloucester, the Dean of York, the Master of the Charter-House, and Dr. Allix, who had the particulars from Mrs. Greenwood.

Doctor Pitcairne is said never to have related the following story without some emotion of mind. His friend, Mr. Lindsey, upon reading with the doctor, when very young, the known story of the two Platonic philosophers, who promised to one another that whoever died first should return a visit to his surviving companion, entered into the same engagement with him. Some years after, the doctor, at his father's house in Fife, *dreamed* one morning that Lindsey, who was then at Paris, came to him and told him that he was not dead, as was commonly reported, but still alive, and lived in a very agreeable place, to which he could not as yet carry him. By the course of the post news came of Lindsey's death, which took place, exceeding suddenly, *the very morning of the dream.*

Some years ago the lady of Colonel Gale, having lost her husband, was going to Kingston, in Jamaica, to administer to his effects. In her way she stopped all night at a friend's house, intending to proceed on her journey the next morning; she accordingly ordered her coachman to be ready to set out at the appointed hour. Mrs. Gale's waiting-woman, who accompanied her mistress, dreamed that night, that her master appeared to her, and inquired where her mistress was; the servant told him that her lady was going to Kingston, and was now on her journey; the colonel replied, she must not go,—she must return with him, for he was come to fetch her; this the servant told next morning to the family where they were. Soon afterwards she went into her lady's room to call her up, but was told by her that she found herself somewhat indisposed, and did not think she should be well enough to proceed on her journey that day: she moreover desired the servant to forbid the carriage being got ready, according to the order given the coachman the night before. When the lady of the house perceived her friend very feverish and indisposed, the doctor was called in, but all to no purpose, for the fever increased upon her to such a degree that she survived little more than a week or ten days.

In the night of the 11th of May, 1812, Mr. Williams, of Scorrior House, near Redruth, in Cornwall, awoke his wife, and, exceedingly agitated, told her that he had dreamed that *he was in the lobby of the Home of Commons, and saw a man shoot, with a pistol, a gentleman who had just entered the lobby, who was said to be the Chancellor;* to which Mrs. Williams naturally replied, that it was only a dream, and recommended him to be composed and go to sleep as soon as he could.

He did so; but shortly after he again awoke her and said that he had, a second time, had the same dream; whereupon she observed that he had been so much agitated with his former dream, that she supposed it had dwelt on his mind, and begged of him to compose himself and go to sleep, which he did.

A third time the same vision was repeated, on which, notwithstanding her intreaties that he would lie quiet and endeavour to forget it, he arose (then between one and two o'clock) and dressed himself. At breakfast the dreams were the sole subject of conversation, and in the forenoon Mr. Williams went to Falmouth, where he related the particulars of them to all his acquaintances that he met. On the following day, Mr. Tucker, of Trematon Castle, accompanied by his wife, a daughter of Mr. Williams, went to Scorrior House on a visit, and arrived about dusk. Immediately after the first salutations on their entering the parlour, where were Mr. Mrs. and Miss Williams, Mr. Williams began to relate to Mr. Tucker the circumstance of his dreams, and Mrs. W. observed to her daughter, Mrs. T., laughingly, that her father could not even suffer Mr. Tucker to be seated before he told him of his nocturnal visitation; on the statement of which Mr. Tucker observed, that it would do very well for a dream to have the

Chancellor in the lobby of the House of Commons, but that he would not be found there in reality. And Mr. Tucker then asked what sort of a man he appeared to be, when Mr. Williams described him minutely; to which Mr. Tucker replied, "Your description is not at all that of the Chancellor, but is certainly very exactly that of Mr. *Perceval*, the Chancellor of the Exchequer; and, although he has been to me the greatest enemy I have ever met with through life (for a supposed cause which had no foundation in truth), (or words to that effect), I should be exceedingly sorry indeed to hear of his being assassinated, or of any injury of the kind happening to him."

Mr. Tucker then inquired of Mr. Williams if he had ever seen Mr. Perceval, and was told that he had never seen him, nor had ever written to him, either on public or private business; in short, that he had never had anything to do with him, nor had he ever been in the House of Commons in his lifetime. At this moment Mr. Williams and Mr. Tucker, still standing, heard a horse gallop to the door of the house, and immediately after, Mr. Michael Williams, of Trevince (son of Mr. Williams of Scorrior), entered the room, and said that he had galloped out from Truro (from which Scorrior is seven miles distant), having seen a gentleman there who had come by that evening's mail from town, who said that he was in the lobby of the House of Commons on the evening of the 11th, when a man, called Bellingham, had *shot Mr. Perceval*; and that, as it might occasion some great ministerial changes, and might affect Mr. Tucker's political friends, he had come out as fast as he could to make him acquainted with it, having heard at Truro that he had passed through that place in the afternoon, on his way to Scorrior.

After the astonishment which this intelligence created had a little subsided, Mr. Williams described most minutely the appearance and dress of the man that he saw in his dream fire the pistol at the Chancellor. About six weeks after, Mr. Williams, having business in town, went, accompanied by a friend, to the House of Commons, where, as has been already observed, he had never before been. Immediately that he came to the steps at the entrance of the lobby, he said, "This place is as distinctly within my recollection, in my dream, as any room in my house," and he made the same observation when he entered the lobby. He then pointed out *the exact spot* where Bellingham actually stood when he fired, and which Mr. Perceval had reached when he was struck by the ball, where he fell. The *dress* both of Mr. Perceval and Bellingham agreed with the description given by Mr. Williams, *even to the most minute particulars.*

The foregoing dream is the more marvellous and astonishing on account of the striking conformity of its details to those of a contemporaneous event, which was performed nearly three hundred miles from the person of the dreamer. Moreover, to silence all those doubts which those who fancy they can theorize upon dreams continually offer to the public, when anything of the kind becomes realized, it must be stated, that *the person who dreamed the dream is now alive; the witnesses to whom he made known the particulars of it at the time are also living;* and the whole comes therefore under the denomination of a special and undoubted type or warning of what afterwards happened. The great respectability of the parties who are ready (as they have assured the author) to make oath on the subject, sets aside every appearance of wishing to impose upon public credulity. It is here recorded as a matter of fact, which may cause the sceptic to pause ere he pronounces all dreams as the offspring of the imagination, or the effects of bodily infirmities.

To these I shall just add the following curious account, published by the "Author of Waverley," in one of his notes to the new edition of the "Antiquary," and thus conclude this introduction.

"Mr. R——d, of Bowland, a gentleman of landed property in the Vale of Gala, was prosecuted for a very considerable sum, the accumulated arrears of tiend (tithe), for which he was said to be indebted to a noble family, the titulars (lay impropriators of the tithes).

Mr. R——d was strongly impressed with the belief that his father had, by a form of process peculiar to the law of

Scotland, purchased those lands from the titular, and therefore that the present prosecution was groundless. But, after an industrious search among his father's papers, an investigation of the public records, and a careful inquiry among all persons who had transacted law business for his father, no evidence could be discovered to support his defence.

The period was now near at hand when he conceived the loss of his lawsuit inevitable, and he had formed his determination to ride to Edinburgh next day, and make the best bargain he could in the way of compromise. He went to bed with this resolution, and, with all the circumstances of the case floating upon his mind, had a dream to the following purpose. His father, who had been many years dead, appeared to him, he thought, and asked him why he was disturbed in his mind? In dreams men are not surprised at such apparitions. Mr. R——d thought that he informed his father of the cause of his distress; adding, that the payment of a considerable sum of money was the more unpleasant to him, because he had a strong consciousness that it was not due, though he was unable to recover any evidence in support of his belief. "*You are right, my son*" replied the paternal shade, "*I did acquire right to those teinds for payment of which you are now prosecuted.* The papers relating to the transaction are now in the hands of Mr.——, a writer (or attorney), who is now retired from professional business, and resides at Inveresk, near Edinburgh. He was a person whom I employed on that occasion for a particular reason, but who never on any other occasion transacted business on my account. It is very possible," pursued the vision, "that Mr.——may have forgotten a matter which is now of a very old date; but you may call it to his recollection by this token, that when I came to pay his account, there was difficulty in getting change for a Portugal piece of gold, and that we were forced to drink out the balance at a tavern."

Mr. R——d awaked in the morning with all the words of the vision imprinted on his mind, and thought it worth while to ride across the country to Inveresk, instead of going straight forward to Edinburgh. When he came there, he waited on the gentleman mentioned in the dream, a very old man: without saying anything of the vision, he inquired whether he remembered having conducted such a matter for his deceased father. The old gentleman could not at first bring the circumstances to his recollection, but, on mention of the Portugal piece of gold, the whole returned upon his memory; he made an immediate search for the papers, and recovered them; so that Mr. R——d carried to Edinburgh the documents necessary to gain the cause which he was on the verge of losing.

The author has often heard this story told by persons who had the best access to know the facts, who were not likely themselves to be deceived, and were certainly *incapable of deception.*

Milton tells us that—

"Millions of spiritual creatures walk the earth,
Unseen, both when we wake and when he sleep"

It is perfectly consistent with our fullest belief of a merciful providence, that some occasional evidences should be given of a state after death; nor does it at all lessen this probability, that instances of such appearances are very rare, because, whenever they have happened, or do happen, it is to be supposed, *that reasons subsist for it which are at present unknown to us.* Witchcraft is perverting nature; but this is not the case with apparitions any more than dreams, and many other proofs that are given of the compound nature of man. It must be confessed, indeed, that this is a subject enveloped in considerable obscurity, and that it is the source of much weakness and imposture but all this will not warrant a peremptory conclusion against the hypothesis of the existence of spirits, because it is a subject of which we are not as yet competent to judge.

I shall conclude in the words of MONSIEUR BAYLE, the celebrated French scholar and philosopher, who was far from being overstocked with credulity, but could not withhold his assent from the doctrine of monitory dreams. "I think," says he, "we may say of dreams the same almost as of enchantments, that they are far *less* mysterious than people believe; and somewhat *more* than unbelievers fancy. THE HISTORIES OF ALL TIMES AND PLACES RELATE, BOTH WITH RESPECT TO DREAMS AND MAGIC, SO MANY SURPRISING THINGS, THAT THOSE WHO OBSTINATELY DENY THEM ALL RENDER THEMSELVES SUSPECTED, EITHER OF WANT OF SINCERITY, OR JUDGMENT TO DISCERN THE FORCE OF THE PROOFS. A violent prejudice or a certain turn of mind blinds their understanding, when they compare the reasons *pro* and *con*.

𝕻𝖆𝖑𝖒𝖎𝖘𝖙𝖗𝖞, 𝕸𝖊𝖙𝖔𝖕𝖔𝖘𝖈𝖔𝖕𝖞,
AND
𝕻𝖍𝖞𝖘𝖎𝖔𝖌𝖓𝖔𝖒𝖎𝖊,
FROM A RARE OLD AUTHOR
No. I.

Hippocrates prince of physick, sayes, that the physician cannot be accomplished in his art, if he have not the knowledge of Astrologie; so I may say that the Chiromancer is not perfect nor accomplished if he have not Physiognomie, which is *scientia quâ natura hominum ex aspectu corporis judicatur, ἀπὸ τον φυσ κιγνω μόνειν, ex facie addivinare, et per natura judicia cognoscere*. Or otherwise, for a more clear definition thereof, it is a science whereby the conditions of men and their temperaments are fully known by the lineaments and conjectures of their faces. It consisteth in two things, that is to say, the complexion and composition of the body of man; both which do manifestly declare and shew the things that are within the man, by the external signs; as by the color, the stature, the composition and shape of the members. These two sciences are so joined together and united, that they never go one without another, and to make profession of the one without the other, is a vain thing. These sciences are joined together by the ancients, even by the satyrist, Juvenal:—

    Spatium lustrabit utrumque.
Metarum et fortes ducet, fronteraque manumque,
Prabebit fati crebrum popysmaroganti.

And yet, when he describes his Zoilus, he doth it by the filthy spots and signs of his body, and not by those of his hand; for the Chiromancer may not see every one's hands; and sayes of this Zoylus,

> Tristis
> Occurras fronte obducta, ceu Marsia victus.
> POST.
> Vultua gravis, horrida sicca
> Sylva comæ, nullus totâ nitor in cute, qualem
> Praestabat calidi circumlita fascia visci,
> Sed fruticante pilo neglecta, et squallida crura.

> How
> Like conquered Marsia, with a cloudy brow?

And afterwards,

> A heavy countenance and brisled hair,
> Like a rough wood, naught fashionably fair,
> But as ore laid with birdlime: on thy thighs
> Though meagre, ugly shrubs of hair arise, &c.

So Martial describes his,

> Crine ruber, niger ore, brevis pede, lumine luscus,
> Rem magnam præstas Zoile si bonus es.

> Squint-ey'd, club-foot, red hair, and swarthy face,
> A wonder Zoylus! if the least of grace.

Homer in the second of his Iliads, and the eighteenth of Odusses, describes Thersites and Irus mischievous and evil speakers by the lineaments and composition of their bodies: see here the description.

> It seemed here that nature needs would be,
> Employ'd to forge out all deformity,
> He was purblind, crump shoulder'd too, and lame,
> Sharp head, and ill-bon'd body out of frame.
> But little hair, a long and folio ear,
> In brief so ugly as to wonder were.

As for the second, he sets him, forth without ought of beauty, big, and cowardly, and such as Lucian represents his Happelopin; for the greatness of the body diminishes the courage, as Aristotle says, and the soul follows the composition of the body, that is to say the marks: so the same poet describes Ulisses and Achilles of a middle stature, and consequently couragious.

By Physiognomie, the humours and the inward part of the soul is so truly known, that Socrates the most vertuous Philosopher, whereof the oracle itself hath given this testimony, $Aνδρων$ $απάντων$ $Σωκράτηδσο$ $φώτ$ $αγος$, Socrates the most wise among men, yet being described by his Physiognomy (by a philosopher skilled in that science) was the most nasty and unhandsom of all men living, and totally lost as to lust and luxury. His disciples laught at this judgement, as utterly false. Socrates reproving them, said. My friends, these things according to nature should be so indeed, but I have corrected the vices of my nature by the rule of reason: as if he should say, the imperfections of nature may be reformed by virtue, and that a man may in some sort resist his destiny, if he be wise, and allay his ill fate with a syrrup of the punishment or shame that must follow. There is a story to this purpose taken out of the learned Pasquier in his curiosities of France. In the reign of Lewis the 12th, the Duke of Nemours, nephew to the said king, and his Lieutenant General, in all the countries beyond the mountains, deliberating to give battell to the Spaniard, some days before the battel was at Capry, together with most of his captains: the lord of that town was called Albert Mirandula, a very learned man, and cousin germain to the great Picus Mirandula. This lord, in his entertainment of the said Prince and his captains, mentioned a judicary Astrologer which was with him; a man very expert in that science, aged sixty years, and very famous for his predictions. At the request of the Duke of Nemours he was sent for, to whom the Duke presented his hand, who after many words of complement, told him, that he should give battel to the Spaniard and the Viceroy of Naples, and that he should gain the victory; but he advertized Monsieur de Pasise and de Bayard, to have a care of him, for he should be killed in that battel; he told the said gentlemen all that should come to pass; and more particularly he told one called Jacquin Caumont, an ensign bearer in the company of Captain Mollard (who had done him some injury,) that he should be hanged within three moneths, which happened accordingly: and to all those to whom he had told their fortunes, it happened according to what he said; and he looked as well upon the face as the hands, as the said Pasquier says, and yet he did not look upon the hand of the said Jacquin, but only on his face.

In the same manner H. Sanurenda the good monk, revealed to Charles the 8, King of France, his adventures by his Physiognomy; and told him the success of his voyage, and return from the kingdom of Naples, which business rendered the said Sanurenda suspect to the Pope. Therefore not to insist any farther on these discourses and histories, which the reader may finde if he please, in the authors before mentioned; I shall only for to conclude, say, that I may without tediousness advance into my instructions, that no man can well fortell any thing, and judge of Chiromancie without Physiognomie. Therefore I shall give an epitome and abridgement, such as I shall conceive necessary for instruction.

AN EPITOME OR ABRIDGEMENT OF PHYSIOGNOMIE

The Hebrews have extremely honoured this science of Physiognomie, and the Scripture gives you the Physiognomie of Jacob, Moses, David, Absalom, Jonathan, and many others. The compilers of the Talmud have made a treatise of it, both of Chiromancie and Physiognomie, called מסכה ידים Massecheth Jadaim, that is to say, the treatise of the hands; where they distinguish Physiognomie from Metoposcopie, which is indeed but a part of Physiognomie, which the Greeks understood well, saying, μετωπόσκοπος ἀπὸ του μετόπου και επισκοπειν i.e. a science whereby things to come are known by the aspect of the forehead. These Greeks knew also Umblicometry, and divers others; but as for Physiognomie, they placed it according to this figure.

And to represent it more clearly, the whole is placed after this manner.

Part Two: Divination

The forehead............. ♂ Mars.
The right eye ....☉ Sol.
The left eye................☽ The Moon.
The right ear.............. ♃ Jupiter.
The left ear................♄ Saturn.
The nose ....♀ Venus.
The mouth.................☿ Mercury.

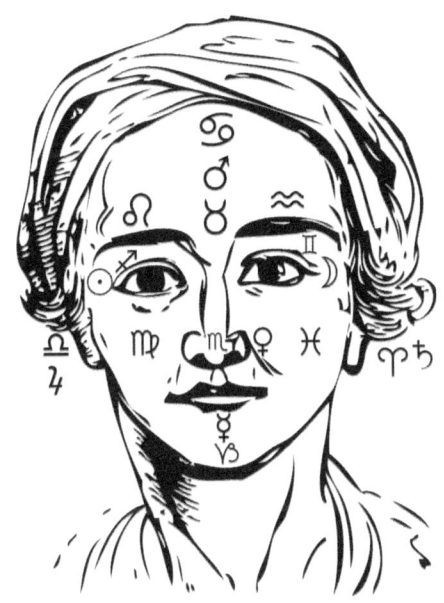

And as for the signs of the zodiac upon the face, they are attributed, accomodated, and placed thus.

♋ Cancer..................... In the forehead the zenith.
♌ Leo.........................The right eye-brow.
♍ Virgo......................The right check.
♎ Libra......................The right ear.
♏ Scorpio...................The nose.
♐ Sagittary.................The right eye.
♑ Capricorn................The chin which is nadir.
♒ Aquarius................The left eye brow.
♓ Pisces....................The left cheek.
♈ Aries......................The left ear.

♉ Taurus......................The middle of the forehead.
♊ Gemini.....................The left eye.

So the Greeks and Hebrews have ordained and constituted them for the profit of the knowledge of this science, of which Part the *Second* shall treat.

Palmistry, Metoposcopy
AND
Physiognomie
VERBATIM FROM RARE OLD AUTHORS.
No. II.

How the Nativity may be found by Physiognomie; the which is demonstrated by that of a Prince done by this Science with its true significations advanced in this place for an example to the curious

♄ Ruling in the several temperaments.

First, he that is cholerick having Saturne in his radix ruling, is pale, having his eyes deep in his head, looking downwards, slow-paced, red eyes, or like those of a cat, and little. Secondly, if Saturn be in the nativity in the flegmatick radix of any person of either sex, he is naturally fat, the colour of the eyes, and the eyes themselves like lead, and all about them there is as it were a bruisedness; he is slow in all his actions, and carries himself herein in a courtly manner. 3. When Saturn rules, is in the nativity of a melancholick person, it causes the man to have his face awry, ill favoured, and a fool, being of divers colours, sad, fearfull, having the eyes most commonly asquint. He is nasty, slovenly, clownish, unconstant, hath a stinking breath, is thoughtfull, desiring great things, but most mischievous, nay shall be hard to believe any thing of the Divinity, but a mocker and insolent, going proudly and gravely; he shall have thick lips, the shoulders very fleshly; and marks at the knees and heels; he shall pass away his life in a tavern, or in a cloyster for to carowse it. 4. But Saturn participating of the sanguine humour, which is the royal one, and the best of the temperaments, the properties are these: they have the voyce sharp and strong, they are merry and jovial; but there are very few that have Saturn chronocrator, are of a sanguine humour; as for the face, they have it fair enough, but the colour like an olive, red eyes with bloody spots in them. So much for the physiognomy of the Saturnines; now for the Jovialists.

♃ Ruling in the several temperaments.

1. He that hath Jupiter in his nativity, in the cholerick significant, is of a white complexion, hath a long beard, and is bald in the forehead, the hair reddish or yellowish, very soon angry, yet wise. 2. If the said Jupiter rule in the nativity of a flegmamatick person, he is of a good stature, and well proportioned, fair-haired, his nose like a trout's, black eye-brows, a green eye, and bleared. 3. For the melancholy, Jupiter is seldom in such nativities. 4. As for the sanguine humour, 'tis there that Jupiter governs most; a sanguine person hath the body white, the face somewhat red, the eyes not altogether black, white teeth, high forehead with four apparent lines therein, the which signifie good husbandry, wisdom, and liberality.

♂ Ruling in the several humours.

1. When Mars is lord of the nativity of a choleric person, the party is red as if he were sunburnt, hath a round face, cat's eyes, and bleared; a cruel countenance, arrogant and proud; he is bald on the crown of the head, of a middle stature, the forepart of his head big, the nostrils issuing out, and when he goes he makes but short paces, he goes lightly and is of himself given to evil. As for the woman of this humour, she is described by Martial in these verses, upon the kisses of Philena.

Car non basio te Philena? calva es.
Cur non basio te Philena? rufa es.
Cur non basio te Philena? lusca es.
&c.

2. But being in the root of the nativity of a flegmatick, he makes him reddish, or yellowish, of a small and sudden nature, a great contester, talkative and a lyar; he is bald on the crown of the head, hath a broad face and great head, he looks on the one side in an arrogant manner: this nature is much given to be vicious. 3. When Mars is Lord of a melancholick nativity, it makes the party have a threatening countenance, and have the marks in the face. If Aries be ascendant, he is crump-shouldered, hath a long face, the head in the form of a pyramid, the hair of a chestnut colour, great eyes and yellowish; to be short, the person is guilty somewhat of folly. 4. If Mars be in a sanguine nativity, which happens very seldom, the person will he very well featured, round-faced, flaxen-haired, green-eyed, the countenance gentle at first, but the speech bold, proud, and menacing.

☿ Ruling in the several Constitutions.

As for Mercury, he never is but in three complexions; if it be a cholerick, the person is of a great stature, lean and of a leaden colour, and sad, having not much hair, wild eyes, and deep in the head, with narrow lips and short teeth. 2. When he is in the nativity of a melancholick and is retrograde, the party is incredulous, subject to many vices, and is always marked by nature, looking a squint, wry mouth'd, wry neck'd, and crumpshouldered: such was Richd. the 3. King of England. 3. When it is a sanguine humour, the man is well disposed, both in his corporal and spiritual proportions, when Mercury is lord of his nativity.

The ☉ ruling in the Cholerick.

But for the Sun when he is alfridary or lord of a cholerick, he causeth him to be of a brown colour with some small redness, fleshy, having very great eyes, well bearded and well haired, the head great and round, and of a middle stature; he is a great dissembler and cautious.

The ☽ ruling in the flegmatique.

1. The Moon is most commonly significatrix in flegmatick nativities, for which reason they are called Lunar; they are very white, intermingled with a little red, having the head great and thick, the eyebrows joyning together, fair eyes, but haply unequal: if Cancer be the ascendent of those persons, they are fat beyond measure. 2. When she is in that of a melancholick, she makes him corpulent, fleshy, fit to make a monk on, having the head fit to wear the cowle, curled hair; a long beard, but not handsom; there may be also some signification of gluttony, as having a great mouth and thick lips, especially the under lip.

♀ Ruling through the several humors.

1. Venus is never but in flegmatic nativities; the persons are fair, courteous, amiable, gentle, having the body white, gentle speech, the hair thick, handsomly curling or crisping; their natural mark is in the neck, which is very fair: they have black eyes, whereof the ball is yellowish, which doth as it were burn or shine. A maid born in this constellation will not long keep her virginity, if she be high-nosed, which commonly happens. Now by these physiognomies well considered (which he must needs do, who pretends to the knowledge of these sciences) one may make the horoscope very easily, taking one or more questions concerning some one whom we wish well unto, and would know his present and future contingences.

First, having by the lineaments of the face known what planet was lord, let us see if he derive of the nature of that planet, having the lineaments of the face such as we have described; if they are conformable without any difference, then infallibly that person is born in the first house or face of that sign of the Zodiak which is referred to that planet. As here we have a man that is white, fair spoken, having a long nose, fair hair and thick, a brown eye; he is born, Venus being *ad instar*, in the first part of Taurus, which is the first house of that planet: so proceed by way of question, having proposed it to yourself, and observed the hour and minute, taking the month and the day, you will certainly finde this sign Taurus, whether it be in the house of life which is the first, or it be the tenth which is Hilygiak, and is the house of dignities and honours; and from the figure you shall thereupon erect, you may draw most certain significations, as Belot did for a young German Prince, whom he had the honour to see in the suburbs of St. Germain at Paris. "My proceed (saith he) was thus, without desiring to know the day or hour of his nativity, or his age. Having observed his physiognomie; I saw he was flegmatique, had black hair, red eyes, great eye brows, the mouth sufficiently rising up, great teeth, a fat neck, and all the body full enough; my question being made the 18 day of March, at 7 of the clock in the morning, in the year 1623. I found that the ascendant of this physiognomical question was Libra in the 10 degree, which is the last of the first part. My question was to know how long this Prince should live, what should be his actions, fortunes, and misfortunes; briefly what should happen in his days: I erected this figure, and thereupon made certain quadrains and resolutions, that my friends might understand the significations of the said figure, and the things portended to this young Prince. Which here for the obscurity thereof I have omitted, the figure will inform you. I confess he hath left it dark, but there is a key to unlock this mysterie.

The Figure is thus to be conceived.

The Tenth House   12 of ♋

Eleventh House	19 of ♌
Twelfth House	17 of ♍
Ascendant	10 of ♎
Second House	3 of ♏
Third House	3 of ♐

The opposite signs and degrees make compleat the Figure.

THE POSITION OF THE PLANETS.

♄ in the 5 of ♑, the North Angle.
♃ in the 13 of ♍.
♂ in the 2 of ♈.
☉ in the 2 of ♐.
♀ in the 13 of ♑, the North Angle
☿ in the 22 of ♐.
☽ in the 3 of ♊, the Angle of the 9 House

This Figure is Geomantically formed.

Of the Head and its Judgements.

The learned and knowing Hippocrates, in the sixth Book which he wrote concerning ordinary Diseases, says that by considering the head of a man, it may be judged of the whole body, that being the most apparent of all the parts of the body, and is not covered nor masked, and especially the face, which at the first sight is seen of all, that so may be judged of the temperament and actions of the person. Now in our science of Physiognomie, the form, proportion, and dimensions of the head are to be considered; for by it, and its form, we judge of the minde contained therein, which is that that distinguishes us from beasts, and makes us know the breath which is said to have been blown into our face by the perfection of all things, that so he might give us the epithite of Saints, which is the mark which all wise men aim at for the obtainment of that immortality which is desired by pure wisdom. That therefore we may come to this discovery, it is thus:

A little head is never without vice, and most commonly is guilty of little wisdom, but rather full of folly, which is naught and malicious.

A great head doth not signifie any perfection of manners, though there may be sometimes, but not often, goodness of nature; the most perfect is the round head, which is somewhat depressed on both sides after the fashion of a sphear compassed about with its zodiack. The best form of a head is moderate, as greatness and thickness, and of a decent and convenient roundness, which before and behinde is tempered with a little compression.

The brain, one of the noblest parts of the body, is according to the form of the cranium, for if the cranium be corrupted, the brain is so too. The head of man, hath proportionably more brains then all other living creatures; and men have more brains then women, and the head of man hath more joynts then any other creature. So the well formed head is like a mallet or sphear, there being some eminency before and behinde; the form of the middle ventricle should be a little compressed, so the cogitative faculty is the more notable. If the forepart be depressed, the man is of no judgement; if the hinder, he hath no memory, having a great weakness in the motion of the nerves, and consequently of all the parts of the body. The strength of the brain is demonstrated by the strength of the body and nerves, as also by the breadth of the shoulders, the breast, and the lateral parts, called hypocondres, which are the junctures of the liver to the spleen. The head which is of a handsom and decent form, augments the sense and virtue, and denotes in the man magnificence and honour; but if deformed, the contrary; the judgements we shall thence draw are these.

1. A head not beyond measure great, denotes persons fair, wise, and well conditioned, studious, having a strong and great memory, given to the reading of good books.

2. Those that have the head out of measure big, are commonly foolish, indocile, not far from a little madness: they do nothing that speaks any gentility of spirit, but live sadly in a perpetual melancholy, or happily gluttony.

3. When the head is big proportionable to the body, the sinews of the neck big, and the neck it self strong, it is a sign of strength, choler, magnanimity, and a martial humour.

4. When a man or woman have the head long and sharp like a pyramid, or sugar loaf, it denotes a man shameless, who in his youth had a vivacity of spirit enough, which at the age of twenty years vanished away: many such heads may be seen amongst us; such persons are gluttons and great eaters, rash and bold, which proceeds from the dryness of the brain.

5. A head well composed, and of a good form, according to the dimensions of the body, and if the ventricle before be well formed and well tempered; for the apprehension of species proceeds from heat and moysture, and the retention proceeds from the draught in the hinder part; a head thus formed, signifies goodness and wisdom.

6. A head having the middle ventricle somewhat compressed towards the sides, denotes the cogitative faculty, natural, diligently comprehensive, rationative and eloquent, which proceeds from the union of the spirits that are in that place; those who have the head thus, are learned and knowing,

7. A head that is altogether spherical, signifies mobility, inconstancy, forgetfulness, little discretion and wisdom.

8. The head very little is necessarily an evil sign; and the less it is, the more folly there is; the person is subject to sickness, because of the small quantity of brains, the ventricles being narrow, wherein the spirits being pressed, cannot exercise their functions, as being shuffled together and smothered; whence it comes that their imagination is neither free nor good, and their memory is slippery: such persons are very cholerick, and hasty in all their actions, and are more like St. Mathurin then Socrates, and are commonly vertiginous, and exceed not 56 years at most.

9. A head out of measure long, and oblique in the organs, denotes impudity and imprudence, they are like the swine, as Porta says, wearying themselves in the defilement of venereal actions.

10. A head that is low and flat, denotes impudence and dissoluteness: a head high before, folly and stupidity of spirit.

11. A head that hath as it were a ditch behinde, and is depressed and hollow, denotes a man subject to wrathfulness, being of a melancholick humour; this head hath some likeness to that of a camell.

12. A big head with a broad forehead, is like that of an ox, having a large face like a gyant, it denotes a man slow, gentle, yet laborious and extreamly indocile.

13. When the head is straight, and almost flat in the middle, of a middle size, it denotes that man hath a good strong understanding, that he is couragious, and fears nothing as to the affairs of the world, that he is indefatigable in the vicissitude of fortune, and that all the afflictions that can happen to him, cannot make him quit his constancy and conduct, but is firm amidst the most outragious accidents; if he have a high forehead, he is perfectly martial.

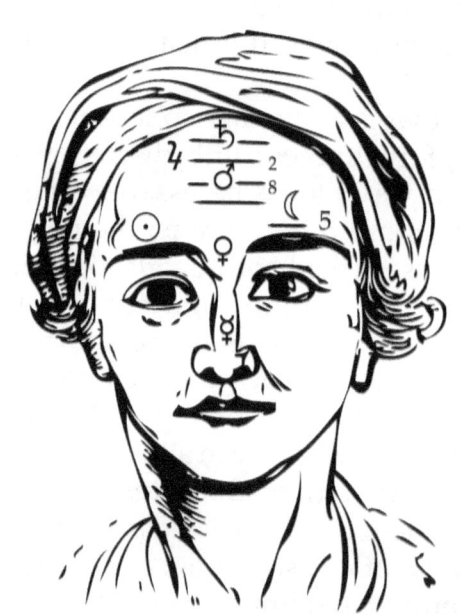

Of Metoposcopy, and the significations of the forehead, and the Planets placed thereon, according to this Science.

Metoposcopy is a science depending of Physiognomie, which we have defined to be a science of judging of things to come by the aspection on the forehead, as also of knowing the temperaments of any one. No divination is certain, unless it be joined with, and assured by Astrology, which at present is the certainest science for the prediction of things to come; and the joyning it to the other sciences of divination, renders them more recommendable and more perfect; *for Astrology is the foundation of what ever concerns the prediction of things to come*. That is the reason that in our Metoposcopy, for the greater perfection thereof, we accommodate the seven planets, as you finde them in this figure. Of the significations of the said planets, we shall discourse after the description of the forehead. The forehead is a part of the face, situate in the *sinciput*, confined by the eyes, the root of the nose, and the temples; and by the accidents thereof, is discovered sadness, joy, clemency, gentleness, severity, humanity, frowardness, wisdom, folly, silence, whence came these proverbs, *Frontem exporrigere, frontem extrahere*: and Aristotle says, *Frons verecundiæ et honoris sedes*; for it is a neighbour to the place of the fancy, being, as it were, the enclosure of the common sense in the hither part of the brain. The forehead hath its dimensions, that is to say, latitude, longitude, roundness, and fulness; the latitude begins at the root of the nose, where the eyebrows discontinue; and ends with the first hairs neer a branch of the hollow vein ; the longitude is from one temple to the other; the longitude and latitude make the roundness, when all thing are well joyned together; and the plain foreheads are such because they are depressed and without elevation. The diversities of foreheads are, the great, the little, the round, the ovall, the lean, the fat, the broad, the narrow, the collected, the confused; as for the lines and veins, they are, the cloudie, the straight, the concave, the slender vein. Upon the forehead we place the seven planets upon the lines as is to be seen in the figure; on the first line neer the hair is ♄, on the second ♃, on the 3. ♂, on the 4. ☉, on the 6. and lowest ♀, and ☿ upon the nose.

The Moon on the left eye, and the Sun on the right. Venus at the root of the nose. Of the situation of the said planets and their significations we shall speak of after the significations of the diversity of foreheads, sith these two are all that is comprehended in all the science of Metoposcopy.

1. A great and spacious forehead signifies a sluggish and fearfull person, that is compared to the Ox; most of those that have the forehead such, are people of good consciences, not given to do any hurt, they are very fit to become lawyers.

2. The little forehead denotes the person indocile, wicked, and given to mischief; believing nothing but his own foolish opinions; they are compared among the beasts to the cat or rat of Pharaoh. The Emperour Caligula had it so; so also was he an epitome of all cruelty and cowardise, and would never believe any person of authority.

3. The broad forehead represents a person gluttonous and unclean, (especially in the intercourse of the sexes,) as having somewhat of the nature of the swine: such persons are given to flattery, professing in shew all manner of friendship, but behinde a mans back they are his enemies, speaking evil and offensive words, and scandalous to those whom they pretend an affection to. Bartholomew Cocles of Bulloigne says, that a forehead great and broad on all sides, without any hair, or as it were, bald, signifies an audacious and understanding person, but sometimes malicious and very wrathfull, and not legal, and oftimes a great lyar.

4. A forehead pointed at the temples of the head, so as the bones do almost appear without the flesh, signifies vanity, inconstancy, little capacity, and not much resolution in business, but changeableness every moment.

5. He that hath the forehead somewhat swollen by reason of the thickness of the flesh, at the temples, as if he had jaws or cheeks full of flesh, it denotes the person very couragious and martial, it is one of the marks that a great captain should

look for in the choice of his soldiers; moreover those that have such foreheads are proud, easily angry, and forward to engage themselves in combats.

6. A square forehead, denotes according to Aristotle, magnanimity: *Quadrata frons* (saith he) *pro faciei ratione mediocris magnanimos ostendit ob similitudinem leonis*. Those that have such a forehead are couragious as lions, and are compared to them because of their strength, courage, and prudence. See Porta.

7. He who hath the forehead wrinkled and low in the middle, and seems as it were double in the face, neer the nose, that is to say frowning, wherein there is a valley or descent, is a simple person, magnanimous in adversity, and fortune is very cruel and cross to him.

8. He that is bald, or hath little hair on the forepart of the head, having the forehead plain, and the skin delicate and smooth, which the Greeks call δερμάτιον, unless it be the superficies of the nose, is unconstant, wrathfull, and ill-conditioned.

9. He that hath the forehead gathered together and wrinkled, is a flatterer, and hath somewhat of the nature of a dog; he flatters, but it is for to deceive.

10. The concave forehead, which hath pits and mounts, is a signe of fearfulness, deceit, cheating, and ambition. Adamantius saith, *Asperâ fronte ne gaudeas, neque quæ fossas monticulos habeat; omnia namque hæc signa versutiam et infidelitatem nunciant, et interdum stultitiam et insaniam*: he which hath a frowning, wrinkled, and capred forehead, which is a word comes according to Varro, from *caperata, et crispis carprarum comibus assimilatur*, is of a Saturnine humour and melancholick, and denotes one that thinks more than he speaks, premeditating his conceptions before he effects them. Such a one was Philip Melancthon; these persons are of a gentle humour and familiar conversation; if the person be very rich, the greater is the melancholy, as saith Albertus Magnus; *Qui semper frontis rugas contractor habent, melancholici et res magnas cogitare consueti*.

12. A clear forehead without wrinkles, signifies a fairness of minde as well as of body, but a malicious disposition given to debates, suits, and contentions; the most part that have it so, have not much devotion; the great Sidonius Apollinaris saith, that Epicurus had it so.

13. A forehead neither strait, nor lean, nor smooth, nor rough, but between all, signifies a round-dealing friendship without deceit or circumvention.

14. The cloudy forehead, and having black marks, signifies boldness; and such persons are likened to bulls and lions, who are in perpetual choler.

15. Those who have much carnosity about the eyes, so that their eye-brows hang down like those of hounds, are fraudulent, cruell, and unmercifull: deriving their cruelty from beasts of prey. Selymus, the emperour of the Turks had them so, and he was cruel, bold, a great, indefatigable, and severe warriour. It is said also that Charles Duke of Burgundy had them so too.

16. A forehead, that upon the first sight appears sad, severe and austere, shews a strange and barbarous humour, prone to all cruelties. Such are the Arabians, Cannibals, Anthropophagi, people that know no pitty; if it happen they be of a melancholick humour, they are likely to devour their own children, as saith a learned author, "Which I have myself observed in one of that humour, who was executed at Eureux. His name was Taurin, living neer a town called Le Ventes, who transported with madness and cruelty, had eaten his own children; there were some thought him wizard, which was not true, it being only folly seconded by melancholy and solitude had transported him to that inhumane action."

17. A depressed and low forehead, denotes an effeminate person; this kinde of forehead suits well with a woman; for a man that is so, hath a low and abject soul, is fearfull, servile, effeminate, cowardly, and carried away with the many words of a great talker, for there is not much assurance in their words, yet he is overcome by the speech of the most simple man that he stands in fear of.

Now seeing we have represented all the forms of the forehead, in pursuance of our Metoposcopy, we must treat of the lines of the forehead and their significations, and afterwards of the characters of the Planets, and the Planets themselves, which signifie, according to the places where we shall place them in the forehead, an abridgement of this great world.

The lines of the forehead have longitude, latitude and profundity, and begin at one temple and end towards the other; the which lines by their aspect, represent unto us the evil or good fortune of the person; those veins are Planetary. A Planetary line is that which is referred to some of the Planets, which are placed on the forehead, as is before mentioned: but because that in all foreheads there doth not appear perfectly all the lines, we shall draw our more particular judgments from those of the Sun and Moon which infallibly appear on all foreheads; upon the eye-brows, that of the Sun upon the right, and that of the Moon on the left; but it is more easie to judge of those who have all the lines, some having them more apparent, others less. The first line which is that of Saturn, appears neer the hair; that which is under it is Jupiter's, the third belongs to Mars, the other four are in the superficies of the forehead, as the Sun and Moon upon the eyes, Mercury neer the grissell of the nose, Venus above it between the eyes. So there you have the number of the planets observed, and them placed according to the celestial rule; Saturn highest, Jupiter next, then Mars, the Sun under Mars, Venus fift, Mercury under her, and the Moon neer the left eye-brow, and the Sun at the right, and Venus at the root of the nose; and by these places we are shewed the analogy and proportion which there is between the great and little world, even as experience confirms it, and reason demonstrates these motions, being like those of the heavens; the nose and the bone of the Vertex being the imaginary poles whereon these planets move.

In these lines we must observe the characters which are given them as marks of the planets, and are the infallible signs of the temperaments, and of man's life, that we can discover; whereby we also know the duration and length thereof. These marks are crosses, circles, warts, and such like characters, which commonly are found in men's foreheads; and it is to be considered upon which veins they are; for without doubt, the man shall derive somewhat from that planet where the character shall be, rather then from any other. The significations of the planetary lines are either general, when they are accommodated to all the lines of the planets, or special. The general significations of the lines of the planets, afford us these canons and aphorisms.

1. The lines of the planets either all in general, or each in particular, some are fortunate, others unfortunate: those which are fortunate, are those which are strait, or bend a little towards the nose, if they be equal, continued, and not dissected, nor distracted, nor barred in like obelisks.

2. Those that are not well placed and unfortunate, are those that are much winding, approaching a semicircle globe, or obelisk.

3. Simple and straight lines denote a simple, good, and honest soul, without any malice.

4. The oblique, indexed, and sometimes the distorted lines denote variety: craft, cheating, to be short, all mischief and deceit.

5. If the right line of the forehead be oblique, that is, on the side attributed to the Sun, it signifies malice.

6. If the veins of the masculine planets look towards the left side, and be plain; and if that of Mercury, which is sometimes masculine and sometimes feminine, look towards the feminines in the same manner, it denotes nothing but evil.

7. Many lines signifie nothing else but a multitude of changeable affairs.

8. The fewness and simplicity of the lines, denotes a certain simplicity in affairs.

9. When the lines encrease and decrease, they represent some great affair, according as the character of the planets shall denote.

10. Jupiter's line being mean and reflected, shews some great and happy gain with honour and good report.

The general significations of the planets most commonly include the special; that is to say, some planets are referred to certain lines, as we said, or judged of them.

1. If the lines be great and not winding, long (especially that of Saturn and Jupiter, as also those of Saturn and Mars ;) and very apparent, they denote most exorbitant and mischievous actions.

2. If the line of Jupiter be longer then that of Saturn, it denotes riches, and all other things that are obtained by Jupiter.

3. If the line of Mars exceed the others, let the captain that chooses souldiers observe it; for those that are so, are great warriours, and have no other ambition then to raise a fortune by the war; and especially, if there be a cross upon that line, and not a semicircle, it speaks a very cholerick humour, and a good fortune by following Bellona.

4. A line broken or discontinued, especially that of Saturn and Mars, denotes misfortune in war.

5. If two lines or three be in the place of Mercury, and if they be apparent and straight, simple and equal, they denote the person eloquent and wise, and very honest.

6. If there be more then three lines, and be straight, and bending at the extremity, they signifie loquacity, prating, detraction, deceit, inconstancy, lying, simulation, and dissimulation.

7. If the lines be such in the forehead of a woman, she is talkative, abusive, prating, a scold, a sorceresse, given to unlawfull arts, knowing some foolish verses, useless in incantation.

8. Two or three lines being at the root of the nose and cut in the middle, signifie a lascivious person, and one much transported with that vice.

9. The line of the Sun being perfect, long enough, and not interrupted or cut, signifies honours and riches given by Kings and Princes.

10. The Moon line being dear, distinct and perfect above the left eye, signifies much travel into strange nations, and some abode by the way.

And this is all we have as to the judgements of the forehead, of which depends Metoposcopy. Yet to satisfie the ingenious reader, I will particularly demonstrate the same, and then I shall bestow the next chapter for to treat of what is supernatural in this science.

That the seven Planets, being placed on the forehead, the twelve Signs of the Zodiac are there also with their Spirits and Intelligences.

There can be no greater sympathie, then is between the celestial and elementary bodies. There is (as I have often said before) such an analogy between all our members and the superiour bodies, that there is no member which is not governed by those influences either generally or particularly The harmony of these stars is the total of our body; as to the particular parts, all in all, as the face in general, and in particular the forehead. And therefore the ancient Hebrews called these celestial bodies by the names of spirits, and have attributed to them secret intelligences and genii; and those over whom any particular star, as ♄, ♃, ☿, &c. do powerfully govern, are powerfully actuated by the influence of that star, or its Genius. Now upon the forehead may be discovered the spirit or governing genius; as if it be Saturn, it is Sabathiel who hath two under him, which are referred to his two houses, that is Capriel to ♑, and Aquariel to ♒, or else Gediel and Deliel. If it be Jupiter that governs the forehead, it is Zedekiel, who hath these two, Sagitariel and Pisciel, or Acabiel, Dagimiel. If it be Mars, it is Madirniel, and his houses, Teleteriel, Acabriel, or else Ariel, Scorpiel; if it be the Sun, it is Semeliel, or Leoniel. If it be the Moon, Jarchael, or Levanael, her house Sartamiel; if it be Venus, Mogahel, her houses Suriel, Maniel. If Mercury, Cochabiel, his houses Tomiel, Betuliel; the latter of these referred to Mercury, was that which governed Appollonius Thianneus, which he knew by the Brachmanes; and that is it which with that of the Moon that is next the earth, and consequently easie to be allured and drawn to us: Arbatel gives the faculties of this Spirit, Betuliel to Aratron, whose faculties and spirits are 1. To transform the most vile mettals into fine gold and silver. 2. To turn treasures into charcoal, or charcoal into treasures. 3. It teaches Chymistry, Magick, and Physick. 4. It appears like little men as pigmeys. 5. Makes men invisible, and 6. Makes sterile things fruitful. It is an easie matter to know whether the person be governed by it; for if he have four lines above the root of the nose, and if those lines be hollow, and make the extremity wrinkled, doubtless the person is governed by it; if besides he be melancholick; sometimes the lines are fair and clear, as Apol. Tyan. had them. And that denotes a great force in the possession of this spirit, nay speaks apparent miracles. I believe that the brothers of the Rosecrusian possesse it; it is an order sprung up within these late years in Germany, that at present doth miracles through all Europe. These brothers have some admirable secrets of the sciences mentioned before, together with an ardent zeal towards the superior powers, and enter acquaintance with all knowing men who acknowledge the true God, and part not from them without doing them some good. They know almost all things to come, as may be seen by their predictions. They have taken the name of brothers to avoid the vanity of that name of fathers forbidden in the Scripture; they know the languages of the countries where they are to dwell; they are well acquainted with the tongues, the Hebrew, Chaldean, Syriak, Arabick, and all the Oriental languages, the Greek, Latine, Italian, Spanish, French, Sclavonian, Germane, and make Lexicons of them, moreover they are skilled in the Civil Law, the Galenick and Paracelsick Physick, the Aristotelick and Ramick philosophy, the liberal arts; to be short, they are an epitome of all sciences. As for their religion, their tenets are very pure. Henry Nehusio a German physician accuses them for Anabaptists, for having the opinions of Socinas; tis true they have no certain place for their prayers, which require great meditation; they live in an unanimous society, abounding with money; their vows are somewhat neer those of Appollon. Tyan. but besides the plurality of the Gods they also possess his genius; they have the lines before mentioned above the root or grissel of the nose, and so they are discovered, as also may be known the diversity of the lines where the Planets are situated, and their characters which may be seen in Cor. Agrip. in the 3 book, and 29 chap, of his Philosoph. Occult, which I would not put down here, to avoid prolixity. But when once they are known, it may be judged of the Genius and temperament by the inspection of the forehead, which is the only subject of Metoposcopy.

Of the Judgements, of the Manners and of the Body, by the Colour, and other Accidents.

The colours of the body, and especially of the face, denote the humour and inclination of the person; and by the external colour and accidents, the Physiognomist must judge of the internal and faculties of the soul. As blackness in a man if it be shining, is a sign of adustion, as well in the members as in the hair. The black colour denotes a man slow in his actions, not much given to war, as being of a heavy and fearfull humour, without courage, if not occasionally; but he is cautious, neat, and subtile, and fit for counsel, or for some secret enterprise, nay a treason if need be; such was Ulysses, who carried the garland in the Trojan victories, and was preferred before Ajax; the most part of those who are so coloured are born towards the south parts. A green colour that is obscure and black, speaks a cholerick person; those who are ruddy or altogether red, and are lean withall, are neat, cunning, and subtile; which is the reason of this proverb : Few little men are humble, and red faithfull; but those that are big, fat, and have the hair of the head of another colour whether it be chesnut or olive colour, are jovialists and honest people, open without painting or cheating; but if the hair be black, beware; the proverb saith.

> Of a red beard and black hair,
> If th'art wise, thou'lt have a care.

Those that have the face pale, and leady, yet have the forehead red, and the eyes depressed, are extreamly shamefaced, much subject to passion and choler; they are never at rest with themselves, thinking always that some others plot and conspire against them; all fancies are phantasmes to them if melancholick; the fingers of their hands seem mountains; the least sight unaccustomed to them seems to be a place full of furies, which is the subject of their discourse; and indeed by such sick minds as these, these doleful places have been invented; poets and others have drawn their descriptions from these fantastick imaginations, and thence described the pains and torments which are there exercised. The Abbot Odo was of such a colour, and he was the first that since the year of salvation, hath given us these descriptions, which have been subscribed unto and received by them that believed them.

A whitish red colour, which the Latines call candidier, and the Greeks λακὸν ὑπερίζςον, signifies a man debonair and familiar, and couragious and gallant as to matter of war. The learned Galen in his Art of Medicine, saith, *Signum optimæ; temperaturæ, id est calidæ; et humidæ, esse colorem commixtion ex albo el rubro*. And Aristotle as to the significations of it, says, *In idea ingeniosi, monstrat candidum colorem, optimum ingenium demotare*: and since him Albertus Magnus: *Color medius inter album et rubrum, declinans ad prunum, si est clarus boni ingenii et bonorum index*. It is held that Alexander the Great was of this colour, though Apelles painted him sordid and dark coloured; but Plutarch represents him to us of this white ruddy colour, a colour whereof the sweat is very sweet and pleasant, and such had the said Alexander, as Aristoxenes represents him: for my part, I am of opinion that such persons are jovial, and of good conversation, desiring nothing so much as mirth; they have a good understanding, but not so much as to employ it in the study of the sciences; they are cholerick and couragious, but their choler lasts not long; most part of your northern people are of this colour and complexion. A high white colour is to be admired among those that profess they love beauties; it is very recommendable in women, and much desired by those who affect to pass half their age in the pleasures of this life, which are for the most part the pains of their lives, that they may afterwards, bait the hook for the zealous ones of these times to catch others. Tis true this colour is very fit for a woman, who of her self is luxurious and fearfull; but not to a man, for it would speak him effeminate: Arist. in his Physiog. says, *Albus color in homine excedens, demonstrat foemineum.* We have amongst us some kindreds that are thus excessively white; and the women are extremely luxurious; and the men tender, fearfull, short-sighted, and like to take the occasion of doing any imposture.

The brown colour mingled with pale, which the Latines call *sublividus*, the Greeks ὑπόχλωςον, i.e. *subslavus*, denotes a glutton, a great talker, one easily angry and one that speaks immoderately; it also signifies folly joyned with cruelty; and the most part of those that embrace novelty in matter of divine worship, are of this colour: they will have men receive whatever they conceive in their corrupt imagination, and advance with their flattering speeches, as articles and decrees of heaven; by this reason, and by their sottish inventions they make men beleeve and adore things whereof antiquity that adored a plurality of Gods, would be ashamed, and Herodotus would blush to write, as being too apparent impostures. These persons do much envy others, and especially those of their profession; as for the pale, Martial says,

Omnibus invideas Livide, nemo tibi.

Those that have a flushing colour, are not far from madness, as having extraordinary heat. Polemon says, *Color flammens furiosos indicat:* Alber. Magnus, *Ignitus color cum lucentibus oculis ud insanium vergentem hominem notat*. This colour denotes not only an ardent desire of things present and of small consequence, but also things to come; for there wants not a vivacity of spirit. Tis thought the prophetess Cassandra was of this colour, having shining eyes; such were David, Daniel, and Esdras, who in their fury have spoken great things at certain times. A squallid colour doth not signifie any thing but strength, as Aristotle witnesses, *Qui in figura fortis viri tribuit colorem squallidiorem* αυχηρώτερον. The most part, of those that are given to the wars, are no sheep or cowards, and hate those that trim up and varnish their complexion: as for them, they are squallid, and all dusty through their military exercises, not studying any thing but stratagems and feats of war, to the end they may transmit an immortal fame to posterity.

The Judgements of the Hairs according to their substance and colours.

The hair is one of the parts that adorn the head of man, but especially of a woman; for a woman of quality husbands them to the advancement of her beauty: the Apostle permits her to please her husband. The ancient Gauls wore long hair in token of their liberty; in the Old Testament there is mention of the hair of Sampson and Absalom, which was also bestowed upon the daughters of Jerusalem for to adorn themselves withall. Lycurgus commanded his citizens to wear their hair long, that so they might be more fair and decent. Charilaus being asked why he wore his hair long, answered, *Quia ex omni ornatu hic pulchrior foret, &c.* Silvius Italicus in the commendation of Scipio, says,

> Maitia frons, faciesque coma, nec poue retorquet,
> Cæsaries brevior.

Fair hair, as the poets say, are the prisons of Cupid, and heretofore, nay at present the ladies make rings and bracelets of it, as Martial witnesses.

Unus de toto peccaverat orbe comarum
Annulus, incertâ vix bene fixas aeu.

The hair therefore being a part of Physiognomie, we draw these Judgements from their substance, which we shall lay down here by way of aphorisms and canons.

1. Hair that is thick, and soft, denotes a man of much mildness, and of a constitution cold and moist; for the farther the brain is from heat, the head is more hairy; the heat of man that goes to the superiour parts pierces everywhere the skin of the head, and makes a certain humour to issue out of the pores; and the more subtile part of this humour vanishes away, but that which is more gross remains within and turns into hair, which is more solid then the fleshy skin, and the hairs are broader then the pores, so long as the impetuosity and force which drives them out is great.

2. When the hair hangs down and is soft, it denotes a humid complexion and sanguine; and when they grow fast, it is a sign the body will shortly decline to dryness, and not to moisture. And when the heat and draught are joyned, the hair comes out fastest, and more thick.

3. Much hair denotes a hot person, and the bigness thereof his choler, and that he is soon angry: this plenty of hair happens more to young then to old men and children; for in these the matter is more vapourous then moist, but in young men the contrary; wherefore contraries follow their contraries

4. Abundance of hair in young children, shews their complexion increases, and augments with melancholy.

5. Curled hair and black, denotes heat and drought; the people of the south have it for the most part alike, especially the Ethiopians; it proceeds from the crookedness of the pores; as for their signification, Aristotle says, *Qui capillos nimis crispos habent timidi sunt, et ad Æthiopes referuntur.*

6. Hair standing up an end like the prickles of a hedge-hog, signifies a fearfull person, and an ill courage; of the hair that falls upon the forehead towards the nose[...]

7. Smooth and plain hair, denotes a person of a good understanding, placable, courteous, tractable, and somewhat fearfull.

8. When the hairs are delicate and clear, they signifie a man of a weak complexion, and subject to sickness. As for the colours of hair, we must in the first place consider the climate; for the meridional people are for the most part black and curled; the northern, who inhabit cold countries, are flaxen-haired, of a yellowish colour, their hair being full and close, and therefore they are not altogether cold, but rather their temperament and humour is very hot, the heat in the Winter time, being locked up as we see in the bosom of the earth. As for the rest, the Oriental have their hair of a chestnut colour, fair and very small; the Occidental have it blacker and more rough; yet it is not absolutely assured that all those countries should have them so; for such a one is black that hath black hair; he that hath them yellow or flaxen, white; red or brown, may be said to have them fair, &c. As for their significations they are these.

1. White hair signifies a great frigidity, as may be seen in old men, whose hair becomes white by reason of frigidity and siccity, as it happens to vegetables which when they dry, change their black or green into white; and that happens many times after great drying diseases.

2. We are to mark that there are but four principal colours of hairs, *viz.* black, red, flaxen, and white or grey: the white proceeds from want of natural heat, or corrupted flegm, yet they signifie slippery and evil conditions.

3. Black hair proceeds from an excessive adust choler, or adust and hot blood.

4. Red hair denotes a head not adust but diminished and moderate.

5. Hair of the colour of gold, denote a treacherous person, having a good understanding but mischievous. Red hair enclining to black, signifies a deceitfull and malicious person, whose sweat is most loathsom and fit to make the narcotick unguent with the blood of the line of life of a dead man, and other ingredients, as may be seen in Porta's Natural Magick.

6. Chestnut coloured hair, denotes a fair and just person without deceit. So much shall suffice as to the hair.

Of the Eyes, and their significations.

The principal efficacy and perfection of Physiognomie consisteth in the eyes, as being κάτοπιρον της ψυχης *Speculum Animi*, the doors or outlets of the brest, the index of the countenance, the conservators and dispensators of the cogitations, the minde is as apertly conversant in the eyes as in a market, they being indexes of love, mercy, wrath, and revenge: the minde resolute, the eyes prosiliate, being humble, they subsidate, in love they are amorous, in hatred revengefull, the heart cheerfull they smile, being sorrowfull they languish. Wherefore we may from the eyes discover the good or ill disposition of persons; therefore Homer calls Minerva a blue-eyed lass, and Venus black-eyed, αγων ελικωπιδα, to represent the prudence of the one and luxury of the other. And that is the reason the left eye is attributed to Venus; for if in a woman that eye be shining, and move, the eye-lids fat, it signifies much inclination to lasciviousness, especially if that woman be olive-coloured or yellowish with her black eyes, as Venus is described by Hesiod Διαχρυσην Αφροδιτας, never look for any shamefastness in such a woman.

1. Great and big eyes, denote a slothfull, bold, and lying person, and a rustick and unsavory minde.

2. Eyes of divers colours, especially the right, which is attributed to the Sun, denote a man agitated with divers passions and opinions, especially in matters of religion; it is said that Michael Servet had them so.

3. Eyes deep in the head, that is to say, hollow, denote a great minde, yet full of doubts; if they are green, they signifie admirable knowledge, yet accompanied with malice, luxury, and envy; if they are red, it discovers the nature of the cat.

4. Eminent and apparent eyes of a wall colour, denote a simple, foolish, and prodigal person.

5. Sharp and piercing eyes that decline the eyebrows, denote a deceiver, and a secret and lawless person.

6. Little eyes like those of a mole, or pig, denote a weak understanding, and one fit to be made a cuckold, as who believes all is said to him.

7. Beware squint-eyes, for of a hundred there are not two faithfull.

8. Eyes that move much, and look slowly, yet sharply, and that with some reclination of the flesh of the eye-brows, denote an unfaithfull, slothfull, and riotous person.

9. The worst of all eyes are the yellowish, citron, and cerused; beware of them, as also of those who when they speak to thee twinkle; for those that have such eyes are double minded; if it be a woman that doth so with her left eye, trust her not as to the faithfulness of her love, and observe where she casts her amorous looks

Physiognomical signs taken from the parts of the Eyes.

1. The angles of the eyes over long, indicate malevolent conditions.

2. The Angles being short, a laudable nature; if the angles neer the nose are fleshy, they intimate a hot constitution, and improbity.

3. The balls of the eyes equal, declare justice; unequal, the contrary.

4. The circles in the eyes of divers colours, and dry, declare fraudulency and vanity; but moyst, demonstrate fortitude, prudence, and eloquence.

5. The lower circle green, and the upper black, it is a certain sign of a deceptions and fraudulent person.

6. And lastly, eyes of a mean bigness, clear and shining, are signs of an ingenious and honest man.

Of the Face.

A face very fleshie, signifies a fearfull person, merry, liberal, discreet, luxurious, faithfull to another, importunate to obtain his will, but presumptuous.

2. A lean face, denotes a man wise, of a good understanding, but rather cruel than mercifull.

3. A round and little face, denotes a man simple, weak, and of an ill memory.

4. Who hath a long and lean face, is audacious in words and deeds; he is riotous, injurious, and luxurious.

5. He that hath a broad and thick face, is clownish, and a boaster.

6. He that is of a pale coloured face, is not healthy, and hath an oppilation of the spleen.

7. He that hath it Vermillion, is good, wise, and capable of all good things.

8. He that hath it white, womanish, soft and cold, is tender and effeminate; this colour suits well with women; for such are good natured, but fit for men.

9. A red face, denotes according to the proverb, a hot complexion.

10. A violet or leady colour, signifies a mischievous person and Saturnine, who does nothing but plot treasons and pernicious enterprizes: such was that of Brutus and Cassius, as also of Nero. So much for that, now we come to speak of the humours.

Of the four humors, or Temperaments of Man.

The Hebrews transported with deep meditations in their ghematry, attribute high and secret things to the quartenary, which Pythagoras, who had been a little nursed in their school, had observed as a most mysterious number, calling it Tetractin; and their great and solemn oath was by that number, as may be seen by these verses,

> Juro ego per sanctum parti tibi mente Quaternum,
> Æternæ fontem naturæ, animiám parentem.

Now the reason why the Hebrews honoured this number, was because God had appeared to them in this name, יהוה four-lettered, which was so venerable that no nation hath translated into its proper idiom and natural language, but they have given it four letters, that they might correspond with the Hebrews, as the Egyptians, Arabians, Persians, Mages, Mahometans, Greeks, Tuscans, Latines, French, Italian, Spanish, &c.; that is to say thus, Theut, Abla, Sire, Orsi, Abdi, Θεός, Esar, Deus, Dieu, Dios, &c. by the four letters of the name of God; the Hebrew mecubalists comprehend this all, as well the celestial world as the elementary, and by the secret of their ghematry, placed their table thus.

	Jod	He	Vau	Cheth
	י	ה	ו	ה
The Elementary World	Fire	Air	Earth	Water
The Celestial World	Michael	Raphael	Gabriel	Uriel
The Epitomised World	Choler	Blood	Melan-choly	Flegme

These worlds thus placed, represent unto us what we should look for as the greatest secret of them; for this great world, called by the Greeks Megacosmos, composed of the first number, is of four elements: the second, according to R. Joseph of the four principal angels; and the third, of the four temperaments or humours, which compose this little world, which is man's body.

1. From these complexions, we shall for our physiognomical learning, observe, that the cholerick humour dryes a man, hinders not his growth, but causes it to be without bodily strength, and the person to be hasty in all his actions.

2. The sanguine or aerial humour, causes the body to grow with a beauty in the face and fatness: the person changeth not in his misfortunes.

3. The humid complexion, which is according to the nature of water or flegme, causes the bodie to be soft, and of little strength; the persons are fearfull, and sleep not too fast, but are lightly awaked, and through fear.

4. The melancholick humour, causes the body to grow slowly, but the minde advances, and these are the men that are worthy of great speculations (yet without fidelity) for such men do not much regard truth, when they would pleasure those whom they are obliged to, but only look on what they themselves imagine.

I have now done with Physiognomie, the rules which have been delivered, being enough for those who would comprehend this Art, without any further discourse. Let then the desirous to learn, read and peruse them.

Part Two: Divination

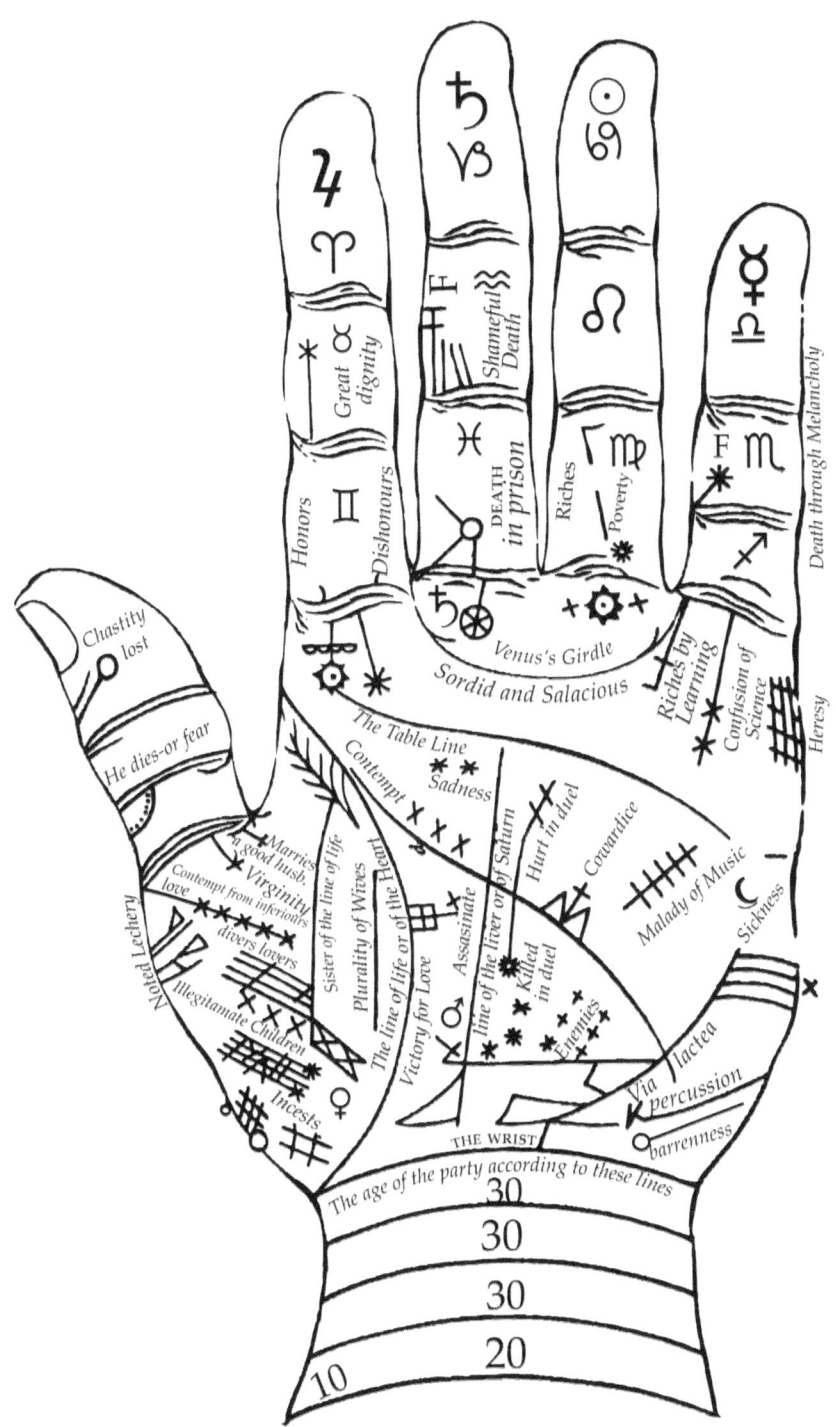

Palmistry.

THE LINES AND THEIR SITUATION IN THE HAND.

1. The line of the heart, or of life, encloses the thumb, and separates it from the plain of Mars.
2. The middle natural line begins at the rising of the fore-finger, near that of life, and ends at the mount of the Moon.
3. The line of the liver begins at the bottom of that of life, and reaches to the table-line, making this triangular figure Δ.
4. The table-line, or line of fortune begins under the mount of Mercury, and ends near the index, and the middle finger.
5. Venus girdle begins near the joynt of the little finger, and ends between the fore-finger, and the middle-finger.
6. The percussion is between ♀ and ☽. Also called the ferient, *à feriendo*, from smiting.
7. The wrist contains those lines that separate the hand from the arm, called *rascetta*.

As for the judgements and significations of the said lines, we shall see them elsewhere: let us now see our other figures.

The true and perfect Description of the Hand.

The hands are the principal parts of the body: the anatomists divide them into three principal parts, that is to say, the wrist, the body of the hand, and the fingers; the best description of them is in the Theology of Hippocrates; but by Chiromancers these three parts are called the palm; a word which Apuleyus useth in his Golden Asse, calling that part Dea Palmaris, which we in Chiromancy call the plain of Mars. The second is called the hollow of the hand, which is from the extremitie of the other side of the thumb towards the little finger, which we call the mount of the hand, or of the Moon. The third are the five fingers, which are to be noted by their names, which according to the physitians are such,

Pollex, Index, Medius, Annularis, Auricularis, which I have represented before in three fingers, and not with any more, because I would be guilty of no confusion, as Indagine, Codes, Corvus, and many others. You are then to note, that the thumb, as being the first, greatest, and strongest, is so called, and dedicated to Venus, and hath such a mark ♀. The next is called Index, the indicative or demonstrative finger, because with it we point at any thing: the old philosophers have called it so, and among others Socrates, who for that reason is painted, pointing with that finger at a woman, that represented nature: and this finger is attributed to Jupiter, and signated with the character of ♃. The third is called the middle finger, because in the middle, some call it physitian, because that with it are touched the privy parts, when something is amiss. The Latines call it verpus, from the word verro, which signifies to rub. And Oras Apella in his Hieroglyphick, represents an infamous person by that finger. But in old time this finger with the thumb and fore-finger represented the Trinity, or the hand of Justice of our Kings. It may be yet seen in some ancient edifices, and particularly at Plaisy in Galie, whereof the president Fauchat, in the seventh book of his history of the declination of the House of Charlemaigne treats at large. This finger is Saturn's, the mark ♄. As for the ring-finger, which is so called, because commonly a ring is worn on it, especially on the left hand; the physitians and anatomists give the reason of it, because in the finger there is a sinew very tender and small that reaches to the heart; wherefore it ought to wear a ring as a crown for its dignity. But besides observe, that in the ceremonies of marriage, they first put the matrimonial ring on the thumb, whence they take it, and put it on every one till they come to this, where it is left. Whence some who stood (as Durand in his Rational of Divine Offices) to discourse on these ceremonies, say it is done because that finger answers to the heart, which is the seat of love and the affections. Others say, because it is dedicated to the Sun, and that most rings are of gold, a mettal which is also dedicated to it: so that by this sympathy it rejoyces the heart: this finger hath for the Sun this mark ☉. The last and least of all is called the ear-finger, because commonly we make use of it to make clean our ears, as if it were some instrument. We read that Dionisius or Denis the Sicilian tyrant, would never make use of any other instrument to cleanse his ears, fearing they should give him some poysoned instrument, as being a Prince very fearfull and distrustfull, whose life was miserable in his tyranny, because of the fear imprinted on his soul. The finger is attributed to Mercury, the sign ☿. In these verses you have a short and learned description.

> Est Pollex veneris, sed ♃ indice gaudet
> ♄ Medium, Sol mediumque tenet;
> ☿ Minimum; ferentem candida Luna,
> Possidet, in Cavea Mars sua castra locat.

Thus Englished.

> Venus the thumb, Jove in the index joyes,
> Saturn the middle, Sol the youthfull toyes;
> Stilborn the least, Luna the ferients.
> In cavea Mars delights to pitch his tents.

Now all these fingers have certain risings at their roots or bases, which are called mounts, attributed to the Planets, to which is added that apparent flesh, which is and belongs to the percussion of the hand; the four principal fingers have twelve joynts or ligaments, to which are attributed the twelve signs of the zodiac, and to each finger one of the seasons of the year: as to the index, which is ♃, we give it the Spring, and to each joynt one of the signs of that season; to the highest Aries, to the middle Taurus, to that of the root Gemini, which are thus marked, ♈, ♉, ♊. The little finger, which is Mercury's, hath the Autumn, and conforms to that of Jupiter, because they represent the two Seasons, which are equally milde and temperate; whereof the two first signs are equinoctial, (that is to say make the nights and days of a length). The signs of the Season of Autumn, which are attributed to this finger, and placed as the others are, Libra, Scorpius, and Sagittary, thus marked, ♎, ♏, ♐. The middle finger, which belongs to

Saturn, represents Winter, a rigorous Season; hath Capricorn, Aquarius, and Pisces, marked thus, ♑, ♒, ♓. The ring-finger, which is the Sun's, hath for signs ♋, ♌, ♍. And these two Seasons have in their first moneths the two solstices, that is, when the Sun neither descends nor ascends, but stands still in the extremities of the zodiac, in the zenith, as to its elevation, and in nadir for its declination. These two angles being represented in the hand, we must imagine the zenith at the end of the middle finger, and the nadir neer the wrist, where ends the line of life, so it represents an ovall figure.

We may represent it according to the third following figure, imagining the zodiac from the forefinger about the thumb and mount of ♀, which shall be comprized in the oval of the zodiac; and we will also imagine our signs placed; Aries on the rising above the wrist; Taurus on the mount of Venus; Gemini on the branches of the line of life, (which denote our life). On the first joynt of the fore-finger ♋, on the second ♌, on the third ♍, leaving the thumb apart, as being an imperfect finger, because it hath but two joynts, which is the first number according to the Arithmeticians, called flat, and hath not so many perfections as the ternary or three, which is the second number. This half circle we call arctick. As for the other half circle meridional, which we call antarctick, we begin it at the top of the ring-finger, and place the first sign, which is ♎, on the first joynt of the finger; on the second ♏, on the third ♐. At the extremity of the table line, Capricorn; in the middle of the mount of the Moon, ♒; and near the wrist on the other side, Pisces; so that the seven Planets will be enclosed within the zodiack.

It is to be noted that every mount, (as I shall shew more at large in the rules of the Science,) signifies and denotes something worthy of special consideration; as that of Venus love, that of ♃ honours, that of ♄ misfortunes, that of ☉ riches, that of ☿ sciences, that of ♂ military atchievements, and that of the Moon afflictions and diseases of mind. I shall pass no further in the notion and significations of these mounts, reserving it to another chapter. But ere I conclude, I will say a word of the lines and observations of the hand, as much as shall be necessary in this place.

In the enclosure of the hand there are six lines or cuts, (as hath been shewed already,) whereon depend the three principal parts of man, that is to say, the head, the heart, and the kidneys, on which depend the three worlds; that is to say, the Intellectual, Celestial, and Elementary; they are thus placed.

The Intellectual	To the Head	To God
The Celestial	The Heart	To Heaven
The Elementary	The Kidneys	To the Elements

SO THE LINES OF THE HAND.

The Table Line The Middle Nat	To the Head	To God
The Line of Life Line of the Stomach	To the Heart	To Heaven
The percussion The wrist	To the Kidneys	To the Elements

To understand these lines, you must know first, that the table line takes its force from the whole head, and that it begins at the percussion of the hand, (where is the mount of Mercury, situate under the little finger,) and reaches with two or three branches, and commonly without, under the fore-finger where it ends; and sometimes it is joyned with the middle natural line, both of them answering to the head, and with that of life make an angle, which ends between the mounts of Venus and Jupiter.

The second line of the head, called the middle natural line, is that which begins at the root of the line of life, and passes through the middle of the palm, between the mount of Mars and the Moon, and advances under that of Venus, and commonly to the table, as hath been said before.

The third, which is the line of life, called also the line of the heart, begins at the mount of the fore-finger, and ends near the wrist, separating the mount of Venus from the triangle or palm.

The fourth, called that of the liver or stomach, begins under the mount of the Moon, and makes the triangle of Mars, thwarting the middle natural, or straite line, joyning with that of life, above the mount of Venus.

The fifth is the wrist, which are those spaces which appear in the joynt of the hand, where there are two lines at least, and four at most, and divers cuts advancing towards the mount of Venus.

As for the sixth, it is the sister of the line of life, which ever follows it, whereto we adde the percussion, which is the outer part, which moves when we strike any thing. These are the most remarkable parts of this science, which are to be much observed in matter of divination, as being the principles of Chiromancy.

Of the Predictions of the Hands in general, and particularly of the Hand-wrist.

You have already known the seven lines of the hands, answering the seven mounts, or seven planets; now you are to learn the judgements which you are to draw from them, that the prolixity may not dispatience any man, and that every one may be easily instructed. I give you first of all this hand before the chapter, wherein is comprized a great and true part of the Chiromantick judgements that I have found infallible; that hand alone can instruct any man whatsoever to make judgements, and to tell particularities and rarities, to make himself to be admired in the eyes of those that affect this science, which he will thereby render much desirable. After the meditation, and the lesson of the hand, I will give you rules and tables upon every line or part of the hand, and demonstrate the whole science in divers figures, and visibly unfold the substance of the truth in near seven hundred aphorismes, for your better instruction, to make you able to judge of things past, present, and to come, with all assurance: which rules I have found true; yet I could not possibly comprehend them in the hand, because of their number and diversity of accidents, both good and bad, which they denote and signifie; therefore I will take them by particulars, in such conspicuous maner, that never was presented to any English eye before this.

1. When there are four lines in the hand-wrist all alike, and well coloured, they signifie to him that hath them, that he shall live eighty or an hundred years; but if there be two little houghs above, making a sharp angle, It denotes that the party shall have the succession of an heritage fall to him by the death of some one; and in his old age be shall rise to honours according as he is capable; he shall be of a good disposition, and healthy.

2. It must be noted here for a second rule, that we allow to every line which is upon the hand-wrist, which separates the hand and the arm, so many thirty years, as it may be seen in this figure. We may also comprehend therein all the ages of the givers of years, as the fifty-eight of Saturn; and by this means also may be known the humour and complexion of the person. The forty-seven of Jupiter, the eighty-two of the Sun, the eighty-three of Venus, the eighty of Mercury, the hundred which the Moon gives, and the forty-nine of Mars, all which may be known according to these lines.

3. When there are but three lines in the head-wrist, if they be superficial and broad, the life shall be sixty years, but abounding in riches in youth, and declining to poverty in that age; if the first line be thick, the second thin, and the third small, that signifies in the first age riches, in the second diminution, in the third augmentation.

4. If there are but two lines, the life will be but sixty years at most, and subject to diseases.

5. To bare but one, signifies death not afar off; but when the first line or the hand-wrist is crooked, and the rest straight, with a right angle and continued, it denotes weakness as to temporal things.

6. if you find the lines scattered abroad in the hand-wrist, it represents a man of little understanding, but couragious enough, and shall not exceed forty years.

7. Let him that hath lines crossing one another in his hand-wrist, take heed of the sword of Justice.

8. When the first line is gross and thick, and the second subtile, and the third thick and broad, it portends in the first age great riches, in the second diminution, and much misfortune, for then Saturn will reign in Alfridary; in the third age he will recover himself again in riches and good fortune; and in the fourth again, misfortune and poverty; if the fourth line be small, death, with the penury of all things, is prenoted.

9. If the lines of the hand-wrist lie scattering and spread abroad, so that they touch not one another, but crookedly passing divers wayes, they signifie a man of a great ingenuity, and guilty of much curiosity; that he entertains high cogitations, and is of a heightened courage, ayming only at the highest things; easie to violate the laws of his Sovereign.

10. When a line crosses the wrist, and crookedly spreads it self towards the line of life, it signifies a sickness; if it be pale, it signifies death near; if it be black, it denotes the approach of a disease, wherein the party shall languish long, by reason of the corruption of blood.

11. When there is a crooked line traverses (after the manner of a bow), the lines of the wrist, it denotes the man shall be of a servile relation, or that he shall be a slave; if there be two, it represents, that he that hath such a thing, shall be by justice condemned to the gallows, or shall end his life miserably.

12. If the lines of the hand-wrist are doubled towards the mount of Luna, and if one line ascend towards the line of the stomach, and be uneven. It portends great tribulations and adversities, nay secret assassinations, cheats, hostilities, and all pernitious actions.

13. If those lines are red and pure, they denote the party martial, and that he shall raise him a fortune by the wars, that he shall be fortunate in all combats as much as he can desire, and that he shall not want the honours of Man.

14. If you find the lines of the wrist in the manner of a chain, especially the first, it signifies a laborious life, yet not unsuccessfull; and he shall by his labour, get together much wealth by his commerce both by sea and land, and especially by sea, if those lines be red and whitish.

15. When it happens that many lines spread themselves abundantly, and end towards the mount of Luna, it demonstrates long expeditions, voyages by sea and land, perpetual peregrinations, and a vagabond life.

16. Among the lines of the hand-wrist if there be one that thwarts them, and all the plain of Mars, and advances even to the mount of the Sun; it presages unexpected honours and riches, which will come suddenly, as also the favour of some great Prince and dignities.

17. Moreover, if any line of the wrist fall down to the palm, and the hollow of the hand, through the line of life, and if it be red, it denotes a debility of understanding, and weakness of body.

18. When there is a triangle near the mount of the Moon, beginning at the lines of the wrist, if it be on the hand of a woman, it denotes she is corrupt even from her tender age, and shall be given to all sorts of unclean actions, in the flowre of her age, and shall be infamous.

19. If there be crosses upon the hand-wrist of a woman, it is a sign she is shamefac'd, chaste; and if there be one in the middle, looking towards the fied of Mars, it denotes that certainly that woman shall be a widdow at twenty-nine years, and in her widdowhood shall take some religious habit, and shall live the rest of her time in great devotion.

20. When the lines of the hand come to the flat of the hand, it signifies diversity of opinions, and a great Inconstancy in resolution.

A TABLE OR ABRIDGEMENT OF THESE RULES FOR THE EASIER COMPREHENSION OF THEM.
THE HAND WRIST IS REFERRED TO ♌.

The long wrist without intersections signifies	*Strength of members and constancy.*
The short wristed, cut, and dissected, signifies	*Weakness of body and minde.*
If the lines of the wrist look towards those of Saturn, they denote	*Vanity, vain-glory, and lying.*
If that line branches itself towards the mount of Jupiter, it denotes	*Honours, dignities, and riches.*
If the contrary,	*Poverty.*
When it casts its branches between the fore-finger and that of Saturn,	*The man shall be wounded in his head; the woman shall die in child-bed.*
If there be crosses or stars in these lines, they denote	*Tranquility of life in old age.*
When there are only stars, it is	*To women, misfortune and infamy.*
When the lines which look towards the mount of Venus make a triangle, it denotes	*Incest, and other sins of dishonesty.*
If those lines lend towards the Hepatick line, it shews	*Integrity of life, and that long.*

A table of the Nails.

THE NAILS BROAD.

1. He or she that hath the nail thus, is of a gentle nature, and good enough, but yet guilty of some pusillanimity, and a fear to speak before great persons, having not his speech at command, and being guilty of a certain bashfulness.

2. If about these nails there happen to be an excoriation of the flesh, which is commonly called points; in these large nails it signifies the party given to luxury, yet fearfull, and commonly guilty of some excesse at his ordinary.

3. When there is at the extremity, a certain white mark, it signifies ruins as to means, that shall happen for want of providence, through negligence; the party hath more honesty then subtility, and fears more a frost in the moneth of May, then the loss of a battel.

THE NAILS WHITE.

1. He that hath nails white and long, is sickly and subject to much infirmity, and especially to feavers; he is neat, but not very strong, because of his indispositions.

2. If upon this white, there appear at the extremities somewhat that is pale, that denotes a short life, that shall happen by sudden death, it may be the squincy; for such persons are fat and of a jovial humour, yet participating with melancholy, or Saturn, and are not merry but by chance.

3. When at the beginning of this nail, or at the root, there appears a certain mixt redness of divers colours, like the rainbow, it denotes the man cholerick and ready to strike, who delights much in combats, battels, conflicts, and duels, contemning every one without any respect.

4. When the extremity is black, it speaks the man given to agriculture, and that his desires are not extraordinary, but content themselves with a mediocrity.

NARROW NAILS.

1. Whosoever hath such a nail, it may be presumed he is a person covetous of the sciences of venery and falconery; that he smells of the bird of prey, viz. is prone to do his neighbour a dammage, and cannot live without hateing his neighbours and kindred.

2. When the nails are long and narrow, the person hath somewhat of the nature of the eagle, will command lesser birds, and kill them; flie high in contempt of those who are more then himself, having the heart always raised to ambition and sovereignty.

LONG NAILS.

When the nails are so, it notes the person well-natured, but distrustful, that wilt not confide in any man, as being from his youth conversant with deceits, yet not practising them, and that because the over goodness of nature which is in him doth rather love reconciliation then differences.

OBLIQUE NAILS.

1. Signifie deceit, and that the person is given to over-reach his neighbour, to make deceitfull bargains, that there may be matter of circumvention and deceit; he hath no courage, nor any greater desire then to see a full parliament, and when he sees it, thinks himself one of the greatest law-givers of the world.

2. When upon these crooked nayls there are certain white little marks at the extremities, it signifies a slothfull person, of little judgement, yet desires most to be heard, though he hath offended no body; there is an inseparable cowardise in his minde, and that through the avarice which governs it.

LITTLE NAILS.

1. Little and round nails denote a person obstinately angry, of a distasteful conversation, that is more enclining to hatred then otherwise, believing all things to be subject to him.

2. If the little nails be crooked at the extremities, it denotes the person fierce and proud, and entertains no desire which doth not speak pride and high dignities.

ROUND NAILS.

Signifie a cholerick person, yet of good nature, and soon reconciled; he is desirous of, and loves the secret sciences, yet with an honest minde, without any design to hurt any body, doing what he doth for his own satisfaction.

FLESHY NAILS.

Signifie a calm person, given to idleness, and will rather sleep, eat, and drink, then take a town by some warlike stratagem, or have any evil design against his neighbour.

PALE AND BLACKE NAILS.

Denote a person Saturnine, subject to many diseases, and withall guilty of many cheats and tricks to deceive his neighbour, for these accidents are derived from Jupiter and Mercury.

RED AND MARKED NAILS.

Signifie a cholerick and martial nature, given to cruelty; and as many little marks as there are, they speak so many evil desires, which tend rather to the hurt then the good of his neighbour; these nails have the nature and complexion of Mars, and of Venus for their variety.

And this shall suffice for the Nails, let us now consider the Hand in generall.

Particular Rules for the Hands.

As for the general predictions of the hands, what my judgement is of them, I shall deliver with as much brevity and truth as I can possibly; the hands being as it were, the looking-glasses wherein we see the soul and the affections.

1. If thou findest any lines at the top of the fingers, beware of drowning or falling into the water; and observe in what finger it is, that thou maist know what moneth this misfortune will happen to thee, and prevent it.

2. If thou find two lines under the joynt of the thumb, it denotes great inheritance and possessions; but if there be but one, it denotes no great wealth. If these lines be great and apparent, the person hath some riches, about which he is in debates and law-suits.

3. If between the joynts of the thumb there be two lines streached out and well united, the person will be a gamester; but by means of his gaming he shall be in danger of his life: but if they be disjoyned, or winding and crooked, he is like to fall into thieves' hands, and be robbed.

4. If there be a hand that hath two lines joyned together, within, under the last joynt of the thumb, it denotes danger by water; but if they are pale, it signifies that it hath happened in childhood, or that it will happen late; half these lines are without, they threaten some loss by fire.

5. A woman that hath lines at the root of the thumb, upon the mount of Venus, so many lines as there are, so many children shall she have: if they verge towards the outside of the hand, so many men shall have to do with her, or marry her.

6. If thou find the first joynt of the thumb having a line that joyns to it within from the part of the fore-finger, he that hath it shall be hanged; and so much the more certain, by how much the more the said line represents it, and descends from the table line: but if the said line be united without, and not within, it is a sign the person shall lose his head; if it be environed all about, the man shall be hanged.

7. When the table-line is crooked, and falls between the middle and forefinger, it signifies effusion of blood, as I said before.

8. When thou findest upon the mount of the thumb, called the mount of Venus, certain lines thwarting from the line of life to it, the person is luxurious, and for that reason shall be hated of his friends and superiors; but when thou findest two lines near the thumb fair and apparent, they signifie abundance of temporal wealth.

9. The mount of Venus swelling up and high in the hand of any one, signifies luxury and unchastity.

10. If thou find a hand that hath a cleft, with three small branches, the person that so hath it, shall be hated of great men; but he shall be a great dissembler, and for that reason shall not fear them much.

11. If thou find the line of life separated, or divided into halfs, the person shall be wounded with a sword in his body.

12. If a woman hath the palm of the hand short, and the fingers long, it is a sign she shall bring forth with great pain and difficulty.

13. When thou seest a hand something long, and the fingers somewhat thick, it is a sign that the person is slow, idle, of a phlegmatick complexion, yet a good body, and very modest.

14. When thou findest the palm of the hand long, and the fingers of a good proportion, and not soft in the touching, but rather hard, the person is ingenious, but changeable, given to theft, and vitious.

15. He that hath the hand hollow, solid, and well knit in the joynts, is likely to live long; but if over-thwarted, it denotes shortness of life.

16. He that hath the hand according to the quantity of his body, and the fingers too short, and thick, and fat at the ends, is denoted to be a thief, a lyer in wait, and furnished with all evill, a paragon of vice, the more he hath the fingers filled towards the ends.

17. When the palm of the hand is longer then its due proportion requires, and the fingers more thick, by how much they are the more short it signifies the man idle, negligent, a fool, and proud, and that so much the more, by how much the hand is more brawny.

18. He that hath the hands long and great, is liberal, good-conditioned, crafty, hath a great spirit, and is a good counsellour, and faithfull to his friends.

19. He that hath the hand shorter then it should be, according to the proportion of his other members, it is a sign of a great talker, and that he is a glutton, insatiable, injurious, and a censurer of other mean actions.

20. He that hath the fingers turning backwards, is an unjust person, subtile, ingenious; and the more neat his fingers seem to be (as being more dry) the more mischievous is he, and advances into all evill, as if he were at enmity with vertue ; when the lines of the joynts are all alike, take heed of such servants.

21. He that hath the fingers well united and close, so that the air can hardly pass between, is a curious person, and very carefull about his affairs.

22. When thou seest one that hath the fingers retorted at the highest joynt, and turned backward orderly, as it appears here, it it a sign of an envious person. Indagines and Savanarola say that he is envious: but it is a vertnous envy or emulation, and the person a professed enemy of vice.

23. If thou find one whose fingers are dispersed, and thicker at the joynts, and between the joynts small and dry, as if the flesh were taken away, it denotes poverty and misery. The men that are thus qualified, are great talkers, and suffer poverty by their over-great wisdom.

24. Who hath the fingers in such a manner as that they strike one another, as if they were beating a drum, it is a sign that he it changeable in his thoughts, and hath ill opinions of others.

25. He that when he is in discourse with others, hath a custom of striking with his hands, and cannot abstain from it, hath some imperfection in his understanding, and his mind being overwhelmed with many affairs, it is as it were confused.

26. If thou find one whose hands shake when he reacheth them forth to take somewhat, it denotes that he is no cholerick person. There are others that have this infirmity through the too much use of wine; therefore caution is to be used.

27. When you see a man who when he eats, opens his mouth, and stoops it to his hand, or to the meat which he holds, it is a sign he is a glutton, and an enemy to all the world; and he that in the same action pulls down his hat over his eyes, is a treacherous person, and given to all manner of vice, and such a one as wise men avoid.

28. Observe the finger of Mercury, or the little finger, if the end thereof exceed the last joynt of the annular or ring-finger, such a man rules in his house, and hath his wife pleasing and obedient to him, but if it be short, and reach not the joynt, that man hath a shrew, an imperious commanding woman, that wears the breeches; if one hand differ from the other, (as

it may do,) having in one the little finger exceeding the joynt, in the other shorter, then it denotes one wife a shrew, and the other courteous; and you may know how to distinguish by observing the hands; for if that hand that shews the lines the most conspicuous, have the little finger long, passing the joynt of the annular, then the first wife is good; if that hand have the shortest finger, then the first wife is a shrew, and so of the other.

The last of these Rules is worthy observation; for on it depends Chironomy, or the science of the slight of the hands, very necessary to those who desire to be gamesters.

The foregoing extracts upon these curious subjects, will be further elucidated by the engraved plate on Palmistry which accompanies these articles, and to which I refer the reader.

ANCIENT DIVINATION
BY THE
WHEEL OF PYTHAGORAS;
Which is said to resolve all Questions, Past, Present, and Future.

PART I.

THE WHEEL.

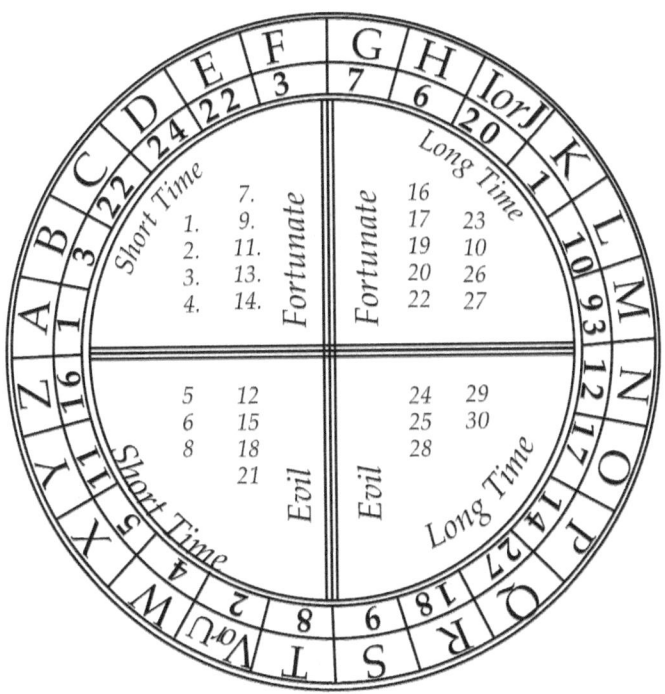

The Ancients, who were extremely fond of divination, were wont to place great confidence in the "Wheel of Pythagoras," which resolves questions by *Arithmancy*, or a species of sortilegy by numbers; wherein the result depends upon the unfettered agency of the mind and will, or intent to know "any difficult thing."

The Wheel of Pythagoras is said by former writers to resolve "all questions the asker may wish to be acquainted with, whether of the past time, the present time, or of the future." The following are said to be

The Questions the Wheel answers.

1. If a horse shall win the race?
2. If a prisoner shall come out of prison?
3. If a sick person shall recover or die?
4. If an absent person shall return?
5. If the city besieged shall be taken?
6. Of two fighters, which shall prevail?
7. If the sickness shall be long or short?
8. If a suit at law shall be gained?
9. If thy wishes shall succeed?
10. If the day shall be fortunate?
11. If stolen or lost things shall be recovered?
12. If it be good to buy or sell?
13. If the asker shall marry?
14. If the undertaking shall succeed?
15. If the asker is fortunate or unfortunate?
16. If any matter or thing whatever shall end good or ill?

Explanation of the Wheel.

The Wheel, it will be perceived, is divided into four compartments, the *upper* half of which contains in order the numbers which are termed propitious, good, and *fortunate;* the *lower* half contains those numbers of a contrary kind, or those which are termed evil, unpropitious, and *unfortunate.*

Round the Wheel are the letters of the Alphabet, to which are placed certain corresponding numbers which are required in the calculations: (these will be explained in Part 2). Besides which, the numbers in the right half of the wheel are said to denote "Long Time," or that the question which has these numbers in the working will be a length of time about; and those in the left half of the wheel are said to signify a short or brief space of time ere the affair is accomplished. Next follow the

TABLES USED IN WORKING THE WHEEL.

1. *The Mystical Numbers of each Day in the Week*

Sunday	106
Monday	52
Tuesday	52
Wednesday	102
Thursday	31
Friday	68
Saturday	45

2. *The Numbers of the Planets ruling the Days.*

Day	Planet	Number	Day	Planet	Number
Sunday	☉	34	Thursday	♃	78
Monday	☽	45	Friday	♀	45
Tuesday	♂	39	Saturday	♄	55
Wednesday	☿	114			

3. *The Numbers to be chosen by Chance (as hereafter explained) in working the Questions.*

1	11	22	28	29
6	2	12	23	30
15	7	3	13	24
19	16	8	4	14
25	20	17	9	5
27	26	21	18	10

The numbers attributed to the days of the week, and of the planet ruling the day, are of very ancient origin; and for which it would be difficult to assign a reason, or even account for in any way consonant with Astrological Science. They are, however, as well as the Wheel, a relic of former *traditional* foreknowledge by lots or numbers; probably invented, like Geomancy, in the monastic solitude of the middle ages. The manuscript from whence this is compiled appears to have been written as early as the fifteenth century.—It was purchased at a high price at the sale of the late Mr. Cosway's library. But Christopher Cattan, a very old author, whose works are rare and expensive, makes some mention thereof; yet he fails in describing the manner of using the numbers, and in other parts of the process.

Arithmancy, or Divination by Numbers, on which the Wheel is founded, was variously practised. Many stupendous "*Tomes*," in the dead languages, now obsolete and forgotten, were to be found, explaining the "Arte and Manner" of these curious proceedings; in which the letters of the party's name were said to contain many hidden arcana, when decyphered by the "mysteries of numbers." The ancients went so far in these particulars, as to declare their belief that each individual may know the chief *secrets* of his destiny by the help of his name, or patronymical appellation; and also that there exists a peculiar sympathy between the name and the pursuits throughout life. These facts are here stated merely to apprise the reader of the unlimited fondness of the ancients for every kind of Aruspicy or Soothsaying, no matter how or where it was accomplished.

There have been several Italian writers of eminence who have treated of the power of numbers when chosen or combined by "lot" amongst whom stands conspicuous Trithemius, the famous Abbot of Spanheim, whose work, entitled "Steganography," is exceedingly mystical, rare, and curious, but has never been translated into English.

The Italians have also made use of the "Wheel of Pythagoras" for finding out fortunate numbers in the Lottery; as the following extract from the life of

The celebrated Count Cagliostro

will sufficiently prove.

"The lottery,' says the count,'was at this time on the point of commencing; the daily discourses of Scot on this subject (who, like Vitellina, was addicted to all games of chance) brought to my mind a manuscript which I had in my possession; it contained many curious cabalistical operations by numbers; by the aid of which, amongst other secrets, the author set forth the actual *possibility* of calculating numbers for lotteries.

"'I had ever considered this as a vague and enthusiastic idea, but had long contracted the habit of suspending my judgment on those things I had not particularly made the object of my speculations.'

"He was resolved, he tells us, to prove the truth or falsehood of those assertions; and, by adhering to the rules prescribed in the manuscript, for the 6th of November he predicted the number 20. 'On this,' says he, 'Scot risked a trifle, and *won*; but by number 26, which was calculated for the ensuing day, he gained upwards of one hundred guineas!

" 'The numbers 55 and 57 were announced with equal *success* for the 16th of November; the profits of which days were equally divided between Vitellina, and the pretended Lady Scot.

" 'Judge my astonishment,' says the Count, 'at perceiving the exactness of those calculations I had believed to be but a mere chimera! The *possibility* of such calculations I must entirely submit to the determination of the reader; but was this uncommon success the effect of human skill or of entire chance?'

"The Count, from a point of delicacy, thought proper to resist the repeated solicitations of Scot, &c., by resolutely refusing to predict other numbers. Scot exerted every effort to strengthen his intent with the Count. He presented Madame Cagliostro with the trimming of a cloak worth four or five guineas; in return for which, as he would not mortify him by a refusal, the Count presented him, on the same day, with a gold box, value twenty-five guineas; and, to free himself from further importunity, ordered his servant to deny him both to Scot and Miss Fry, which was the real name of the pretended lady.

" The latter, however, in a few days gained admission to Lady Cagliostro. She informed her in broken accents, accompanied with tears, that she was for ever ruined; Scot, she said, to whom she had the weakness to be attached, having decamped with the profits arising from the lottery, leaving her with his three children entirely destitute. This imaginary tale produced the intended result. Madame Cagliostro, touched with the pretended misery of her situation, generously interceded with the Count in her behalf, who, at her request, sent her a guinea, and, for the ensuing day, the chance of number 8.

"Flushed with her former success, she now *believed* the calculations of her benefactor infallible; and, having procured cash upon her effects, she boldly risked a considerable sum on the above number. Fate was again propitious! On the 7th of December, the number *eight* emerged from the wheel of fortune!

"This extraordinary chance, on which the Count did not risk a single guinea, returned to Scot and Miss Fry (whose quarrel was fabulous) the full sum of one thousand five hundred guineas!"

Cagliostro's Life, p. 22

WHEEL OF PYTHAGORAS.

Part II.

TO RESOLVE THE QUESTIONS.

In the first place, the inquirer must refer to Table III., page [229]; and, while thinking earnestly upon the question he wishes resolved or answered, let him choose a *number* out of that table, without premeditation; or, what is said to be still better, let the inquirer take thirty pieces of card, and write thereon from No. 1 to 30; and these pieces being so numbered, and mixed together, *let one of them be chosen promiscuously,* and the number thereon taken notice of. This is the first step in the operation; but thereon depends the truth of the whole: therefore the inquirer must be particular in this part of the process.

Secondly. To this number, so chosen, either from the table or otherwise, let the inquirer *add the number answering to the first letter of his proper or Christian name*; which is seen in the Wheel itself, where the numbers stand in the inner circle, under the letters.

Thirdly. To this sum add *the number of the day of the week, and of the planet ruling the day*; which is plainly shown in Tables No. I. and II. page [229], of that day on which they ask the question. Then, *add the whole together*, and divide it by 30, or subtract 30 from it, as often as you can ; and the remainder look for in the Wheel, observing in what part of the Wheel it falls; but if there be no remainder, then the number 30 itself must be looked for.

Now, to know whether the question or demand, which the inquirer or any one else propounds, shall succeed or not; take notice, if the number falls in the *upper half* of the Wheel, your fortune therein is Good, and the lot you have cast will cause your request to be fulfilled. But if it chance to be found in the *lower half* of the Wheel, your lot is evil and unfortunate; and the proposed question shall have an Evil issue.

Note, also, if it be any question wherein time is concerned; as, how long or how short shall be the matter in hand before it be accomplished. Observe, that one half of the Wheel represents numbers of "long time," the other half of "short time;" and even so, in good or evil, shall the matter in hand fall out.

The whole of the questions *but one* in the list are answered thus; but, to No. 3, which is, "If a sick person shall recover or die?" to the above sums must be added, the "Moon's Age" on the day the question is asked; and the result proceeded with in the same manner.

Example 1.

Saturday, March 1, 1828.—It was asked. If an undertaking should succeed? The number chosen was 14; and the first letter of the person's Christian name was R.

>Number chosen.................................. 14
>Number in the Wheel answering to R. ... 13
>Number answering to Saturday............ 45
>Number of the Planet ruling Saturday ... 55
>
>>Sum...... 127

This, divided by 30, leaves 7 for the remainder. Refer to the Wheel, and 7 is found in the upper half of the Wheel, and in the half marked "short time." This shows that the affair would be accomplished accordingly.

Example 2.

A person whose initial was S. asked, on Wednesday, If a sick friend should recover or die? and drew forth a card with the number 23 upon it, as his lot.

>Number chosen........................... 23
>Number answering to S................... 9
>Number answering to Wednesday... 102
>Number answering to the Planet...... 114
>Number of the Age of the Moon...... 20
>
>>Sum... 268

This, divided by 30, leaves 28 for the remainder, which is found to fall in the unfortunate half of the Wheel, and denotes long sickness, and dangerous, or of a doubtful issue.

These examples will be sufficient to illustrate the method of resolving questions by the Wheel of Pythagoras, in which the only difficulty consists in choosing the first number. For which purpose, the manuscript from whence this is taken recommends the inquirer not to "ask but one question on the same day, and to refrain from all gibing, sporting, jesting, and unbelief, while divining," or making use of the Wheel, in order to know the truth.

The reader will remember that this extract is put more for his amusement than for any avouching as to its actual certainty. Let him try it, and judge for himself.

UNFORTUNATE AND EVIL DAYS,

BY THE

WHEEL OF PYTHAGORAS.

The same manuscript also contains *a tradition* relating to the evil days, or days of misfortune, whereon no question should be asked; as follows:—

"There be evil and unfortunate days, so called by the ancient philosophers, in the which, if a man fall sick, he shall be in danger of death, or else to be long sick; or, if any person take upon him a journey, and set forward in any one of these days, he shall have *ill luck* in his doings: neither is it good to plant, to make bargains, or banquets, in any of them.

"January hath five ill days; that is, the 3d, 4th, 5th, 9th, and 11th.
February hath three; that is, the 13th, 17th, and 19th.
March hath three; that is, the 13th 15th, and 16th.
April hath two; that is, the 5th and the 14th.
May also hath two; the 8th and the 14th.
June hath but one ill day; and that is, the 6th.
July hath two ill days; the 16th and 19th.
August hath two; the 8th and the 16th.
September hath three; that is, the 1st, 15th, and 16th.
October hath but one ill day; and that is, the 16th.
November hath two; that is, the 15th and 16th.
December hath three; that is, the 6th, 7th, and the 11th."*

---

* The reader may discover the *really fortunate and unfortunate days*, according to astral causes, by consulting "THE PROPHETIC GUIDE," published annually. That for 1829, contains the *fate* of each day in that year

The foregoing tradition seems to be a relic of ancient augury, or soothsaying, and, consequently, very old in date. In the middle ages, these days were universally shunned, as "ruled by evil influences." As an old writer has it,

> "Days of evil, strife and hate;
> Cruel wrath and fell debate.
> Planets strike and stars annoy.
> Aspects, aught of good destroy.
> Shun their calends.
> Heed their power.
> Nought begun in evil hour
> Ever went well. Spirits o'er
> Those days preside.
> Who sport and gibe,
> With human fate;
> Omens of hate,
> Wrath, and debate."
>
> OLD LEGEND.

TRADITIONS AND SUPERSTITIONS
OF FORMER TIMES
The Planetary Alphabet
OF "TRITHEMIUS THE WISE,"

Which is said to discover the Sign and Planet under which any one is born, and their Good and Bad Fortune in life, by the Letters of their Name.

A	B	C	D	E	F
1	5	22	24	22	3
G	H	I	K	L	M
7	6	20	1	10	23
N	O	P	Q	R	S
12	11	15	27	13	9
T	V	W	X	Y	Z
8	2	4	6	3	4

NUMBERS ANSWERING TO THE PLANETS.

The Sun	☉	1 or 4
The Moon	☽	2 or 7
Saturn	♄	8
Jupiter	♃	3
Mars	♂	9
Venus	♀	6
Mercury	☿	5

NUMBERS ATTRIBUTED TO THE 12 CELESTIAL SIGNS.

Aries	♈	7	♎	8	Libra
Taurus	♉	6	♏	9	Scorpio
Gemini	♊	12	♐	4	Sagitarius
Cancer	♋	5	♑	3	Capricornus
Leo	♌	1	♒	2	Aquarius
Virgo	♍	10	♓	11	Pisces

Among the most curious of the ancient inventions, may be classed the foregoing tradition of the old astrologers "for finding the sign and star under which any one is born;" which is done as follows.

1. TO FIND THE ALMUTEN OR RULING PLANET AT BIRTH, BY NAMES ALONE.

Add together the different sums answering to the *letters of the Christian* (or proper) *names, and those of each parent,* as they are set down in the table called the "Planetary Alphabet," and then divide that sum so found by *nine;* the remainder, which is left after such division, being sought as above, directs you to the planet which is the Almutan, or *planet, who ruled at birth,* as it is termed by the old authors. Thus, if the remainder were 3, that planet would be *Jupiter;* if 1 or 4, the *Sun;* if 2 or 7, the *Moon;* and so of the rest: and if nothing remain after such division is made, the number 9, which you divided by, is the symbol of the planet.

Example. Name of the party inquiring, JAMES; of the parents, ANN and THOMAS. Proceed thus—

Party.		*Parents.*		*Parents.*	
J	20	A	1	T	8
A	1	N	12	H	6
M	23	N	12	O	11
E	22			M	23
S	9			A	1
				S	9
Sum	75	Sum	25	Sum	58

Add these together.

```
         75
         25
         58
        ___
Divide by 9) 158
             ___
             17, and 5 remainder.
```

Therefore 5 is the planetary number, which gives Mercury (☿) for your almutan, or ruling star.

This is too plain to need any other example.

2. TO DISCOVER THE SIGN THAT PLANET WAS IN.

Add together the different sums of your own and your parents' proper names, and divide the sum by 12; the remainder shows the *sign* the planet was in. But if there be no remainder, take 12 itself for that number.

Example. Names as before.

```
          Sum.
Divide by 12)158
             ___
             13, and 2 remainder.
```

No. 2 is attributed to Aquarius (♒), therefore the party in question is born under ☿ in ♒, (Mercury in Aquarius).

Note that this rule is said only to be true when the party inquiring is ignorant of their true nativity, although it may afford much amusement to any other person who is fond of the superstitions of past ages. The *ancient* Chaldee and Babylonian soothsayers, and the modern Persian astrologers, agreed unanimously in drawing certain particulars of the future fate, or the "destinie," of mankind, from the letters of their names; affirming that *"all names were to be found registered in the heavens,* and to be known by the planets reigning at the birth of man." Some of the ancient Magi go even farther than this, and declare that the *Genius,* or the Guardian Demon, which they say every man has allotted him from the instant of his emerging into life as an animal, may be likewise known, and his company sought, by the nomenclature of the native and his parents. It is from a scarce work in the British Museum, that the foregoing is compiled, written in the Italian language, and correctly translated with the different planetary characters.

The signs and planets differ from each other in nature, influence, and description, as various writers also teach. Of the twelve zodiacal signs, some are said to be far more fortunate than others, "in their influence over man's life."

ANCIENT AUGURY AND SOOTHSAYING.

Augury is the art of inspection, and prognosticating or soothsaying, by observation of birds and beasts, and was in great repute among the ancients. The Lacedemonians had always an augur to attend upon their kings; and among the Romans was a college of augurs.

Romulus himself was a soothsayer, and ordained that the choice of magistrates should be confirmed by augury; and so fond were the ancients of this art, as to ordain that nothing of public or private affairs should be transacted without it. In taking the auspices, it was observed whether the beasts came willingly to the altar or not—whether the entrails were of a natural colour, and not exulcerated, or whether any parts were defective or wanting. Thus, when the Emperor Augustus found two galls in his sacrifice, it was considered as prognosticative of peace with Antony, and the amity of state dissentients.

Because Brutus and Cassius met a blackamoor, and Pompey had on a garment of dark colours, at the battle of Pharsalia, these were said to be presages of their overthrow. When Gracoeus was slain, the same day the augurs observed that the sacred chickens that were kept for the purposes of divination, refused to come out of their coop. So the death of Caesar was divined, from the unusual noise and clattering of armour in his house. In like manner, the poisoning of

Germanicus was presaged by the strange circumstance (according to historians) of a trumpet sounding of its own accord.

About anno 1300, a *painted* horse, on the walls of the imperial palace of the Emperor Andronicus, was said to neigh with great loudness,—which was judged a happy omen to that Emperor, and his Chancellor congratulated him in the expectation of future triumphs; and when Baldwin, emperor of the Latins, was beaten out of Constantinople by his father, his horse neighed with a strange and hollow sound, which was thought by his courtiers (as it proved) ominous of great disasters.

An owl screeching in the Senate-house, was deemed ominous and boding ill-luck to the Emperor Augustus. A company of crows following Sejanus to his house with great noise and clamour, was judged to be fatal, and so indeed it proved.—Romulus had the empire promised him before his brother Remus, by the soothsayers, because *he* had seen the double number of vultures.—So our William the Conqueror, when he first stepped on land, his foot slipping, he fell down and got some dirt in his hand, which his attendants fearing to be an evil omen, he said, "No; I have, by this fall, but taken *possession* of this island." Also, a swarm of bees hovering over St. Ambrose, as also Plato the philosopher, when infants in their cradles, was judged to portend "that great wisdom should flow from their mouths, which would enrapture mankind."

Bibliomancy;
OR, DIVINATION BY THE BIBLE.

Amongst other modes of divining the future fate made use of by the ancient Christian Church, the *Bible* formed a most prominent feature: and it is affirmed, that the forty-ninth chapter of Genesis is of singular efficacy therein; for it is said, that if any person beginning life refer to the forty-ninth chapter of Genesis, and choose any verse at random, *beginning with the third verse, and ending with the twenty-seventh verse,* the verse he first chooses shall be typical of his future fate, character, and success in life. Several persons who have tried this method have been struck with the singularity of the result.

Another method practised by the ancients upon almost every occasion, was, to open the Bible at random—especially the Psalms, the Prophets, or the Four Gospels,—and the words which *first* presented themselves decided the future lot of the inquirer. Several remarkable instances of this practice are upon record, from which I abstract the following:—

One Peter, of Tholouse, being accused of heresy, and having denied the truth of the accusation upon oath, a bystander, in order to judge of the truth, seized the book upon which he had sworn, and opening it hastily, met with the words of the devil to our Saviour, " What have we to do with thee, thou Jesus of Nazareth?" and concluded from thence that the accused was guilty; and this was afterwards proved.

The founder of the Franciscan Friars, it seems, having denied himself the possession of anything but coats and a cord, and still having doubts whether he might not possess books, first prayed, and then casually opened upon *Mark*, chap. iv.—" Unto you it is given to know the mystery of the kingdom of God; but unto them that are without, all these things are done in parables:" from which he drew the conclusion, that books were not necessary for him.

The Emperor Heraclius, in the war against the Persians, being at a loss whether to advance or retreat, commanded a public fast for three days; at the end of which he applied to the Four Gospels, and opened upon a text which be regarded as an oracular intimation to winter in Albania.

Gregory of Tours also relates, that Meroveous being desirous of obtaining the kingdom of Chilperic, his father consulted a female fortune-teller, who promised him the possession of royal estates. But, to prevent deception, and to try the truth of her prognostications, he caused the Psalter, the Book of Kings, and the Four Gospels, to be laid upon the shrine of Saint Martin, and, after fasting and solemn prayer, opened upon passages which not only destroyed his former hopes, but seemed to predict the unfortunate events which really afterwards befel him.

In the Gallican Church it was long practised in the election of bishops,—children being employed, on behalf of each candidate, to draw slips of paper with texts on them; and that which was thought most favourable decided the choice. A similar mode was pursued at the installation of abbots, and the reception of canons; and this custom is said to have continued in the Cathedrals of Ypres, St. Omers, and Boulogne, so late as the year 1744. In the Greek Church it was practised upon the consecration of Athanasius, on whose behalf the presiding prelate, Caracalla, archbishop of Nicomedia, opened the Gospels upon these words—"For the devil and his angels," *Matt.* xxv. 41. The bishop of Nice first saw them, and adroitly turned over the leaf to another verse, which was instantly read aloud—"The birds of the air came and lodged in the branches thereof." But this passage appearing contrary to the ceremony, the first became gradually known; and the historian who has recorded the fact, remarks, that the Church of Constantinople was violently agitated by the most fatal divisions during the patriarchate.

The Methodists are said to pay a particular attention to this mode of discovering future events; a singular instance whereof is given in the life of the eccentric but fortunate bookseller, Mr. Lackington, which is recorded by himself as follows:—

" One Sunday morning, at eight o'clock, my mistress, seeing her sons set off, and knowing that they were gone to a methodist meeting, determined to prevent me from doing the same by locking the door, which she accordingly did; on which, in a superstitious mood, I opened the Bible for direction what to do, and the first words I read were these — "He has given his angels charge concerning thee, lest at any time thou shouldst dash thy foot against a stone." This was enough for me; so without a moment's hesitation, I ran up two pair of stairs to my own room, and out of the window

I leaped, to the great terror of my poor mistress. I got up immediately, and ran about two or three hundred yards towards the meeting house; but, alas! I could ran no farther; my feet and ancles were most intolerably bruised, so that I was obliged to be carried back and put to bed. This my rash adventure made a great noise in the town."

The author of this book is well acquainted with many persons of erudition and sound judgment, who, at the present day, *privately* make use of the foregoing method of prognosticating the event of their undertakings, by opening the Bible in a chance way, and placing reliance upon the first passage of Scripture that meets their eye; and they say it is seldom erroneous.

A Marriage Omen

Among the peasantry of Westphalia, and in some parts of Wales, young females knock, on Christmas Eve, at the hen-house. If a hen first cackles, they relinquish all hopes of being married during the ensuing year; but if a cock crow first, they deem it an infallible omen of their being married before the ensuing year expires.

Midsummer Charm, to Know when any one shall die.

To ascertain whether a person will die in the current year, the country folk, in some places, about Midsummer, pluck some of the herb St. John's wort, before sunrise in the morning and hide it in the walls in various parts of the house. The bunches which immediately droop, announce with certainty (it is said) the speedy death of those who placed them there; but if the herb remains fresh and green, then the person who placed it there will not die during that year.

Description and Use of the Ancient Danish Calendar*

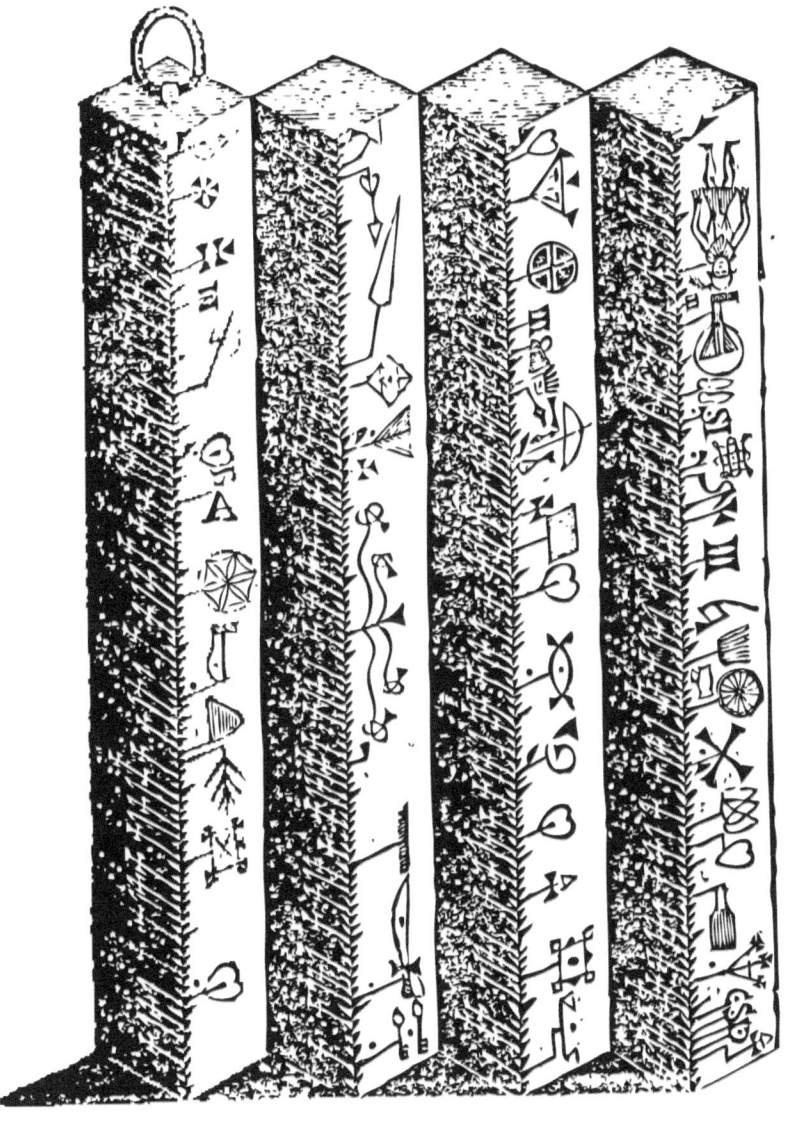

* Formerly used as a powerful charm,

THIS ancient almanack, which was in common use throughout this country, during the earlier part of last century, is a very curious relic of the Danish Government in England. It was called by the "Rimstock," from "Rimur," which, in their language, signified "a calendar."*

By the Norwegians, with whom they are still in use, they are termed "Primestaves," from the introduction of the prime or golden number upon the staff, or walking-stick, which, with them, is the prevailing form of this utensil. I have one of these primestaves in my possession, which consists of the straight branch of a tree, divested of its bark, having the figures of men, animals, birds, fishes, reptiles, flowers, and weapons, neatly incised upon its surface. It is about an inch in diameter, and nearly three feet in length.

These instruments differ from each other in form, size, material, and marks. Olaus Wormius, in his "Fasti Danici," exhibits two; one hexagonal, with an intermixture of Runic characters, and another flat, divided into six columns. He says that there were some very ancient ones made of horn, and others inscribed upon a hollow bone. Mr. Gough has engraved one to his edition of Camden's Britannia.

Dr. Robert Plot, who, in 1686, published "The Natural History of Staffordshire," has descanted very largely on this singular implement, in an additional chapter "Of Antiquities." He says that they were generally made of wood, box, fir, or oak, though he met with some few of brass; that they were of two sizes, one larger, for the use of a whole family; and others private, of smaller dimensions, to carry in the pocket. This work, which has become extremely scarce, was published in one volume, folio. The thirty-fifth plate is a representation of one of the larger sort of clogs, and dedicated "to the worshipful Elias Ashmole, Esq." who was a very distinguished antiquary, a native of Lichfield, and collector of the Ashmolean Museum at Oxford, over which Dr. Plot, at that time, presided.

---

* Vide— "The Pirate," by the author of Waverley.

The above drawing, which is copied from this print, shows the four edges of the square log, each one of which contains three months, which are divided by notches into days, every seventh being of a larger size, to denote the sabbath; and the first of every month is noted by a patulus stroke, inclining upwards. The figures on the left side of the notches show the golden number, or cycle of the moon. If this number be under 5, it is denoted by so many points; if 5, by a hooked line drawn from the notch representing the ancient sigil V. When above 5, and under 10, the hooked line has one or more points appended to it; at 10, the stroke is crossed thus X, points are now placed above it to 14; at 15, the cross is surmounted by a hooked line, making it XV. The dots are still continuous, till at 19, the line is intersected by two crosses, which is the last number requisite to mark these changes.

The other figures remaining to be described on the *opposite* side of the *notches*, are symbolical of the life or death of the *saint*, against whose feast they are opposed, or of some *custom* or *occupation*, in vogue about the time, as follows:—

JANUARY		AUGUST	
Days		Days	
1. *Annulet*	New Years' Day	1. *Bow and Arrows*	Lammas
6. *Star*	Epiphany	7. *Cross*	Transfiguration
13. *Cross*	Hilary	13. *Gridiron*	Lawrence
25. *Axe*	St. Paul	25. *Heart*	Assumption
FEBRUARY		SEPTEMBER	
Days		Days	
2. *Heart*	Purification	1. *Hunting-Horn*	Giles
3. *B.*	Blaize	8. *Heart*	Nativity
5. *A.*	Agatha	14. *Cross*	Holy Cross
14. *Lover's knot*	Valentine	29. *Pair of Scales*	Michael
24. *Leg*	Matthias	OCTOBER	
MARCH		Days	
Days		13. *Man*	Edward the Confessor
1. *Harp*	David		
2. *Bough*	Chad	18. *Guitar*	Luke
25. *Heart*	Annunciation	25. *Shoes*	Holy Cross

April
Days
- 3. *Javelin* — Richard
- 4. *Arrow* — Ambrose
- 23. *Spear* — George

May
Days
- 1. *Branch* — May-Day
- 3. *Cross* — Invention

June
Days
- 11. *Rake* — Barnabas
- 24. *Sword* — John
- 29. *Keys* — Peter

July
Days
- 2. Heart — Visitation
- 7. *A.T.crost* — Thomas a-Becket
- 20. M. — Margaret
- 22. *Cup* — M. Magdalen

November
Days
- 2. S. — All Souls
- 6. *Cross* — Leonard
- 11. M. — Martin
- 23. *Wassail Cup* — Clement
- 25. *Wheel* — Catherine
- 30. *Cross* — Andrew

December
Days
- 6. *Hearts* — Nicholas
- 8. *Heart* — Conception
- 13. *Lute* — Lucy
- 25. *Drinking-horn* — Christmas day
- 26. S. — Stephen
- 27. I. — John
- 29. *Cross* — Thomas-a-Canterbury

It may be remarked, that all the feasts of the *Virgin* are marked with a *heart*.

J.H., Litchfield.

Part Three:
Low Magic

Wonderful Charms, Talismans, and Curious Secrets in Occult Philosophy.

EXTRACTED FROM ANCIENT MANUSCRIPTS AND RARE OLD AUTHORS.

> "When the silent stars are shooting,
> And the answering owls are hooting,
> Shall my soul be upon thine.
> With a power, and with a sign?" —Byron.

* * * * * * *

"The charm works, and now Arthur hie thee to the green wood, keep to the left, and anon on the verge of the sloping pasture, where the *fairy-ring* envelopes its mystic space, thou shalt find the deadly *nightshade*, and the root of vervain; haste, I say, or the hour of *Saturne* will be gone by, and lo the moon has already risen to light thy path.

"*Arthur.*—Father, I speed, winged by love, and all anxiety to try thy potent *spell*—ye stars be favourable."—Old Play.

TRADITIONS AND SUPERSTITIONS OF FORMER TIMES.

In regard to the display of the former popular belief in the mystic power of charms, spells, enchantments, and the occult influences of certain agents; the author is desirous of its being understood that he by no means wishes to revive the gloomy days of superstition, nor to impose upon the unreflecting multitude the principles of ignorance or enthusiasm. Neither does he avouch for the truth or falsehood of the different mystical rites, ceremonials, and such like, that are brought forward in this book for the sole purpose of *recording* the traditional customs of times long past; which most persons certainly feel pleasure in perusing, when they are incorporated in tales or romances, or even in detached fragments of legendary lore, where a small portion of truth is generally mixed with a prodigious deal of fiction. These remarks are necessary for the purpose of freeing the author, and the science he professes, from the charge of superstition; which he well knows his enemies would, but for this explanation, hasten to palm upon him, without reason or reserve.

SECTION I.

THE SINGULAR PROPERTIES OF NATURAL MAGIC,

WITH

A Cursory View of Charms, Talismans, &c.

IN the grand laboratory of nature, there are many singular compositions of herbs and minerals, which have a surprising effect in themselves, without the least assistance from supernatural agency; for, in the commixture of bodies of a *similar* nature, there is a twofold power and virtue; *first*, when the *celestial* properties are duly disposed in any natural substance, then under one form divers influences of superior powers are combined; and *secondly*, when from artificial mixtures and compositions of natural things, combined amongst themselves in a due and harmonical proportion, they agree with the quality and force of the heavens, under certain correspondent constellations. This proceeds from the *occult* affinity of natural things amongst themselves, by the force and sympathy of which many astonishing effects are produced.

* * * * * * *

In the writings of *Paracelsus*, we find many surprising examples of the power invested in sympathy and antipathy, by means of *images*, *talismans*, and *amulets*, compounded of nothing more than natural ingredients; and he very particularly describes an infallible method by the *image* of any bird or beast, to destroy it, or effect its death, though at a distance. So likewise by the hair, fat, blood, excrements, or excrescenses of any animal, the diseases of that animal might be cured, and its life preserved or destroyed.

This is seen in the famous *Armary Unguent** and the *sympathetical powder*; and there are multiplied instances and histories, both at home and abroad, of those who have been burnt, hanged, or otherwise punished, for the use of *waxen images*, which they composed in divers postures, under certain *constellations*, whereby the persons they are made to represent, have been severely tormented, or macerated to death; for, according to the torment or punishment they intended to inflict upon the object of their resentment, so they disposed the *hour* of the *constellation*, the quality of the compound, and the posture or form of the *magical* image ; for instance, if they wished to pine, or consume by slow degrees the health and life of any person they were offended with, they moulded his *image* in wax, of such an *ominous* form and aspect as conduced to their design, making several *magical* characters upon the sides of the head, describing the characters of the *planetary hour* upon the breast of the image, the name of the persecuted person on its forehead, and the intended effect to be wrought, on its back. If they meant to produce violent pains and tortures in the flesh or sinews, they proceeded to stick pins or thorns in various places of the arms, legs, or breast of the image. If to cast them into violent fevers or consumptions, they proceeded in a certain planetary hour, every day to warm and turn the image before a lingering fire, which fire was composed of certain *exotic* gums and *magical* ingredients of sweet odours, and roots of certain shrubs efficient to their purpose. And when the whole image was completed, it is astonishing to human comprehension, what surprising effects they were capable of producing upon the person they intended to represent, and which the reader can only attain a competent idea of, by reading the accounts of the trials and confessions of those who suffered the law in the 16th, 17th, and commencement of the 18th centuries, for transactions of this kind, an incredible number of which are not only recorded in the notes and memorandums of the judges, but attested by a

---

* The receipt for making this famous compound is given hereafter.

great variety of noblemen, gentlemen, clergy, physicians, and others, who were eye-witnesses of these singular proceedings; and for which reason we have spared giving the *minutia* of forming these execrable *images*, lest the evil-minded and malicious should attempt thereby to work some abominable species of revenge upon their unsuspecting neighbours.

Thousands of other strange and uncouth inventions might be here described, and as the Europeans have the ability of effecting such astonishing things by the medium of *images*, *talismans*, *amulets*, and *charms*, so the Asiatic nations have a faculty of producing similar effects by similar rites.

* * * * * * *

The art of *transplantation* is also *magical*, which was formerly much practised, and is still, as we are credibly informed, made use of in the more remote and unpolished parts of this island.* The method is, by giving certain preparations to any domestic animal, they thereby remove fevers, agues, coughs, consumptions, asthmas, &c. from any person applying to them for that purpose; or they can remove them from one person to another, by burying certain *images* in the ground†, or against their houses, with certain ominous inscriptions and Hebrew letters; yet the effects of these are chiefly derived from the sympathies of nature‡, for many persons, without knowing the cause, have been able to remove diseases, take off warts, &c. and to perform many surprising cures at a distance from the patient, and even without ever seeing him; so, by a similar property in the sympathy and antipathy of nature, certain leaves, roots, or juices being rubbed upon warts or excresences, and buried under the ground, remove

---

* It is a singular fact that *rape-seed*, sown with curses and imprecations, thrives infinitely better than when sown in the ordinary way.

† If the object be for hate, this is done in the hour of *Saturn* ; but if for love, *Venus* is chosen well dignified.

‡ It is a tradition amongst the country people, that if a *live* pigeon be tied to the breast of a child which has the hooping cough, and afterwards let free, the child will *recover*, but the bird will die thereof.

or cure the same, which experiments take effect according to their mediums, and their consumption or putrefaction in the mother earth, of which the human source is principally compounded.

The Evil Eye.

Among the qualities attributed to the eye in some persons, and once universally credited, was the power of working evil and enchantment by its glances. The operation of the "Evil Eye" (once so denominated,) upon mankind, as being a pretty general belief in past times, has been recorded by many writers. Bacon says that its effects have, according to some historians, been so powerful as to affect the mind of the individual upon whom they fell; that even after "triumphs, the triumphants" have been made sick in spirit by the evil eyes of lookers on. In most modern European nations, in their earlier ages, the fear of the fascination of children by an "evil eye," made nurses very careful how they permitted strangers to look upon them. In Spain it was called *mal de ojos*, and any one who was suspected of having an "evil eye," while regarding a child, was forced to say, while observing the infant, "God bless it." This notion, however, is far more ancient than the name of England. The Greeks and Romans gave credit to it, when they were in their high career of glory. We find, in many ancient writers, allusions to the malicious influence of what they rail the "vicious" or "evil eye." Theocritus, Horace, Persius, Juvenal, and others, allude to it in a way not to be mistaken in its alliance with the later superstition. I have never heard what charms were used by our forefathers or the ancients against the influence of the "evil eye,"

Vervain and dill
Hinder witches from their will,

was, we know, a sovereign receipt against the daughters of the Lady of Endor. Lilly has the following charm to obviate the effect of an "evil tongue," which, for curiosity sake, I will mention. "Take *unguentem populeum, vervain,* and *hypericon,* and put a red hot iron into it. Anoint the backbone, or wear it on the breast." Notwithstanding this sovereign mode of guarding against an "evil tongue," the evil eye seems to have been as much proof against the wisdom of our forefathers as against our own. It would therefore, in the language of the olden time, be an "insult to Providence," if, after the experience of our ancestors in such matters, we presumed to attempt the discovery of an efficient antidote.

In our times the "evil eye" still survives, though its operation may not be so much a matter of general attention as formerly. It works still, in a manner equally as injurious as when the "irradiations of the visual orb" were supposed to be solely confined to the subtle operations of magic. The "evil eye," in modern days, is observed to be not less dangerous in its consequences to its possessor, than to those whom it fixes upon as victims of its malignity. He smarts in heart-consuming anguish while he regards the happiness of a neighbour, the success of an acquaintance in an honourable calling, or the hard struggle and merited reward of literary assiduity. No rank of life is beyond the glance of the "evil eye" no talent mailed against its deadly malignity, no robe of innocence so pure as to conceal the wearer from its blighting observation. The sensibilities of genius, with whatever art or science they may be linked, are too often scorched by its fatal gaze. It blanches the cheek of beauty, dries up the springs of charity, extinguishes the noblest ardours, withers the fairest blossoms of the soul, and almost renders indifferent the glorious triumphs of virtuous age, by blasting the honours due to its protracted perseverance in goodness. The subjects of Vathek, in the terrible hall of Eblis, had a heart of self-wasting fire, which was disclosed on putting aside the vest. The man with the "evil eye" exhibits the burning heart through the organ of vision. His glances explain what is passing within, as well as if the ribs and pericardium were pellucid crystal, or the transparent summer atmosphere.

The man with the evil eye "always looks obliquely at society. His tongue may be silvery smooth, tipped with velvet, dropping honey, like Nestor's, though blackness be beneath. He cannot conceal the glances that shoot insiduously towards the objects of his hatred—glances, that, were they rays of a pestilence (as he would they were,) must make perish all against whom they are directed. No glance from the basilisk could be more fatal in reality than his glance, had he his wish. To provoke the latent vengeance of the "evil eye," it is a sufficient offence to be fortunate: success is a brand on the forehead of another in its sight. The specious Iago of the "evil eye" may have four senses of the five such as the best might select for themselves; but with him, these only administer to the sovereign lord of vision, and exist subordinate to the "aspect malign." The man of the "evil eye" finds his heart ignite with tenfold violence when excellence of any kind meets due reward. Who but the man of the "evil eye" has, in his own opinion, a right to be fortunate in industry?—who but he has a lawful claim to the suffrages of society and the crown of reward? The bonds of friendship are melted before him; human sympathies dried into dust; envy and selfishness furnish fuel to the heart, and malignant flames rush from the "evil eye" with terrible intensity. Lord of the ascendant, the "evil eye" makes reason its vassal, and never allows the claims of self or self-interest to be balanced against common sense or obligation. Is the object regarded an artist? he may be a far superior one to him of the "evil eye;" is he an orator? he may far excel him; or, is he an author, possessing genius and learning, and patronized by the public? it matters not: the baser passions have put down reason, and drowned even a fool's degree of reflection. The "evil eye" can see nothing but what is tinged with its own green hue, and no longer discriminates colour or form. The result is a consequence mathematically correct—true to the very point: envy and hatred become the guiding star of the soul. Does he pester society with his diatribes? —he mingles in them, to second the desires of his heart, the venom of the snake, with the stratagem of the fox, and the reasoning of the ostrich, which hides its head alone from the hunter and fancies itself unseen. He has no sight but for the objects of his malice, and loses the view of his own interest in the eagerness of ocular vengeance. Is the owner of the "evil eye" a trader?—he looks fatal things to his industrious neighbour's credit; is the owner a female?—she glances away her friend's virtue. Lastly, the owner of the "evil eye" is an universal enemy, whom man cannot trust, time marks out for retribution, and fiends alone can envy.

If society still hold one man to whom this alleged power, anciently attributed to the organ of vision, remains in action, let him be watched. The "evil eye" cannot be mistaken: unsteady as the ocean waves, it rolls around and about in fevered restlessness; now extended, it exhibits its orb clear of the lid, surrounded by the white, in angry convulsion— now half closed, it questions with wariness and shallow cunning—now calm and dead as Lethe, it represses the pale beam of its malice, and with saintly bearing, seems piety itself, the herald of cordiality, the star of friendship and rectitude. But it is all the charmed disguise of the magician, that he may make his spells the surer. The "𝕰𝖛𝖎𝖑 𝕰𝖞𝖊" 𝖎𝖘 𝖘𝖙𝖎𝖑𝖑 𝖙𝖍𝖊 𝖘𝖆𝖒𝖊: its Tophetic beams are less visible, only from the hope that they may more effectually operate on the objects of their malignity. May the readers of the *Familiar Astrologer* ever be preserved from its hated influence! So prays their friend and *well*-wisher,

Raphael.

"WITCHCRAFT".

To speak of witchcraft and witches in the present day raises a smile of incredulity, and an expression of doubt as to the sanity of the person speaking, but, nevertheless, the fables and stories are not all false. Witchcraft is a possible fact. We read of it in many places in Scriptures, and the punishment to be inflicted on those who dealt in this art. Many learned authors distinguish between the *Black Art* and the *White* Art; the former including sorcery, and the tormenting and destruction of others; and the latter, in the relieving of pain, and assuaging the troubles of others. The reader may ask, but how is it possible for one person to affect another? It is quite possible, and is done magnetically, for understand, that witches cannot act, unless they have something to act upon. This something must belong to, or have been in contact with the person whom they would affect, in order that it may contain some of the vital magnetism of that person. For instance, the witches will wrap up images, etc., in a piece of garment, begged from the person they would afflict, and having done this, the connection is established, for *anything* which thou hast handled or used in any way contains some of thy magnetism. Having established this connection (which some witches do by means of blood drawn from their own bodies, as being more potent), the WILL is then set to work, and the desired result follows. No witchcraft can be accomplished without a *strong, continued,* and *persistent* will of thine own; that is, thou must have the desired object continually in thy mind, and excite thy mind to a determination to accomplish thy purpose. Witchcraft is, therefore, simply one person affecting another through the power of *will*, and magnetism is the *conducting rod* by which the mind works; or, in other words, it is putting human magnetism to a bad and injurious purpose. Tradition tells us that there once existed a race of beings who could slay their enemies from afar, without swords or weapons, simply by the power and exercise of their will. It is, therefore, no wonder that any one with a *strong will* can affect another, when once the magnetic link is established between the two.

Animal Magnetism.

As facts multiply, science is unveiled, and theory becomes more easy. We have lately witnessed curious experiments executed at Toulon by Count de B——; and a public document, now in existence, proves a remarkable fact. It describes what took place on the 15th of March, 1830. in the department of Gers, at the residence of the Justice of Peace of the canton of Condon, in the presence of persons, every one of whom are well known to us.

Jean ———, a farmer, aged 23, was afflicted with an abcess from congestion upon the inner and upper part of the thigh. The surgeons who attended him, declared that cure puncture would be practicable, but the operation required great prudence, and much resignation, because the crural artery crossed the tumor, developed in a frightful manner. Count de B——, whose magnetic skill is remarkable, proposed plunging the patient into the magnetic state, thereby to produce somnambulism, and establish insensibility upon the part of the body where the operation was to be performed. In that condition, he said, they might spare the farmer the pain and suffering inevitable in his then state. The proposition was accepted. In about two minutes the patient was placed in the magnetic state; somnambulism immediately followed, but without remarkable lucidity. The farmer said, in answer to a question put by his magnetiser, that he looked in vain for his illness. He could not see it, nor the cause of it. At that moment Doctor Lar—— performed, with the greatest skill, the surgical operation which had been considered necessary. He applied the bistoury several times, and produced the desired effect. The dressing was then made in the usual manner. During the whole of the operation the patient remained immovable as a statue.—His magnetic sleep was undisturbed. Upon the proposition of all the medical men, Count de B—— destroyed the magnetic state in which the patient had been plunged, and awoke him. Doctor R—— then approached him, and asked whether he was willing to submit to the operation. ——"If it must be so," said the patient, "I will submit." Doctor R—— then announced that it was quite useless to recommend it, because it was done. The astonishment of the patient was increased when they made him see the dressing. He had felt nothing, and only remembered the action of Count B——, when the latter applied the palm of his hand to his (the patient's) forehead to make him sleep.

HOW TO CURE WITCHCRAFT, AND BREAK THE SPELL.

If any one suspect that they are bewitched, let them take some of their own water, and cut some of the hair from the nape of the neck, and from the arm-pits, and put all together in a saucepan, with nine new pins or needles, or nine pieces of broken glass, and at twelve at night put the saucepan on the fire, and let it boil all away, but not so that it runs over the side of the saucepan. During this operation, let not a word be spoken, or a sentence be uttered, or the operation will be in vain. Two persons should be present at the time, and all keyholes and crevices into the room should be stopped and plugged. Should there be a knock at the door, or a voice heard, as most, frequently there is, heed it not, but continue on thy work, until the whole of the liquid is exhausted; then go to thy bed, say thy prayers, and rest assured that thy work has not been in vain. If thou suspectest that any of thy beasts or animals suffer from this cursed art, thou shalt take some of their water, and hair from off their necks and tails, and proceed in the manner above taught. And understand this, that if thou proceedest in thy work when the moon is in Scorpio (♏), it shall be so much the more powerful, especially if at the time the moon be afflicted by the planet Saturn.

A LEGENDARY CHARM, USED BY WITCHES IN GATHERING HERBS FOR MAGICAL PURPOSES.

> "Hail to thee, holy herb,
> Growing on the ground,
> All on mount Calvary
> First wait thou found.
> Thou art good for many sores
> And healeth many a wound;
> In the name of Saint Jesu !
> I take thee from the ground."

Taken from an old black letter missal, in the possession of the "Mercurii," which also states, that "the muttering of this charm, while concocting drugs or simples, balsams or elixirs, contributes marvellously to their efficacy."

CHARMING AWAY THE HOOPING COUGH.

An English lady, the wife of an officer, accompanied her husband to Dublin not very long ago, when his regiment was ordered to that station. She engaged an Irish girl as nurse-maid in her family, and a short time after her arrival was astonished by an urgent request from this damsel to permit her *to charm little miss from ever having the hooping cough*—(then prevailing in Dublin)!

The lady inquired how this was performed; and not long after had, in walking through the streets, many times the pleasure of witnessing the process, which is simply this:—An *ass* is brought before the door of the house, into whose mouth a piece of bread is introduced, and the child being passed *three times* over and under the animal's body, the charm is completed; and of its efficacy in preventing the spread of a very distressing, and sometimes fatal disorder, the lower class of Irish are *certain*.

A CURIOUS CHARM TO BIND OR COMPEL A THIEF.

To bind a thief so that he shall have neither rest nor peace till he return thee thy lost goods, go to the place from whence they were stolen away, and write the name of the person or persons thou suspectest upon parchment, and put the same underneath the threshold of the door they went out of. Then make four crosses on the four corners or posts of the doorway, and go your ways saying, "Thou thief, which hast stolen and taken away such a thing from this place, Abraham, by his virtue and the power God gave him, call thee back again,—Isaac, by his power, stop thee in the way,—Jacob make thee go no farther, but bring them again,—and Joseph, by his power and virtue, and also by the grace and might of the Holy Ghost, force thee to come again into this place;—and that neither Solomon let thee, nor David bid thee; but that the same through Christ our Lord do cause thee presently, and without stay, to come again into this place, and bring them with thee. Fiat, fiat, fiat, cito, cito, cito. In the name of the Father, and of the Son, and of the Holy Ghost, Amen." Repeat these words *three* times, and the thief shall not rest, nor delay, till he return thee thy goods.—*Ancient Manuscript.*

A CHARM TO STOP BLEEDING AT THE NOSE.

Touch the nose, and say, *nine times with great faith,* these words,— "Blood abide in this vein as Christ abideth in the Church, and hide in thee as Christ hideth from himself;"— and the bleeding will presently cease, to the admiration of all present.

Charms for Various Occasions.

A Charm AGAINST FURIOUS BEASTS.

Repeat earnestly and with sincere faith these words:—
"As destruction and famine, thou shalt laugh, neither shalt thou be afraid of the beasts of the earth"
"For thou shalt be in league with the stones of the field, and the beasts of the field shall be at peace with thee."—Job, chap. 5, v. 22, 23.

A Charm AGAINST TROUBLE IN GENERAL.

"He shall deliver thee in six troubles, yea in seven there shall be no evil touch thee.
"In famine he shall redeem thee from death, and in war from the power of the sword.
"And thou shalt know that thy tabernacle shall be in peace, and thou shalt visit thy habitation and shalt not err."*—Job, chap. 5, v. 19, 20, 24.

A Charm AGAINST ENEMIES.

"Behold, God is my salvation; I will trust, and not be afraid, for the Lord Jehovah is my strength and my song; he also is become my salvation.

---

* Our version has it "sin" but the original signifies thou shalt not "err."

"For the stars of heaven, and the constellations thereof, shall not give their light; the sun shall be darkened in his going forth, and the moon shall not cause her light to shine.

"And behold, at evening tide, trouble; and before the morning he is not; this is the portion of them that spoil us, and the lot of them that rob us."—Isaiah, chap. 12 and 17.

A 𝕮𝖍𝖆𝖗𝖒 AGAINST PERIL BY FIRE OR WATER.

Thus, also, when we would avoid peril by fire or water, we make use of this passage:— "When thou passest through the waters, I will be with thee, and through the rivers they shall not overflow thee; when thou walkest through the fire, thou shalt not be burnt, neither shall the flame kindle upon thee."—ISAIAH, chap, 43, v. 2.

And as, according to the learned Cabalists, there is not a *verse, line, word,* or even *letter,* in the Holy Scriptures which has not some particular and peculiar meaning, either offensive or defensive (being read in the original Hebrew), so, according to them, the holy and ineffable names of the Supreme Being, drawn from the sacred word according to the rules of theurgic science, are equally powerful to avert impending evils, &c. But they have been very desirous of keeping their writings a profound secret, according as we read in Esdras — "Thou shalt deliver those books to the wise men of the people, whose hearts thou knowest can comprehend them, and keep those secrets." Which is the reason why the greater part of the ancient writings were written in enigmatical language, and must be hieroglyphically understood.

A LEGENDARY CHARM OR SPELL, SAID BY OLD AUTHORS TO BE PROOF AGAINST THIEVES AND ENEMIES.

To be said daily.

"In the power of God, I walke on my way,
In the meekness of Christ, what thieves soever I meet,
The Holy Ghost, to Day shall me keep.

Whether I sitt, or stande, walke or sleepe,
The shininge of the Sun,
Also the brightnesse of his beames, shall me help;
The faith of Isack to daye shall me leade;
The sufferings of Jacob to daye be my speed.
The devotion of the holye Lambe, thieves shall *lett**
The strength of Jesus's blessed passion them besett.
The dreade of death, hold thieves low,
The wisdome of Solomon cause their overthrow.
The sufferings of Job, set them in holde,
The chastitie of Danielle, lett what they woulde.
The speeche of Isac, their speeche shall spill,
The languishing faith of Jherom, *lett* them of their will.
The flaminge fier of hell to hit them I bequeath.
The deepnesse of the deepe sea, their false hands for to lett.
The lighte of heaven against them shall rise.
The dreade of serpentes cause their hearts to grieve.
The helpe of heaven, cause thieves to stand;
He that made the Son and Moon, bind them with his hand,
So sure as St. Bartholomew bound the fiend,
With the hair of his beard.
With there three secret names of God, knowne and unknowne,
Miser, Sue!! Tetragrammaton. Christ Jesus. Amen."

From a curious Manuscript.

A SAFE WAY TO SECURE A HOUSE.

If thou suspectest thy House will be robbed, and would secure it from *Thieves*, as no doubt but thou art desirous, consider the Night what Planet Reigns, and is Lord of the Ascendant, and these are the characters, the *Sun* ☉ on *Sunday*, the *Moon* ☽ on *Monday*, *Mars* ♂ on *Tuesday*, *Mercury* ☿ on *Wednesday*, *Jupiter* ♃ on *Thursday*, *Venus* ♀ on *Friday*, *Saturn* ♄ on *Saturday*. Now, consider on what night thou doest this, as to these Planets, and Write on fair Parchment

---

* "*Lett*", old word; to obstruct, to *hinder*.

these Characters, ♌ ♈ ♑ and suppose it to be on a *Sunday*, add the Planetary Character ☉ with this Number, 1, 3, 5, ¼, ⅐, and at that Night lay this under the Earth, or covered with a Tile in the Middle of the House, as near as may be; sprinkle it over with the Juice of Night Shade, and so go to sleep as soon as thou hast thrice repeated them over, and if the Thieves have power to enter the House, they shall have no power to get out again, or to carry anything away till the Sun Rises, and if thou be watchful, then thou mayest easily apprehend them before they are able to depart.

And this thou may'st do any day of the week, adding the Character of the Planet that Rules that Day, as I have set it down, to what is beside set down in order.

A Safeguard for all Out-houses, to Secure Poultry, Cattle, Corn, or what else is shut up therein.

Consider the day, as in the Former, and set down on a piece of clean Parchment these Characters ♋ ♉, add the Character of the Planet, as for *Monday* ☽, and these figures, 9, 8, 5, 3, ⅙, ⅐, lay this sprinkled with the Juice of Hemlock under the Threshold of the Outhouse, or if there be none, in some secret corner, and if any Thieves Enter, they will be so blinded and amazed that they will not find their way out again, but group in vain till the Sun Rises, before which time thou must be watchful to come thither; for the Sun shooting its Beams through the Air, the Guardian Virtues Retire, and the Force is dissolved for that time; but with changing the Planet will serve for the next Night, and so on.

A Safeguard for an Orchard, Park, Warren, or Field, to take a Thief etc.

The Several Places being Guarded by one and the same Planet, not to be too tedious to thee, one and the same thing will indifferently serve to secure any of them from Thieves that come to make Robbery or Depredation, whether it be for Fruits of the Earth, or any kind of Cattle, or to Steal any Timber in Fields or Woods; to make which, take the following direction: Have a piece of curious clean Parchment, made of a sleek skin, cut it with five points or corners in the form of a star, but so large that thou mayest write in the centre of it what is to be written, viz., ♊ ♐ ♓, the character of the Celestial Signs governing these affairs, add the character of the Planet for the Day, as before directed, and suppose it to be *Tuesday, Mars* that governs that day has this character, which set down thus, ♂, and this number, 1, 7, 11, 12, ½, ⅓; close it up with Virgin's Wax, as I should have told thee, thou oughtest to have done the former, and sprinkle it with the Juice of Fumitory, and place the same (if in a Garden) in the hole of a wall, if in a Field, Forest, Park, or Wood in the hole of a tree, having laid it before in Goose Tansey, and so whatever any Thief takes in these several grounds, he shall not be able to carry off till the Sun rising; but then, if not watched, he may do it.

To Drive Away Ghosts or Spirits that Haunt a House, and Prevent the Nightmare.

This is a curious secret, and I think never before made public, or privately practised but by a few. To do this, take the Wool that grows between the two Eyes of a black sheep, burn it to powder, after it has been steeped a night and a day in Man's Urine, mix this with the Powder of Nightshade, or *Wake-Robin*, an Herb so called, boil then in a Quarter of a Pint of *Aqua Vitæ*, sprinkle the Walls of the Chamber thou fanciest is haunted with it, and no disturbance will happen if thou turn thy face when thou goest to repose, to the *Eastward*, when in Bed, and say thy Prayers.

This is to be carried about One for the Prevention of Witchcraft, being under an ill- Tongue, or Planet Struck.

These Misfortunes generally happen under the Power of the Moon, who (as Ancients hold) is the Favourer of Magic or Enchantment; take the most Opposite Planet to her in allaying her force this way, which is *Jupiter*, write his Character thus, ♃ on a piece of Parchment, and add to it the following Characters, that are the Signs of the Zodiac, viz.,

♍ ♎ ♏, and this number, 1, 3, 7, 5, ½, ⅐, ¼; after this, set down the Number the Figurative Letters in thy name make, wrap it up in as small a compass as thou canst, and sewing it up in a piece of black silk that has been steeped in the Juice of Vervine, hang it about thy neck when the Moon changes, and thou wilt be secure from any Danger of this Nature, if thou leadest a good life.

To prevent Affrighting Dreams and take away Fear in the Night.

Thou must take of *Laudanum* a dram, Frankincense of the like quantity, of *Bezora* stone as much; beat these into powder, and write upon a piece of parchment these Characters, ♄ ♃ ♅ ☿ and under them thy name; put the powder in the Paper thou writest on, and when thou repose, bind them on thy forehead and stomach; for thou must have two papers ordered one and the same way, as directed, putting half the Powder in the one, and the other half in the other.

To help a Person under an ill Tongue, and make the Witch appear, or the Effects cease.

Cut off some of the Party's Hair, just at the nape of the Neck, clip it small and burn it to Powder, put the Powder in Sal Almoniac, write the Party's Name thou suspectest backwards, and put the Paper dipt in Aqua Vitæ into the other two; then set it over a gentle Fire; let the Party afflicted sit by it, and diligently watch it, that it ran not over to catch flame, speaking no word, whatsoever noise is heard, but take notice of what Voice or Roaring is heard in the Chimney, or any part of the Room, and then write how often thou hearest it, and fix before each writing, this Character, ☽, and if the Party who Afflicts thee appears not visible, though thou mayest know the Voice, repeat it again, and if she appear in no visible shape, it may make her Charm impotent, and give Relief to the afflicted Party.

To Prevent or take Vermin, that come to destroy Poultry, or Coney Warrens.

Thou must take a piece of Wolf's Skin, the Hair on, the breadth of the palm of thy Hand, or somewhat more, prick a great many Holes in it with a bodkin, in the three corners, but leave the middle entire, scrape the middle part to the fleshy side, so that it may be smooth enough to write on; then write these Characters, 2 3 4 7 5; this done, write the Guardian (△ ☉ ∧ Ⅱ L) Name underneath them, viz., *Azmeros*; then burn the wool of Fox's-tail, with some Feather few, and the seed of Henbane; lay the Powder on the Characters, that it may cover them pretty well, then fold the corners, and stitch them up close, with the Powder in it, and this done sprinkle it with the juice of Hysop, and hang it up with a couple of horse-hairs, drawn out of the middle of the Tail of a live Stone-Horse, and hang it up in thy Hen-House, Dove-cot; or, for a Warren, on a Pole, or a Tree, as near as thou canst in the middle of the Coney-Burrows, and the Vermin will either fear to approach, scenting it at a distance, or being come near it, will continue snuffing and endeavouring to get at it, then you may come and destroy them with a Gun, Dogs, Crossbow, or other ways as thou findest most practicable; instead of a Wolf's-Skin, thou mayest use a Badger's, if the other cannot be had.

To prevent a Dog barking at thee in the Night-time.

Thou must take the Skin off the Forehead of an Hyena, a beast so called, which may be had at the Furrier's shop, boil it in the urine of a young Stone Colt, and smoke it over the burnt hoof of a cow, twice or thrice, till it is dry, and so carry it about thee, and so long as thou doest this, wherever thou comest in the night, the Dogs will not only be silent, but run away from thee as fast as they can, when thou approachest anything near them: For if they once scent it (as certainly they will), the great aversion they have to it will make them tremble and avoid thee, without being able to open at thee.

To draw Cats together, so that they shall not escape Hands.

So soon as ever the new moon appears, gather the Herb Nepe, and dry it a little in the heat of the ☉, when it is temperately hot, then take a fair piece of Parchment, and cut it in the shape of a half-moon, write on it these Characters, ☿ ♄ ✴, wrap the Parchment up close, and put it amongst the Herb, which hang up in a Net, in a convenient place, and when one of them has scented it, her Cry will soon call all those about her that are within hearing, and there they will rage and ran about, leaping and capering, to get at the Net, which must be so hung, or placed, that they cannot easily do: for they will certainly tear it to pieces; and in this thou wilt have pleasant pastime, as well as to take and destroy them, if they are offensive to thy Gardens, Houses, Dove-cots, etc.

A Pledget to wear about one's Neck, to present Bugs, Fleas, or Gnats biting in the Night-time.

This to many People may prove no less advantageous than any, especially where these Insects are a second Plague of *Egypt* to People. To do this, gather Arsmart or Hounds Tongue, an Herb with a long, sharp-pointed little Leaf, that grows in ditches, in moist places, in summer. Dry it to a powder, add to it as much of the Powder of Sarsafax Wood as will lie upon a shilling, sprinkle them a little with Juniper Water, mix it with the Wool of a black sheep, cut off betwixt the Horns, in the Wane of the Moon, write on a piece of paper these Characters, ♒ ♂ ♏ ✴ ♄ ½, ⅓, sprinkle the paper, when thou has folded it up, with Juice of Rue, and sew it up in a thin silk bag, and with a little small Cat's-gut hang it about thy neck, when thou goest to sleep; and if thou art awake, the power is the same: thou wilt rest without being disturbed with these, or other Insects.

Part Three: Low Magic

To drive away Mice or Rats, in a House or Granary,

If thou canst set a He Weasel, about the Increase of the Moon, kill him, and take out his fat, then dry his skin, that thou mayest write, on the fleshy side of it, these Characters, ♉ ♈ ♊ ♋ ☽ ✶, do it over with Weasel's Fat, and stuff up the skin with Moss, taken from the Root, or lower part of an Oak-tree, and place it on a sharp Haw-thorn stick, put the sharp end into it Belly wards, and stick the other end in the Floor, in a little hole made with a Gimlet in the place of their resort: let it not be placed more than six Inches above the Floor, and as many as come there will immediately avoid the House, or Out-house; and if thou wouldest kill them there, it is but strewing Pot-ashes on the Floor, and it will work so powerful, that they cannot get away; but there thou mayest kill them at pleasure.

To prevent being robbed on the Road, or meeting with any bad Accident.

Consider (in this case) what Planet thou settest out under, ruling as to the Days, and its influence. The Moon ruling *Monday,* denotes inconstancy in success; *Mars, Tuesday,* violence; *Mercury,* on *Wednesday,* deceit and fraud; *Saturn,* on *Saturday,* envy and malignaminity; but the *Sun, Jupiter,* and *Venus,* governing *Sunday, Thursday,* and *Friday,* are very friendly Planets, promising success; however, other Days are proper enough, with the cautions I shall give thee hereafter; and this is as followeth, to prosper and prevent Ill Fortune, in being Robbed, Falling from thy Horse, or Sick, falling into any Pit, Water, or the like.

Now note, That the Malignant Planets are friendly to others, and befriended of them again; *Sol* is friendly to *Jupiter* and *Venus; Luna* to *Jupiter, Venus,* and *Saturn; Mars* is friendly to *Venus; Mercury* is friendly to *Jupiter, Venus,* and *Saturn; Jupiter* is friendly to *Sol, Luna, Mercury, Venus,* and *Saturn, Venus* is friendly to *Sol, Luna, Mars, Mercury,* and *Jupiter; Saturn* is friendly to *Jupiter, Sol,* and *Luna,* and these are temporising to hinder the malignamity of each other; therefore the Promises considered; now as to what thou art to put in Practice for thy security.

Gather Vervine, an herb so called, in the New of the Moon, hang it up in the Chimney to dry, then powder it, and steep it in the water of *Agaus Castus*, then dry it again, and reduce it to fine Powder; these temporise with the Planets *Venus* and *Mercury*, which are so powerful in their influence for the protection of Travellers. Put this Powder into a Hollow Ring, of any kind of Metal, and have these characters engraved on the inside of it, ♀ ☿ ♄, then thou mayest go or ride safe without danger of any violence, keeping thy mind on Good Things.

To find out a Thief, or make him or her bring back the Goode stolen.

Thou must set down the Day, Hour, and Minute, if thou canst, when the Goods were stolen, and the name of the Planet ruling the Day, as I have before set down, to direct thee; this being done, set down these following Characters in a fair piece of Parchment, ☽ ☉ ♄ ✶ △ Σ; this done, Turn Round thrice, and if thou hearest no news in 44 hours, of the Thief, as ten to one thou wilt, then prick the Parchment full of Holes, and hang it up in the Chimney, where the Heat of the Fire may a little scorch it, and the Thief is held to be so restless in his mind, and tormented, that he or she will discover the Thief to be at Ease, or bringing home thy Goods, throw them privately into thy house, or some place appertaining to thee.

THE MIGHTY ORATION,

TO MAKE A THIEF BRING BACK THE STOLEN GOODS.

By the most Great and Almighty Power of Alpha and Omega, Jehovah and Emanuel, and by Him that divided the Red Sea, and by that Great Power that turned all the waters and rivers in Egypt into blood, and turned all the dust into lice and blains, and by that Power that brought frogs all over the land of Egypt, and entered into all the king's palaces and chambers, and by that Great Power, that terrible thunder and lightning and hailstones mixed with fire, and sent locusts which did destroy all green things in the whole land of Egypt; and by that Great Power that destroyed all the first born in the land of Egypt, both of man and beast; and by that Great Power that divided the hard rocks, and rivers of water issued out of the same in the wilderness: and by that Great Power that led the Children of Israel out of Egypt into the land of Canaan; and by that Great Power that destroyed Sennacherib's great host; and by the Great and Almighty Power of Him who walketh on the sea as on the dry land; and by that Great and Almighty Power that raised dead Lazarus out of his grave; and by that Almighty Power of the holy, blessed, and glorious Trinity, that did cast the devil and all disobedient spirits out of heaven into hell, that thou thief return immediately and restore the goods again that thou hast stolen away. Therefore in and by the names of the Almighty God before rehearsed, I charge thee, thou thief, to restore the goods again immediately, or else the wrath of God may fall upon thee, and cause thee to be consumed. Amen.

—*From a very Ancient Old M.S.*

TALISMANS.

The extraordinary interest which has been excited by the author of Waverley's celebrated romance of "The Talisman," has, it appears, created a pretty general desire for becoming acquainted with those mysterious agents (as they are said to be) in the laboratory of nature. And hence also, the author of this book has toiled amidst many a dusky and worm-eaten memorial of former times, in order to give an accurate description of the most esteemed Talismans, which those ancient manuscripts treat of. In addition to which, he has chosen such as appear to be facile in construction; and by the ease with which the reader can thus make them, it will be soon manifest whether their powers are real or imaginary.

TALISMANS.*

In the whole circle of the theurgic art, there is scarcely anything more abstruse or intricate than the mystical science of talismans. The practice has occasionally received much opposition from those persons who are either unable to comprehend the secret yet sublime mysterys of nature, or unwilling to give credence to any thing beyond the immediate sphere of their own comprehension; and, on the other hand, the art has stood its ground with firmness amidst the change of ages.† Mourning rings, miniatures, lockets, devices‡,

---

* The late celebrated romance of *"The Talisman,"* by Sir Walter Scott, evinces a singular instance of the faith mankind formerly had in these mysterious agents, which were formed under appropriate *constellations*. The editors of this work, particularly the *Mercurii*, are acquainted with many scientific persons who have proved *talismanic agency* both in preservation from dangers and accumulation of good fortune. Mr. V—y, the astrological champion, has also had proofs thereof.

† Amongst mankind in general, there is much of talismanic belief, witness the avidity with which the *caul* of an infant is sought after, to preserve from danger by water. There is also a belief that persons born at or near *midnight*, are apt to see spirits, and have supernatural omens. This *Raphael*, the astrologer, supposes may proceed from the sun being then near the fourth house, or house of secrets and secret discoveries. There seems much truth in this general opinion which the sceptic will find difficult to disprove.

‡ It is reported by credible persons, that when Napoleon went to Egypt, he was there presented with a *talisman*, by a learned rabbi, the effect of which was designed to protect and defend him from *sudden attacks, assassinations,* and all manner of hurts from *fire-arms*. Whether or no this was really the case, we of course cannot decidedly avouch; but the persons who related it, we believe to be incapable of falsehood. And it certainly was very singular, that although so many attempts were made to wound him, and although he has frequently been seen in battle, when "the balls tore up the ground under his horse's feet," and although he had frequently horses shot under him, yet he uniformly escaped free from harm; and he seems indeed to have been inspired with a belief that he was under some special supernatural agency. The talisman was supposed to have been formed under the power and

mottos, armorial bearings, and the "boast of heraldry,"* are but so many relics of talismanic learning.

 Sunt lachrymae rerum et mentem mortalia tangunt.—
   Virgil.

The Imperial Talisman of Constantine.
Which is said to give Victory over Enemies.

 This Talisman must be engraved on pure iron. The metal must be moulded into the above form on the day of Mars (which is *Tuesday*), and in his hour (which is the first and eighth hour of that day), while the moon is in sextile, or trine to Mars, which every astrologer knows, and which the ephemeris will teach. It must be engraven at the same time, or under similar aspects, and in the increase of the moon.

 When completed (the utmost care being taken that it is began and ended under the required aspects), the person for whom it is made must retire to some secret place, and fumigating it with the magical suffumigation of the spirits of Mars, which consists of red saunders. frankincense, and pepper, must proceed to suspend it from some part of the body, where it will be kept clean and secret; or it may be worn on the finger as a ring, the characters being engraven inside (the size of the Talisman being of no consequence) next to the finger.

---

influence of the Sun.

 * It is singular that in the science of *heraldry* they make use of *houses*, the same as in the astrological science.

This is said to be the identical sign which the Emperor Constantine saw in the heavens, previous to his embracing Christianity. And it is also said to "give victory over every earthly enemy, being rightly formed."—*MSS. Key to Agrippa.*

The writings of the ancients are filled with the various effects and descriptions of Talismans, many of which were formed of the most costly materials; as of "gold, silver, and rubies." The following, worn in a ring, is said to prove of great and surprising efficacy in the way of acquiring powerful friends, and overcoming the evils of life: it is termed by an old manuscript

"THE RING OF STRENGTH."

"Let a ring be formed of virgin gold; on the day of the sun, and in the hour of Jupiter, in the moon's increase, wherein thou shalt place seven precious stones—the DIAMOND, the RUBY, the EMERALD, the JACYNTH, the SAPPHIRE, the BERYL, and the TOPAZ. Wear it about thee, and fear no man; for thou wilt be invincible as Achilles."—*MSS of Philadelphus.*

AN AMULET OR CHARM
FOR LOVE.

"He that beareth this charm about him, written on virgin parchment, shall obtain love of lord and lady."—*Ancient MSS.*

TALISMANS.

THE SPIRAL SEMAPHORA.

An Hebrew Talisman.

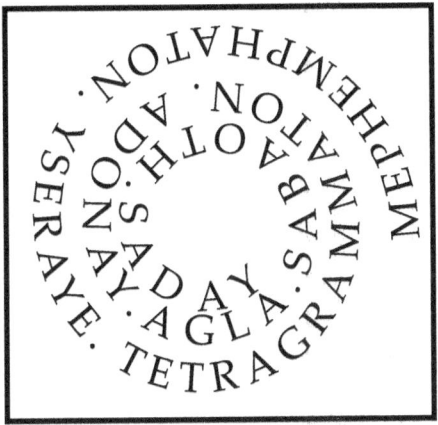

AMONG the Hebrew Cabalists, the following charm is said to be of singular efficacy towards *success in life*. "Procure a piece of virgin silver in the increase of the moon; let it be well guarded, and kept free from contamination with other metals. Then, on the day when the sun is in trine to the moon from the signs Scorpio and Pisces, mould the metal into the form of a medal, and engrave the words thereon. It will be more precious to thee than the gold of Ophir." —*Manuscript of the late Dr. Tilloch.*

A TALISMAN

FOR DESTROYING ALL KINDS OF VENOMOUS OR TROUBLESOME INSECTS OR REPTILES.

THIS talisman is to be made of *iron*, when the *sun* and *moon* enter the sign *Scorpio*. It has been proved to be very powerful in effect; so much so, that, where it is buried, no kind of venomous reptile or troublesome insect can come within certain yards thereof.* It is also said to be efficacious in *saturnine* diseases, especially if made when the MOON enters the constellation CANCER, conjoined with the SUN.

---

* The MS. from which this is taken cost fifty guineas, and a medical gentleman to whom it belonged, affirms that he had himself *proved* the truth of this observation; for being at one time much annoyed with *beetles*, he made this talisman, and screwed it to the floor, when these troublesome insects immediately disappeared; but afterwards, when the servant removed it, through ignorance, they returned in great numbers, when he again mailed it to the floor, and they again disappeared ! ! This talisman is easily made.

A TALISMAN AGAINST ENEMIES.

According to the opinion of the ancient theurgists, this talisman is under the dominion of the sun and Jupiter. It is to be cast of the purest grain tin, in the day and hour of Jupiter, at a time when these planets are in mutual aspect to each other, from the signs ♈, ♌, ♐, and during the increase of the moon. The characters are to be engraven on the same in the day and hour of Mercury, likewise during the moon's increase.

It may be suspended about the neck, or worn about any part of the body, so that it may be kept secret to all but the wearer. Its *effects* are, to give the most decisive victory over enemies, to defend against their machinations, and to inspire the wearer thereof with the most remarkable confidence.

☞ *It is to be remembered, that in this and the following talismans, the embellishments or scenery are to be omitted when they are made.*

A TALISMAN FOR LOVE.

> "But this most sweet and lighted calm,
> Its blue and midnight hour,
> Wakened the *hidden* springs of his heart,
> With a *deep* and *secret* power." — IOLE.

THIS talisman is said to be wonderfully efficacious in procuring success in amours and love adventures; it must be made in the day and hour of *Venus,* when she is favourable to the planet *Mars*. It should be made of pure *silver,* or purified copper. If *Venus* be in the sign of *Taurus* or *Libra,* it is still better.

A TALISMAN FOR WAR AND BATTLE.

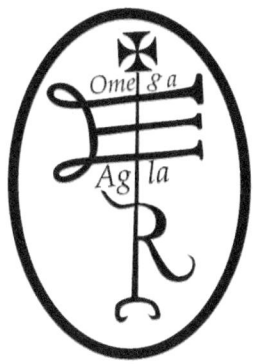

"But ye whose art th'enchanted *moon* obeys,
Who summon Heav'n to bless your *magic* blaze.
Help me, O help!"—Propertius.

"He that beareth this sign about him, shall be holpen in every need, or necessity."

Ancient mss.

A Charm for healing Diseases.

Taken from a curious MS. of the Twelfth Century, in the Possession of the Mercurii.

```
A b r a c a d a b r a
 a b r a c a d a b r
  a b r a c a d a b
   a b r a c a d a
    a b r a c a d
     a b r a c a
      a b r a c
       a b r a
        a b r
         a b
          a
```

The letters which compose this charm must be written in a pyramidal form, as above, on virgin parchment, with the *quill* of a *raven*, and with *ink* formed out of the smoke of a consecrated wax-taper; then let the party who is afflicted of the disease, which he would have cured, wear the charm hung around his neck during the time that the *moon* performs one circuit through the twelve signs of the zodiac; and let it be performed on the day of the *full moon*, and, if possible, while the moon is in the magical signs 𝖘𝖆𝖌𝖎𝖙𝖙𝖆𝖗𝖎𝖚𝖘 or 𝖕𝖎𝖘𝖈𝖊𝖘.

It is necessary that the wearer have a firm and confident faith in the power of Divine Omnipotence; and the following oration must be said upon first beginning to wear the above holy charm, and in very difficult cases the patient should repeat the oration daily, with great devotion.

𝕿𝖍𝖊 𝕺𝖗𝖆𝖙𝖎𝖔𝖓.

"O, sweet Lord **Jesus Christ**, ✠ the true God, who didst descend from the kingdom of thy Almighty Father, being sent to wash away our sins, to release those who were in prison and afflicted, to console the sorrowful and the needy, to absolve and to liberate me, thy servant, from my affliction and tribulation, in which I am placed. So, O, Omnipotent Father, thou didst receive us again, by his expiation, into that paradise, by thy blood, O, **Jesu**, ✠ obtained, and didst make us equal among and angels and men. Thou, O, Lord **Jesus Christ**, ✠ wert worthy to stand between me and mine enemies, and to establish my peace and to show thy grace upon me, and to pour out thy mercy. And thou, O Lord, didst extinguish the anger of mine enemies, which they contained against me, as thou didst take away the wrath of Esau, which he had against Jacob, his brother. O, Lord **Jesus**, ✠ extend thine arm towards me, and deliver me from my affliction, even as thou didst deliver Abraham from the hands of the Chaldean, and his son, Isaac, from the sacrifice, and Jacob from the hand of his brethren; Noah from the deluge; and even as thou didst deliver thy servant Lot; thy servants, Moses and Aaron, and thy people Israel, from the hands of Pharoah, and out of the land of Egypt; David from the hands of Saul, and the giant Goliath; or as thou deliveredst Susannah from her accusers ; Judith from the hands of Holofernes;

Daniel from the den of the lions; the three youths from the fiery furnace; Jonah from the whale's belly; or as thou deliveredst the son of Cannanea, who was tormented by the devil; even as thou deliveredst Adam from hell, by thy most precious blood; and Peter and Paul from chains. So, O, most sweet Lord **Jesus,** ✠ Son of the living God, preserve me, thy servant, from my affliction, and mine enemies; and be my assistant, and my blessing, by thy holy incarnation, by thy fasting and thirst, by thy labours and affliction, by thy stripes, by thy thorny crown, by thy drink of gall and vinegar, by thy most cruel death, by the words which thou spakedst upon the cross, by thy descent into hell, by the consolation of thy disciples, by thy wonderful ascension, by the appearance of the Holy Spirit, by the day of judgment, by thy great gifts, and by thy holy names, **Adonay** ✠ **Eloym** ✠ **Heloym** ✠ **Yacy** ✠ **Zazael** ✠ **Paliel** ✠ **Saday** ✠ **Yzoe** ✠ **Yaras** ✠ **Caelphi** ✠ **Saday** ✠, and by thy ineffable name יהוה **Jehovah.** ✠ By all these holy, omnipotent, and all-powerful names of singular efficacy and extraordinary power, which the elements obey, and at which the devils tremble: O most gracious **Jesu,** ✠ grant, I beseech thee, that this holy charm which I now wear about my person, may be the means of healing my lamentable sickness: so shall the praise thereof be ascribed, O Lord, to thee alone, and thou alone shalt have all the glory." **Amen.** *Fiat, fiat, fiat.*

By making use of the above occult and sacred remedy, the most miraculous cures have been heretofore performed; and as there is nothing therein which is in any way derogatory to the power of the Supreme Being, or inimical to our fellow-creatures, there certainly can be no harm in making continual use thereof, upon every occasion.

ANOTHER WAY.

If it were required to perform a cure upon one at a distance, or without the afflicted party's knowledge thereof, let the charm be written on virgin parchment, and then you may perform the cure without their knowledge, by scraping out one line of the charm every day with a new knife, kept for the express purpose; and at scraping out each line, say as follows: —

"So as I destroy the letters of this charm, Abracadabra, so, by virtue of this sacred name, may all grief and dolor depart from A. B. in the name of the Father, and of the Son, and of the Holy Ghost. In the name of the Father, I destroy this disease. In the name of the Son, I destroy this disease; and in the name of the Holy Spirit, I destroy this disease." Amen.

Many have healed divers diseases this way; the disease wearing, by little and little, away. Therefore keep it secret, and fear God. — *Ancient MS. supposed to have been an original of Friar Bacon.*

The following curious, and very ingenious device, may amuse some of my readers. The sentence *"Reform alone can save us now,"* may be read 484 different ways, beginning at the letter R in the centre: —

```
w o n s u e v a s n a c a n s a v e u s n o w
o n s u e v a s n a c e c a n s a v e u s n o
n s u e v a s n a c e n e c a n s a v e u s n
s u e v a s n a c e n o n e c a n s a v e u s
u e v a s n a c e n o l o n e c a n s a v e u
e v a s n a c e n o l a l o n e c a n s a v e
  v a s n a c e n o l a m a l o n e c a n s a v
  a s n a c e n o l a m r m a l o n e c a n s a
    s n a c e n o l a m r o r m a l o n e c a n s
    n a c e n o l a m r o f o r m a l o n e c a n
    a c e n o l a m r o f e f o r m a l o n e c a
    c e n o l a m r o f e R e f o r m a l o n e c
    a c e n o l a m r o f e f o r m a l o n e c a
    n a c e n o l a m r o f o r m a l o n e c a n
    s n a c e n o l a m r o r m a l o n e c a n s
  a s n a c e n o l a m r m a l o n e c a n s a
  v a s n a c e n o l a m m a l o n e c a n s a v
e v a s n a c e n o l a l o n e c a n s a v e
u e v a s n a c e n o l o n e c a n s a v e u
s u e v a s n a c e n o n e c a n s a v e u s
n s u e v a s n a c e n e c a n s a v e u s n
o n s u e v a s n a c e c a n s a v e u s n o
w o n s u e v a s n a c a n s a v e u s n o w
```

A CHARM TO PROTECT AGAINST THIEVES.

Whoso will protect himself against thieves by night or by day, let him wear this charm (written on virgin parchment) about him, and repeat the words thereof every morning, so shall no theft happen to annoy him." —*Original Manuscript, dated May, 8, 1577, in the possession of Mr. Graham, the Aeronaut.*

THE CHARM.

Deus autem transiens per medium illorum, ibat ✠ **Ihus Xpus** ✠ benedictus Deus quotidie prosperus iter facit **Deus** salutaris noster ✠ **Ihus** ✠ obstinenter occuli eorum ne videant, et dorsum eorum ni curva ✠ **Ihus** ✠ effundus supra eas irs tua, et furor ire tue com-prehendat eos ✠ **Irrnat** ✠ supra inimicas meos formido et pavo in magnitudine brachii fiant eniobiles quasi Lapis, donee per transeat famulus tuus ✠ quern redemisti ✠ dextera tua magnificata est, in virtute **Domini** per crusist inimicus in multitudine virtutis tuae deposuisti omnes adversarious meos ✠ **Ihesu** ✠ eripe me et ab in surgentibusque in me libera me ✠ **Ihesu** ✠ custodi me, et de manu peccatoris et ab hominibusque iniquis eripe me ✠ **Ihesu** ✠ eripe me de opera tibis que iniquitate et a viris sanguine salva me ✠ gloria **Patri** ✠ **Anthos** ✠ **Anostro** ✠ **Morio** ✠ **Bay** ✠ **Eloy** ✠ **Apen** ✠ **Agia** ✠ **Agias** ✠ **Yskiros** ✠.

MARVELLOUS PROPERTIES OF HERBS, STONES, ROOTS, MINERALS,

&c. &c.

ST. JOHN'S WORT.

The herb St. John's Wort, being carried about any one, is said to protect the wearer against all invisible beings.

TO CAUSE TRUE DREAMS.

The seeds of flax and flea-wort, finely powdered, and often smelt to, occasion prophetic and ominous dreams. The manuscript from whence this was taken deems it infallible.

A RING FOR POWER, AND TO OVERCOME ENEMIES.

Let the character of Saturn (♄) be engraved upon a magnet, or piece of loadstone, in the time of the moon's increase; and, being worn on the right hand, no enemy or foe shall overcome the wearer.

FOR THE SIGHT.

Fennel, rose, vervain, celandine, and rue.
Do water make which will the sight renew.

ACONITE, OR WOLFSBANE.

It is said by old herbalists, that these herbs are so extremely pernicious and poisonous, that if either man or beast be wounded with an arrow, knife, sword, or any other instrument, dipped in the juice of this herb, they die incurably within half an hour afterwards.

MULLETT, OR FLEA-BANE.

This herb, burned and smoked where flies, gnats, fleas, or any venomous things are, doth drive them away.

HERBS THAT ACT AS A CHARM AGAINST SPIRITS.

—" There is an herb called corona regis (or rosemary); the house that is suffumigated therewith, noe devil nor spirit hath power over the same. *Piony* hath the same virtue."—(*Manuscript.*)

TO MAKE A SAD PERSON MERRY.

For dull, melancholy men, take the flowers of rosemary, and make them into powder; bind them to the right arm in a linen cloth, and this powder, by working upon the veins, shall make a man more merry and lightsome than ordinary.

MYSTERIOUS PROPERTIES OF THE SUNFLOWER.

Albertus Magnus relates that the heliotropium, or sunflower, is endued with wonderful virtues; for, if gathered when the sun is in the fifth sign of the zodiac (♍), and wrapped in a laurel leaf, thereto being added a wolf's tooth, the person who carries it about him shall find that nobody can have the power of using any other than mild language to him. Moreover, if anything has been taken from him by stealth, let him lay it under his head at night, and he shall see the thief, and all the circumstances of the theft.

THE NETTLE.

The second herb he notices is the *nettle.* By holding this herb, together with *milfoil,* in your hand, you are free from apparitions. Mix it with the juice of sen-green, and smear your hands therewith, putting a part into any water where there are fish, it will not fail to attract them; withdraw it, and they will disperse immediately.

MARVELLOUS PROPERTIES OF HERBS, STONES, ROOTS, &c.

TO SLEEP WITHOUT DANGER.

"Whosoever weareth vervain or dill.
May be bold to sleep on every hill."

The herb Dill is said to procure sleep, sound and secure; and in ancient times it was thus that garlands were used to be worn at riotous feasts, that thereby they might not only sleep, but sleep without danger.

SECRETS OF ALBERTUS MAGNUS

THE HERB CELANDINE.

No less extraordinary is the property of the herb celandine; which, it is said, if suspended over the head of a sick person, will set him singing aloud if he be likely to live; but, if to die, it will make him weep.

THE HERB PERIWINKLE.

The herb periwinkle, Albertus Magnus tells us, being pulverized with earth-worms and sen-green, creates affection between man and wife, by putting a portion of it in their food. A small quantity of the above preparation, with some sulphur, being thrown into a fish-pond, will destroy the fish.

THE HERB HENBANE.

The herb henbane, mixed with wild saffron, and given to a mad dog, kills him instantaneously; and mixed with the blood of a leveret, is said to fascinate hares.

THE LILY, ASTROLOGICALLY GATHERED.

Gather the lily while the sun is in *Leo* (which is from the 23d of July to the 21st of August), mix it with the juice of the *laurel;* which done, bury it for some time under dung, and worms shall be bred from it, which worms being reduced to a powder, and applied to one's neck, will not let the bearer sleep. If put into a vessel containing cow's milk, and covered with the hide of a cow of one colour, it will dry up the udders of the whole herd.

THE MISLETOE.

It is said, that if the above herb be put into the mouth of any person, and that he think of a certain thing, it will dwell upon his memory if it be to happen; if not to happen, it will escape his remembrance entirely. Let it be suspended from a tree with the wing of a swallow, and birds without number will flock thither.

THE HERB CENTAURY.

The same writer mentions many wonderful virtues of the herb centaury; as, for instance, if it be put into a lamp with the blood of a female *puet*, all the bye-standers will imagine themselves *enchanted*, in such a manner that it will appear their position is inverted, supposing their heads to be where their feet are. Again, if thrown into the fire, —" the stars shall seem a tilting at one another:" moreover, when applied to the nose of any one, it will operate so as to make him run himself out of breath for fear.

VERVAIN, ASTROLOGICALLY GATHERED.

Vervain, he says, has, among others, a salutary property. Gather it when the sun is in *Aries* (from the 21st of March to the 21st of April), and mix it with a grain of *piony* of one year's growth; it is a specific for those who are afflicted with epilepsy or fits. If put into a rich mould, it will produce worms in eight weeks, which are immediate death to whoever touches them. Another property of it is, to attract pigeons, which it does surprisingly when put into a dove-cot.

TO FASCINATE OR CHARM DOGS.

The herb *dog's-tongue*, with the heart of a young frog, and its matrix, will, in a short time, collect a multitude of dogs to wheresoever it is laid. Put the same herb under your great toe, and it will prevent a dog's barking. Tie it to a dog's neck, in such a manner that he cannot get at it with his teeth, and he will not cease wheeling round until he fall as it were dead.

WONDERFUL PROPERTIES OF SAGE

Sage, being rotted under dung, and put under a glass, will produce a worm, or a bird having a tail like a blackbird's; the blood of which, if it touch a person's breast, renders the person so touched senseless for a fortnight. Another property of it is, that if the powder be put into a lamp, the room in which it burns will seem full of serpents.

PROPERTIES OF THE AMETHYST.

The amethyst, which is of a purple colour, is supposed to prevent drunkenness and inebriation, which property must greatly enhance its value, and render it an invaluable acquisition to the possessor. Our author also adds, that it aids the understanding; as does likewise the pale transparent beryl.

THE CORAL.

The coral, inheriting a virtue from that element in which it is found, is said to allay tempests, and to be a safeguard to those who journey by water. It has, moreover, been used to stop bleeding; and is said to be of marvellous efficacy for children to wear during their infancy and the period of their teething. The latter virtue is also mentioned by many writers of the eighteenth century.

AN ADMIRABLE AMULET TO STOP BLEEDING.
(*From an old Author.*)

Take a toad, and kill him; then take three bricks, put them into the fire, and take out one of them, and put the toad upon it. Then take out another, and put him again upon that; and when the brick is nearly cold, take off the toad, and put the brick again into the fire; then take the third brick and do so, till the toad be consumed to ashes. Then take the ashes and put them carefully into a silk or taffeta bag; and when any one bleedeth, apply the bag upon the heart of the party, and it will instantly stay the bleeding, either of the nose or of any other wound whatever.

[Herb footnote]
The following extraordinary magical virtues of herbs, &c. are extracted from an ancient manuscript in the possession of *"Raphael:"* —

"Anoint thee with the juice of *canabus* and *archangel*; and, before a mirror of steel, call *spirits*, and thou shalt see them, and have power to bind and to loose them.

"The fume of *fleniculis* chaseth away spirits.

"Take the herb *avisum,* and join it to *camphire,* and thou shalt see spirits, that shall dread thee. It helpeth much to the achieving of secret things.

"*Coriandrum* gathereth spirits together; a fume being made thereof with *apio nisquio,* and *lazias cicuta,* urgeth spirits, and therefore it is said to be the herb of spirits.

"*Petersilion* chaseth away all the spirits of riches.

"Take *coriandrum* of the second kind, which maketh one to sleep; and join thereto *croco, insgreno,* and *apio,* and grind them together with the juice of *hemlock*; then make a suffumigation therewith, and suffume the place where thou wilt hide any treasure in, when the ☽ is joined to the ☉, in the angle of the earth; and that treasure, so hidden, shall never be found

MARVELLOUS PROPERTIES OF HERBS, STONES, ROOTS, &c.

TO SEE SPIRITS.

"Take the juice of Dill, Vervaine, and St. John's grease, (St. John's wart), and anoint your eyes for three days, and you shall see spirits visible " — *Old MSS.*

SINGULAR PROPERTY OF PENNYROYAL.

"In winter, when all things wither and drie up, Pennyroyal flourisheth "

VIRTUES OF THE MANDRAKE.

"Whosoever can get any of this rare plant, shall have continued joy without sorrow, wealth without want, and be warded from all evil and sudden death, or mischances. He shall never be robbed, nor killed, but overcome all his enemies, in what nature soever: this is clearly proved." — *MSS. Key to Agrippa.*

THE SLEEP OF PLANTS.

"The common chicken weed, with white blossoms, affords a notable instance of what is called '*the sleep of plants,*' for every night, the leaves approach in pairs, so as to include within their upper surface the tender rudiments of the new shoots, while the uppermost pair but one, at the end of the stalk, are furnished with longer leaf stalks, than the others, so that they close on the terminating pair, and protect the branch." — *Literary Chronicle.*

THE MYSTERIOUS LETTERS DELIVERED BY HONORIUS,

CALLED THE

Theban Alphabet

A	B	C	D	E	F	G	H
I	K	L	M	N	O	P	Q
R	S	T	V	X	Y	Z	

Of Mysterious Writing.

THERE is among Theurgists a writing which they call celestial, because they show it as placed and figured amongst the stars. There is also another kind of character received by *Revelation* only, and which cannot be found out any other way; the virtues of which are from the Deity revealing them, of whom there are some secret works breathing out an harmony of the divinity, or they are, as it were, some certain agreements or compacts of a league between us and them. Of this kind, was the *sign* in the Heavens revealed to *Constantine*, "In hoc vince." Also, that revealed to *Antiochus*, in the figure of a *pentangle*, signifying *health*; for, being resolved into letters, it speaks the word ὑγίεια, i. e. *health*. In the faith and virtue of which *signs*, both kings obtained a great victory against their enemies. So, also, Judas, who by reason of that was afterwards surnamed Machabeus, being to fight with the Jews, against *Antiochus Eupator*, received from an angel a notable sign, מבבי, in the virtue of which they first stew 11,000, with an infinite number of elephants, and afterwards slew 35,000 of their enemies. For that sign did represent the name of **Jehovah**, and was a memorable emblem of the great name of seventy-two letters, by the equality of number; and the exposition thereof is מי כמיד באלי סיהיח, *i. e. who is there among thee strong as* **Jehovah**?

The *seals* of spirits are widely different from the above, being formed out of magical squares, circles, and pentacles: they are chiefly dependent upon the power, virtue, and efficacy, of certain mysteries relative to numerical powers; and others depend upon the office of the ruling angel, being essentially different in their formation, as well as use; for each of the planetary spirits is accompanied by an *intelligence* to *good*, and a *spirit* to *evil*; which are also used for various peculiar purposes. But the seals of the evil and familiar spirits are more subject to arbitrary formation, being void of any other demonstration, than as having been handed down to us by the learned in those mysteries.

𝕮𝖆𝖇𝖆𝖑𝖎𝖘𝖙𝖎𝖈𝖆𝖑 WORDS OF GREAT EFFICACY

1. *To cause Destruction to Enemies.**

Out of the following passage, *"Let their ways be dark and slippery, and let the angel of the Lord pursue them"* they draw forth the name of the evil angel and messenger of mischief **Mirael** or **Midael**, מידאל, of the spiritual order of warriors: and, when they would destroy an enemy, they made a talisman, cast at the time when the moon was in evil aspect to Mars, affixing thereupon the above name **Mirael**, and the name of the enemy also whom they would subvert or destroy, and the effect soon followed.

---

* Ancient MSS. in the possession of the Mercurii

2. To give Divine Protection.

The Cabalists draw forth a name of great efficacy from the following sentence: "*You are everlasting power, God.*"

From the above verse is drawn forth the great name of God, **Agla**, (*Alga* transposed), and whoso would protect himself against enemies must wear this great name continually about him, written on parchment.

אדני לעולם גברד אהה
א   ל   ג   א
A   L   G   A

3. 𝔒𝔱𝔥𝔢𝔯 𝔇𝔦𝔳𝔦𝔫𝔢 𝔑𝔞𝔪𝔢𝔰.

The word or name **Jesu** is extracted from the following sentences of Holy Writ: "*Until the Messiah shall come,*" and "*His name abides till the end,*" by taking the first Hebrew letters of each word in this manner:—

לוכלו אש בי and כודיה וש יכו
ו   ש   י   ו   ש   י

By which the name J**ESU** is formed.

Also the word **Amen** is extracted from the following verse: "*The Lord, the Faithful King*:—

באכן מור אחגי
י   מ   ן

By taking the three heads or three first letters of each word collected and compounded together, which proves that the word Amen is of great efficacy, and not without just cause used at the end of all prayers by the Church of England. Thus, in like manner, did the ancient Cabalists proceed in determining the names and powers of good or evil spirits, and thus did they proceed in adjuring or binding them, as they found occasion.

THE INFLUENCE OF THE MOON,
IN AFFAIRS OF IMPORTANCE AND MAGNITUDE
According as she is Increasing, or in the Wane.

Not only does the moon claim the most powerful pre-eminence, in every part of Astrological Science whether as it relates to the fate of the new-born infant, or to the fate of any individual enterprise; but those who are skilful in husbandry well know that plants or herbs which are sown, or even trees which are planted in the decrease or *wane* of the moon, seldom thrive, or afford hopes of fruitfulness. But my readers are not aware that her occult influence extends even to affairs of business in a general way. Therefore, let those who would have any pursuit or undertaking successful, observe the course of the moon; and, above all things, *begin nothing of consequence in the decrease*, which is from the second day of the full moon to the next new moon (which the commonest almanack will show); for long experience *proves*, that, with very few objections, there does not exist half the chance of success to any pursuit during that time; and, on the contrary, affairs and business of any kind, *which are began in the increase of the moon*, that is, from the second day after the new moon to the time of the full, have a far better prospect of success, allowing for natural obstacles, than at the opposite period.

This, if well understood and duly observed, may save a world of trouble; and it is a singular fact, that nearly all the *unsuccessful* literary publications, especially newspapers and periodicals, which are so continually appearing, and as constantly failing, are ushered forth to public notice *while the moon is in her decrease:* I leave this to the notice and verification of my readers.—It is a fact denying contradiction, I can assure them; and a slight observation of events will enable them to prove it. The reason for which, in an astrological point of view, is, because the moon signifies not only the community at large, of every nation, but also those changes in fashionable and popular opinion which result from no apparent origin; but which, although whimsical, are yet too powerful for a thinking person, well acquainted with the foibles and vices of mankind, to despise.

" For he made the moon also to serve in her season, for a declaration of times, and a sign of the world."—*Ecclesias.* xliii. 6.

The celebrated Dr. Mead, well known as one of the most skilful of his day, whose portrait is hung in the new assembly room of the Royal College of Physicians, has these remarks upon the " Influence of the Moon."

"To conclude, the powerful action of the moon is observed not only by philosophers and natural historians, but even by the common people, who have been fully persuaded of it time out of mind. Pliny relates, that Aristotle laid it down as an aphorism, *that no animal dies but in the ebb of the tide!* And that births and deaths chiefly happen about the new and fall moon, is an axiom among women. The husbandmen, likewise, are regulated by the moon in planting and managing trees; and several other of their occupations. So great is the empire of the moon over the terraqueous globe."

OF PERSONS BORN FORTUNATE, ACCORDING TO THE MOON'S COURSE.

In every almanac, there is given the time of what is termed the *"moon's southing:"* this is the time when the moon crosses the meridian; now those persons who are born *within an hour and a half preceding the southing of the moon, and within half an hour succeeding it,* have the moon in the tenth house of heaven, and are fated to be travellers, to see far distant countries, and to have a most remarkable life; replete with diversities, changes, and, in many respects, a great variety of good and evil fortune. But for changes, publicity, notoriety, and extensive acquaintances, their horoscopes are generally remarkable; the moon having wonderful power when in, or near the meridian, over the lives and fortunes of all who are born under such a celestial position.

Again, those who are born *within half an hour of the moons rising and setting,* (which is also easily seen by the most common almanac), have the moon angular either in the first or seventh house; and consequently are certain to be either seafaring persons, travellers, or subject to the most extraordinary changes. But it is more fortunate of the two, to be born near the moon's *rising*, rather than the setting; as the ascendant in all nativities has the greatest efficacy.

By attention to those foregoing simple rules, those persons who know nothing of astrological calculations, may learn something of the fate to which they are destined. The following curious facts, which have already been noticed in the different periodicals of the day, are sufficient to prove the theory of

LUNAR INFLUENCE.

If an animal, first killed, be exposed to the full effulgence of the moon beams, it will in a few hours become a mass of corruption; whilst another animal not exposed to such influence, and only a few feet distant, will not be in the slightest manner affected.

Fruits also, when exposed to the moonshine, have been known to ripen much more readily than those which have not; and plants, shutout from the sun's rays and from light, and consequently bleached, have been observed to assume their natural appearance if exposed to the rays of a full moon.

In South America, trees cut at the *full moon*, split almost immediately, as if torn asunder by great external force. The writer of these observes, *"all these are remarkable and well established facts*, but have never as yet been accounted for."

TRADITIONS AND SUPERSTITIONS OF FORMER TIMES.

PROGNOSTICATIONS FROM THE MOON'S AGE.

Moon's Age.

1st day. THE child born is said to be long-lived. The dream true, and the event satisfying.

2d day. The dream will be unprofitable. The child born on this day grows fast. It is a fortunate day for searching after remarkable things.

3d day. The dream good. The child born this day is said to be fortunate with great men or Princes.

4th day. Unhappy, evil, and perilous, especially to those who fall sick. The dream will not be effected.

5th day. Good to begin any work, or to voyage on water. A *good* dream will be effected and brought about; but a bad dream will have no meaning. The child born this day proves a traitor.

6th day. The fugitive shall be recovered. Dreams suspended. The child born will, it is said, be short-lived.

7th day. The sick person whose sickness began on this day shall soon be well. The dream must be kept secret. The child born this day will be long-lived and liable to trouble.

8th day. The dream true and certain. The child born long-lived.

9th day. The dream will turn out good next day.

10th day. The dream will be soon effected. The sickness perilous. The child born this day is said to be fated to long life. The ☉ being Alchochodon.

11th day. Here rules Babiel, enemy to dreams; hence the dreams will be of no effect. The child born this day shall be afflicted in travelling, and irreligious.

12th day. The dream good and effective. The child ingenious and long-lived.

13th day. The dream true and effective. The child then born will be foolish or a zealot.

14th day. The dream shall be ambiguous, doubtful, and the effect suspended. The child born this day will be an extraordinary genius. His fate is ruled by the demon or angel Cassiel, in the hierarchy of Uriel.

15th day. He who falls sick this day it shall be unto death. The dream true. Fortune indifferent. The child under ♀, handsome, fair, and fortunate.

16th day. The dreams will be accomplished. The child long-lived. ♀ is said to be Alchochodon.

17th day. If this fall on a Saturday, it is said to prove very unfortunate. The dream not effected for three days. The child born on this day is said to be unhappy.

18th day. The dream is said to be true and certain. The child, through much labour and travel, will come to high dignity and honours.

19th day. Hiel rules. The day dangerous. Dream forbodes ill fortune. The child likely to prove mischievous, or a thief.

20th day. The dream true. The child, as before, a cheat.

21st day. The day is said to be good. The dream unprofitable. The child corpulent, strong, but a cheat.

22d day. Gebil rules. The dream is true. The child good, docile, and long-lived.

23d day. A fortunate day. The dream, nevertheless, is false. The child born this day will be deformed, but clever.

24th day. The dream of no effect. The child then born soft-tempered, and voluptuous.

25th day. Unfortunate dream. Adversity for the child then born.

26th day. Dream certain. The child, when adult, will be rich and honoured.

27th day. A good day. The child fortunate, but a great dreamer. Dreams prevail.

28th day. The sick will die. The dream bad, as the spirits are troubled with religious whims. The child born this day will die young; and if it live past five months, will prove a zealot, or an idiot.

29th day. Fortunate; Raphael predominates. The child born long-lived, and fated to riches. Dreams true.

30th and last day. Unfortunate. Child short-lived. The sick person will die. Cassiel predominates.

With respect to the foregoing traditions, they are very ancient, and are therefore curious. Their truth or falsehood may be proved by observation.—The days of the *moon's age* may be known by the commonest almanack.

THE THEORY OF

FORTUNATE AND UNFORTUNATE DAYS,

BY THE LUNAR MOTIONS.

I HAVE already spoken of the powerful influence which *the Moon possesses over the earth and the whole of its inhabitants*; this daily experience proves, beyond the shadow of a doubt: for which reason, the Moon is a chief significator in every horoscope, or theme of heaven, and as such the student must invariably observe her aspects, ere he can obtain the truth of the matter. I shall, probably, give many instances thereof in the course of these pages; but, for the present, I shall confine myself to the diurnal lunar aspects, or the configurations the Moon is perpetually forming with the remaining seven primary planets, the Sun, Mercury, Venus, Mars, Jupiter, Saturn, and Herschel.

The theory of fortunate and unfortunate days has, therefore, a real foundation in nature; since those days *only* are considered as fortunate, on which the Moon forms a favourable aspect with a fortunate planet; and the unfortunate ones are those on which her configurations are malignant and evil.

To be more explicit: the *best*, or most fortunate days, are those on which the Moon is in ✶*, △, quintile or ☌ of Jupiter; the *next* in power, when she is in the like configurations with Venus; and the *worst*, or most malignant and unfortunate, are those days whereon the Moon is in ☌, semiquartile, □ or ☍ of Saturn or Mars; and next to those, when she is in □ or ☍ of Herschel; the ☌ of Herschel not being near so evil.

Those days, also, whereon the Moon is in ☌, □, semiquartile, or of the Sun, are eminently evil. But of these, the ☌, and next the □, are the worst; the ☍ being beneficial in some cases, such as where publicity is concerned, &c.

Again, on those days that the Moon comes to the □, semiquartile, or ☍ of Mercury, astrologers account it unfortunate for business, or travelling, or writings and speculations of any kind. Also, those days when she is in evil aspect to Jupiter or Venus, as the □, semiquartile, or ☍ are accounted far from *good*; but the quartile, in these cases, acts worse than the opposition.

On the other hand, even the fortunate aspects of the *evil* planets, as the ✶ or △ of Saturn, Mars, or Herschel *are rarely considered as benevolent*; the ☌, ✶, or △, of Mercury is good for business; and the like aspects of the Sun for affairs connected with requests, petitions, or affairs where patronage is concerned. And on those days whereon the Moon forms no aspect, but is *void of course*, as astrologers term it—which is, when she in no aspect whatever with any planet,—it is generally accounted that the chief or reigning influence is *evil*. Seldom does any new undertaking prosper or come to maturity which is *then* commenced.

---

*[Ed. The symbols are astrological aspects:
 △ is Trine, or 120 degrees,
 □ is Square, or 90 degrees,
 ☍ is Opposition, or 180 degrees,
 ☌ is Conjunction,
 ✶ is Sextile, or 60 degrees,
 "Semiquartile" is 45 degrees,
 "Quintile", or Quincunx , is 150 degrees]

It follows, therefore, as a mathematical consequence which should be well remembered, that *there is nothing superstitious in attending to the choice of times and seasons, since the celestial configurations do exist in the heavens,* and are by no means chimerical; and he that rejects them, or laughs at the student who (by consulting his Ephemeris) appoints a peculiar time when the heavenly influences are fraught with fortunate aspects; might with equal propriety make sport of the patient who attends to the mandates of his physician; as to his choice of the vernal sunshine, or refreshing breeze of summer, in preference to the dews of the night; or the chilling airs of the humid and streaming atmosphere: when he ventures abroad for the restoration of his health.

To settle at once, and set aside the noisy and incredulous laugh of the disbeliever in the celestial influences, I will give one instance of the lunar configurations in a case still fresh in the minds of my readers, from the dreadful scene of death and destruction it caused; a scene truly of horror, and fraught with dire remembrances. I allude to the Royal Brunswick Theatre, which opened with unusual splendour on Monday, the 25th of February, 1828, and within a few days was nothing but a pile of ruins!

On the 25th of February, 1828, at noon-day, the Moon was in seven degrees thirty-six minutes of the sign *Cancer*, and Saturn was in thirteen degrees thirty-nine minutes of the same sign. Consequently, the Moon was fast hastening to the malignant conjunction of that evil star. The aspect, or the meeting of those two planets, took place at a quarter past twelve o'clock that night; consequently, the whole of that day, during the opening, the rehearsal, and the first performance, *the Moon was terribly afflicted*. The Moon also signifies the community at large (as all astrological authors teach); and what could more truly depicture the unfortunate end of this ill-fated commencement, than the above evil configuration? To an unprejudiced mind, this single instance, which every Almanack or Ephemeris of the year can prove, will be sufficient to entitle my theory to *attention*—and attention is all that is wanting to prove its truth.

To calculate the aspects of the Moon with the other seven planets, the student should make use of *"White's Ephemeris,"* wherein the places of the heavenly bodies are set down for noon for each day in the year. [...]

A Table of the Moon,
FROM THE OLD ASTROLOGERS,
FOR NATIVITIES.

☽ in ♈ in Nativities.	☽ in ♉ in Nativities.
Then she is a mighty queene of great renowne and reputation; fair, lightsome, pleasant, great bodied, and well made, and will be quickly angrie.	She is then queen of a great and mighty realme, of good humanitie, keeping her realme in good peace and tranquilitie; she doth good justice, and is of all men well beloved; loveth rest and joy, and is something given unto the pleasure of the flesh.
☽ in ♊ in Nativities.	☽ in ♋ in Nativities.
When she is in ♊, she is poore and miserable, having lost some of her members, doing her business and affairs very ill and unprofitable. She is of ill nature and condition, ill clad and of ill conversation in life, and against eating and drinking.	In ♋ she is a queene of great power and a great realme, taking from and giving unto whom she pleaseth, and is of an absolute power and authoritie; a lady of wisdom, beautie, and prudence, and is well beloved, authorised, and obeyed in her realme

☽ in ♌ in Nativities. In ♌, she is a queene crowned, but yet without authoritie to do or command, but is in contempt and despised of all them of her realme, each one living at pleasure as he listeth.	☽ in ♍ in Nativities. When she is in ♍ she is very melancholia and pensive, slumbering, ill-apparelled and clothed, loving pick thanks and doing nothing that is good.
☽ in ♐ in Nativities. When she is in ♐, she taketh pleasure to shoot in cross-bows, and to bear the pike and halberd, and to joust in tourney.	☽ in ♑ in Nativities. When she is in ♑ she is a noble and mighty lady, fair, handsome, well made, well clothed, and of good name and fame.
☽ in ♎ in Nativities. She is then a queene crowned, and doth none other thing eat and drink too much, nothing at all minding her business: she is carelesse and recklesse, taking no pleasure but in mirth, as in ignorance, dancing, ribaldry, songs, ballets, rounds, companie of women, and of other things of pleasure.	☽ in ♏ in Nativities. When she is in ♏, she is a woman of great and evil thoughts, being the cause of much evils which comes to her and to others, and all by her ignorance.

☽ in ♒ in Nativities.	☽ in ♓ in Nativities.
When she is in ♒, she is a lady loving hunting and great pursuit of them, which avoide afore her, she never stayeth in one place, she always goeth and cometh without rest, and taketh things in hand which serve to no use, as well in her diet as in her affairs.	When she is in ♓, she is a woman out of order, and careth nothing for faire clothes, but all her pleasure is to hunt, and to play at cards, dice, and such other games which wasteth her substance, and she careth not much for her business.

Talismanic Effects of the Moon over the Vegetable World.

To prove the wonderful occult power which "the empress of the night" possesses over the vegetable creation, proceed as follows:—

Take any given quantity of common peas, and divide the same into four parts, keeping them separate. Then, on any spot of ground at all fit for vegetation, when the season approaches for sowing them, sow the contents of the *first* parcel on the *first* or *second day* of the *new moon*. The *second* parcel sow near the same spot on the first or second day of the *second quarter*; the *third* parcel sow on the second or third day before the *full moon*; and lastly, sow the fourth parcel on the second or third day before the *moon* is out. Now the *first* parcel, sown under the *new moon*, will grow very fast, *blossom most beautifully, but will* not *bear fruit*. The *second* will *blossom and bear very little*. The *third* parcel will not only *blossom* beautifully, but *will bear fruit in abundance,* and the *fourth* and last parcel *will scarcely rise from the ground* ! Likewise all fruit trees set at the *new moon* blossom, but never bear fruit; while all others set three days before the *full* bear abundantly. And in pruning trees the same effect takes place, for a tree pruned at the *new moon* will shoot forth branches, but *unbearable*, and if pruned at the *full*, they will be prolific.

This curious experiment has been tried by the *Mercurii* and several other philosophers; it at once decides the moon to possess the most powerful influence over sublunary affairs, and whether relative to the animal or vegetable creation, or to the world at large, still is this influence perceptible to every searcher after Nature's secrets, and the discovery thereof will repay the curious inquirer.

ARGUMENTS CONCERNING STARRY INFLUENCE, DRAWN FROM THE TIDES.

By the term *tide*, as here used, we are to understand the periodical approaches of the water of the ocean to, and their alternate recessions from, the shores of every country of the earth. The *tides* of the ocean have a very immediate connection with *lunar* astronomy; for, where their course is unimpeded, it is commonly high water when the moon is about on the south-south-west point of the compass of the *horizon* of any place: consequently, the *greatest* elevation of the waters will be about twenty, or from that to twenty-five, degrees *eastward* of the moon. All the operations of the tides are confined between determinate limits, which are called *high* and *low* water. The interval between high water at one time, and the high water following, is half the time of the moon's apparent circuit round the earth, which is 12 hours 25 minutes; so that, in 24 hours 50 minutes, the tide ebbs and flows *twice* upon every coast.

Thus far we have considered the phenomena of the tides as resulting from *lunar influence* alone; but there is a force in the sun as well as in the moon, which is constantly operating to disturb the ocean, and which produces special effects, according as it is combined with, or counter to, the *lunar* influence. General experience has shown that the *lunar* is to the *solar force* about as 5 to 2. It is also found that the sun, in *quadrature* with the moon, causes a depression or diminution of *lunar* effect, of 30 1/2 inches in the height of a tide, it being at these times that the two luminaries are acting at right angles to one another, as they do in all *quartile* aspects. The lunar effect of itself causes a rise of about six feet; consequently, the mean spring-tide, where there are no obstructions, should be 30 1/2 + 72=102 1/2 inches, and the mean neap-tide 72 — 30 1/2=41 1/2 inches; and this is found to correspond with observation in a general way, and setting localities out of the question.

But the distance of each *luminary* from the earth being variable, occasions different intensities of force to be constantly employed, so that neither these nor any other proportions are to be esteemed constant. They are, however, quite sufficient for the present purpose, which is that of giving general ideas of the nature of the solar and lunar influences, as they happen to be in conjunction or quadrature, and exerted in these positions upon terrestrial matter.

Considerable difference in the magnitude of a tide is caused by the **moon's** distance, so that the ratio of the disturbing force in the **moon** to that in the **sun** is sometimes 6 to 2, and at others not more than 4 to 2: thus, in the former instance, instead of the mean spring-tide being 8 1/2 feet, it would be 10 feet; and in the latter case only 7 1/2, But as well as that of the **sun** and **moon**, every planet has a gravitating power on the waters of the ocean; and the combined influence of the ten primary planets, were it all brought into action at one time, would be, to that of the **sun** and **moon** conjointly, about as 1 to 100; so that, in a mean spring-tide of 102 inches, the united influence of the planets would raise it about one inch.

When the **moon** is in *perigree* at the time of spring-tide, such tide may be expected to rise at least 2 3/4 feet higher than a mean spring-tide; and, on the other hand, a difference of 2 3/4 feet deficiency will be generally experienced in spring-tides, which happen at the time of the **moon's** *apogee*.

If the **moon** has a *northern declination*, and the *latitude* of the place is also *northern*, the tide which happens when the **moon** is above the horizon is greater than that which happens on the same day when she is below it: and, when the *latitude* of the place is *contrary* to the *declination* of the 𝔪𝔬𝔬𝔫, the effect is reversed.

APPLICATION OF THE FACTS CONCERNING THE TIDES TO ASTROLOGY.

HAVING thus presented some of the most obvious facts relative to the action of the 𝔰𝔲𝔫, 𝔪𝔬𝔬𝔫, and 𝔭𝔩𝔞𝔫𝔢𝔱𝔰 severally, upon the waters of the ocean, it cannot fail to be observed, that all the inequalities of motion—of distance—of declination—of phases—and of mutual aspects, agreeing, as they do, with observation as to their various proportional effects, afford a mass of evidence which places the theory of siderial influence upon terrestrial matter upon a foundation which nothing can destroy, or even shake. Indeed, no one acquainted with the peculiar and nicely corresponding ratio between cause and effect relative to the tides, and having, at the same time, skill in mathematics, and acquaintance with the mechanism of nature, sufficient to discover these sympathetic relations, and to generalize them to questions in *astrology*, will, for a moment, hesitate to own, that every star has an influence which is not to be restrained by human power—that this influence is constantly producing some mutation in the earth—and, like the ebbing and flowing of the sea, is impetuously running, without intermission, round all the regions of the world.

Pythagoras maintained that the world is actuated by a divine soul; and, when we come to examine that miraculous sympathy in nature so admirably manifested between the heavenly bodies, and the amazing body of water, surrounding our earth, which is incessantly agitated by sympathetic influence, we are involuntarily brought to think of the doctrine of this eminent sage. In looking deeply into the sympathies which we are constantly experiencing, we can hardly quarrel with those who have ascribed them to an agency more than we can comprehend. We see a gift of foreknowledge strongly implanted in the badger, the hedgehog, the hare, and almost every animal with which we are acquainted. We see, also, that birds and reptiles have a surprising forecast: and who can fail to perceive effects constantly working between the *heavenly* bodies, and the bodies and souls of mankind? Whether there exists an *ethereal* effluvium that is communicated from one body of matter to another, and which produces those strange *sympathies* we are witnessing, is not necessary to be declared ; we know they *are* produced, and being able to connect them with what we term *planetary influence* is sufficient to show we have sound groundwork for forecasting the effects incident to known causes.

𝔉airy 𝔏egends and 𝔊oblin 𝔏ore

" *Puck.* How now Spirit! whither wander you?
Fai.   Over hill, over dale.
            Through bush, through brier,
            Over perk, over pale,
            Through flood, through fire,
            I do wander every where.
            Swifter then the moone' s sphere;
            And I serve the fairy queen,
            To dew her orbs upon the green:
            The cowslips tall, her pensioners be
            In their gold coats spots you see;
            Those be rubies, fairy favours,
            In those freckles live their savours
        I must go seek some dew drops here,
        And hang a pearl in every cowslip' s ear.
        Farewell, thou lob of Spirits, I'll, be gone!
        Our queen and all our elves come here anon."
                            A Midsummer Night' s Dream.

THE ELVES IN IRELAND.

The *Elves*, which, in their true shape, are said to be but a few inches high, have an airy, almost transparent, body: so delicate is their form, that a dewdrop, when they dance on it, trembles, indeed, but never breaks. Both sexes are of extraordinary beauty, and mortal beings cannot be compared with them.

They do not live alone, or in pairs, but always in large societies. They are invisible to man, particularly in the daytime; and as they can be present, and hear what is said, the peasantry never speak of them but with caution and respect, terming them "*the good people*," or the friends, as any other name would offend them.

If a great cloud of dust rises on the road, it is said by the peasantry that the Elves are about to change their residence, and to remove to another place, and the invisible travellers are always saluted with a respectful bow. They have their dwellings in clefts of rocks, caves, and ancient tumuli. Every part within is decorated in the most splendid and magnificent manner; and the pleasing music, which sometimes issues from thence in the night, has delighted those who have been so fortunate as to hear it.

During the summer nights, when the moon shines, and particularly in the harvest time, the Elves come out of their secret dwellings, and assemble for the dance in certain favourite spots, which are hidden, and secluded places, such as mountain-valleys, meadows near streams and brooks, and churchyards, where men seldom come They often celebrate their feasts under large mushrooms, or repose beneath their shade. In the first rays of the morning sun they again vanish, with a noise resembling that of a swarm of bees or flies. Their garments are said to be as white as snow, sometimes shining like silver: a hat or cap is indispensable; for which purpose they generally select the red flowers of the *foxglove*, and by it different parties are known.

The secret and magic powers of the Elves, tradition asserts to be so great as scarcely to know any bounds. They can assume in a moment, not only the human, but every other form, even the most terrific; and it is easy for them to convey themselves, in one second, a distance of five leagues.

Before their breath, all human energy fails. They sometimes communicate supernatural knowledge to men; and if a person be seen, walking up and down alone, and moving his lips, as one half distraught, it is said to be a sign that an Elf is invisibly present, and instructing him.

The *Elves* are, above all things, fond of music. Those who have heard their music, cannot find words to describe the power with which it fills and enraptures the soul. It rushes upon them like a stream; and yet the tones are simple, even monotonous, and in general resembling natural sounds. Among their amusements, is that of playing at ball, which they pursue with much eagerness, and at which they often differ so as even to quarrel.

Their skill in dancing far exceeds the highest art of man, and the pleasure they take in this amusement is inexhaustible. They dance without interruption till the rays of the sun appear on the mountains, and make the boldest leaps without the least exertion. They do not require any food, but refresh themselves with dewdrops, which they collect from the leaves.

They severely punish all who inquisitively approach or teaze them; otherwise they are friendly and obliging to well-meaning people, who confide in them. They remove humps from the shoulder, make presents of new articles of clothing, undertake to grant requests; though, in such cases, good humour on the applicant's part seems to be necessary. Sometimes, too, they appear in human form, or allow persons who have accidentally strayed amongst them during the night, to join in their dances; but there is always some danger in this intercourse. The person becomes ill in consequence, and falls into a violent fever from the unnatural exertion, as they seem to lend him a part of their power. If he forget himself, and, according to the custom, kiss his partner, the whole scene vanishes the instant his lips touch hers.

The *Elves* have another peculiar and more intimate connexion with mortals. It seems as if they divided among themselves the souls of men, and considered them thenceforth as their property. Hence, certain families have their particular Elves, to whom they are devoted; in return for which, however, they receive from them help and assistance in critical moments, and, often, recovery from mortal diseases. But as, after death, they become the property of their Elves, the death of a man is to them always a festival, at which one of their own body enters into their society. Therefore they require that people shall be present at funerals, and pay them reverence. They celebrate an interment like a wedding, by dancing on the grave: and it is for this reason that they select churchyards for their favourite places of resort. A violent quarrel often arises, whether a child belongs to the Elves of the father or of the mother, and in what churchyard it is to be buried. The different parties of these supernatural beings hate and make war on each other, with as much animosity as nations among mankind: their combats take place in the night in cross roads, and they often do not separate till daybreak parts them. This connexion of men with a quiet and good tribe of spirits, far from being frightful, would rather be beneficial, but the Elves appear in a dubious character; both evil and good are combined in their nature, and they show a dark as well as a fair side. They are said to be *angels expelled from heaven, who have not fallen into hell*, but are in fear and doubt respecting their future states, and whether they shall find mercy at the day of judgment.

This mixture of the dark and the malevolent is visibly manifested in their actions and inclinations. If, in remembrance of their original and happy condition, they are beneficent and friendly towards man, the evil principle within them prompts them to malicious and injurious tricks. Their beauty, the wondrous splendour of their dwellings, their sprightliness, is nothing more than illusive show; and their true figure, which is frightfully ugly, inspires terror. If, as is but rarely the case, they are seen in the day-time, their countenances appear to be wrinkled with age, or, as people express it, "like a withered cauliflower," a little nose, red eyes, and hair hoary with extreme old age.

One of their evil propensities consists in stealing healthy and fine children from their mothers, and substituting in their room a *changeling*, who bears some resemblance to the stolen infant, but is, in fact, only an ugly and sickly Elf. He manifests every evil disposition,—is malicious, mischievous, and though insatiable as to food, does not thrive. When the name of God is mentioned, he begins to laugh, otherwise he never speaks till, being obliged to do so by artifice, his age is betrayed by his voice, which is that of a very old man. The love of music shows itself in him, as well as extraordinary proficiency: supernatural energies are also manifested in the power with which he obliges everything, even inanimate objects, to dance. Wherever he comes, he brings ruin: a series of misfortunes succeed each other; the cattle become sick, the house falls into decay, and every enterprise proves abortive.

If he is recognized, and threatened, he makes himself invisible, and escapes. He dislikes running water; and if he is carried on a bridge, he jumps over, and, sitting upon the waves, plays his pipe, and returns to his own people.

At particular times, such as *May* eve, for instance, the evil Elves seem to be peculiarly active and powerful. To those to whom they are inimical, they give a blow unperceived, the consequence of which is lameness; or they breathe upon them, and boils and swellings immediately appear on the place which the breath has touched. Persons who pretend to be in particular favour with *"the fairies,"* undertake to cure such diseases by magic and mysterious journeys.

THE CLURICAUNE.

In this quality the *Elf* is essentially distinguished from the Shefro, by his solitary and awkward manners: the CLURICAUNE is never met with in company, but always alone. He is said to be much more corporeal, and appears in the daytime as a little old man, with a wrinkled countenance, in an antiquated dress. His pea-green coat is adorned with large buttons, and he seems to take a particular delight in having large metal shoe-buckles. He wears a cocked hat in the ancient French style. He is detested on account of his evil disposition, and his name is used as an expression of contempt. People try to become his master, and therefore often threaten him: sometimes they succeed in outwitting him; sometimes he is more cunning, and cheats them. He employs himself in making shoes, at the same time whistling a tune. If he is surprised by *man*, when thus engaged, he is, indeed, afraid of his superior strength, but endowed with the power of vanishing, if he can contrive to make the mortal turn his eyes from him, even for an instant.

The *Cluricaune* possesses a knowledge of hidden treasures, but does not discover them till he is pressed to the utmost. He frequently relieves himself, when a man fancies that he is wholly in his power. A common trick of his, is infinitely to multiply the mark showing where the treasure lies, whether it be a bush, a thistle, or a branch, that it may no longer serve as a guide to the person who has fetched an instrument to dig up the ground.

The Cluricaune has, it is said, a small leathern purse, with a shilling which, however often he may pay it away, always returns, and which is called the lucky shilling. He frequently carries about him two purses, the one contains the magic shilling and the other a copper coin; and if compelled to deliver, he cunningly presents the latter, the weight of which is satisfactory; and when the person who has seized it is examining whether it is correct, he watches the opportunity and disappears.

His enjoyments consist in smoking and drinking. He knows the secret, which the Danes are said to have brought into Ireland, of making beer from heather. The small tobacco pipes of antique form, which are frequently found in Ireland, in digging up or ploughing, especially in the vicinity of those circular entrenchments called Danish forts, are supposed to belong to the Cluricaunes; and if they are discovered broken, or in any way damaged, it is looked upon as a sort of atonement for the tricks which their pretended owners are presumed to have played.

The Cluricaune also appears connected with men, and then attaches himself to a family, with which he remains as long as a member of it survives, who are at the same time unable to get rid of him. With all his propensity to mischief and roguery, he usually has a degree of respect for the master of the house, and treats him with deference. He lends a helping hand, and wards off secret dangers; but is extremely angry and enraged if they forget him, and neglect to put his food in the usual place.

THE BANSHEE.

The *Banshee* is considered the " white woman," or the chief of the Elves. A female spirit, said to belong to certain families, generally, however, of ancient or noble descent, which appears only to announce the death of one of the members.

The Banshee shows herself in the vicinity of the house, or at the windows, of the sick person, clasps her hands, and laments in tones of the greatest anguish. She wears an ample mantle, with a hood over her head.

THE PHOOKA.

The *Phooka* is said, by a celebrated author of fairy lore, to be extremely obscure and indefinite in representation. People are said to recollect it imperfectly, like a dream, even though they have experienced the strongest sensations, yet the Phooka is palpable to the touch. It appears as a black horse, an eagle, a bat, and compels the man of whom it has got possession, and who is incapable of making any resistance, to go through various curious adventures in a short time. It hurries with him over precipices, carries him up into the moon, and down into the bottom of the sea. If a building falls in, it is imputed to the Phooka. There are numerous precipices and and rocky caverns, called "Phooka Caves:" even a waterfall formed by the Liffey, in the county of Wicklow, has derived its name from this spirit. The people prohibit their children from eating blackberries after Michaelmas, and ascribe the decay of that fruit, which takes place after that season, to the Phooka! *Shakspeare* records these fairy, phantasies admirably, thus:—

> "About, about,
> in Windsor Castle, *Elves*, within, without;
> Strew good luck, *Ouphes*, on every sacred room.
> That it may stand till the perpetual doom
> In state as wholesome, as in state 'tis fit.
> Worthy the owner, and the owner it.
> The several chairs of orders, took you scour,
> With juice of *balm* and every precious flower.
> Each fair instalment, coat, and several crest.
> With loyal blazon evermore be blest.
> And nightly, meadow fairies, look you sing,
> Like to the garter's compass, in a ring:
> The expression that it bears, green let it be,

More fertile, fresh, thou all the field to see.
And *"Hony soit qui mal y pense"* write,
In emerald turfs, flowers purple, blue, and white;
Like sapphire, pearl, and rich embroidery.
Buckled below fair knighthood's beading knee,
Fairies use flowers for their charactery.
Away, disperse! but, till ' tis one o' clock,
Our dance of custom, round about the oak
Of Herne the hunter, let us not forget."

Merry Wives of Windsor.

THE FAIRY LAND OF YOUTH.

Beneath the water (*tradition relates*) there is a country, as well as above the earth, where the glorious sun shines forth in splendour, beautiful meadows flourish in luxuriance, trees put forth their gaudy blossoms, fields and woods vary the goodly scene, splendid cities and gorgeous palaces arise aloft in beaming splendour, equalled by none on earth, which are inhabited by legends of *Fairies* and myriads of *Elves*.

Tradition relates, that if you have found, at the proper moment, the right spot upon the banks of the water, the splendid scene may be easily beheld. Persons who are said to have fallen in, and reached this sub-aqueous world without accident, on their return have related wonders of this enchanted region.

It is called *"the Fairy Land of Youth"* for it is affirmed that time has no power there, over years, or months, or weeks, or days, or hours, or moments; no one ever, *there*, becomes old; no one regards time as passing fleetly; and those persons who have passed whole years there, nay, even an age, have fancied the enchanted period as only a moment.

On particular days, *at the rising of the sun*, it is said, the fairy inhabitants appear above the surface of the water, decked forth in all the resplendent colours of the Rainbow, and apparelled like immortals, in never fading garments, bright, ethereal, and magnificent. With the song, the dance, and the sweetest strains of enlivening music, they are said to pass joyously, in a certain track along the water, which no more yields to the pressure of their little feet, than the solid earth under the foot of frail man, till they at length vanish, and disappear in *mist*.

> "He ask'd how many charming hour, had flown
> Since on her slave her heaven of beauty shown.
> 'Should I consult my heart,' cried he, 'the rate
> Were small — a *week* would be the utmost date;
> But when my mind reflect, on actions past,
> And counts its joys, time must have fled more fast:
> Perhaps I might have said *three months* are gone,'
> 'Three months!' replied the fair; 'three months alone.
> Know that *three hundred years* have roll' d away.
> Since at my feet my lovely phoenix lay.'
> 'Three hundred years!' re-echoed back the prince,
> 'A whole three hundred years completed since I landed here!!"
>
> The Enchanted Lake.

THE LEGEND OF O'DONOGHUE.

In an age, so distant that the precise period is unknown, a chieftain, named O'Donoghue, ruled over the country which surrounds the romantic Lough Lean, now called the Lake of Killarney. Wisdom, beneficence, and justice, distinguished his reign, and the prosperity and happiness of his subjects were their natural results.

He is said to have been as renowned for his warlike exploits as for his pacific virtues; and as a proof that his domestic administration was not the less vigorous because it was mild, a rocky island is pointed out to strangers, called "O' Donoghue's Prison," in which this prince once confined his own son for some act of disorder and disobedience.

His end (for it cannot correctly be called his death) was singular and mysterious. At one of those splendid feasts, for which his Court was celebrated, surrounded by the most distinguished of his subjects, he was engaged in a prophetic vision of the events which were to happen in ages yet to come. His auditors listened to his relation,—now wrapped in wonder, now fixed with indignation, burning with shame, or melted into sorrow,—as he faithfully related the heroism, the injuries, the crimes, and the miseries, of their descendants.

In the midst of his predictions, he rose slowly from his seat, advanced with a solemn, measured, and majestic tread, to the shore of the lake, and walked forward composedly upon its unyielding surface. When he had nearly reached the centre, he paused for a moment, then turning slowly round, looked forward to his friends, and waving his arms to them, with the cheerful air of one taking a short farewell, *disappeared from their view.*

The memory of the "*good O'Donoghue,*" has been cherished by successive generations with affectionate reverence; and it is believed that, at sun-rise, on every May-day morning, the anniversary of his departure, he revisits his ancient domain : a favoured few only are in general permitted to see him, and this distinction is always an omen of good fortune to the beholders. When it is granted to many, it is a sure token of an abundant harvest—a blessing, the want of which, during this prince's reign, was never felt by his people.

Some years have elapsed since the last appearance of O'Donoghue. The April of *that* year had been remarkably wild and stormy, but on May morning the fury of the elements had altogether subsided. The air was hushed and still, and the sky, which was reflected in the serene lake, resembled a beautiful but deceitful countenance, whose smiles, after the most tempestuous emotions, tempt the stranger to believe that it belongs to a soul which no passion has ever ruffled.

The first beams of the rising sun were just gilding the lofty summit of Glenaa, when the waters, near the eastern shore of the lake, became suddenly and violently agitated, though all the rest of its surface lay smooth and still as a tomb of polished marble. The next moment a foaming wave darted forward, and, like a proud high-crested war-horse, exulting in his strength, rushed across the lake towards Toomies mountain. Behind this wave, *appeared a stately warrior fully armed, mounted upon a milk-white steed*, and at his back fluttered a light blue scarf. The horse, apparently exulting in his noble burthen, sprung after the wave along the water, which bore him up like firm earth, while showers of spray, that glittered brightly in the morning sun, were dashed up at every bound.

The warrior was O'Donoghue; he was followed by numberless youths and maidens, who moved light and unconstrained over the watery plain, *as the moonlight fairies glide through the fields of air*. They were linked together by garlands of delicious spring flowers, and they timed their movements to strains of enchanting melody. When O'Donoghue had nearly reached the western side of the lake, he suddenly turned his steed, and directed his course along the wood-fringed shore of Glenaa, preceded by the huge wave that curled and foamed up as high as the horse's neck, whose fiery nostrils snorted above it. The long train of attendants followed, with playful deviations, the track of their leader, and moved on with unabated fleetness to their celestial music, till gradually, as they entered the narrow straight between Glenaa and Dinis, they became involved in the mists which still partially floated over the lakes, and *faded from the view* of the wondering beholders! But the sound of their music still fell upon the ear, and echo, catching up the harmonious strains, fondly repeated and prolonged them in soft and softer tones, till the last faint repetition died away, and the hearers awoke as from a dream of bliss.

From Crofton Croker's delightful Fairy Legends.

INVOCATION OF THE FAIRY QUEEN.

From the Life of the celebrated William Lilly.

"Since I have related of the Queen of the Fairies, I shall acquaint you that it is not for every one, or every person, that these *angelical creatures* will appear unto, though they may say over the call over and over; or, indeed, is it given to very many persons to endure their glorious aspects. Even very many have failed just at that present time when they are ready to manifest themselves: even persons, otherwise of undaunted spirits and firm resolution, are herewith astonished, and tremble, *as it happened not many years since with us.* A very sober discreet person, of virtuous life and conversation, was beyond measure desirous to see something in this nature.

"Accordingly he went with a friend into my Hurst Wood. The Queen of Fairies was invoked: a gentle murmuring wind came first, after that, amongst the hedges, a smart whirlwind; by and by a strong blast of wind blew upon the face of the friend, *and the Queen appearing in a most illustrious glory,* 'No more, I beseech you,' quoth he, 'my heart fails—I am not able to endure longer.' Nor was he; his black curling hair rose up, and I believe a bullrush would have beat him to the ground.—He was soundly laughed at.

"There was, in the times of the late troubles, one Mortlack, who pretended unto speculations, had a *crystal,* a *call* of Queen Mab, one of the Queens of fairies: he deluded many thereby. At last, *I* was brought into his company: he was desired to make invocation. He did so: *nothing* appeared, or would. Three or four times, in my company, he was put upon to do the work, but could not: at last, he said he could do nothing as long as *I* was in presence. I, at last, showed him his error, but left him, as I found him, a pretended ignoramus."

I may seem, to some, to write *incredibilia;*—be it so: but knowing unto whom, and for whose sake only, I do write them, I am much comforted therewith, well knowing you are the most knowing in these curiosities of any now living in England."

Lilly's Life and Times.

> "Fairy King, attend and mark,
>   do hear the morning lark;
>   Then, my Queen, is silence sad,
>   Trip we after the night's shade!
>   We the globe can compass soon,
>   Swifter than the wandering moon."

Shakespeare.

THE TYLWYTH TEG.

In the mountains, near Brecknock, there is a small lake, to which tradition assigns the following tale:—

In ancient times, a door in a rock, near this lake, was found open upon a certain day every year: I think it was *May*-day. Those who had the curiosity and resolution to enter, were conducted by a secret passage, which terminated in a small island in the centre of the lake. Here the visitors were surprised with the prospect of *a most enchanting garden*, stored with the choicest fruits and flowers, and inhabited by the *Tylwyth Teg*, or fair family—a kind of fairies whose beauty could be equalled only by the courtesy and affability which they exhibited to those who pleased them. They gathered fruit and flowers for each of their guests, entertained them with the most exquisite music, disclosed to them many secrets of futurity, and invited them to stay as long as they should find their attention agreeable. But the island was *secret*, and nothing of its produce must be carried away.

The whole of this scene was invisible to those who stood without the margin of the lake. Only an indistinct mass was seen in the middle, and it was observed that no bird would fly over the water, and that a soft strain of music, at times, breathed with rapturous sweetness in the breeze of the morning.

It happened, upon one of these annual visits, that a sacrilegious wretch, when he was about to leave the garden, put a flower, with which he had been presented, into his pocket; but the theft boded him no good. As soon as he had touched unhallowed ground, the flower vanished, and he lost his senses.

Of this injury, the fair family took no notice at the time. They dismissed their guests with their accustomed courtesy, and the door was closed as usual. But their resentment ran high: for though, as the tale goes, the Tylwyth Teg and their garden undoubtedly occupy the spot to this day, though the birds still keep a respectful distance from the lake, and some broken strains of music are still heard at times, yet the door which led to the island was never re-opened; and, from the day of this sacrilegious act, the Cymry have been unfortunate.

Some time after this, an adventurous person attempted to draw off the water, in order to discover its contents, when a terrific form arose from the midst of the lake, commanding him to desist, or otherwise he would drown the country.

> "Come now a roundel, and a *fairy* song;
> Then for the third part of a minute, hence:
> Some war with rear-mice for their leathern wings.
> To make my small Elves coats; and some keep back
> The clamorous owl, that nightly hoots and wonders
> At our quaint spirits. Sing me now to sleep;
> Then to your offices, and let me rest."
>
> *A Midsummer Night's Dream.*

SINGULAR AUTHENTICATED APPEARANCE OF A FAIRY.

For nearly half a century, a weekly dinner party of literary men took place at the house of Joseph Johnson, a respectable and honest bookseller in St. Paul's Church Yard. Johnson was the publisher of Captain Steadman's Work on Surinam ; and as the Captain lived at Hammersmith, he usually came to town on the rooming of the weekly dinner by the Hammersmith stage.

As the coach was proceeding at its usual rumbling rate towards London, Captain Steadman was aroused by a very uncommon sound in the air; and on looking out of the coach door, his surprise was increased by the apparition of a little fellow, *about two feet high*, dressed in a full suit of regimentals, with a gold-laced cocked hat, and a gold-headed cane, striding along the footpath, "and raising such a devil of a sough," that the Captain's astonishment knew no bounds. He rubbed his eyes, looked, doubted, and looked again; but there, to visible certainty, was the little man striding away, swinging his arm, and "swishing his cane" in full force, going at the rate of nine miles an hour, and leaving the coach far behind him. Away he went at this prodigious pace until he came to a green lane which led to Holland House, up which he whisked with the greatest nimbleness. When the coach came opposite to the lane, the little man was nowhere to be seen.

This was related by Captain Steadman at dinner the very day it occurred, and he continued to affirm his belief in the appearance of the goblin, to the day of his death.

Crofton Croker, Esq., author of "The Fairy Legends," gives this relation on the authority of the late Mr. Fuseli, the celebrated artist, who was then present.

Part Four:
High Magic

The World of Spirits.

CELESTIAL MAGIC.
Part 1.

Copied verbatim from a beautifully illuminated magical Manuscript, formerly in the possession of the celebrated Mr. Richard Cosway, r. a.

Isagogical instructions how to know good Spirits from bad, when they appear.

Signs.

The Signs of appearance, both of GOOD ANGELS and EVIL SPIRITS are, and ought, carefully to be well observed by reason, they are foregoers of such appearances, and whereby are, known the differences thereof, which is a matter of material consequence, as hereafter shall be more plainly shewed forth.

Good Angels moved.

If *good Angels*, or elemental powers, or otherwise dignified spirits, of a benevolent or symbolizing nature with celestial powers, and allied to the welfare and preservation of mankind, are moved and *called forth to visible appearance* in a CHRISTALL STONE, or glass receiver, as one usual way or *customary* form is among the learned Magicians, then the sign of their appearance seemeth most like *a vail, or curtain, or some beautiful colour hanging in or about the glass or stone,* as a bright cloud, or other pretty kind of hierogliphical shew, both strange and very delightful to behold.

It is therefore to be remembered, that the Magical student ought to have for his purpose a *christal stone*, of a round globick form, very clear and transparent, or other of like diaphanity, or ball of clear and solid glass, with a little hole on the top, of like form, of any convenient bigness or diameter, according as can reasonably be obtained or made, and the same to be set in a form; and also the Glasses to be made with a stalk or shank fixed thereto, and so to be put into a socket with a foot or pedestal to stand upright; the stone being catted by the name of a shew stone, and the glass by the name of a glass receptacle; or in practice or action upon invocation or motion, made for spiritual appearance, there shall either be a wax candle on each side thereof, or a lamp behind the same, burning *during the time of action*, set on a table apart, fitted and furnished for this purpose. But if appearance hereof aforesaid be moved for by invocation, *out* of the shewstone or christal glass; or if yet, notwithstanding appearance happen to shew themselves out of them, yet *the sign of their appearance will be very delectable and pleasant*; various, amazing the senses to behold, as a shining brightness or sudden flashes, or such like similitudes, very splended in shew, or in the place where action is made, or appearance moved.

Invocation.

When *Invocation* is made to any of the CELESTIAL POWERS, or dignified elemental spirits of light, and appearance accordingly is presented, and visibly showeth itself, either in the shew stone or christal glass, or otherwise out of them; then view the same very well, and also take notice of its corporature physiognomy, or features of the face, vestures or garments, deportment, language, and whatsoever else may be worthy of note, by reason of making a fine distinction between the appearance of good Angels or Spirits, and others that are evil, and of knowing the same without being deceived; for although evil powers or spirits of darkness may be invocated, moved, or called forth to visible appearance, and consulted withal and made use of, in such concerns or upon such actions, wherein by nature and office they may be commanded to serve in all such matters as thereupon are dependent, and as the necessity thereof shall be suitable and requisite; but then actions with them are different both in time, and place, and order, and also the manner of operation, which by them are diversly and severally else where, hereafter inserted and shewed forth in its proper place; therefore do the magick philosophers give this caution, saying, beware that one action, operation, or secret in the art, be not mixed with another.

Action Apart.

But let celestial, elemental, and infernal actions, operations, and invocations, be used and kept apart, according to the method and manner as are in particular ascribed, and properly referred unto each of them. Now then, *observe*, that the appearance of celestial and benevolent angels, and other dignified elemental spirits of powers of light, are to be thus known or distinguished from those that are infernal, or evil powers, or spirits of darkness. *The good angels, or dignified powers of light as aforesaid, are in countenance very fair, beautiful, affable, smiling, amiable, and usually of a flaxen or golden coloured hair*; in behaviour or gesture, courteous and friendly; in speech, very gentle, mild, grave, and eloquent, using no vain, idle, or superfluous language in their discourse; in their corporature very handsome, straight, comely, well-favoured; and in every limb most exactly formall and well composed; their motions, sometimes to be plainly perceived, sometimes swift, and sometimes interceptable, both in their appearance, countenance, and departure; and their garments, of what fashion, form, and colour soever, are likewise very fair and beautiful, or Oriental; and if it be of many colours or strange fashion, yet they are also very splendid and rare, and lively to behold; and, in short, they are celestial and dignified in all their appearances, as they are in countenance and corporature, without the least deformity either in hairyness in the face or body, or a swarthy complexion, or any crookedness, or any ill shaped member of the body; so also their garments are clean and unsoiled, without spot or blemish, and untorn or ragged, or anywise dirty with any filthy soil, and always embrace the word *MERCY!*

Appearance.

When the appearance of any celestial angels, or angelic powers of light, or dignified elemental spirits, are visibly shewed forth, and by good testimony or diligent observation well known to be so, then, with due reverence given thereto, may be said as followeth:—

Receive thus.

WELCOME be the Light of the Highest, and welcome be the Messengers of Divine Grace and Mercy unto us, the true servants and worshippers of the same, your God, whose name be glorified, both now and for evermore.

Good or Evil.

And if the appearance be *good*, then it will stay; but if not, then *it will immediately vanish* away, at the rehearsing of the word MERCY. But if any evil power shall appear in the place of that which is good, or instead, and impudently withstand and opposing, then vanish it as in this case. Evil spirits are to be dealt with in manner and form as hereafter is inserted in its place, by reason those powers or spirits, who are by nature evil, and so are contrary to those by nature good, *may not be dealt with* as in those actions or operations; nor those powers of light, by nature good, to be moved in reference to that otherwise properly appertaineth, or belongeth by nature and office to the evil spirits or powers of darkness, more than as for their assistance, and so according for deliverance from any violent surprize, assaults, illusions, or other infernal temptations, or envious attempts.

Expected appearance.

Now then, if by those observations *the expected appearance* is understood, and found to be celestial and of good, or to be dignified elemental spirits, or powers of light, and so likewise of good, as accordingly was invocated, moved, or called forth to visible appearance by name, order, and office, to such appearance say thus:-

Demand.

Are you the same whom we have moved and called forth to visible appearance, here before us at this time, the name (N) or who else are ye, and *of what order, and what else is your name*, that we may so note of you, either as you may be ranked in order amongst the blessed angels, or otherwise known or called by any of mortal man: if you be of celestial or elemental verity, and so of charity, you cannot mislike or deny these our sayings.

Answer.

Then if it maketh any answer, as peradventure it may, then make reply according as the nature of discourse requireth. But if it make *no* answer, then repeat the words aforesaid, Are you the same, &c. &c.; then it will shew forth or tell its name, order, and office; the which when it is known by hearing, then it will speak or otherwise shew forth; say then as followeth:

Who it is.

If you be (N) as you say, *In the name of Jesus, say that all wicked angels are justly condemned; and yet by the mercy of God in the merits of Christ, mankind elect are to be saved.*

Whereunto it will then return a satisfactory answer, or else it will *depart* and be gone away; then if the appearance be good, as may be known by the answer and the reasons thereof, that was made or given to the aforesaid proposition, say as followeth:

Speak to the appearance.

O ye servants and messengers of Divine grace and mercy, and celestial angels, or angelic powers of light, or dignified elemental spirits, and mediums of benevolence to mankind, servants of God, you both now at this time, and always are and shall be unto truly and sincerely welcome, humbly desiring you to be friendly unto us, and to do for us in whatsoever it shall please God to give by your order and office unto you, for the better knowledge of mankind living on earth, and to make us partakers of true science and sapience, in the undefiled and secret wisdom of the Creator.

Answer made.

And if any answer shall be made hereunto, or any discourse from hence should arise or proceed hereupon, then both wisdom and reason must be the principle conduct in the management thereof; but if there be silence, and no discourse arise from thence, then begin to make humble request for answer to such desires and proposalls, as in a certain writing is contained, which ought to be in readiness with you, and then will the effects of all things be undoubtedly, and with good success be determined.

Intrusion.

The *sign of intrusion, or appearance of evil,* when action or invocation is otherwise made for moving or calling forth celestial angels or intelligences, or their dignified powers, or elemental spirits of light, are not apparent or visible, to be any ways discernible than your shapes, forms, gestures, or other little principals in appearance, quite contrary in behaviour, language, cloathing, or vestures, to those above related, and to be observed of the good, &c.; neither are they herein otherwise to judge of them than as intruders, tempters, and illuders, on purpose, if possible, to deceive and also to destroy the perseverance and hopes of obtaining any benefit, by celestial and good mediums, by reason they are degraded and deprived of power to send or shew forth any foregoing sign of their appearance, in those such superior actions, invocations, or moving only celestial or dignified elemental powers, and to visible appearance, herein no ways to have farther notice of them, to be vanquished or sent away as before has been said. Observe then the corporative forms and shapes of evil powers, or spirits of darkness, in their appearances, by forcible intrusions of the kind *are easily discovered from the good powers* and spirits of light, as now shall be declared, as followeth:

Of Evil Powers.

EVIL POWERS, or *spirits of darkness, are ugly, ill favoured, and beastly in shape* and appearance; wherein observe, if they do appear in upright or human stature, then either body, face, or covering, are quite contrary to the other, before specified of good; for although an evil or infernal spirit may appear in the likeness of an angel of light, especially in the time and place when good angels or spirits of light are moved, invoked, or called forth, forming themselves very nearly, so even almost imperceptibly to sight and appearance, except ingeniously discovered by any curious observation, and clearly may be discerned quickly by their ragedness, uncleanness of their garments, and difference of their countenance in beauty, features, and other decent composures of the body, language, and behaviour, and the corporal difference of the limbs, or bestial similitudes, who in times do usually and suddenly make their appearance, and as readily shew forth motions, gestures, and speakings unusually blasphemous, ridiculous or different language, altogether dissonant and contrary both in manner and matter, to that of the celestial angels, which also *may be soon discovered* by the diligence of a sober and curious speculator, which notable intrusions they make on this action, properly to destroy the reason, hope, and judgement of the invocation, and by great errors, and other ignorant mistakes, not only to deceive and confound the more solid and genuine knowledge, and capacitys of man labouring therein, but also to distract the senses, and thereby lead the understanding into a meander, and therein to weary and tire us with verity of doubt and desperation, not knowing how to unravel the Gordian knot, or to be satisfied or delivered from the hopeless pilgrimage, but by the help of Icarian wings; from hence it may be understood, that *evil spirits and powers of darkness, sooner appear as impudent intruders in time of good action,* and in place where invocation is made for the moving and calling forth of any good angels, or dignified elemental spirits or powers of light, to visible appearance, than at any other time and place, which as unto themselves they shall be indifferently by order, office, and name: invocated, moved, and called forth to visible appearance, for such their assistance, as by nature and office, wherein they are accordingly serviceable and suitable to the occasion, wherein they are commanded. Therefore, in such actions are to be only referred unto those of evil powers or spirits of darkness, those actions we say are differently set apart, and to be distinguished both in time, place, order, and method, and other aforesaid, &c. so they may be moved and called forth, commanded and constrained, and according so dealt withall, and used as the present action shall require, and the discretion of the invocant shall find agreeable to the nature and office; so then it is observable, that the evil spirits may be invocated and dealt withall, differently, or apart by themselves, according as aforesaid; but not in such place, or in such time, as when action or motion is made for the appearance of any celestial spirit of light, and other elemental powers or different spirits by nature good as well as evil, and other wandering spirits, none resident in orders certain of like nature, &c. may be constrained and commanded by invocation properly thereto referred, with several appurtenant rules and observations inserted therein, as ample and at large shewed forth; but celestial angels and other elemental powers, by nature and office benevolent or good, may not be commanded nor constrained by any invocant; they are only to be moved and called forth by humble entreaties, thereby acquiring favour and friendship.

When wicked Intruders come.

KNOW THEN, if at any time and place, where action or motion is made, and humbly entreated, earnestly besought, for the appearance of any celestial power, &c., and wicked intruders shall impudently thrust themselves in place, and would enforce credulity into the speculator, and that it shall be plainly discovered, *then shall the magician dismiss, discharge, send away, and banish them from hence,* after the manner hereafter shewn, in the second Part of this magical formula.

The World of Spirits.

CELESTIAL MAGIC.

PART 2.

Copied verbatim from a beautifully illuminated magical Manuscript, formerly in in the possession of the celebrated Mr. Richard Cosway, r. a.

To banish the Evil Spirits

SAY THIS ORATION.

The vengeance of God is a two-edged sword, cutting rebellious and wicked spirits of darkness, and all other usurping powers, in pieces; the hand of God is like a strong oak, which, when it falleth, breaketh in pieces many shrubs; the light of his eyes expelleth darkness, and the sweetness of his mouth keepeth from corruption. Blessed are all those to whom he sheweth mercy, and reserveth from temptation, and illusion of wicked intruders, defending them by his mighty power, under the covert of divine grace; not suffering his humble servants to be overcome or overthrown by any infernal assaults. Now therefore, because you have come hither, and entered without license, seeking to entrap and ensnare us, and secretly conspired by these your subtleties, to deceive and destroy us and our hopes, In the true meaning of these our sober, Innocent, honourable, and celestial actions, we do, in the great mighty name, and by the power of the most high God, triumph imperially over you; and by the virtue, force, and efficacy whereof, be you and your powers banished, overthrown, and utterly defeated; and behold, by virtue of that celestial power, by divine grace given unto us, and wherewith we are potently dignified; and as heirs of God's promise, through faith containing inherent with us, we do hereby wholly deface and overthrow you, and ye are totally vanquished: therefore we say depart, and immediately begone from hence in peace, without noise, turbulence, injury, harm, violence, or other damage to us, or this place, or any other place or person whatsoever; and as you are of darkness, and the places of darkness, and have without any charge or permission enviously intruded, seeking thereby to ensare, deceive, or overwhelm us, the divine Judgement and vengeance of the most high God, for your wicked and malicious conspiracy and intrusion, be your deserved reward; and as it was delivered to you, so take it with you, that the malice which you have shewn us may heap your own destruction; be ye therefore dismissed, and immediately we say depart hence unto your orders, and there to continue in the bonds of confinement during the divine pleasure of the Highest.

If they are yet obstinate and impudent, and will not depart, but rather will withstand the commands of the Magician, let him say as followeth.

To Banish.

Do you thus impudently withstand, and obstinately refuse, to depart from our presence, and from the place, and perniciously attempt yet farther against us: in the name of Jesus, we say, depart ye wicked seducers, and be ye immediately gone away from hence; and so be it unto you, according to the word of God, which judgeth righteously, from evil unto worse, from worse unto confusion, from confusion unto desperation, from desperation unto damnnation, from damnation unto eternal death. Depart therefore, we say, unto the last cry, and remain with the

Prince of Darkness, in punishment justly due, as a fit reward unto your wicked, malicious deservings, and the God of mercy graciously deliver us from you.—**Jehovah Tetragrammaton Sadai**

And if no celestial angel, or other dignified spirit of light, appear in place to vanquish and send away, or seal up any wicked or infernal spirit or spirits of darkness, when appearance is presented, a notorious intruder in the time and place, when celestial or elementall actions, with dignified powers of light, are in agitation and operation.

Rules to be observed.

Then let the discreet Magician, with prudent passion, have diligent regard to himself, and consult the foregoing rules, according to respective and serious observations; who, by the office of himself, will undoubtly, not only contract the sight and friendship of the celestial angels, and dignified, elemental, and other benevolent spirits of light, to his relief and comfort, and to vanquish and overcome all evil spirits and powers of darkness: but also he shall have power to command, call forth, and constrain all sublunary spirits and powers, of all natures, orders, and offices, both good and evil, light and darkness, or otherwise relating thereunto, and bring them to such obedience, as according to their severall and respective natures and offices, they may be so commanded and constrained to serve and obey.

A second Introduction.

When invocation, and replication thereunto, is amply made, according to time, method, and order, and the celestial angel or intelligence thereby moved, doth appear, or any other angel or intelligence of the same hierarchy, then mark and observe well the manner, shape and form, corporature, gesture, vestments, and foregoing sign thereof, and if in all symbolical likelyhood and probable symptoms, the apparition seemeth to be no less otherwise conjected, that which is from hence to be expected, although that very intelligence that was moved and called forth by name, doth not appear, by reason it is of the superior order of the hierarchy, who are not always sent, are usually go forth, neither are moved to visible appearance, but of especial grace and divine pleasure, more immediately unto choice and peculiar vessels of honour accordingly appointed immediately by the Holy Ghost, to fulfill the command of the Highest, but yet some or other or more of the celestial powers of the same order as aforesaid, more inferior in degree, may be moved hereby to descend and appear, at the earnest request of the Magician, and perform whatsoever shall be requested, according to its nature and office.

Good or Bad.

It cannot be unknown to any discreet Magician, that whensoever any good angel or celestial intelligence is moved, or called forth to visible appearance, but also that evil spirits, and infernal powers of darkness, are immediately ready to encroach and appear in the place of good angels; therefore, it behoveth to be very careful, and greatly observing thereof, both the method and manner how to know rightly and distinguish the appearance, and how to vanquish and banish evil spirits when they intrude, and enter into place and presence, to deceive and overwhelm us, we have sufficiently and at large inserted and shewed forth in our Isogogicall Preface, before annexed thereunto; therefore, we shall in this place only shew forth a method of our greeting the apparition of any celestial angel, or dignified power of light; and when, by all the prescript rules given, that apparition is truly known to be celestial, and of good, then humbly receive it with ample benevolence, saying as followeth.

To receive a good appearance.

Welcome be the light of the Highest, and welcome be the messengers of Divine Grace and Mercy unto us the true servants and worshippers of the same your God, whose name be glorified, both now and for evermore.

When known to be good.

If the appearance is perfectly known and understood, and by all signs and tokens perfectly known to be celestial or angelical powers of light, then with due reverence, say as followeth.

Receiving good angels.

O thou servants and messengers of divine grace and mercy, and celestial angels or intelligence, powers of light, or dignified elemental spirits and mediums of benevolence to mankind, servants of God, you, both now at this time, and always are, and shall be unto us, truly and sincerely welcome. Humbly desiring you also to be friendly, and to do for us in whatsoever it shall please God to give by your order and office unto you, for the better knowledge and benefit of mankind living here upon earth, and make us partakers of true science, In the undefiled and sincere sacred wisdom of your Creator.

Answer.

And if any answer shall be made thereunto, or any discourse from hence should arise or proceed thereupon, then both wisdom and reason must be the principal conduct of the management thereof; but if there be silence, that no discourse ariseth from hence, then begin to make humble request for answer to your desires and proposals; then will the effects of all things, undoubtedly, and with good success, be determined.

fear or mistrust.

But if there should any fear, doubt, or misprission, or just cause or jealousy be had or made of any expected apparition, or any angel or intelligence of celestial orders, or other elemental power of light, celestially dignified, or otherwise; if at any time there should appear a spirit which you do not think is of good, nor of the order you moved for, or have any mistrust of it, the which you may easily perceive by form, and also by its answering you in your question, and then you may say as followeth.

To know who it is.

In the name of Jesus, who art thou? then, perhaps, it will say, I am the servant of God; then you may say, art thou come from God? art thou sent from him with good tidings or messuage? then, perhaps, it will say to you, or some such like words, what I am, he knoweth of whom I bear witness! Then you may ask its name, saying then, what is your name, either as it is notified among the blessed angels, or called by any mortal man? if you be of verity, and so of charity, you cannot dislike my speeches. Then it will tell you its name, or say nothing at all: but if it doth tell you its name, then you may say to it, if you be in the name of Jesus, say that all wicked angels are justly condemned, and that by the mercies of God in the merits of Christ, mankind elect is to be saved! Then it will give you a sufficient answer to satisfy you, or else it will be gone from you; and then, if it be of good, and hath answered your request, then, perhaps, it will say, thus much thou hast required; then you may say, I did so, for so is his judgement and justice against the impenitent, and his mercy to his elect, testify truth.

Then you may ask your desire.

We thought good to instance thus much, for better information and instruction, although a full narrative hereof is amply and at large shewed forth, in the foregoing Isogogicall Preface, both as to knowledge, and receiving of good angels, or celestial intelligences, or other elemental spirits or powers of light, angellically or celestially dignified; and for the knowledge, vanquishing, and driving away of all evil spirits and infernal powers of darkness, whensoever any such shall forcibly intrude, or make entrance or appearance, instead of celestial and good angels, or other dignified elemental powers of light, in the time and place of these actions, purposely to deceive, confound, and, if possible, destroy the hopes, and expectations, and benefits of the philosophers, in their elaborate industry, and care, and earnest addresses unto the celestial angels and blessed intelligence, or dignified elemental powers, or other spiritual mediums or messengers of divine grace, for the true knowledge and finding out the use of all physical and metaphysical arcanums, or secrets in a superior profound mistery, which can not otherwise be known or found out, but by the divine light and conduct of angellical ministry, and other spiritual revelation and instruction by such mediums and benevolence to mankind; and through the divine grace, mercy, and goodness of the Highest, as are by nature, order, and office, thereunto pre-ordinately decreed and appointed. But as touching the insisting any farther of this matter, we think it needless; since it is more fully treated in the foregoing preface, which we advise to be well understood, by a due and serious consideration, before any progress or unadvisedly proceedings are made herein. Observe, also, whereas we have severally and particularly mentioned celestial angels, or blessed intelligences, and other dignified spirits of light, who are by nature and office good, and also friendly unto mankind, and generally inserts them together with material distinction; yet let grave and sober Magicians take notice what consideration be first had, of what angel or intelligence, of what spirits, and of what orders, office, he would move or call forth; and so in particular to make mention thereof according, and not otherwise, whereunto every thing ought by nature, degree, order, and office, properly to be referred.

Here endeth the Isogogicall Preface, or Second Introduction.

The nine great celestial Keys, or angelicall Invocations.

Moving or calling forth to visible appearance the governing angels or blessed intelligences, and all other of the celestial ministring angels and mediums spiritual of divine light;

grace, and virtue, located, residing, and bearing rule in the seven orbs, heavens, mansions, or spheres, as they are primarily, attributed and properly referred to in the seven Planets, the starry firmament, and first mover, who therein acccording to every and each of their respective hierarchies, orders, and offices, whereunto they distinctly appertain, do serve and obey the commands of the most high God, and both immediately and mediately, as messengers and servants spiritual of divine grace and light, and mercy, fulfilling his omnipotent decrees, determinations, and appointments, as dispensable and disposed of at his omniscience, will, and pleasure, and who are frequently conversant and familiar with such holy, pious, and devout—living on earth, whensoever they are by them called forth to visible appearance, as either may or fitly shall be qualified therefore, or otherwise endowed with celestial gifts, blessings, and confirmations, by angelical mystery or divine grace, more superior.

A prayer to be said before the moving, or calling forth any of the celestial intelligences to visible appearance, by the following keys or provocations.

O almighty, immortal, immense, incomprehensible, and most high God, the only creator of heaven and earth, who by thy word alone hast in thy omniscience, among the rest of the marvellous and wonderful works, placed and appointed many hierarchies of sacred celestial angels, from this mighty and unspeakable throne unto the fiery region, as ministering spirits of severall names, natures, degrees, order, and offices, residing in those eleven orbs, or spheres, placed one above the other, and the proper mansions of those blessed angels or mediums, or superior messengers, both mediate and immediate of divine grace, light, and mercy, and amongst the sons of men, from the beginning of time, called sacred, celestial intelligences, from the orb, region, or element of, from the superior to the inferior, in the severall and respective orbicular mansions, orders, and offices, do serve before thee, to obey thy commandments and most high commands, as in thy divine will and pleasure, in the unity of the blessed Trinity, is decreed and appointed; and also by thy most gracious and merciful permission to minister unto, and to illuminate the understanding of thy servants, the sons of men; and by their frequent appearance, verbal converse, friendly community, angelicall archidoctions, and other spiritual justincts, continually from time to time, and at all times, directing, instructing, and inspiring them in all true science and sapience, and also to fulfil thy divine will and good pleasure therein, to all such of thy humble and true servants, whom thou art graciously pleased to shew forth thy bountiful and paternal mercies, we, thy most sinful and undutiful servants the least of thy blessings; yet with an assured confidence of thy heavenly benignities, do, in thy holy fear, humbly prostrate ourselves before thy almighty presence, at the sacred feet of thy fatherly goodness and clemency, in all contrition of heart and earnestness of spirit, humble beseeching thy omnipotent majesty to have mercy, pity, and compassion upon us, and to pardon all our sins and offences that we have committed against thee; and in thy infinite goodness, graciously to dignify us with celestial dignity, by the power of thy holy spirit, and grant that these thy glorious ministring angels, or blessed intelligences, who are said to govern and reside in the nine orbs, orders, and hierarchies, as they are severally and respectively therein placed and set over, that is to say, **Methratton** in the ninth moveable heaven, in the order of seraphins, **Razael** in the highest orb, or starry firmament, in the order of cherubims; **Cassile** or **Zaphkiel**, and **Tophiel** in the seventh orb or heaven of Saturn, in the order of thrones; **Sachiel** or **Zadkiel** in the sixth orb, or heaven of Jupiter, in the order of dominations; **Samael** in the fifth orb or heaven of Mars, in the order of potentates; **Michael** and **Uriel** in the the fourth orb of heaven, of Sol, in the order of virtues; **Anael** in the third orb, or heaven of Venus, in the order of principalities; **Raphael** in the second orb, or heaven of Mercury, in the order of archangels; **Gabriel** in the first orb or heaven of Luna, in the order of angels; messengers of divine grace, from the superior to the inferior, residing and bearing office in each respective orb of heaven, and hierarchies, severally and distinctly, in general and particular, and also all others, thy benevolent messengers, spirits of light, residing in the orbicular spheres, angels, orders, mansions, divisions, and the heavens, by thy divine goodness and permission, and at our humble request, invitations, and invocations may descend and appear to us, in this **christall Stone or glass**, which we shall call receptacles, as being all convenient for the receiving of all angellical and spiritual presence in their appearance, and so for that purpose set here before us, for that they which we beseech thee Lord to bless and to dignify, first with thy omnipotent confirmation, and secondly, by the influence of the angelical confirmations, by them conveyed therefore, and conjoined thereunto; and also by their splendid presence, and that in and through the same, they may transmit their luminous rays, or true and real presence, in appearance, to the sight of our eyes, and their voices to our ears, that we may plainly and visibly see them, and audibly hear them speak unto us, or otherwise to appear out of them, and besides them visibly to be seen and heard of us, as shall please thy divine will, and shall best and most benefit our benefit and comfort, and also befitting our conveniency in these actions, inquisitions, matters of things that we thus humbly beseech thee to give and grant unto us, and all things else that shall be necessary for us, which great benefits thou hast been pleased mercifully heretofore, to omit and give our ancestors and forefathers, and also, lately to such of thy servants as we have humbly, faithfully, unfeignedly, and obediently besought thee for true wisdom, by divine and angelical inspiration and instruction, which they have fully enjoyed by the ministry of thy sacred angels.

The first Key.

Moving or calling forth to visible appearance the celestial hierarchies of angels, of the order of seraphins, whose principal governing angel or blessed intelligence, bearing rule, is Mithratton, and residing in the ninth orb, mansion, or sphere, called the primum mobile of the first moveable heaven.

The Prayer, or Invocation.

O you glorious, great, sacred, and celestial angel, or blessed intelligence, who art called **Mithratton**, and all other, the celestial angels, servants of the most high, omnipotent, incomprehensible, immense, eternal God of hosts, the only creator of heaven and earth, and of all things whatsoever, both celestial, elemental, animal, vegetable, mineral, and reptile, or insects that is contained therein, or comprehended, and serving as ministering angels, present always before at his most high, superior, and divine commands and appointments, in the order or hierarchies of angels called **Seraphims**, and residing in the ninth heaven, and bearing office, rule, and power, in the mansion, orb, or Sphere, called the first mover; we, the servants also of the Highest, reverently here present in his holy fear, do call upon, humbly request, earnestly entreat, and move you to visible appearance, in, by, and through this most excellent, ineffable, great, mighty, signal, sacred, and divine name of the most high God, **Eheia**. and his numerical attribute, **Kether**, who sitteth in the most imperial and highest heaven, before whom all the hosts and choir of celestial angels incessantly sing, **O-amp-la-man-halleluja**. And by the Seal of your creation, being the mark of character of holiness unto you, and by the occult mystery, secret virtue, and efficacy and influence thereof, dignifying and conforming you in orders, offices, name, nature, corporality, with divine, celestial, angellical, immortal, eternal, and sublime excellency, glory, power, purity and perfection, good and love, first unto the service of the most high God, and his divine laws and commands, and next unto the charge, care, conduct, council, comfort, benefit, and assistance of his servants, the sons of men, living on earth, to inspire, instruct, and give them unto the knowledge and way of truth, and all true physical and metaphysical science, either immediately from the Holy Ghost, unto more choice vessels of honour, or mediately by divine grace and permission from your self or selves, unto the sons of men, servants of God dwelling on earth, whensoever you shall be of them invocated and called forth, and thereby moved to descend and appear unto them, and by all aforesaid, and by the great signal virtue, power, dignity, excellency, and efficacy thereof, both immediately, primary, and mediately, secondary, by respective mediums of divine light, grace, and mercy, as ordinately dependent, and so thereby flowing, and accordingly diffusing by several emanations proper, a simbolizing power and virtue, from the superior to the inferior, we do humbly beseech, earnestly request, and incessantly intreat you, O you magnificent, benevolent, and sacred angel, or blessed intelligence, **Methratton**, who, said to be the principal celestial angel, or blessed Intelligence, governing the ninth heaven, mansion, orb, or sphere, called the first mover, together with all others, the benevolent, sacred, and celestial angels or intelligence, ministers of truth, or true science and sapience, both celestial and terrestrial messengers spiritual of light, and mediums of divine grace, located, bearing rule, and residing in the order, or hierarchy, and office, called **Seraphins**, in the ninth heaven, orb, or sphere, of the first mover, from the superior to the inferior, in general and particular, jointly and severally, every, each one, by office and degree respectively, and to gird up and gather yourselves together, and some one or more of you, as it shall please God, by divine permission, to move and descend from your celestial mansion, or place of residence, in this Christal Stone, or Glass Receiver, and therein to appear visibly unto us; and we do also entreat you would be favourably pleased, in and through the same, to transmit your true angellical and real presence, plainly unto the sight of eyes, and your voice to our ears, that we may visibly see you, and audibly hear you speak unto us, or otherwise to appear out of the same, as it shall please God, and you his servants of divine grace, and messengers of mercy, as seemeth most meet, proper, pertinent, or best befitting this action, appearance, occasion, or matter, and the shew plainly and visibly unto us, a foregoing sign, or test of your appearance; and we also yet farther humbly request, earnestly entreat, and beseech, and undeniably move you, O you benevolent and glorious angel, and blessed Intelligence, **Methratton**—together with all others, the sacred celestial angels, or intelligences, from the superior to the inferior in power and office, residing in the ninth orb, or sphere, called the first moveable heaven, and serving the divine decrees, commands, and appointments of the highest, in the office and order of Seraphims, in, through, and by this divine signal majesty, and powerful name of your God, **Eheia**, and his attribute, **Kether**, and the great efficacy, virtue, excellent power, prevalency, and superiority thereof to gather together every, each one jointly, and by itself, respectively and severalty to move and descend from your celestial mansion, or place of residence, apparently visible to our eyes in this **Christal Stone, or Glass Receiver**, standing here before us, as being sent for your purpose, or otherwise out of the same, as it shall please God; and by you, his servants of Divine Grace, Light, and Mercy, seemeth best befitting this action; and also be friendly unto us, and by your angelical benevolence and celestial Illumination, and favourable assistance, familiar Society, mutual correspondency, verbal converse, continual community, and sacred instructions, both now, at this present time, and at all other times to inform and more rightly direct our more weak, depraved, stupid, and ignorant intellect, judgements, and understandings; and to conduct us by your angelical instincts and archidoctions, into the luminous pathway of truth, leading and giving entrance into ports, cities, and palaces of wisdom, and true sapience; and to make us partakers of undefiled knowledge, without whose angelical guide, spiritual conduct, blessed assistance, and benevolent advertisement, it is very difficult, if not impossible for us, or any mortal on Earth, to find, or obtain, or to be esteemed worthy of entrance into your testimony: wherefore we humbly entreat and move you, O you great, sacred, and celestial ministring angel or intelligence **Mithratton**, and all other the president and inferiour angels and servants of the most High God, presiding and officiating in the ninth Heaven, mansion, orb, or sphere of the first mover, in the order of hierarchy of angels called **Seraphims**, who all obediently serve and readily fulfil his omnipotent decrees and commandments in his divine dispensations, and appointments according to your general and respective offices, in, by, and through his ineffable, imperial, great, signal, and divine name, **Eheia**, and his numeral attribute **Kether**, and by power, virtue, and efficacy thereof, we the servants of the same your God, and by the strength and force of our hope and faith in him for Divine assistance, grace, and mercy therein, do earnestly request, powerfully invocate, and confidently move you, and call you forth to visible appearance here before us in this **Christal Stone, or Glass Receiver**, or otherwise out, as it shall please God, and is given unto you so to do, and likewise to shew visibly unto us a foregoing sign of your appearance; O you servants of mercy, **Methratton**, and all other the celestial ministring angels, messengers, and mediums of Divine grace and light from the superior power and permission in the name of the Highest, descend and appear, and visibly shew yourselves jointly, and severally, and respectively, unto us in this **Christal Stone, or Glass Receiver**, standing here before us; or otherwise out of the same, as it shall please God to appoint and permit you; and to shew us a proceeding sign thereof, and by your immediate angelical inspiration, and information, and chief teaching, to instruct, help, and aid, and assist us both now, at this time present, and also at all other times, and places, whensoever and wheresoever we shall invocate, move, or call you forth to visible appearance, and to our assistance in whatsoever truth, subject, matter, or thing appertaining thereunto in all wisdom and true sapience, both celestial and terrestrial, and that shall be necessary for us;

and also as any other emergent occasion shall properly and duly require, to the advancement and setting forth the glory of God, and the improvement of our welfare, comfort, and benefit of our worldly and temporal estate and condition, while yet we live; and likewise in all such matters or things whatsoever else you shall be necessary for us to know and to enjoy, even beyond what we are able to ask or think, which the Almighty Giver of all good gifts shall, in his bountiful and paternal mercy be graciously pleased hereby to give you, and reveal, and shew forth unto us, or otherwise to bestow upon us, O you great angel, or blessed intelligence, **Methratton, and all other you celestial angels of the order of Seraphims, Mediums of Divine grace and mercy, Ministers of true light and understanding, and servants of the Most High God**, particularly recited and respectively spoken of, invocated, moved, and called forth to visible appearance aforesaid, **Descend we say**, and by the power of superior commission from one or more of you appear visibly here before us as for the servants of the Most High God, whereunto we move you all, jointly and severally in your power and presence, whose works shall be a song of honour, and the praise of your God in your Creator. **Amen**.

Let the foregoing Invocation he devoutly and seriously read; then make a pause for about 9 minutes of time, or a little more than half a quarter of an hour; and if nothing appear neither within the Christal stone, or otherwise out of the same to visible appearance, then read with good devotion the following replication, 4 or 5 times observing the like time aforesaid betwixt each replication.

Replication.

O ye glorious angel or blessed intelligence, who by name is called **Methratton**, and all other ye sacred celestial angels of the order of **Seraphims**, residing or located by mansion, orb, or sphere of heaven, called the **Primum Mobile, or the first moveable heaven**, particularly recited, mentioned, moved, and called forth to visible appearance, as in the foregoing invocation; and hath been of us lately, and more at large, rehearsed, humbly solicited, and earnestly requested by the virtue, power, force, and efficacy whereof, and of all the royal words and sentences therein contained; and also by the mighty, great, powerful, and excellent name of the Most High God, **Eheia**, and his numerall attribute **Kether**; or otherwise by the truest and most especial name of your God, we, the servants of the Highest, reverently, here present, in his holy fear, attending his divine grace, mercy, and good pleasure, paternally unto us herein, do, by the strength and power of our faith, hope, and confidence of, and in our God, and our confirmation in his holy spirits, dignifying us with superior power and perfection, humbly entreat, and earnestly request, and powerfully move you, O you great angels or blessed intelligence, from the superior to the inferior, in general, and particular, every, each one, for and by itself, respectively by degree, nature, and office, residing in the mansion or 9th orb of the first moveable Heaven, and serving the commands of the Highest in the order and hierarchy of angels called **Seraphims; move, therefore, O you great and glorious angel**, **Methratton**, or some one or more of you, O ye sacred celestial angels of the order of **Seraphims**, by degree, nature, and office; and by the power, virtue, and efficacy of all aforesaid, descend and appear visibly unto us, In this **Christal Stone, or Glass Receiver**: or otherwise out of the same here before us, as it shall please the Most High God, and also you, **his celestial Messengers of Divine grace and mercy**, and to shew forth plainly unto us, some remarkable sign or token foregoing your **coming and appearance**; and to be friendly unto us, and to do for us as for the servants of the Highest, whereunto in his name **we do again earnestly request and move you both in power and presence** whose friendship unto us herein shall be a song of honour, and the praise of your God in your Creation. **Amen**.

The manuscript here ends with the example of "the first key:" but this will no doubt, leave *Celestial Magic* sufficiently exemplified for the amusement of my readers.

THE BONDS OF SPIRITS, THEIR ADJURATIONS, &c.

THE bonds by which spirits are *bound*, besought, or cast out, are *three:** some of them are taken from the *elemental* world, as when the Theurgist would adjure a spirit by any inferior and natural thing of affinity with or adverse to them, inasmuch as we would call up, or cast them out, as by fumigations of *flowers*, *herbs*, *animals*, *snow*, *ice*, or by *fire*, and such like; and these also are often mixed with divine praises, and blessings, and consecrations, as appears in the Song of the Three Children, and in the psalm *"Magnificat,"* and in others of the same signification. This bond works upon the spirits by an apprehensive virtue, under the account of love or hatred, inasmuch as the spirits are present with, or favour, or abhor, any thing that is natural, or against nature, as these things themselves love or hate one another.

The *second* bond is taken from the *celestial* world, viz. when they are adjured by their *heaven*, by the *stars*, their *motions*, *rays*, *light*, *beauty*, *clearness*, *influence*, and *wonders*, and such like. And this bond works upon spirits, by way of admonition and example. It hath also some command, especially upon the ministering spirits, and those who are of the lowest orders.

The *third* bond is from the *intellectual* and *divine* world, which is perfected by religion; that is to say, when they are adjured by the *sacraments*, *miracles*, *divine names*, *sacred seals*, and other mysteries. Wherefore, this *bond* is the highest of all, and the strongest, working upon the spirits by command and power; but this is to be observed, that, as after the *universal* Providence, there is a *particular* one, and after the *universal* soul, *particular* souls; so, in the first place, we *invocate* by the *superior* bonds, and by the names and powers which rule the things; then by the *inferior*, and the things themselves. Thus, also, by these *bonds* and *adjurations*, not only *spirits*, but also all creatures, are bound; as *tempests*, *burnings*, *floods*, *plagues*, *diseases*, force of arms, and every animal, by assuming them, either by *adjuration*, or *deprecation*, or *benediction*, as in

---

* Barrett's Magus, page 67.

the charming of serpents, &c. besides the natural and celestial, by rehearsing out of the mysteries of religion, the cure of the serpent in terrestrial paradise, the lifting up of the serpent in the wilderness; and, likewise, by assuming that verse of the 91st Psalm, *"Thou shalt walk upon the asp and the basilisk, and shalt tread upon the lion and the dragon."*

Method of Raising and Invocating Spirits.

THE various manuscripts relative to the fact of spiritual intercourse which we have consulted for the purpose of introducing the chief formula used upon this occasion all agree in declaring, that those who would invocate spirits must, for some days previously, prepare themselves to these high and mysterious ceremonies by living, in a manner, secluded from the rest of the world, being religiously disposed, and for *three* days at least must live free from sensual gratifications.

The *place** chosen must be secluded, solitary, and isolated from the resort of men, where no businesses carried on, where no unhallowed eye must enter, and where the pryings of curiosity remain ungratified. For this reason, dilapidated buildings, free from the tread of human footsteps;† or in the midst of forests, lonely caves, or rocks by the sea-shore; or amidst the ruins of ancient buildings, where the owl and the night raven alone are tenants, and where the general appearances indicate desolation and darkness: these are the

---

* Some Theurgists affirm that the place used for invocation must be either on a ground-floor or in some place where no rooms that are inhabited may be on the same level; and thus a forest or retired grotto has been frequently used.

† The late learned Mr. R. Cosway, R.A. hired a room, which he kept always consecrated for the purpose of raising spirits. On the floor he had the magic circle drawn, and it was never entered by any idle or curious intruder. This we have been assured by a gentleman, who was an intimate friend of Mr. Cosway, was actually the case.

most proper places that can be chosen for the provoking of spirits to appear; it being remembered that all and every order of these unearthly agents are averse to visible appearance, and, when they do appear, make use of the most terrific forms to affrighten the student, and swerve him from his purpose: all which, as well as the loudest thunders and most furious lightnings, the Invocator must accustom himself to see and hear without the least appearance of agitation; for, should his fears alarm and overpower him, the evil spirits would suddenly obtain the mastery, and, if they succeeded in getting him out of the sacred limits of the *magic circle*, his chief fortress and safeguard, his instant destruction would be sure to follow; instances of which are not wanting on record: so that the magic operator must be a man of firm and undaunted courage, of quick foresight, and accustomed to hideous objects. He must also have two associates with him, who must be well acquainted with the magic rites, and particularly in dismissing the spirits; for, it must also be known, that it is far more easy to *raise* than to *dismiss* or lay a spirit, through the unaccountable antipathy which these invisible agents have towards the human race: and when once the settled laws of nature are broken through by invoking these supernatural beings, the Invocator is certainly in some considerable danger, having subjected himself to other powers, who will not be backward in using every advantage they may casually obtain.

The *place* being chosen, secure and free from interruption, the Invocator or Theurgist must choose the proper *day* and *hour* for working, according to the nature, order, and office of the *spirit* he would invoke, not forgetting that in the *increase* of the moon he must raise *good*, and in the decrease of the moon, *evil* spirits. He must also be provided with the *seals* of the *earth*, the *seals* of the *spirit*, and the sacred *lamen* or *pentacle*, the magic sword, vestment, and other instruments for the performance of his purpose, the whole of which must be made and completed in the hour of 𝔐𝔢𝔯𝔠𝔲𝔯𝔶.

The *day* and *hour* being chosen, the Theurgist must also provide himself with the proper *perfume* agreeable to the spirit, and must exorcise or consecrate the place he would invocate in, after the accustomed manner (which, however, we shall not here describe, as it would be dangerous so to do, and would put too much power in the hands of evil-minded men, on account of the simple and facile means, yet wonderful power, which these consecrations contribute, when rightly performed). He must then proceed to draw his *circle*, nine feet in diameter; within the outer circle, two concentric circles of a hand's breadth must be made, and the four quarters of the world marked therein by a correct compass. In the midst, for divine protection, must be described the great and powerful names of God, **Jehovah**, **Tetragrammaton**, **Adonai**, **Sadai**, and appropriate inscriptions; taking care that the circles* be correctly formed, and duly joined and fortified with sacred crosses, within and without; the chalk or coal being first properly consecrated. The lights used upon the occasion must be of wax, and each candlestick inclosed in a magic pentacle. The *sword* must be of pure steel, made expressly for the occasion; and, indeed, none of the instruments used must be ever devoted to any other purpose. All things being ready, he must, with his associates, enter the circle in the proper planetary hour, and, having entered, must with the sword proceed to consecrate and close the circle in the accustomed manner, after which he must proceed as he thinks fit to adjure, constrain, and force the spirits to visible appearance;† in doing which he must, as said before, be undaunted, firm, and confident, not despairing or impatient, but determined to bring his will and purpose to the desired effect.

---

* Some Theurgists describe the circle on *virgin* parchment, and secure it to the floor with *virgin* wax.

† Vide *Magus*, p. 96, *Ceremonial Magic*, and *Agrippa's Occult Philo*, lib. 4; also, *Pope Honorius* on Magical Rites, and *Solomon's Key to Magic*.

TO RAISE AN EVIL OR FAMILIAR SPIRIT.

Now, if the Theurgist would call an evil spirit to the *circle*, he must first consider and know its nature, and to which of the planets it agrees; and what offices are distributed unto it from the planet. This being known, let there be sought out a place fit and convenient and proper for the invocation, according to the nature of the planet, and the quality of the offices of the same spirit, as near as it can be done; as if their power be over the sea, rivers, or floods, then let the place be the sea-shore, and so of the rest. Then choose a convenient time, both for the quality of the air (being serene, quiet, clear, and fitting for the spirits to assume bodies), as also of the quality and nature of the planet and the spirit, as on his day and time in which he rules; for he may be fortunate or unfortunate, sometimes in the day, and sometimes in the night, as the stars and spirits do require.

These things being judiciously considered, let the *circle* be made at the place elected, and in the circle write the proper names and characters, fortifying the same by proper pentacles and divine inscriptions; then let the Theurgist consecrate the circle and everything he uses, which being done in a firm and solemn manner, he must proceed with his incantations, turning to each of the four quarters, reiterating the same. Then let him look around, to see if any spirit does appear, which if he delays, then let him repeat his invocation, as above said, three times; and if the spirit is obstinate and will not appear, then let the Theurgist begin to *adjure* it with divine power, but so that all his adjurations do agree with the nature and office of the spirit; and thus he shall effect his purpose. When the spirit appears, let the Theurgist turn himself towards it, courteously receiving it, and demanding answers to his questions; but if the spirit shall be obstinate, ambiguous, lying, or else refractory, let the Theurgist bind it by repeated conjurations, and, if you doubt any thing, make, without the *circle*, with the consecrated sword, the figure of a *triangle* or *pentagon*, and compel the spirit to enter into it: then, having obtained of the spirit that which you desire, *license** it to depart, with courteous words, giving it command that it do no hurt; and, if it will not depart, compel it by powerful conjurations; and, if need require, expel it by *exorcisms* and suffumigations. And, when it is departed, go not immediately out of the circle, but make a stay, and use some prayer, giving thanks to God and the good angels, praying also for your future defence and preservation, after which being done, you may depart.

Of Intelligences and Spirits,
In their different Orders; also of Subterraneous and Infernal Agents.

ACCORDING to the theory and belief of the ancient Theurgists, an **Intelligence** is an intelligible substance, free from all gross terrestrial matter, immortal, and of supernatural influence, and the nature of all **Intelligences**, **Spirits**, and **Angels**, is the same. From this term, however, the infernal spirits are exempted. Of the **Angels** there are three kinds: the first of which we call supercelestial, and minds altogether separated from a body, being, as it were, intellectual spheres worshipping only one God, as it were, their most firm and stable unity or centre. Wherefore they even call them Gods, by reason of a certain participation of the Divinity, for they are always full of God, are always about the Supreme Being, infusing the light received from Him unto the inferior orders, making an equal distribution of power and duty.

The **Celestial Intelligences** follow in the second order, which are called *mundane* angels, viz. being appointed, besides the divine worship, for the spheres of the world, and for the government of every heaven and star; whence they are divided into so many orders as there are heavens in the world, and as there are stars in the heavens. Thus, the ancients termed those *Saturnine* who ruled the sphere of **Saturn**; others *Jovial, Martial,* and so on throughout the whole order

---

* They who neglect *licensing* the spirits to depart are in very greaqt danger, because instances have been known of the operator experiencing sudden death.

of the heavens. And the ancients also placed in the starry heavens angels who might rule the signs, triplicities, decans, quinaries, degrees, and stars. Therefore they established twelve princes of the angels, who rule the twelve signs of the zodiac, and thirty-six who rule the decans, and seventy-two others who may rule so many quinaries of heaven, with the tongues of men and nations, and four who may rule the triplicities and elements, and seven governors of the whole world, according to the seven planets; and they have given to all of them *names* and **seals** which they call **characters**, using them in their invocations, incantations, &c. &c. For instance, if at any time they operated for the **sun**, they invocated by the name of the **sun**, by the names of the solar angels, and so of the rest. *

Thirdly, they established angels, as ministers for the disposing of those things below, which Origen called certain invisible powers, to which those things which are on earth are committed to be disposed of. For, according to them, sometimes they, being invisible, do direct our journeys, and all our business, are often present at our battles, and by secret helps do give the desired success to their friends; for at their pleasure they can procure prosperity and inflict adversity.

In like manner they distribute these into more orders; so some are **fiery**, some **watery**, some **aerial**, and some **terrestrial**: which *four* species of angels are computed according to the *four* powers of the celestial souls, viz. the *mind, reason, imagination,* and the vivifying or *mobuce* faculty. Hence the **fiery** follow the mind of the celestial souls, concurring to the contemplation of more divine things. But the **aerial** follow reason, favouring the rational faculty, after a certain manner, separating it from the sensitive and vegetative. Therefore it serves for an active life, as the fiery for the contemplative; but the **watery** follow the imagination, serving for a voluptuous life; the **earthly** following nature, and favouring vegetation.

---

* Vide Psellus de Operatione Dæmonium

Some of these are also **oriental**, some **occidental**, some **meridional** some **septentrional**. Moreover, according to the ancients, there is no part of the world destitute of the proper assistance of these angels, not because they are alone, but because they reign there especially; for they are every where, although some especially operate and have their influence in this place, and some elsewhere. Neither, truly, are these things to be understood as though they were subject to the influence of the stars; but, as they have corresponded with the heaven above the world, from whence especially all things are directed, and to which all things ought to be conformable: whence, as these angels are appointed for divers stars, so also for divers places and times, not that they are limited to any place or time, neither by the bodies which they are appointed to govern; but because divine wisdom hath so decreed; therefore they favour more and patronize those bodies, places, times, stars, &c. and hence are called *diurnal, nocturnal, meridional,* and *septentrional*. Thus, the ancients termed some woodmen, some mountaineers, some fieldmen, some domestics. Hence the Deities of the Woods, Satyrs, Familiars, Fairies, Nymphs, Naiades, Dryades, Pierides, Hamadryades, Muses, the Graces, Genii, and such like; some of whom they affirm are so familiar with men, that they are even affected with human perturbations; by whose instructions *Plato* thinks that men do wonderful things, even as by the instruction of men. And they report that there are so many legions as there are stars in the heaven, and so many spirits in every legion as there are in heaven itself stars. Yet, according to *St. Athanasius,* the number of *good* spirits is according to the number of men, ninety-nine parts, according to the parable of the Ten Goats; others suppose the number of the angels equal with men, because it is written, he hath appointed the bounds of the people according to the number of the angels of God; and concerning their number others have written many things; but the modern theologians, following *Austin* and *Gregory,* easily resolve themselves, saying, that the number of the *good* Angels transcendeth human capacity, to the which, on the contrary, innumerable unclean spirits do correspond, there being as many impure spirits in the inferior world as good spirits in the superior; and some divines do not scruple to affirm that they have received this by revelation.*

Under these they place a kind of spirits subterraneous, or obscure, which the Platonists call angels that failed, revengers of wickedness and ungodliness, according to the decree of divine justice; and they call them evil angels and wicked spirits, because they often annoy and hurt, even of their own accord. Of these, also, they reckon more legions, and in like manner distinguishing them according to the names of the stars and elements, and parts of the world. They also place over them kings, princes, and rulers, of which four most powerful and evil spirits rule over the other, according to the four quarters of the world. Under these many more princes of legions govern, and many private officers, as the **Gorgones**, **Statenocte**, **Tisiphone**, **Alecto**, **Megara**, and **Cerberus**.

This kind of spirits, according to Porphyry, inhabit a place nigh to the earth—yea, within the earth itself; there is no mischief which they dare not commit: they have altogether a violent and hurtful nature, therefore they plot and endeavour violent and sudden mischiefs, and, when they make incursions, sometimes they lie hid, and sometimes offer open violence, being very much delighted in all things done wickedly and mischievously.†

---

* Vide Orac. Magica. Zoroas, and Bodin's Daemonomania.

† Vide Delr. Disq. Magic, 1. 14. also Schot. Physic. Curios; and *Philostrat. in Vitâ Apoloni.*

Of the Names of Spirits,

AND THEIR VARIOUS DESCRIPTIONS;

ALSO OF

SPIRITS THAT RULE THE STARS, SIGNS, AND ELEMENTS.

MANY and different are the names of good and bad spirits, but their proper and true names, as those of the stars, are known only to God, who alone numbers the multitude of stars, and calls them by their names, whereof none can be known by us, but by divine revelation; very few are expressed to us in sacred writ. But the Hebrew Rabbis think that the names of angels were imposed on them by Adam, according to that which is written, "The Lord brought all things which he had made unto Adam, that he should name them; and as he called any thing, so the name thereof was." Hence the Hebrew *Maecubals** think, together with magicians and cabalists, that it is in the power of man to impose names upon spirits, but of such a man only who is dignified and elevated to this virtue by some divine gift or sacred authority; but because a name that may express the nature of divinity, or the whole virtue of angelical essences, cannot be made by any human voice, therefore names for the most part are put upon them from their works, signifying some certain office or effect which is required by the order of Spirits; which name then, and not otherwise, obtains efficacy and virtue to draw any spiritual substance from above, or beneath, to make any desired effect.

Thus, an intelligent writer on magic† declares, he has seen and known some persons, who, writing on *virgin parchment*, the name and seal of some spirit, in the hour of the moon, which they afterwards gave to be devoured by a water frog, and rehearsing a certain verse, letting the frog go into the water, great rains and showers followed. Also, the same person, inscribing the name of another spirit with the seal

---

* Wier de Proest. Dam. 2, c. 4, et seq.
† Barrett's Magus, book 2, page 55

thereof in the hour of **Mars**, which was given to a crow, upon the crow being set at liberty, and a verse applicable thereto rehearsed, there followed from that part of heaven whither it flew, lightnings and horrible thunders, with thick clouds.

Also, the names of some angels are **Raphael, Gabriel, Michael, Haniel,** which is as much as to say, the *vision* of God, the *virtue* of God, the *strength* of God, the *glory* of God, &c. In like manner, in the offices of *evil* demons, are read their names, viz. a *player*, a *deceiver*, a *dreamer*, a *fornicator*, and many such like.

So we receive from many of the ancient fathers and the Hebrews, the names of angels set over the planets and signs:

Thus the spirit of **Saturn**	is **Cassiel**, in the order of *Thrones*.
the spirit of **Jupiter**	is **Zadkiel**, in the order of *Dominations*.
the spirit of **Mars**	is **Samael**, in the order of *Potentates*.
the spirit of **Sol**	is **Michael**, in the order of *Virtues*.
the spirit of **Venus**	is **Hanael**, in the order of *Principalities*.
the spirit of **Luna**	is **Gabriel**, in the order of *Angels*.
And the spirit of **Mercury**	is **Raphael** in the order of *Archangels*.

These are those *seven* spirits which always stand before the face of God, to whom is entrusted the disposing of the whole celestial and terrene kingdoms which are under the region of the **moon**; for these (as the more curious theologians say) govern all things by a certain vicissitude of *hours, days,* and *years*. As the ancient astrologers teach concerning the planets which they are set over, which *Mercurius Trismegistus* calls the *seven* governors of the world, who, by the heavens as by instruments, distribute the influences of all the signs and stars, upon their inferiors.

Again, the ancients have two other* superior orders of spirits, answering to two spheres of the Heavens, distinct from the planetary regions, namely **Methratton** in the ninth orb of Heaven, in the order of *Seraphims*, and **Razael**, in the starry orb of Heaven, in the order of *Cherubims*.† And every one of the planetary spirits ‡ governs the world 354 years and 4 months, the government beginning from the *intelligence* of **Saturn**; afterwards, in order, the *intelligences* of **Jupiter**, **Venus**, **Mars**, **Sol**, **Luna**, and **Mercury**, the government again returning to the spirit of **Saturn**.§¶

TRITHEMIUS, the famous Abbot of Spanheim, wrote a special treatise concerning these, which he that will thoroughly examine may from thence draw great knowledge of future times. Over the **twelve** signs of the Zodiac, are set these—viz. over **Aries** the spirit **Malahidael**; over **Taurus** the spirit **Asmodel**; over **Gemini** the spirit **Ambriel**; over **Cancer** the spirit **Muriel**; over **Leo** the spirit **Girchiel**; over **Virgo** the spirit **Gamaliel**; over **Libra** the spirit **Luriel**: over

---

* This singular order of *other* spiritual rulers, in addition to the seven planetary spirits, making in the whole *nine* orders, proves that the system of the ancients was not founded in delusion; for, as above shown, they have two *other* orders of spirits, which are not attributed to *any* star or planet, but merely to the sphere of Heaven. So that the discovery of an *eighth* planet does in no way overturn the ancient system of magic, but seems to hint that there is a possibility of the existence of *another* planet still more remote than HERSCHEL; whose immense distance, as it wanders through the boundless regions of infinite space, has hitherto hindered its discovery by our best astronomers, but which we firmly believe will, by its future discovery, give a new and enlarged idea of the now generally received solar system.

† **Razael** is thus the spirit of **Herschel** according to the above division, and is more powerful than the spirit of **Saturn**, even as the influence of **Herschel** exceeds that of **Saturn**.

‡ Trinum Magicum; also Peucer de Divinatione, &c

§ Vide Agrippa de Occul. Philosoph. lib. 4.

¶ *Steganographia, Ars per Occullam Scripturam, &c. &c.per Joanne Arithemio, &c.*

𝕾𝖈𝖔𝖗𝖕𝖎𝖔 the spirit **Barahiel**; over 𝕾𝖆𝖌𝖎𝖙𝖙𝖆𝖗𝖎𝖚𝖘 the spirit **Abdachiel**; over 𝕮𝖆𝖕𝖗𝖎𝖈𝖔𝖗𝖓 the spirit **Hanael**; over 𝕬𝖖𝖚𝖆𝖗𝖎𝖚𝖘 the spirit **Cambiel**; over 𝕻𝖎𝖘𝖈𝖊𝖘 the spirit **Barchiel**.

Of these spirits set over the planets and signs, St. John makes mention of in the Revelation, speaking of the former in the beginning, and the *seven* spirits which are in the presence of the throne of God, which we find are attributed to the *seven* planets in that part where he describes the platform of the heavenly city, saying, that on the *twelve* gates thereof are *twelve angels*.

There are, again, *twenty-eight* angels, who rule in the *twenty-eight* mansions of the moon; there are also *four* Princes of the Angels, which are set over the *four* winds, and over the *four* parts of the world. Thus, **Michael** is placed over the *east* wind, **Raphael** over the *west*, **Gabriel** over the *north*, and **Ariel** over the *south*. There are also assigned to the *elements* these,—to the *air* **Cheub**, to the *fire* **Seaph**, to the *earth* **Aries**, and to the *water* **Tharris**. Now every one of these spirits is a great prince, and has much power and freedom in the dominion of his own planets and signs, and in their times, years, months, days, and hours; also in their elements, parts, and winds. Every one of these princes bears rule over many legions of immortal spirits; likewise, after the same manner, amongst *evil* spirits, there are *four*, who, as most potent *kings*, are set over the rest, according to the *four* parts of the world, whose names are these: **Oriens**, king of the *east*; **Paymon**, king of the *west*; **Egin**, king of the *north*, and **Amaymon**, king of the *south*.* Which the Hebrew Doctors affirm to be most powerful spirits, under whom many others rule as *princes* of legions. Likewise there are innumerable demons of private offices; moreover, the ancient Grecian Theurgists reckon up six demons, which they call *Telchines* or *Alastores*, "who, bearing ill will to men, take up (as they figuratively express it) water out of the river *Styx* with their hands, and sprinkle it upon the earth, whence follow calamities, plagues, and famines;" and these are said to be *Acteus, Magalezius,*

---

* Vide Cicognae Magia Omnifaria, &c. also Psell de Oper Daemon.

Ormenus, Lycus, Nicon, and *Minon*; and, although in the exact nomenclature of these spirits some ancient authors are found to differ, yet both the ancient and modern Theurgists are unanimous in the description of their several orders and offices.*

𝔄ppearances of 𝔖pirits.

ACCORDING to an ancient MSS. the appearances of the four potent rulers of the four *mundane* quarters are these:—

1. THE SPIRIT **Oriens**, KING OF THE 𝔈ast,

HE appeared with a fair and feminine countenance, and a goodly crown upon his head; he rideth upon an elephant, having before him numbers of musical instruments. Sometimes he appeareth in the similitude of a horse; and, when he is constrained by magical incantations, assumeth a human shape, He hath under him 250 legions of inferior spirits. His power, according to the ancients, is great, and he can answer truly to all demands, both past, present, and to come.

2. THE SPIRIT OF **Paymon**, KING OF THE 𝔚est.

This spirit is powerful to evil, appearing in the likeness of an armed soldier, riding upon a camel or dromedary, being crowned with a bright crown; his countenance is feminine, but his voice hoarse and uncouth. Before him goeth all kinds of musical instruments: yet, when constrained by art, he readily performs the desired wishes of the invocator, and hath under him an infinity of spirits.

3. THE SPIRIT **Egin**, KING OF THE 𝔑orth.

This spirit is high and mighty. He appeareth in the form of a man riding upon a dragon, with a regal crown: on each side of him are hissing serpents. He cometh with a fearful and tremendous noise, with many inferiors around him; and

---

* Does not this seem to prove that there is something more than mere mystery in these curious systems?

under him are countless legions of mighty spirits. When constrained by powerful incantations, this spirit assumes the form of a child, and the raising of this spirit is less dangerous than of either of the preceding, and has proved of great use to the magician, when rightly invoked. He discovers treasures of the earth, and is very tractable.

4. THE SPIRIT **Amaymon**, KING OF THE South.

The spirit **Amaymon** is great, high, and mighty, and terrible in appearance. He usually assumes the form of an old man, with a long beard, his ears being like to those of a horse, with a royal diadem on his head. His first appearance is unusually tremendous; forked lightning and deep-mouthed thunders, shaking the earth apparently to the centre, announce his awful appearance. Then suddenly the earth will appear to vomit forth gushes of flame, and sulphureous odours taint the charmed atmosphere. Anon, are heard all sorts of musical instruments; then an uncouth clatter of creaking wheels and horrid crashes, will every instant astound the invocator; but on a sudden will all be again calm; and, clothed in the whole pomp of his spiritual grandeur, attended by countless legions of invincible spirits, **Amaymon** will be seen riding furiously on a fierce and roaring lion. He will approach to the utmost limits of the space assigned him, and it will well become the Theurgist to preserve his wonted calmness; for, if he powerfully constrain, and urgently invoke, this furious spirit, he may be brought to the most submissive obedience. He has power to give knowledge, dignity, and great promotion.

These four powerful spirits are difficult to be constrained, or urged to visible appearance. They are dangerous to contend with, and are "powers of evil," "swift to destruction." They bear an inveterate hatred to human kind, will delude the Theurgist with lies and deceit, and in every other way strive to render his work abortive. But if the Theurgist shall be able to make them enter a consecrated pentacle, or a circle fortified with divine names, they will be forced against their will to reveal the truth: and he need fear no harm, if he be born under a right constellation.

FORMS AND APPEARANCES OF THE
Planetary Spirits.

These spirits, which are attributed to the seven planets, are more easily called forth than the before-mentioned mighty princes of the invisible world. And, in fact, the ceremonies necessary for the incantations and constrictions for these assume a far more facile and certain character than for the others. Neither can there be anything so dangerous in the process of invocation; for these spirits are almost entirely subservient to human skill, especially where the invocator wishes to converse with the spirits of that planet under which he was born.*

SPIRITS OF Saturn.†

The spirits of Saturn usually appear with a tall, slender, lean body, very unwillingly, and having an angry countenance; having four faces, hosed or beaked. They appear and disappear incessantly, and their colour is black and shining, but of very imperfect form. Their motion is as swift as the wind, attended at times with an earthquake, or extraordinary tremulous motion of the earth.

Their particular shapes are—
A king, bearded, riding on a dragon.
An old man with a beard.
An old woman, leaning on a crutch.
An hog.

---

* One argument brought forward against astrology, is, that the planets are inert and senseless masses of matter, and devoid of any power to move the intellectual faculties of mankind, born under them. Does not the above singular theory of the ancient Magii—that the planets are governed by spirits—account, in a great measure, for the demonstrable effects of their decided influence over human life?

† Vide Agrippa, book 4, and Barrett's Magus.

A dragon.
An owl.
A black garment.
A hook or sickle.
A juniper-tree.

The spirits of Saturn are under the *south-west* wind. They usually come at first with very terrific appearance; and the sign of their appearance is white earth, whiter than snow. Their office is to sow discords, hatred, evil thoughts, and cogitations; to kill, murder, and commit every heinous crime, which the divine Providence shall permit. They rule over *Saturday,* and are invoked the 1st, 8th, 15th, and 22d hours of that day.*

SPIRITS OF THE Sun.

The spirits of the sun generally appear in a large full body, sanguine and gross, in a gold colour, with the tincture of blood. They are very terrific and majestic in their appearance. Their motion is as the winged lightning, accompanied by fearful thunders, and a burning atmosphere.

Their particular forms are,
A king, with a sceptre, riding on a lion.
A king crowned.
A queen with a sceptre.
A bird.
A lion.
A cock.
A sceptre.
A yellow garment.

The spirits of the sun are under the *north* wind; their sign is causing a profuse perspiration upon the invocator.

---

* The hours of the planets have undoubted influence in astrology, as anyone who tries the experiment may soon prove; an explanation of which will be given hereafter.

Their nature is to procure gold, gems, carbuncles, diamonds, and rubies; and to cause one to obtain favour and benevolence, to dissolve enmity, raise to honours, and take away infirmities. These spirits are said to bear rule over Sunday. The hours are the same as those of Saturn.

SPIRITS OF THE 𝕸𝖔𝖔𝖓.

The spirits of the MOON appear generally of a great and full stature, soft and phlegmatic, of colour like a black obscure cloud, having a swollen countenance, with eyes red and full of water, bald heads, and teeth like those of a wild boar; their motion is like an exceeding great tempest of the sea. For their sign there will appear an exceeding great rain about the circle.

Their particular forms are,
A king, like an archer, riding upon a doe.
A little boy.
A huntress with bow and arrows.
A cow.
A little doe.
A goose.
A green or silver-coloured garment.
An arrow.
A creature with many feet.

The spirits of the moon rule over Monday. They are accompanied by tremendous and furious blasts of the *west wind,* * with clouds, showers, and hail, and, when powerfully

---

* The following curious facts were related to us by *three* gentlemen students, of undoubted veracity, with whom we are well acquainted, and who actually experienced them:—

"On the night of September 22, 1822, we resolved upon invocating the spirits of the moon, and accordingly, having prepared the circle, and used the necessary ceremonies and incantations, there suddenly came such a furious storm of rain and hail, and such a dreadful tempest arose, with such fearful blasts of wind, that the elements seemed as if waging war with each other; we every moment expected the dome skylight over our heads would be shattered into a thousand pieces. The rain continued to fall in gushing torrents, the wind howled mournfully, and the lightning flashed in our faces, while the thunder actually

invocated, their appearance has been known to have caused a most furious tempest, so much so that the elements seemed involved in a general confusion.

The nature of the lunar spirits is to give silver, and to convey things from place to place, to make horses swift, and to disclose the secrets of persons both present and future.

SPIRITS OF 𝔐𝔞𝔯𝔰

The spirits of Mars appear, for the most part, in a body tall and choleric, a filthy countenance, of colour brown, swarthy, or red, having horns like harts, and griffin's claws; they come furiously bellowing like wild bulls. Their motion is like fire burning, and the signs of their appearance are thunder and lightning about the magic circle.

Their particular shapes are,
A king armed, riding on a wolf.
An armed warrior.
A female with spear and buckler.
A she goat.
A horse.

---

shook the building to its foundations. Expecting these occurrences, we were nothing dismayed thereat, but persisted, notwithstanding this fury of the elements, to urge the spirits more powerfully, to visible appearance. What followed we cannot at present reveal: suffice it, we had ample proof of the reality of spiritual agency. At the close of our mystic labours, as we were *dismissing* the spirits by powerful restrictions, we were suddenly astonished by a tremendous noise, evidently supernatural; for, had twenty parks of artillery, a hundred loaded waggons, or a thousand pedestrians, passed by at this period, the noise we heard could not have been equalled. It resembled the most furious crashes, incessant cracking of whips, trampling of horses, sound of organs, and innumerable voices, united in an unintelligible jargon. It lasted for nearly twenty minutes, without intermission, and then suddenly ceased! As soon as we could (which was almost on the instant the noise ceased), we rushed into the street, eagerly inquiring of the guardians of the night if any vehicles or if any particular company had passed; but they all agreed none had gone by. This was a little before two o'clock in the morning (our ceremonies began at midnight), and the experiment was performed in a now dilapidated, but once fashionable place of public resort, at the west end of the town."

A stag.
A red garment.
A quantity of wool.
A cowslip.

These spirits bear rule over *Tuesday*, and are under the *east* wind; they are best invocated upon that day, in the hour of Mars. Their nature is to bring or cause war, mortality, death, combustions, and to perform strange exploits.

SPIRITS OF Mercury.

The spirits of Mercury appear, for the most part, in a body of a middle stature, cold, liquid, and moist, fair, and of an affable speech, in a human shape and form, like an armed knight, of clear and bright colour. Their motion is like silver-coloured clouds, and the sign of their appearance is an *unaccountable* horror and fear upon the invocator.

Their particular forms are,
A king, riding upon a bear.
A fair youth.
A woman holding a distaff.
A dog.
A she bear.
A magpie.
A garment of various changeable colours.
A rod or staff.

These spirits are generally accompanied by a *south-west* wind, and are said to bear rule over *Wednesday*. Their nature is to give all sorts of metals, to reveal all earthly things, past, present, or future, to pacify judges, to give victory in war, to teach experiments and all ancient sciences, to change bodies mixed of elements, conditionally, out of one thing into another, to give health or infirmities, to raise the poor and humble the rich, to bind or loose spirits, to open constrictions, &c. They are easily brought to visible appearance.

SPIRITS OF 𝔍𝔲𝔭𝔦𝔱𝔢𝔯.

These spirits appear with a body sanguine and choleric, of a middle stature, with a horrible fearful motion, but with a mild countenance and a gentle speech, and of the colour of iron. Their motion is accompanied with tremendous thunders and vivid lightnings. The sign of their appearance is generally announced by numbers of imperfect and horrid forms, lions, &c.

Their particular forms are,

A king with a drawn sword, riding on a stag.
A man wearing a mitre, clothed in long garments.
A virgin adorned with flowers, and crowned with laurel.
A bull fiercely roaring.
A stag.
A peacock.
An azure garment.
A sword.
A box-tree.

They are said to bear rule over *Thursday*. They are accompanied by a *south* wind, very strong and powerful, resembling an hurricane: their nature is to procure the love of women, to cause men to be merry and joyful, to pacify strifes and contentions, appease enemies, to heal diseases and cause sickness, to procure losses, and to restore what is lost. They are very difficult to be invocated or constrained.

SPIRITS OF 𝔙𝔢𝔫𝔲𝔰.

The spirits of *Venus* appear with a fair body, of mean stature, with an amiable and pleasant countenance, of colour white or green, their upper parts golden: their motion is like a clear star. For the sign of their coming there will appear innumerable forms of handsome maidens, in the most enticing forms.

Their particular shapes are,

A king with a sceptre, riding on a camel.
A naked female.
A she goat.

A camel.
A dove.
A white or green garment.
Flowers.
The herb savine.

They bear rule over *Friday*, which is the day of *Venus*; they are accompanied by a furious west wind, mingled with gentle zephyrs and invisible music, delightful to hear. Their nature is to give silver, to incline men and women to luxury, to cause marriages, to procure love, to take away infirmities, and to aid all things of a gentle and pacific nature. They are easily invoked, and, according to the ancient Theurgists, may be constrained to visible appearance, in less space of time than other spirits.

Magical Suffumigations
AND THEIR WONDERFUL EFFICACY.

The ancient philosophers affirm, that "no one should wonder how great things suffumigations (the burning of certain perfumes or substances) can do in the air, especially when he shall with *Porphyry* consider, that by certain vapours exhaling from proper suffumigations, airy spirits are presently raised; as also thunderings and lightnings, and such like things.

The liver of a *camelion* being burnt upon the top of a house, doth, as it is manifest, raise showers and lightnings;—in like manner, the head and throat, if they be burnt with the wood of the oak, cause lightnings and tempests.

There are also suffumigations under opportune constellations and benevolent influences of the stars, that make the images of spirits forthwith appear in the air, or other mediums. It is said, that if a fume be made of *coriander, smallage, henbane,* and *hemlock,* spirits will presently come together, and become visible: hence are they called "the spirits' herbs." Also make a fume of the root of the reedy herb sagapen, the juice of hemlock and henbane, tapus, barbetus, red sanders, and black poppy; it makes spirits and strange shapes appear. If smallage be added thereto, it chases away spirits from any place, and destroys their visions.

Again; a fume made of *mint, calamint, piony,* and *palma christi* (herbs easily obtained), it drives away all evil spirits, and vain or fearful imaginations. Hermes affirms, that there is nothing better than the fume of *spermaceti* for the raising of spirits; and if a fume be made of that, and lignum aloes, pepper, musk, saffron, and red thorax, tempered together with the blood of a lapwing, it will quickly gather aerial spirits together. And if it be used about the graves of the dead, it gathers together spirits, and the souls of the dead. Some say, that a fume made with linseed and fleabane seed, and the roots of violets and parsley, it maketh one to *foresee things* to come, and doth conduce to prophesying.

If a house, or any place, be smoked with the gall of a cuttle fish, made into a confection with red storax, roses, and lignum aloes, and if there be some water or blood cast into that place, the *house* will seem to be full of water or blood; and if some earth of a newly-ploughed ground be cast there, the earth will seem to quake, and be convulsed as in an earthquake.

Others write, that if any one shall hide gold or silver, or any other precious thing, on Sunday, Monday, or Tuesday, days attributed to ☉, ♂, and ☽, and shall fume the place with coriander, saffron, henbane, smallage, and black poppy, of each *like* quantity, bruised together, and tempered with the juice of hemlock, that which is so hid, shall never be discovered or taken away; for they affirm that spiritual intelligences shall continually bear watch over it; and if any one shall endeavour to take it away, he shall be hurt by these invisible agents, or will become possessed of an incurable frenzy.—*MSS. of Cornelius Agrippa.*

THE MYSTICAL PERFUMES OF THE SEVEN PLANETS,
(According to Hermes).

♄ Saturn..........Pepperwort.
♃ Jupiter..........Nutmeg.
♂ Mars............Lignum Aloes.
☉ Sol...............Mastio.
♀ Venus...........Saffron.
☿ Mercury........Cinnamon.
☽ Luna............Myrrh.

" These are said, by the old herbalists, to render that place fortunate wherein they are burnt, during the right *planetary hour*." — *Key to Agrippa*.

METHOD OF RAISING THE MIGHTY AND POWERFUL SPIRIT
Egin, King of the North.
EXTRACTED FROM AN ANCIENT MS.*

"THE Theurgist must call this spirit in a fair chamber or quadrant, twenty or twenty-four feet at the most in breadth, in every part a window, a cubit wide, or a little more, east, west, north, and south. The floor of the chamber must be paved, bordered, or plastered, very plain and close, so that

---

* It is to be remembered that the surrounding scenery has nothing to do with the CIRCLE, but is merely an embellishment

he may make his circle thereon with chalk or coal, that it may be perfectly seen. This house or chamber must be in a void place, and not near the intercourse of men; for the opinion of some expert men in this art is, that spirits are more willing to appear in some waste place, as in woods, heaths, fens, moors, downs, or in any place where there is no resort, nor where any of the sacraments have been administered; for otherwise thy purpose will not be effected. Therefore be warned.

"The weather must also be observed, for all weathers are not good for thy work; wherefore, when thou wilt begin thy work, see that the air is clear, and, if it be in the day, see that the sun shine; and, if it be in the night, let the moon be unobscured, or the sky full of stars; but take heed of foul or close weather, for in those the spirit will not be visible; and why? because it cannot receive bodily form or shape from the elements; wherefore select fine weather, for the spirit much delighteth therein.

"The spirit must also be invocated on even days of the moon, and in his proper hour, although some Theurgists say they have began in the new moon, and it hath been thirty days' labour before they could effect their entire purpose; therefore, let not this work seem tedious, nor think for one day being spent fruitlessly that thou wilt not effect thy purpose, seeing that expert clerks have spent several days before they could obtain an appearance." This being performed, thy circle must be of the above form.

The Incantations.*

1. TO BIND THE GROUND, WHEREBY NEITHER MORTAL NOR SPIRITUAL BEINGS CAN HAVE POWER TO APPROACH WITHIN A LIMITED DISTANCE.

"Having made your necessary suffumigations and mystic preparations, describe a circle of a hundred feet or more in

---

* The MS. from which this is taken is valued at five hundred guineas, and was formerly in the possession of R. Cosway, Esq. R. A. but is now in the possession of the Mercurii.

diameter, or as much more or less as you may think fit; and, if you wish to keep all living creatures from within a quarter of a mile or more of your experiment, make, at the four parts of the same, east, west, north, and south, proper crosses, and devoutly pronounce thrice the following incantation:—*

"In the name of the **Father**, and of the **Son**, and of the **Holy Ghost**, Amen. I bind all mortal and immortal, celestial and terrestrial, visible and invisible beings, except those spirits whom I have occasion to call, to avoid and quit this space of ground, which I now mark, and wherein I now stand, and that with all possible speed and despatch. I bind you to avoid and no longer to tarry, by the unspeakable power of Almighty by the most high and mighty name of ✠ **Tetragrammaton** ✠ by the all-powerful names ✠ **AGLA** ✠ **Saday** ✠ **Jesu** ✠ **Messias** ✠ **Alpha** ✠ and **Omega** ✠. By all these most high and powerful names, I charge, adjure, bind, and constrain both mortal and immortal, terrestrial, celestial, visible, and invisible beings to avoid, quit, and depart this ground, and do request that none of you, except those I have occasion to call at this time, be suffered to come within these sacred limits, These things I request in the name of the **Father**, of the **Son**, and of the **Holy Ghost**, Amen.

"Then dig a certain depth at the four parts of the compass, and bury the seal of the earth in each part, and no power, either visible or invisible, shall have power to come near thee, or to interrupt thy proceedings."

---

* These curious proceedings are copied literally from the MS before spoken of, and the Editor has thought proper to give the same orthography to the *Latin* and *Hebrew* words as in the original, and, notwithstanding some part may be found rather defective when compared with these languages as they are *now* used, yet the high antiquity of the MS. will be a sufficient excuse for the difference in point of *elegance*, should there be any.

INCANTATIONS FOR INVOKING THE SPIRIT TO VISIBLE APPEARANCE.

I conjure thee, **Egin**, Rex Borealis, and also charge thee that thou appear here before me, and before this circle, by the sufferance of Almighty God, and by the virtue of his passion and other sentences which here shall be rehearsed, to bind and constrain thee.

I conjure thee, **Egin**, by the **Father**, the **Son**, and the **Holy Ghost** and by the heavens, the air, the earth, and the sea, and by all that therein is contained, that thou come shortly, and appear to me and my fellows, not terrible nor fearful, but in mild and peaceable form, without hurt or envy to any of us.

I conjure thee, **Egin**, by all the holy words that **God** spake in the creation of the world, and by all creatures visible and invisible, and by the four elements, and by the virtue of heaven, and by all the holy words that **God** spake unto Moses, and to all other prophets, and by the incarnation, passion, death, and resurrection, of the mild and ineffable Saviour of all mankind.

I conjure thee, **Egin**, by the general resurrection, and by the dreadful day of judgment; I conjure thee, **Egin**, by the coming of the **Holy Ghost**; I conjure thee, also, by the virtue of all the spirits of the just, and by the most holy patriarchs, apostles, evangelists, and by the most holy saints of all ages.

I conjure thee, **Egin**, by the mercy, grace, and power of God; I conjure thee, thou spirit **Egin**, under the pain of condemnation, and thy fearful doom at the great day of judgment; I conjure thee, **Egin**, by the great curse of God; I conjure thee, **Egin**, by all the high names of God; I conjure thee by the high power and strength of our Lord Jesus Christ, the Son of God, the heavenly King of glory; and I conjure thee by the whole of these, in what place of the world soever thou art, to appear instantly before me in the likeness of a child of three years old; and that, without fear, hurt, or envy, thou fulfil my request.

𝕽𝖊𝖕𝖑𝖎𝖈𝖆𝖙𝖔𝖗𝖘 𝕴𝖓𝖈𝖆𝖓𝖙𝖆𝖙𝖎𝖔𝖓𝖘.

If, at the *third* rehearsal of the above mystic ceremonial, the spirit refuses to appear, prepare a fume of sweet-smelling savours, such as frankincense, aloes, cinnamon, oil olives, nutmegs, musk, cassia, roses, saffron, and white wax; which must be burnt, commixed together, on a fire consecrated for the purpose; and, while the fume is forming, and the fire fiercely burning, repeat what follows:—

I conjure thee, **Egin**, and command thee instantly to appear before me, by the virtue of the sentences and words hereafter written, upon pain of the most awful and bitter maledictions of Almighty God.

I conjure thee, O thou spirit **Egin**, that thou arise and appear to us, by the might, majesty, and power of the FIRST word that our Lord spake, in the creation of the world, when he made the light to shine, and said, "Lux et facta, est lux."

I conjure thee, by the SECOND word that he spake when he made the firmament, and said, "Fiat firmamentum in medico aquas, et deinde aquas ab aquis."

I conjure thee, by the THIRD word, when he gathered all the waters that were under heaven into one place, saying, "Congregentur ague que sub coelo sunt et apparia mida."

I conjure thee, by the FOURTH word, which he spake when he made to spring forth trees and herbs, "Germinat terram herba vercli facientur semen cum semendi teipso sit super terram."

I conjure thee, by virtue of the FIFTH word, when he made the ☉, ☽, and ✱✱✱[Stars/Planets–ed.], saying, "Fiat luminaria magna in firmamento cedi ut illuminare terram."

I conjure thee, by the SIXTH word, which he spake when he made birds, fishes, &c. "Producat ague reptile a tire virentes et voluntate super terram sub firmamento coelo."

I conjure thee, by the virtue of the SEVENTH word, which he spake when he blessed them, saying, "Crescite et multiplicamini et reptili aquas maris oves multiplicantur super terram."

I conjure thee, by the EIGHTH word, which he spake when he made beasts, worms, and serpents, "Ducat terram aliam in genero suo irnmenta et reptilia secundum specias scias."

I conjure thee, by virtue of the NINTH word, when he made man in his own image, saying, "Faciamus homo ad imagine et similitudine nostra et per sit pissibus et volatibus que coeli et bestias terre et universe creature qui reptile que monentur in terra."

I conjure thee, O thou spirit **Egin**, instantly to appear, by virtue of the TENTH word, which he spake when he placed Adam and Eve in Paradise, saying, "Crescite et multiplicamini et replete terra subjugate earn et Semite vivi pissibus maris, et volatibus coeli et bestias terre, et universus animalihus que quern monentus super terra." Et per hac verba, conjuro te, spiritus **Egin**."

Lastly, I conjure, charge, bind, and command thee, O thou mighty and invincible spirit **Egin**, by these most high, powerful, and ineffable names of the most highest— ✠ **Jesus** ✠ **fons** ✠ **Salvator** ✠ **Christus** ✠ **Sabbath** ✠ **Adonay** ✠ **Craton** ✠ **Messias** ✠ **Victor** ✠ **Osanna** ✠ **Nazarenes** ✠ **Theas** ✠ **Emmanuel** ✠ **Unigenitus** ✠ **Primogenitus** ✠ **Alpha** ✠ **et Omega** ✠ and by the great, supreme, and all-powerful name להוה which all creatures obey, at which the elements are moved, and the devils fear and tremble. By all these tremendous and awful names, I charge thee, finally, to appear before me. Fiat, fiat, fiat. Amen.

These things being rightly performed, with a rushing sound, "as of many waters," and a tremendous noise, will the spirit appear, and by powerful invocations thou shalt obtain what thou wishest. But let thy proceedings herein be secret, and beware of vain curiosity; for these mysteries are sacred.

Part Four: High Magic 387

TO INVOKE OR RAISE THE SPIRIT

Oberion.

From an ancient MS in the possession of *"Raphael."*

THE CIRCLE FOR RAISING Oberion*

This mighty spirit is chiefly under the dominion of the sun and moon, He appears in great pomp and terror, generally in the form of a scaly monster, the face of a woman, and a royal crown upon his head, attended by innumerable and countless legions.

The Theurgist who would raise or invocate this powerful spirit must, in the first place, draw out his seal and character, and the different offices subservient to him, in the first *Monday* after the *full moon*, and in the hour of the Moon, Mars, Mercury, or Saturn: and when these are made, he must repeat the following ceremonial words:—

---

* From an ancient Ms. in the possession of *"Raphael."*

O ye angels of the **Sun** and **moon**, I now conjure and pray you, and exorcise you, that by the virtue and power of the most high God, **Alpha** and **Omega**, and by the name that is marvellous ✠ **El** ✠, and by him that made and formed you, and by these signs that be here, so drawn forth in these resemblances, and now in the might and virtue of your Creator, and in the name of him the most shining God, and by the virtue of the Holy Ghost, that now, or whensoever that I shall call on **Oberion**, whose image is here pictured, made, or fashioned, and his name that is here written, and his signs here all drawn and graven, written, or made, that **Oberion** be compelled now to obey me, and here to appear openly before me, and fulfil my request.

The *next* day, write or make the name of his *first* counsellor, **Gaberyon**, and that on the right side of Oberion's character, saying,

I exorcise thee, **Gaberyon**, by the power of God, and by the virtue of all heavenly kings, earthly kings, and infernal kings, and by king Solomon, who bound thee, and made thee subject unto him, and by all his signs and seals, and by the four elements, by which the world is sustained and nourished, and by the serpent that was exalted in the wilderness, — that thou, **Gaberyon** now help to give true council to thy Lord **Oberion**, that he do show himself instantly unto me, and fulfil my request.

This must be said three times each day, and three times each night, over the writings.

The *third* day, in the *third* hour, write and make the name of his other counsellor **Geveyron**, with his signs and characters, and do and say as before rehearsed.

This done, suffumigate your seals and writings with a suffumigation of *saffron, aloes, mastic, olibanum,* and *orpient*; and note that the fire used for this purpose must be of *elder-wood* or *thorns*.

Then choose a *secret* and retired place, where no human footsteps may interrupt thee, and make thy circle of the following form. [pg. 386]

INCANTATIONS.

The circle being made, and consecrated according to the rules of ceremonial magic, enter therein, in the hour of Mercury, and begin thy invocations in this manner, on bended knees, and with great devotion.

I conjure, invocate, and call thee, **Oberion**, by the Father, the Son, and the Holy Ghost, and by Him who said, and it was done; who commanded, and it stood fast; who willed, and it was created; and by his Son Jesus Christ, in whose name, all heavenly, earthly, and infernal creatures do bend and obey; and by the unutterable name of ineffable majesty ✠ **Tetragrammaton** ✠ O thou spirit Oberion, I command thee, withersoever thou now art, whether in sea, fire, air, or flood, whether in the air above or in the region beneath, to appear instantly unto me, and my fellows, without hurting me or them, or any other living creature which God has made. This I thrice command thee, in the name of the ineffable Adonai. Amen.

If, at the *third* repetition of this invocation, the spirit gives no visible token of his appearance (for generally, previously to the actual appearance of the spirit, there are heard tremendous noises and frightful hissings, tumultuous yellings, and fearful shrieks); then begin to rehearse the following great bond or incantation, and if the spirit were bound in chains of darkness, in the lowest pit of the infernal regions, he must appear, when this great sentence is rehearsed."

THE GREAT AND POWERFUL INCANTATION,*

For compelling Spirits to visible Appearance.

O thou rebellious and fearful spirit, prince amongst the fallen angels, **Oberion**, I conjure and bind thee to visible appearance by the following most high, most terrible, and mighty invocation:—

---

* This great call or invocation is said to be equally powerful in raising any other spirit.

Hear, O ye heavens, and I will speak, saith the Lord, and let the sea, the earth—yea, hell, and all that is within them contained, mark the words of my mouth: Did not I, saith the Lord, fashion you, and make you? Did not I, as an eagle, who stirreth her nest, fluttereth over her young ones with her wings, and carrieth them on her shoulders? have I not so nourished you, that you were fat, and loaden with plenty? Why have you, then, so spurned with your heels against me, your Maker? Why have you seemed to coequal yourselves with me? What thereby have you reaped? Have you not purchased, instead of that heavenly felicity, hellish perplexity? How have you that fire kindled which doth and shall for ever, at my pleasure, burn you in the bottomless pit of perdition? Why are you so unfaithful and disobedient to my most holy names and words? Know you not that I am God alone, and that there is none but me? Am not I the only יהוה. Is it not in my power to kill and make alive—to wound and to heal—to oppress and to deliver? If I whet the edge of my sword, and my hand take hold of it, to do justice against them who disobey my holy name, who are able to abide the same? To have their sword, eat their flesh, and my sharp arrows of hell fire to be drunk in their blood? Which of you that are disobedient to my name (saith the Lord) is able to withstand mine anger? Am not I Lord of Lords, and omnipotent, and none but I? Who can command the heavens to smoke, the earth to fear, the waters to flow, and hell to tremble? Are not the corners of them all in my hands? O thou obstinate and stubborn spirit, why hast thou dealt so froward with me (saith the Lord), to urge me to command my faithful servant MICHAEL, my valiant champion, to expel and put thee out of the place where thou wast filled with wisdom and understanding, continually beholding my wondrous works? Didst not thou see my glory with thine eyes, and did not thy ears hear the majesty of my voice? Why art thou gone out of the way? Why art thou become an open sepulchre? With thy tongue dost thou deceive my servants, for poison is under thy lips, thy mouth is full of cursing and bitterness, and thy feet are swift to shed innocent blood. Is this the obedience thou owest unto me, and the service thou offerest? Verily, for this thy obstinacy, disobedience, pride, and rebellion, thou shalt be bound, and most cruelly tormented with intolerable pains and endless and eternal perdition.

Then, if the spirit be still rebellious or refractory, make a fire of brimstone and stinking substances, thorns, and briars, &c. Then write the name of the spirit in virgin parchment, and burn it thrice, repeating the following adjuration:—

I conjure thee, creature of God, FIRE, by him who commanded and all things were done, and by the LIVING God, and by the TRUE God, and by the HOLY God, and by him who made thee and all elements by his word, by him who appeared to Moses in a fiery bush, and by him who led the children of Israel in a fiery pillar, through the wilderness, and by him who shall come to judge the world, by fire and brimstone, that thou perform my will upon this refractory and disobedient spirit; till he come unto me, and show himself obedient in all things as I shall command him. O heavenly God, father and author of all virtues, and the invisible king of glory, most strong and mighty captain of the strong and triumphant arm of angels, God of gods, Lord of hosts, which holdest on thy hands the corners of the earth, which with the breath of thy mouth makest all things to shake and tremble, which makest thy angels lightnings, and thy spirits flames of fire, vouchsafe, I beseech thee, O Lord, to send thy holy angels into this place of fire, to torment, vex, and persecute this disobedient spirit, Oberion, and overcome him, as Michael the archangel overcame Lucifer, the prince of darkness, till he come to me, and fulfil all my will and desire. Fiat, fiat, fiat. Amen.

O thou most puissant prince Radamanthus, which dost punish in thy prison of perpetual perplexity, the disobedient spirits, and also the grisly ghosts of men dying in dreadful despair, I conjure, bind, and charge thee, by Lucifer, Beelzebub, Satan, Tamanill, and by their power, and by the homage thou owest unto them; and also I charge thee, by the triple crown of Cerberus, by Styx, and Phlegethon, by the spirit Barantos, and his ministers, that you torment and punish this disobedient spirit Oberion, until you make him come corporeally to my sight, and obey my will and commandment in whatsoever I shall charge or command him to do. Fiat, fiat, fiat. Amen.

These things being rightly performed, the spirit will be constrained to visible appearance: but, after the above incantation, he will come in a very horrible and ghastly form, and attended by terrible convulsions of the elements, raging furiously, and assuming every terrific appearance that is possible, to frighten the invocator. And for which purpose, roaring lions, hissing serpents, and furious beasts, with all the mighty horrors of the infernal regions, and every other possible attempt, will be made to cause terror and alarm. At this juncture, if the magic circle be not well made and fortified, the Invocator will be in the utmost peril, and if he escape with his life may deem himself fortunate; but, if the circle be properly made, there is no fear from the assaults of this rebellious and wicked one, who must become obedient when thus exorcised.

After the spirit has appeared, and performed thy will and request, it is to be well observed, that the utmost caution must be used in quitting the limits of the magic circle. For this end, the Theurgist must devoutly rehearse the following license.

A LICENSE FOR TO DISCHARGE SPIRITS.

I CONJURE thee (Oberion) by the visible and holy temple of Solomon, which he did prepare to the most holy God, by all the elements, and by that most holy name that was graven on Solomon's sceptre, that, for this time, thou do depart quickly, quietly, and peaceably, without lightnings, thunder, rain, wind, storm, or tempest, or any noise or terror whatsoever; and, whensoever I shall call thee, I charge thee that thou do come to me and my fellows, without delay or tract of time, not molesting me or any other creature that God hath made to his glory and praise, and the use of man, or without disordering any thing, putting up or casting down any thing, or doing hurt any other way whatsoever, either in thy coming or going, not hurting, troubling, or molesting me, or any other creature, neither by thyself, nor any other spirit or spirits for thee, or at thy procurement, at any time or times, now or hereafter; by the virtue of our Lord Jesus Christ, the Father, and the Holy Ghost, go thy way in peace to the place which God hath appointed for thee, and peace be between thee and me. In nomine patris ✠ et filii, ✠ et spiritus sancti ✠ Amen.

The Theurgist must repeat this license three times, and afterwards repeating the Lord's Prayer, must leave the circle, walking backwards. He must then destroy all traces of the circle, and remove all instruments used for the purpose, keeping the whole as secret as possible; and must also return home by a different path to that by which he came. So shall no spirit have power to harm him, but let him upon no account neglect any of the foregoing rules, for they are essential to his safety.

Such were the mystic rights, ceremonies, and incantations, used by the ancient Theurgists to burst asunder the bonds of natural order, and to obtain an awful intercourse with the world of spirits,—a study, to the wild sublimity of which modern times afford no parallel,—a study which at once evinces the bold and lofty daring of our courageous ancestors, who, not content with vanquishing earthly foes and quenching mortal feuds, strove to tear asunder the restrictive bonds of this elementary world, to combat with the dread inhabitants of the spiritual regions, and to subject to their service the invincible powers of light and darkness—mighty spirits, who, according to their account, came attended with such tremendous powers, and such awful attributes, that the mere mention of their appearances is enough to cause two-thirds of the present sceptical generation to shrink back and tremble.

THE METHOD OF INVOCATING THE DEAD,

OR

Raising the Spirit of a Departed Person.

Having previously shown and elucidated the rites and ceremonies made use of by magicians for invocating both celestial, terrestrial, and familiar spirits, we will now treat of the *necromantic* art which teaches the method of holding an intercourse with the *spirits* of *departed* persons.

To the honour of the *present* century, we have had but few instances of persons openly and publicly entering into a compact with spirits, or of professing to resolve questions in futurity by means of their agency; neither have we but one *authenticated* instance of *necromancy*; but, in former times, these practices were no uncommon thing, and those who had an opportunity of blending classical learning and scientific speculation with it, were esteemed the most elevated characters of their day, and were frequently honoured with the protection and confidence of princes and nobles.*

The cause of the paucity of these attempts, and also of the appearances of evil spirits, in our days, is because "the fulness of time" and the brightness of Christianity has been gradually dispelling the mists of heresy and idolatry, even as the sun doth the fogs, which vanish on his appearance; not by any violence or compulsion, but from a cause implanted in the nature of things and their opposites. Even so the kingdom of *light*, as it overspreads the soul in power and dominion, closes up the centre of darkness, and scatters the influence of the devil before it, who becomes, as it were, entirely passive as to the works and will of man.

In a former part of this circle, we have given a concise illustration of the nature and offices of spirits, both good and evil, which will serve as matter of much curious inquiry to the inquisitive reader, and which, indeed, is the *substance* of

---

* It is not accounted *sinful* to invoke spirits, unless a compact be formed with them. Vide p. 112, the ghost of Marshal Saxe raised by Schrepfer.

those numerous stupendous tomes which mystified the world in the sixteenth and seventeenth centuries, but which are now only to be found in the libraries or cabinets of the curious. Yet, notwithstanding we have been as copious as possible, this subject is so intricate and diversified in itself, that to attempt an *ample* demonstration of the matter would require deeper speculation than the subject deserves, or than we are masters of, particularly as the inhabitants of these spiritual kingdoms are never in one regular stay, continuance, or property, but, from one hour to another, are continually floating and changing. Like the swiftness of the winds, or the gliding along of running waters, which pass away as a thought, and are no more remembered; so, also, it is with the devils and infernal spirits, in that *lachrymable* state of darkness, where their existence is a continual anguish and torment, shifting from the pangs of one sorrow to the bitterness of another, to all eternity!

The most remarkable instance of *necromancy* in former times is that related by Weaver, in his "*Funeral Monuments.*"

He there records that Edward Kelly, a *magician*, with one Paul Waring (who acted in the capacity of companion and associate in all his conjurations), went together to the church-yard of *Walton-le-dale*, in the county of Lancaster, where they had information of a person being recently interred, who was supposed to have hidden or buried a considerable sum of money, and to have died without disclosing to any person where it was deposited. He proceeds to state, that they entered the church-yard exactly at twelve o'clock at night; and, having had the grave pointed out to them the preceding day, they exorcised the *spirit* of the deceased, by magical *spells* and *incantations*, till it *appeared* before them; and not only satisfied their wicked desires and inquiries, but delivered several strange *predictions* concerning persons in that neighbourhood, which were literally and exactly fulfilled.

PROCEEDINGS IN THE
Necromantic Art

The process in this respect differs materially from the *theurgic* art before explained; for, in the first place, the person being fixed on whose *apparition* is to be invoked, or brought up, the magician, with his assistant, must repair to the church-yard or *tomb* where the deceased was buried, exactly at midnight, as the ceremony can only be performed in the night, between the hours of twelve and one.

The *grave* is first to be opened, or an aperture made, by which access may be had to the naked body. The magician having described the circle, and holding an hazel wand in his hand, of one year's growth, while his companion or assistant beareth a consecrated torch, he turns himself to all the *four* winds, and, touching the dead body three times with his wand, repeats as follows:—

The Necromantic Spell or Incantation.

By the virtue of the holy resurrection, and the torments of the damned, I conjure and exorcise thee, spirit of (N.) deceased, whose body here lies, to answer my liege demands, being obedient unto these mystic and sacred ceremonies, on pain of everlasting torment and distress.

Then let him say, "Berald, Beroald, Balbin gal gabor aguba;" *Arise, arise, I charge and command thee.*

After which forms and ceremonies the ghost or apparition will become visible, and will answer to any questions put to it by the exorcist.

But, if it be desired to put any interrogatories to the spirit of any corpse that hath hanged, drowned, or otherwise made away with itself, the *incantation* must be performed while the body hangs, or on the spot where it is first found after the suicide hath been committed, and before it is touched or removed by the coroner's jury.

CEREMONY FOR RAISING THE SPIRIT OF ONE WHO HATH COMMITTED SUICIDE.

In this case, the exorcist, being prepared with the *pentacles* of Solomon, the two seals of the earth, and other necessaries, he must bind upon the top of his wand, a bundle of St. John's wort (*milies perforatum*), with the head of an owl; and, having repaired to the spot where the corpse of the self-murderer lies, at the solemn hour of *midnight*, precisely at twelve o'clock, he must draw the circle, and, having entered it, solemnly repeat the following words:—

THE INCANTATIONS.

By the mysteries of the deep, by the flames of **Banal**, by the power of the east, and the silence of the night, by the holy rites of **Hecate**, I conjure and exorcise thee, thou distressed spirit, to present thyself here, and reveal unto me the cause of thy calamity, why thou didst offer violence to thy own liege life, where thou art now in being, and where thou wilt hereafter be.

He then, gently smiting the carcass nine times with the wand, says as follows:—

I conjure thee, thou spirit of (N.) deceased, to answer my demands that I am to propound unto thee, as thou ever hopest for the rest of the holy ones, and case of all thy misery; by the blood of ✠ **Jesus** ✠ which he shed for thy soul, I conjure and bind thee to utter unto me what I shall ask thee.

Then, cutting down the carcass from the tree, they lay his head toward the *east*; and in the space that this following incantation is repeating, they set a chafing dish of *fire* at his right hand, into which they pour a little *wine*, some *mastic*, and *gum aromatic*, and, lastly, a vialful of the sweetest *oil*, having also a pair of bellows, and some unkindled charcoal, to make the fire burn bright at the instant of the carcass's rising. The third *incantation* is thus:—

I conjure thee, thou spirit of (N.) that thou do immediately enter into thy ancient body again, and answer to my demands: by the virtue of the holy resurrection, and by the posture of the body of the Saviour of the world, I charge thee, I conjure, I command thee, on pain of the torments and wandering of thrice seven years, which I, by the force of sacred magic rites, have power to inflict upon thee, by thy sighs and groans, I conjure thee to utter thy voice; so help thee God, and the prayers of the holy church. Amen.

Which ceremony being *thrice* repeated, while the fire is burning with *mastic* and *gum aromatic*, the body will begin to rise, and at last will stand upright before the exorcist, answering with a faint and hollow voice the questions propounded unto it: why it destroyed itself,—where its dwelling is,—what its life is,—how long it will be ere it enter into rest,—and by what means the exorcist may assist it to come thereto: also of the treasures of this world,—where they are hid. Moreover, it can answer very punctually of the places where *ghosts* reside, and how to communicate with them; teaching the nature of astral spirits and infernal beings, so far as its capacity reacheth. All which, when the ghost has fully answered, the exorcist ought, out of commiseration and reverence to the deceased, to use what means can possibly be used, for the procuring rest unto the spirit.

To which effect he must dig a *grave*, and, filling the same half full of *quick lime*, with a little *salt* and common *sulphur*, he must put the carcass naked into it; which experiment, next to the burning the body into ashes, is of great force to quiet and end the disturbance of the astral spirit.

TRADITIONS RELATING TO NECROMANCY
Or Invocating the Dead

Translated from Cornelius Agrippa. (MSS.)

"The souls of men do still love their relinquished bodies after death, as it were a certain affinity adhering to them: such as are the souls of noxious men, that have violently relinquished their bodies, and wanting a due burial, their souls do still wander in a liquid and turbulent spirit about their dead bodies; for those souls, by the known means, by the which heretofore they were conjoined to their bodies by the like vapours, liquors, and savours, are easily drawn into their bodies.

"But the souls of the dead are not to be called up without blood, or by the application of some part of the *relict* body; therefore, to *invocate the dead*, thou shouldest suffumigate with new blood, with the bones of the dead, with flesh, eggs, milk, honey, oil, &c. which do attribute to the soul a means apt to receive their bodies.

"It is requisite this work should be done in those places where those souls are most conversant, or for some alliance alluring those souls into their forsaken bodies, or for some kinds of affection which, in times past, was impressed in them, in their life, drawing the said souls to certain places, things, or persons, or for the forcible nature of some place fitted and prepared for to purge or punish their souls. Which places are known from *nightly visions*, presentiments, apparitions, and such like prodigies seen.

"*Apt* places for these things are churchyards; and better than this, places where there hath been an execution of criminal judgments; and better still, those places where of late years murders have been done, and for which no expiation has been made, nor right burials performed. For the expiation of those places is a holy rite, duly to be adhibited to the burial of the bodies, and oftentimes prohibiteth the souls coming into their bodies, and expelleth them far off unto the places of judgment. But the souls of the dead are not easily to be raised up, except it be the souls of them whom we have known to be evil, or to have perished by a violent death, and those whose bodies want a right and due burial.

"Therefore, what place soever you make use of, *take some principal of the relict body* to make a suffumigation with, using other rites. But those things are not always sufficient for the raising up of souls, because of an extra-natural part of reason and understanding, which is above, and known only to the ruling powers of heaven.

"The souls, moreover, ought to be allured by celestial powers duly administered, which do move the harmony of the soul, such as are songs, sounds, inchantments, or holy rites, prayers, conjurations, exorcisms, &c."

The author, wishing to give every possible elucidation relative to the extraordinary superstitions of past ages, *the belief in which, it is said, no longer exists*, has been indefatigable in perusing the various magical manuscripts that has fallen under his immediate notice. This he has done the rather, because hitherto the different authors who have written upon the theory of charms, enchantments, spectral apparitions, and fairy lore, have merely confined their labours to narrative alone, forgetting that the best illustration of those subjects lies in the elucidating their singular ceremonials.

A MAGICAL EXPERIMENT.

The following strange experiment is *copied from a very scarce and curious manuscript*. In the present enlightened age, the rehearsal thereof cannot possibly do any harm, as we presume it would be difficult to find any one who would go through the disgusting process of "raising the dead spirit," even should they place faith in its performance. It is word for word with the original, which was deemed a most profound secret, in the reign of Popery and Inquisition; the betrayal of which would have subjected the party to imprisonment for life, or to a cruel death.

To Invocate and Converse With The Dead.

"When any one dieth, *whom you would have the spirit of when dead*, Go wheare the grave *will* be made, and make sure to take a handful of the first earth that is digged when the grave is first begun to be made; then rehearsing the person's name that is dead, saying as followeth:—

"'O (N) I doe take of the earth in which thou must enter into, that thy spirit may come unto the churche to speake unto me, and fulfill my will, and that it shall never have power to rest, or be quiet, until thou come to speak with me, and fulfill my will and commandments.'

"Afterwards goe into the churche with the earthe in thy hande, and there beholde untill the bodie of the dead person be brought into the Churche; and thou shall see a two-foulde spirit cominge. And the Spirit of the dead like Catts. Then rehearse the names of God followinge, afterwardes they will departe and go with the funerall to the grave. But thou must beholde still, and walke untill the corpse be buried, and everyone departed, and gone awaye.

"Then the Spirit will come to thee again, whom doe not feare, for it cannot hurte thee. Then calle it by the person's name that is buried, and say as followeth,

"' O (N) *I doe conjure thee* by the Passion of our Lord Jesus Xt, and by the virginitie of the sweet Virgin Marye, and by the twelve Apostles, and by the four Evangelists, and by all Martyrs and Confessors, and by this Earthe which I have in my hande, which is of the Earthe wherein thy bodie is buried in, O (N) and by all the Constellations of heaven, and by all the Virtues and Powers, which are in heaven and earth, and by all the Angelles, and their falle, in which was the cause of Man's creation, and by the wordes which Christ spake as he hung on the Altar of the Crosse, That is, Ely, Ely, Lama-zabacthani, Semiforas, that thou doe not offende me by any manner of lyinge or deceit, but that thou declare the truth of all things that I shall aske thee, and that thou doe come unto me at all times when I doe calle thee, by this name, O (N). And in answeringe me trulye with an understanding voice, and true tongue or speeche, which I do best understande, and thus I doe bind thee and conjure thee by all the wordes aforesaid, and I commande thee by our Lord Jesus Xt, and by his most precious bloude, and by him that will come to judge the quicke and thedeade, and the worlde by her. Amen.'

"Then carrye the earth in thy hande to the grave again, and say unto him. Go in peace, O (N), and the peace of God be between me and thee, and as often as I will speake with thee, be thou readie, and when I call thee by this name O (N) with this conjuration. Go in peace, and the crosse of Xt. be betweene me and thee, nowe and always. Amen. Fiat, fiat, fiat."

"Note firste of all when the spirits do appeare, rehearse these names of God followinge to bind them, and thou shalt be safe from all dangers after-wardes. These be the names followinge.

"Tetragrammaton, Anronadall, Draconium, Alliam, fortissam, fortisson, figa, Sache, frege, Pronisioni, Sucreon, Dracosu, Eloy, Sachee, Emanuell, Anathanathout, Semaforas, Amen."

ANOTHER STRANGE NECROMANTIC SPELL.

"If thou be disposed to speake or meete with anye person lyvinge or deade, you muste goe into the Churche yarde on a frydaye at night, at 9 or 10 of the Clocke, and walke rounde aboute the alley seven times, and when you come to a corner, you muste stande still, and saye the Lordes prayer, and the Creede, and before you have gone seven times aboute, you shall meete them you woulde meete withall, personallye as they were wont to goe. Finis."

The Magic Bell for invoking Spirits.
FROM A RARE GERMAN MSS.

"This bell must be formed of *electricum magicum*, and fashioned as above described, round it the words ✠ *Tetragrammaton* ✠ and ✠ *Sadai*, ✠ must be engraved in relief, and also the sign and planet under which you were born. Also inside thereof the word ✠ *Elohim*, ✠ and on the clapper *Adonai*. It must be kept in a clean chamber, and when thou wouldest invoke the celestial agents or good spirits, make a fire with incense and proper perfumes, then rehearse devoutly an appropriate incantation, and ring the bell *thrice*, when the spirit will instantly appear before thee, and thou wilt be enabled to have thy wishes performed. But keep this a secret."

Beaumont, in his "Treatise of Spirits," mentions this singular magical bell, and relates a history of a certain monk who made use of it.

A REPRESENTATION AND DESCRIPTION
OF THE
Urim and Thummim.

FROM A RARE GERMAN ALCHEMICAL MANUSCRIPT.*

THE above illustration exhibits a correct view of the *Urim and Thummim*; it consists of a pedestal formed according to the rules of the magical science, of a composition termed by

---

* In the possession of the Mercurii.

the theurgists, *electrum magicum*, with the word ✠ **Elohim** ✠ on the pedestal; in the centre of this is placed a pillar, which supports an oval *chrystal*, or polished surface set in gold, and around which must be inscribed the mighty name of supreme majesty ✠ **Tetragrammaton** ✠

Round it are five small chrystals, to represent the *animal, vegetable, mineral, and astral* kingdoms, and the one on top to represent the △ of the Lord. The whole must be preserved in a case free from dust.

The Composition of the Electrum Magicum,

Being a rare MS. Secret, that has never yet been made Public.

"Take four half ounces of ☉ which must be poured through the *antimony*, melt it on a *Sunday*, in the hour of the ☉, when it is well fused, throw purified *saltpetre* into it, until it emits sparks of all kinds of colours, when it is well purified—and take care that you do this in the proper hour, then pour it into a *new* vessel, afterwards melt in it, on a *Monday*, in the hour of the ☽, four half ounces of refined silver; purify it with salt of tartar, which has no culinary salt in it, and when the *hour* is *past cease*. On a *Tuesday*, in the hour of *Mars*, melt clean pure *iron* with potashes, and cleanse it further with pitch or tar. On the *Wednesday*, in the hour of ☿, melt four half ounces of *quicksilver*, which purify with pitch. On *Thursday*, in the hour of ♃, melt three half ounces of *tin*; purify it with the fat of a ram. On a *Friday*, in the hour of ♀, take four half ounces of virgin *copper*, purify it with vinegar and saltpetre carefully; then strain it through a piece of leather. On the *Saturday*, in the hour of ♄, melt pure *lead*, throw a good deal of pitch or tar upon it, and put it by, and take care on the *hour* in which the *new moon* is light, to melt in the same hour all the metals together. Put, therefore, your purified *lead* first into the crucible, afterwards the *tin*, before it is too hot, pour the *quicksilver* into it, and stir it about with a *hazel* stick, then put the *copper* into it, and give it a strong heat, afterwards the *silver*, and next the *gold*. While all this is fusing, throw into it the eighth part of an ounce of *mineral steel*, and cast therefrom the pedestal.

After this get two large *chrystals* ground on a *Friday*, and well polished; now observe when the ☉ gets into ♌, place in the same hour a crucible in the fire, which crucible must be well glazed therein; take from the same, four stones, which were before put into the *electrum*, from each one half an ounce; put first the *mineral* in, then the *vegetable* and *animal*, and last of all the *astral*, and when you pour this into the mould, it will seem as if the stone was red hot, like a glowing coal, and it is wonderful, since it never changes, but so remains continually. Then make the instrument as seen in the drawing, and call it the *urim* and *thummim*. This wonderful secret is but little known in the world, and neither kings nor emperors can obtain it for money.

Use of this Famous Secret.

When thou wouldest *divine* by this art, take the *urim* from the case, place it on the table, with two *wax-lights* burning beside it, constrain your imagination, and fall down with reverence before the Father in heaven, then having a brazier at hand, filled with hot embers, throw therein *frankincense, mastic, benzoin* and *myrrh,* and begin to fumigate to all four parts of the world, and with the *incense* pan also three times towards the *urim,* then bend thyself, and devoutly say as follows:

The Incantation.

O! ✠ Tetragrammaton, ✠ thou powerful God and Father! we praise, love, and pray to thee, we also here are collected laying before thee, like poor earth and ashes. We honour thy holy and majestical name, and exclaim with all the saints and elect, three times Holy, Holy, Holy.* Then sing a song of praise to God, such as the Psalm, *We praise thee O God, &c.* And with thy brethren place thyself round a table, and remain a little while quite still, each having his eye directed towards the *urim,* and whatever thou desirest or wishest to

---

* This is supposed by antiquarians to be the mode practised by the high priests amongst the Jews, and to be the same *urim and thummim* as described in Scriptures.

see or know, shall be manifested unto thee, and thou shalt become acquainted with all hidden things, *and wilt be enablad to see anything that is being done in any part of the world, no matter how distant, or whether past, present, or future.* But when this is done, all must be kept a profound secret, the lights must be put out, and all present must fall down and praise God. This is the hidden mystery of the *urim and thummim.*"

Biography

OF

FAMOUS ASTROLOGERS.

LIFE OF HENRY CORNELIUS AGRIPPA.

HENRY CORNELIUS AGRIPPA, a learned philosopher and astrologer, was born at Cologne, on the 14th of September, 1486, and descended from a noble and ancient family of Nettesheim, in Belgia; desiring to walk in the steps of his ancestors, who for many generations had been employed by the princes of the house of Austria, he entered early in the service of the Emperor Maximilian. He had at first the employ of secretary; but as he was equally qualified for the sword and the pen, he afterwards turned soldier, and served the Emperor seven years in his Italian army. He signalized himself on several occasions, and as a reward of his brave actions, he was created knight in the field. He wished to add the academical honours to the military; he therefore commenced the study of law and physic.

He was a man possessed of a very wonderful genius, and from his youth applied himself to learning; and by his great natural talents, he obtained an extensive knowledge of almost all arts and sciences, and was early engaged in the search of the mysteries of nature. The prodigious compass of his knowledge astonished every one who conversed with him. He carefully informed himself of every science, and of course was profound in the Rosycrusian and Alchemical arcanas. He was celebrated throughout Europe, most of the Courts of which he visited. The history of his life, as recorded by Bayle, is curious and interesting:—sometimes, in all the pride of literature, he was disputing in schools and universities; and other times, in courts and camps; then, in the shops of projecting mechanics, and in the laboratory of hermetic philosophers.

The prejudices of the times in which he lived often brought him into trouble; and he was sometimes cited before the civil tribunal for a sorcerer, and his poor dog was even dreaded as an evil demon. At other times, it is recorded, that he practised"Magic, Necromancy, and similar arts."—Although it was, probably, his surprising skill in Judicial Astrology, that caused these absurd rumours, since we find he was daily consulted by, and cast the horoscopes of, kings, princes, and warriors. He was here in England in 1510, and did wonders in the astrological art; and in 1529, so great was his reputation as a prophet, that having cast the nativity of Henry VIII., and predicted many surprising things (all of which came to pass) to the knights and retinue of the Court, the King of England gave him an invitation to settle here, and offered him a magnificent pension, to become the"Astrologer Royal." Which invitation, however, he thought proper to decline; most likely, on account of his knowledge, by means of his scientific skill, of Henry's real character.

He practised astrology at most of the Courts of Europe; and many marvellous legends are on record of his profound knowledge of the stars. He is even said to have predicted the very day and hour of the death of a highly celebrated hero of those times. However, be it as it will, he was the first mathematician of his age. He died in 1535. Some of his works evince admirable skill, and are filled with proofs of his extraordinary genius. The most celebrated of these, in Latin, is his treatise of"Occult Philosophy;" *a rare work*, and calculated to hand this author's name down to the latest posterity.

The World of Spirits

THE LEGENDARY STORY OF THOMAS PERKS.

Authentic Copy of a Letter sent to the Bishop of Gloucester, by the Reverend Mr. Arthur Bedford, Minister of Temple Church, in Bristol.

Bristol, August 2, 1703,

MY LORD,

Being informed by Mr. Shute of your Lordship's desire that I should communicate to you what I had known concerning a certain person, who was acquainted with spirits to his own destruction, I have made bold to give you the trouble of this letter, hoping my desire to gratify your Lordship in every particular, may be an apology for the length thereof. I had formerly given an account to the late Bishop of Hereford, in which there are probably some things contained, which I do not now remember, which, if your Lordship could procure from his Lady, (who now lives near Gloucester,) would be more authentic.

About thirteen years ago, whilst I was curate to Dr. Read, rector of St. Nicholas in this city, I began to be acquainted with one Thomas Perks, a man about twenty years of age, who lived with his father at Mongatsfield, a gunsmith; and contracted an intimacy with him, he being not only a very good-natured man, but extremely skilled in mathematical studies, which were his constant delight, viz. arithmetic, geometry, gauging, surveying, astronomy, and algebra; he had a notion of the perpetual motion, much like that wheel in Archimedes's Mathematical Magic, in which he had made some improvements, and which he has held was demonstrable from mathematical principles, though I could never believe it. I have seen an iron wheel, to which he intended to add several things of his own invention, in order to finish the same; but, thinking it of no use, and being otherwise unfortunately engaged, it was never perfected. He gave himself so much to astronomy, that he could not only calculate the motions of the planets, but an eclipse also; and demonstrate any problem in spherical trigonometry from mathematical principles, in which he discovered a clear force of reason. When one Mr. Bailey, minister of St. James's in this city, endeavoured to set up a mathematical school, I advised him to this Thomas Perks, for an acquaintance; in whom, as he told me, he found a greater proficiency in those studies than he expected or could have imagined. After this, he applied himself to astrology, and would sometimes calculate nativities, and resolve horary questions. When, by the providence of God, I was settled in Temple-parish, and had not seen him for some time, he came to me, and, we being in private, he asked my opinion very seriously concerning the lawfulness of conversing with spirits; and, after I had given my thoughts in the negative, and confirmed them with the best reasons I could, he told me he had considered all these arguments, and believed they only related to conjurations, but there was an innocent society with them which a man might use, if he made no compacts with them, did no harm by their means, and were not curious in prying into hidden things; and that he himself had discoursed with them, and heard them sing to his great satisfaction; and gave an offer to me and Mr. Bayley at another time, that, if we would go with him one night to Kingswood, we should see them, and hear them both talk and sing, and talk with them whenever we had a mind, and we should return very safe; but neither of us had the courage to venture. I told him the subtilty of the devil to delude mankind, and to transform himself into an angel of light; but he would not believe it was the devil. I had several conferences with him upon this subject, but could never convince him; in all which I could never observe the least disorder of mind, his discourse being very rational; and I proposed (to try him) a question in astronomy, relating to the projection of the sphere, which he projected and resolved, and did afterwards demonstrate from the mathematics, so as to show at the same time, that his brain was free from the least tincture of madness and distraction.—Having this opportunity of asking him several particulars, concerning the methods he used, and the discourses he had with them, he told me had a book whose directions he followed, and accordingly, in the dead time of the night, he went out to a cross way, with a lanthorn and candle consecrated for this purpose with several incantations. He had also consecrated chalk, consisting of several mixtures, with which he made a circle at what distance he thought fit, within which no spirit had power to enter. After this he invoked the spirit by several forms of words, (some of which he told me were taken out of the holy Scriptures, and therefore he thought them lawful, without considering how they might be wrested to his destruction;) accordingly the spirits appeared to him which he called for, in the shape of little maidens, about a foot and a half high, and played about a circle. At first he was somewhat affrighted; but, after some small acquaintance, this antipathy in nature wore off, and he became pleased with their company. He told me they spoke with a very shrill voice, like an ancient woman. He asked them if there was a heaven or hell? they said there was. He asked them what place heaven was? which they described as a place of great glory and happiness; and he asked them what hell was? and they bade him ask no questions of that nature, for it was a dreadful thing to relate, and the devils believe and tremble. He further asked them what method or order they had among themselves? they told him they were divided into three orders; that they had a chief, whose residence was in the air; that he had several counsellors which were placed by him in form of a globe, and he in the centre, which was the chiefest order; another order was employed in going to and from thence to the earth, to carry intelligence from those lower spirits; and their own order was on the earth, according to the directions they should receive from those in the air.

This description was very surprising, but, being contrary to the account we have in Scripture of the hierarchy of the blessed angels, made me conclude they ware devils, but I could not convince him of it. He told me he had bade them sing, and they went to some distance behind a bush, from whence he could hear a perfect concert of such exquisite music as he never before heard; and in the upper part he heard something very harsh and shrill, like a reed, but, as it was managed, did give a particular grace to the rest.

About a quarter of a year after, he came again to me, and wished he had taken my advice, for he thought he had done that which would cost him his life, and which he did heartily repent of; and indeed his eyes and countenance showed a great alteration. I asked him what he had done. He told me that, being bewitched to his acquaintance, he resolved to proceed farther in this art, and to have some familiar spirit at his command, according to the directions of his book, which were as follows:— He was to have a book made of virgin parchment, consecrated with several incantations; likewise a particular ink-horn, ink, &c. for his purpose; with these he was to go out as usual to a cross way, and call up a spirit, and ask him his name, which he was to put in the first page of his book, and this was to be his familiar. Thus he was to do by as many as he pleased, writing their names in distinct pages, only one in a leaf; and then, whenever he took the book and opened it, the spirit whose name appeared should appear also; and, putting this in practice, the familiar he had was called Malchi, a word in Hebrew of an unknown signification. After this they appeared faster than he desired, and in most dismal shapes, like serpents, lions, bears, &c. hissing at him, and attempting to throw spears and balls of fire, which did very much affright him, and the more when he found it not in his power to stay them, insomuch that his hair (as he told me) stood upright, and he expected every moment to be torn in pieces; this happened in December about midnight, when he continued there in a sweat till break of day, and then they left him, and from that time he was never well as long as he lived. In his sickness be came frequently to Bristol*, to consult with Mr. Jacob, an apothecary in Broad Street, concerning a cure; but I know not whether he told him the origin of his sickness or not; he also came to me at the same time, and owned every matter of fact until the last, and insisted that, when he did any thing of this nature, he was deluded in his conscience to think it lawful, but he was since convinced to the contrary. He declared he made no compacts with any of those spirits, and never did any harm by their means, nor ever pryed into the future fortune of himself or others, and expressed a hearty repentance and detestation of his sins; so that though those methods cost him his life in this world, yet I have great reason to believe him happy in the other. I am not certain that he gave this account to any other person but myself, though he communicated something of it to Mr. Bayley, minister of St. James's, in this city; perhaps your lordship may be further informed by his relations and neighbours of Mangotsfield, which lies in Gloucestershire, not above a mile out of the road to Bath.

I have frequently told this story, but never mentioned his name before; and therefore, if your lord-ship hath any design of printing such accounts as these, I desire it may be with such tenderness to his memory as he deserved, and so as may not be the least prejudice to his relations, who have the deserved character of honest and sober people. I am

    Your Lordship's dutiful

        Son and Servant,

            ARTHUR BEDFORD.

---

* I have myself seen a very curious Telescope, and a very ingenious Fowling Piece, made by this said Thomas Perks; and in my last tour to the West of England (1880) I found numerous versions of this particular account still extant among the peasantry of Kingswood—*Raphael*.

THE PHILOSOPHERS STONE!

Part the First.

At the request of the Editor, a gentleman of perfect chemical skill, and well versed in classic lore, as also in mathematical and philosophical knowledge, and of no mean talents in the astrological art, has undertaken a series of papers to illustrate the possibility and truth of the Alchemical Art, which has for its grand object the *Transmutation of Metals, the Elixir Vitae,* &c; which the ancients are said, by *credible historians,* to have known, and performed wonders therewith.—The Editor of this work trusts these singular essays will prove highly agreeable to the readers of the Familiar Astrologer, as they are at once rare, curious, extraordinary, and learned! He would also just mention, what the writer of the disquisitions did not seem aware of: viz. that Dr. Woolaston and Sir Humphry Davy each pursued the Hermetical Science for a considerable period; and during the pursuit thereof, hit upon most of their invaluable chemical discoveries. The Editor's informant was a Mr. Wagstaff, a highly respectable bookseller; formerly residing in Brown's Lane, Spitalfields, London; who was well known, a few years back, for having the choicest collection of Alchemical works and MSS. of any one in England. He knew many persons who had followed up the theory of the Hermetic art, as given by the old authors ; but with little success, as the Alchemical writers above all other authors clouded their dissertations with far-fetched enigmas, difficult to penetrate, or even guess at, except by adepts.—He informed the Editor, that Sir Humphry Davy, and other great chemists, were constantly purchasing these Alchemical works of him, and employed him to collect those publications, whether in print or MS., whenever and wherever he could procure them. He likewise told the Editor (of this work) that he could prove these gentlemen believed in Alchemy secretly, whatever were their public opinions: and that he was credibly informed, a series of experiments were generally carried on at His Majesty's Mint, to ascertain the growth of gold, and its chemical foundation, &c.

SECTION I

AN ESSAY ON THE
Sacerdotal Science.

It may perhaps appear singular, that in these times, when knowledge is so generally diffused, that men believe but those things which can be proved with almost mathematical exactness; that the sciences generally, have attained to such a height of perfection, and that the deep and mysterious studies of our forefathers, are now, by most men, treated as idle chimeras, and children of a sickly fancy; that a man should dare to run the risk of being thought a fool or an impostor, by attempting to revive again the long condemned and long forgotten **Science of Alchemy**. But I write for those men who read and *judge for themselves*; for those who will not allow their ideas to be enslaved by the trammels of modern philosophy; which were forged by men, who, in their own self-love and self-sufficiency, believed it to be impossible, *that sciences should exist*, which their all-powerful, all-penetrating genius could not fathom: and who, unwilling to own their insufficiency, condemned as futile those things which had baffled their utmost endeavours to attain. How have they condemned *the profound science of Astrology*? How the science of *Hermetic Philosophy*? How all the other sciences that the ancient wise men and magi followed? I answer, that they have condemned them from their ignorance of their simplest laws or precepts! Let them, if they can, bring forth their proofs of the untruth of the mystic sciences; let those who condemn the ancient art of Astrology be put to the test; and it will be found that not one of them is capable of bringing up a direction, or even of casting a figure. How then is it possible that these men, possessing no knowledge of these arts, can have the power of reasoning on them, or of showing their defects? it would be just as reasonable, to take as a law the opinion of a child on the intricacies of Algebra! But let their criticisms be what they may, let them attempt what they will, THESE ARTS HAVE REMAINED, AND WILL REMAIN, BRIGHT

AND RESPLENDENT AS EVER; even when the progeny of those who have condemned them, shall have passed from the memory of man, and their puny and ephemeral slanders and inventions shall have been forgotten, and not one trace of them existing, to cause the student to smile at their ineffectual endeavours. I have taken upon me the pleasing task of laying before the unprejudiced reader, the history, theory, and application of the **Hermetic Art**; and I shall endeavour to prove, that it is not so impossible to attain to the knowledge thereof, as those who have failed in the study have endeavoured to prove

SECTION II
Of the History of Alchemy.

If I were to endeavour to trace **The Science of Nature** to its origin, it would be vain and foolish; as its commencement is lost in those times which form the infancy of the world. The patriarchs of holy writ possessed it; and it was to the influence of it, that they owed the enjoyment of that lengthened life that strikes us in the present day with wonder.

Hermes, who is supposed to have been cotemporary with Abraham, is the first author who has traced its principles, and who has placed them in order; but being unwilling to disclose it openly to the world, he invented hieroglyphics and symbolical characters, under the veil of which he sent it forth to the people; it was from his writings, that the various schools and temples among the Egyptians, the Greeks, and the Druids, were formed, and where the Priests alone explained it to their disciples.

The Arabians studied it with enthusiasm; and **Geber** seems to have been the inventor of distilatory apparatus, which no doubt he contrived, to aid him in his complicated experiments, before he had discovered the simplicity and facility of the art. After the crusade, the study of this science became common in Europe; and a philosopher or learned man, in those days, would have been very little thought of, if he had not some smattering of the art.

From the toils and labours of these men, from their unremitting exertions and multiplied experiments, we have gained the arts of Pharmacy and Chemistry; and the names, *Raymond Lully, Count Bernard of Trevisan, Sendivogius, Philalethes*, will always be remembered: I cite these names in particular, as I am certain, that **they had a perfect knowledge of the art**. The manipulation, theory, and all the technicalities of the science, exist in their works; and all is explained and laid open to the student, except the real names of the first matters to be employed. This they have *all zealously concealed*; and the ignorance of it, has been the stumbling-block of almost all who have endeavoured to attain a knowledge of Alchemy. Towards the middle of the seventeenth century, the study of the art began to decline; and at the present time, a man would hardly credit you, if you told him, that there was existing, a single **Alchemist**.

SECTION III.

The Theory of the Art.

I now arrive at that part of my Treatise, which must give to the reader an idea of the possibility of the existence of an ART; by means of which, the operations of nature may be performed in less time than she takes to bring the stubborn metals to perfection in the Earth's womb. It is evident, that all things must have a beginning, and likewise different stages of perfection: Man is not born at once in force and vigour, neither does the tree bring forth its fruit at once ripe and fit for food! We are all positive of this, and we know that all things, whether vegetable or animal, require time to come to perfection: why then should we believe that mineral productions are exempt from this law? If we look at **a piece of Gold** can we for a moment consider it as the work of an instant? is it possible that it has gained its metallic splendour, its ductility, maleability, and beauty all at once? or is it to be supposed that the metals were all created at the moment when our terrestrial planet was launched from the Creator's hand into immensity?

This cannot be possible; as we have on record instances of mines having been worked for a considerable number of years until nearly exhausted, and shut up for a length of time; and when re-opened they have been found abundant in ore, and fit for working. **THIS PROVES THAT METALS DO GROW AND INCREASE.** Our next object is to ascertain what their beginning or root is, where it is to be found, and what is its nature. The root is a substance which is neither metallic or mineral, but partakes of both; and arises from the putrefaction and decomposition of both mineral and vegetable bodies; it is soft and maniable, sometimes one colour, sometimes another: the metallic germ is frequently found in it, and it is so common that there is not a child but what knows of it; and yet this plentiful and well known production, is the womb or vehicle which is most fit for the 𝕬𝖘𝖙𝖗𝖆𝖑 𝖆𝖓𝖉 𝕱𝖗𝖚𝖈𝖙𝖎𝖋𝖞𝖎𝖓𝖌 𝕱𝖎𝖗𝖊 𝖔𝖋 𝖙𝖍𝖊 𝖂𝖔𝖗𝖑𝖉; to work its slow and secret operations in, on the formation of metals; it may be found and seen everywhere; it is common in fields and marshy places; it is not necessary to dig deep in the bowels of the Earth for it, as it is frequently found at the depth of a man's leg.

This matter the philosophers called their 𝖁𝖆𝖘𝖊 and with reason *too*—for it holds the 𝕬𝖘𝖙𝖗𝖆𝖑 𝕾𝖕𝖎𝖗𝖎𝖙 in itself, and contains it in all its workings, until it putrifies with it, and becomes one body with it, and then it acquires the name of the first matter, which is so earnestly sought after by those who devote themselves to the study of the 𝕬𝖗𝖙 𝖔𝖋 𝕳𝖊𝖗𝖒𝖊𝖘. I must now say something of the Astral or universal spirit— the **LIFE, FIRE, AND SOUL OF PROCREATIVE NATURE**; by means of which all things are brought forth, live, and increase ; and whose generative power is felt to the very centre of the Earth. All men know that they cannot live upon food alone; and that if they were deprived of air they would droop and die. Neither would a plant live or thrive without it. We must not pass over the action of light in silence: let a vegetable be planted and kept in the dark, it will grow, because it has sufficiency of air, but it will come forth sickly and yellow; but let but one small ray of light fall on any of its leaves, and it will be found that that part will quickly assume its healthy garb of green: and if a man be exposed to continual darkness, its effects on his mind and spirits is quickly visible

We have now convinced ourselves that light and air are necessary for the growth, well being, and life of men and vegetables; and those who have read the Emerald Table of Hermes will remember that he says the following words: "**That which is above is like that which is beneath**" so that subterranean productions likewise require the assistance of these two agents of nature. Now this leads us to the following enquiry: do the invigorating principles of light and air act, one independent of the other? or, do they from their union give birth to a third, which affects all things, whether above or below the earth, in an equal manner? We must naturally conclude that this is the case, as neither light nor air in an isolated state can penetrate the depths of the earth. The generative essence of nature then, is a subtle fluid, compounded of light and air, which is capable of penetrating all things. This is what the Philosophers call their **Astral Spirit**, their water of the Sun and Moon, &c.; and this is what the hermetic student must learn to obtain, before he can commence his operations in the art; for this purpose **The Philosopher's Loadstone** must be discovered, for it has the power of attracting this fluid, and of giving it a substantial form. I cannot disclose openly what this is, but I can tell the student that it frequently takes the form of the **CROSS**; and in this emblem are contained *more mysteries than it would be right to divulge openly to all men*; for this reason, it is called the sign of Redemption, as by its power and assistance, the Philosophers prepared their medicine, which had the universal power of bringing to a perfection, far beyond that which nature alone can do, both animals, minerals, and vegetables; and it restores man to his primitive state, and adds new fire and vigour to his body and mind.

The proper time for the *recolt* of this fluid, begins when **the Sun enters the sign of the Ram**, on the 20th or 21st of March, and continues till he quits the sign of the Twins, about the 20th of June. It must be gathered after sunset, when the Moon is at or near her full; and the wind must not blow violently at this time; the Sun's rays are reflected by the Moon, and the air is strongly impregnated with the **Astral fluid, Or Nitre**: it is adviseable to turn to the north during the time of gathering; and if the student has been fortunate enough to divine the attractor of this fluid, let him seek it in A MINE OF THIRTY YEARS STANDING, and he will then be able to obtain the spirit in the form of a viscous fluid: and the **Stone of the Magi**, their medicine and universal solvent, is nothing more than this fluid, carried to its highest pitch of concentration and fermentation: it may be considered like condensed fire, and is brought to this state of purity, by being frequently fermented and putrified with the mineral matter.

ZADKIEL.

THE PHILOSOPHER'S STONE.

Part 2.

The Practice of the Art of Alchemy.

Nature presents us with one of the materials necessary for the practice and perfection of this art, ready formed to hand and fit for use, as the body, matter, or **Vase** in which we work, is found in the bowels of the earth, according as I have stated in the former part of this treatise. The astral spirit is a liquid, fair and clear, like water, and without the enjoyment of which, no man could live. With these two materials we begin the work of Hermes, and for this commencement we must take nature for our guide; for in like manner as she softens and gives to the earth its fructifying property, by rain and dews, so we imbibe our solid matter with our astral spirit.

By this means our matter becomes incorporated and combined with the generative essence of nature, contained in our water; in this manner, by frequent imbibitions and desinations, our matter becomes dead and putrifies, and in putrifying it arises again to a more perfect state of existence, according to the universal law of sublunary things. It must not be supposed that because the matter becomes dry, that it retains nothing of the virtue of the former imbibitions: it merely looses the aqueous part: and I will endeavour to prove this to those who may not understand the science of Chemistry, Glauber's salt.

If you take a portion of Caustic or Carbonate of Soda, on one part, and some Sulphuric Acid on the other, and you imbibe the Soda with the Acid, they will mutually neutralize one another, and you will obtain a liquid which is neither acid nor alkaline; and an intimate and electrical combination will have taken place between the two bodies from this liquid. By evaporation you may obtain crystals, which will be composed of one part or atom of Soda, two of Acid, and twenty of Water: if you suffer these crystals to dry, or even if you calcine them, you will never be able to make them loose more than the 20 parts of water; the Acid will remain in a fixed and solid state with the calcined salt. So we must conceive the theory of our imbibitions; when our matter dries, it still retains to itself the astral essence contained in our water. Having conducted the unbiassed reader thus far, we will proceed to the practice of the

Imbibitions, or Preparations of the Philosophical Mercury.

For this, it will be necessary to have a small box, with a floor, about a foot high, having its top and bottom pierced with holes, and a shelf of wire grating placed rather more than halfway up on the inside; on this shelf you can place an evaporating dish, of glass or Wedgewood ware, which will contain the mineral matter, and at the bottom of the box a common night lamp, with a small floating wick, will cause sufficient heat for all the practice of the work, which ought never to exceed that of the egg whilst hatching; this may surprise some persons, but I do not write for charcoal burners, or for those who send gold up their chimneys by the intensity of heat they employ; this sort of work is merely destroying nature, and cannot be called an imitation. But to return to our subject:—the mineral matter must he divided into small pieces about the size of peas, and watered with our liquid; care must be taken not to give too much or too little, but just as much as it will suck up and no more; it must then be placed in the warm air oven, and suffered to dry completely. This process must he continued until such time as the matter becomes saturated and pregnant with the astral spirit; this will sometimes after forty, at others after fifty imbibitions, often take from two to three days drying, and frequently upon watering it, it will make a small crackling noise; if small, white, and brilliant spots be observed, it shows that too much water has been added at a time; when it begins to be saturated, it becomes clammy, sends forth a foetid smell of graves, and gradually changes colour, becomes blackish, as I have sometimes seen it, as if ink had been spotted over it. This is the beginning of the putrefaction; it proceeds on, and at last becomes brown, black, scaly, and crusty, like pitch. This the old adepts called by divers names, such as crow's head, &c. When it has attained to this, it must no longer be watered, but left in the gentle, oven heat, it will again change colour, and a light colour will soon be perceived to encircle the vessel in which it is placed. This will extend itself through the whole matter, which will shortly become light coloured and white all over; this is called the first sublimation, and is in fact the **Philosophical Mercury,** which requires to be sublimed six other times to bring it to its perfection. These sublimations are the same as the first; this white mercury must again be imbibed until it putrifies, changes colour, and becomes white again; it must thus go through the seven purifications, which is sometimes called loosing the white doves of Diana, &c. When you have arrived at the seventh sublimation, you must next proceed to separate the pure from the impure, which is done in the following manner: the white substance proceeding from the seven sublimations, must be dissolved in our astral spirit, and suffered to crystalize, when there will form on the top a sort of cottony mass, very brilliant, and floating; this is the long desired, and much sought for, Philosophical Mercury. Underneath will be found other salts, which may be brought to perfection by a continuation of the work, and below all, a pulp will subside which you must keep carefully, as it contains the sulphur of the Magi. Hermes tells you, *"not to throw away your ashes, for they contain the crown of your heart."* The next step is

The Preparation of the Sulphur.

The above-mentioned pulp must be imbibed with our astral spirit, until it becomes putrescent; it will then gradually change its colour to that of red, and is in this case the tinging spirit and blood of the pelican, spoken of with so much secrecy by all hermetic writers. It must be gathered carefully, and separated from the earth which remains, which is called the Terra dominate, is of no use, and may be thrown away.— We have now shown how the ancients prepared the two first matters for their work; and the next is, to unveil the mystery of the Philosophical Marriage of Basil Valentine, where he tells us the white man and red woman must be joined together: to accomplish this, the hermetic workman must proceed in the following way:—the sulphur must be divided into two parts; one part of which must be put aside; the other must be placed in a glass vessel, and must be imbibed with the mercury, dissolved in astral water: this, as in the former case, will require forty or fifty imbibitions; after which it will turn color and purify. It is then that the marriage is completed, and you have obtained the first philosophical matter; it will become black and shining, and is then called the blacker than black, according to the enigmatical language of the adepts, when it has attained this state, it must be left to itself; it will soon pass from the Reign of Saturn to that of Luna, and will become a powder of most brilliant whiteness.

The Reign of ☽

Having succeeded that of dusky ♄, the preparation has now acquired its first stage of perfection, and has not only become a medicine of supernatural force, for the human body; but it has likewise attained the power of acting on metals, and converts them, in proportion to its degrees of multiplication, to the nature of silver. Still must the process be continued; the brilliancy will vanish, and whiteness will subside, and a greenish colour will pervade the whole. This is the sign of your entry to

The Reign of ♀

Care must be taken that your fire be not too strong; the matter has already gained a high degree of subtility, and it ought to be governed so that the mass remains at the bottom of the vessel; by judicious and careful working, the colour again changes; a yellowish tint ensues, then reddish, lemon colour, and thus begins the

Reign of ♂

An igneous nature is now abundant in the matter; it marches on towards the red; the fire must here be strengthened, and it is here that the portion of sulphur which was formerly put aside, will be found necessary, and it will be necessary to continue the work with the solar liquid. This being done, the red colour will become deeper, a tint of regal purple will be seen, then let the student's heart rejoice, as this is the sign of

The Reign of ☉

We have now arrived at our last labour, and the harvest is at hand; the purple colour grows darker, and at last the matter will remain in the vase, of a black red colour, not unlike a freshly precipitated powder of Cassius, containing;

a large portion of gold. If the student still wish to proceed on, and to advance as far as this part of the science will admit, he must here commence the

Multiplication;

Which is merely an exact recapitulation of the foregoing manipulations; but he must beware of proceeding beyond the ninth multiplication; here the medicine becomes too strong and subtle to be contained in any vessel, it passes through glass like olive oil through paper. My limits have not allowed me to treat of this subject in so detailed a manner as I could have wished, or I would have pointed out to the student its intimate relation with the mysteries and ceremonies of religions. I would have shewn that the mythology teaches this art in enigmas; but, however, I leave gone as far as my time and place will allow for the present, let others do the same on this, or what subjects they have a knowledge of, and it may be the means of mutual improvement to us all, in the sciences and learning of the ancient Magi, of which there is not a more ardent and zealous admirer than

Your well-wisher,
ZADKIEL.

[Miscellaneous section on Alchemy]

"I wal tell you as was me taught also.
  The four spirits, and the bodies sevene
  By ordne, as oft I herd my Lord hem nevene.
  The **first** spirit, quicksilver cleped is;
  The **second**, orpimente; the **third** yevis
  Sal amnoniack; and the **fourth**, brimstone.

"The bodies sevene eke, when here anon,
  Sol, gold is; and **Luna**, silver we threpe;
  Mars, iron; **Mercurie**, quicksilver we clepe;
  Saturnus, lede; and **Jupiter**, is tin.
  And **Venus**, copper, by my fader kin."

The following are the directions of a celebrated writer on Alchemy, George Ripley, who wrote his *Compound of Alchemie* in the 15th Century, and addressed it to Edward IV.

"First *calcyne*, and after that *putrifie*,
Dissolve *dystill, sublyme, descende*, and *fixe*;
With aqua vitae oft tymes both weet and drie,
And make a marriage the bodye and spirits betwixte:
Which thus together naturally, if ye can myxe
In losing the bodie, the water shall congealed be.
Then shall the ladie dy utterly of the flyxe.
Bleeding and changing colours as ye shall see.

The *third day*, again to lyfe he shall uprise.
And devour byrds and beastes of the wildernesse;
Crowes, popingayes, pyes, pecocks, and mevies;
The phenix, the eagle whyte, the gryffon of fearfulnesse ;
The green lyon and the red dragon he shall distresse.
The whyte dragon also; the antelope, unicorne, panthere,
With other byrds, and beastes, hoth more and lesse.
The basaliske also, which almost each one doth feare.

In bees and nubi, he shall arise and ascende
Up to the Moone, and sith up to the Sunne,
Thro' the ocean sea, which rounde is without ende,
Onely shypped within a little glassen tonne;
When he cometh thither, then is the maistrie wonne.
About which journey greate goode shall ye not speede.
And yet ye shall be glad that it was begonne,
Patiently if ye list to your work attend."

The following is extracted from GEBER, a renowned *Philosopher* of the olden time.

"Now let the high God of nature, blessed and glorious, be praised: who hath revealed the series of all medicines, with the experience of them, which, by the goodness of his instigation, and by our incessant labour, we have searched out, and have seen with our eyes, and handled with our hands, the completement thereof sought in our magistery. But if we have concealed this, let not the son of learning wonder; for we have not concealed it from him, but have delivered it in such speech, as it must necessarily be hid from the evil and unjust, and the unwise cannot discern it. **Therefore Sons of Doctrine search ye! and ye will find the most excellent gift of God, reserved for you only.** Ye sons of folly, and wickedness, and evil manners! fly away from this science, because it is inimical and adverse to you, and will precipitate you into the miserable state of poverty. For this gift of God is absolutely by the judgment of Divine Providence, hid from you, and denied for ever."

KING GEBER.

The celebrated RAYMOND LULLY is said, while on a visit in London, to have *converted a mass of* 50,000 *pounds of Quicksilver into Gold;* from which Edward I. is said by the Alchemist, to have coined the first rose-nobles, or according to others, the first guineas. He is said to have rendered his name famous by this exploit, as well as by the following feat:

> "Such art of multiplying is to be reproved,
> But holy Alkimy of right is to be loved;
> Which treateth of a precious medicine,
> Such as truly maketh gold and silver fine.
> Whereof example, for testimony,
> Is in a city of Catalony;
> Which *Raymond Lully*, knight, men suppose
> Made in seven images the truth to disclose;
> Three were good silver, in shape like ladies bright
> Everie, each of them were gold, and like a knight
> In borders of their clothing, letters did appear,
> Signifying in sentence as it sheweth here:

First Statue.—"Of *old horshoes* (said one) I was yre,
    Now I am good *silver*, as good as ye desire.
Second Statue.—I was (said another) *Iron* set from the mine,
    But now I am *golde*, pure, perfect, and fine.
Third Statue.—Whilome was I, *copper* of an old red panne.

Now am I good *silver*, said the third woman.

Fourth Statue.—The fourth said, I was *copper*, grown in the filthy place, now I am perfect *gold*, made by God's grace.

Fifth Statue.—The fifth said, I *silver*, perfect, thorough fine, now am I perfect *gold*, excellent, better than the prime

Sixth Statue.—I was a pipe of *lead* well nigh too hundred yere, and to all men good *silver*, I appeare.

Seventh Statue.—The seventh, I *lead*, am *gold* made for a mastery. But truly my fellowes are nearer thereto than I."

I shall conclude this article by another extract from **Geber**. "If they say," exclaims he, "philosophers and princes of this world have desired this science, and could not find it, we answer, **they lie**. For princes, though few, and especially the ancient and wise men in our time, have, as is manifest, by their industry found out this science, but would never by word or writing discover the same to such men because they are unworthy of it. Therefore they not seeing any to possess this science, conceive an error in their minds, and thence judge that none hove found it. But if they otherwise argue that *species* is not changed into *species*, we again say **they lie**; as they are more accustomed than to speak truly of these things; for SPECIES IS CHANGED INTO SPECIES in this manner: namely, when the individual of one species is changed into the individual of another.

We see a *worm* both naturally and by natural artifice *to be turned into a fly*, which differs from its species, and a *calf* strangled, to be turned *into bees, wheat into darnet*, and a *dog* strangled *into worms*; by the putrefaction of ebullition. **Yet we do not this, but Nature, to whom we administer both the same.** Likewise also, *we* alter not metals, **but Nature**, for whom according to art we prepare that matter: for she by herself acts, not **we**; yet we are her administrators, *etc.*

THE FAMOUS ALKAHEST,

OR,

UNIVERSAL DISSOLVENT OF THE ANCIENTS.

According to Paracelsus and Van Helmont, there is a certain fluid in nature capable of reducing *all* sublunary bodies, or dissolving them into their original matter; or into an uniform portable liquor that will unite with water, and the juices of our bodies.

Van Helmont, declaring that *he* himself possessed the secret, excited succeeding chemists and alchemists to the pursuit of so wonderful a menstruum; and Mr. Boyle, the celebrated chemist, is said to have declared, that , "he had rather have been master of it than of the philosopher's stone."

The different conjectures of chemists, with regard to the *matter* of the alkahest, are innumerable; some expected to obtain it from sea-salt and mercury; others wrought on equinoctial dew; others on rainwater; others on talc, on zinc, on antimony, &c.

Kunkel, in ridicule of the universal dissolvent, asks, "If the alkahest dissolves all substances, in what vessel can it be contained?" But this question maybe partially set aside, when it is considered that the menstruum might be weakened so as to be occasionally kept in that vessel which has the greatest power to resist its effects, or it might be contained in a continuous number of vessels, as it is not to be supposed that the effect would be instantaneous. And the fact of so great a man as *Boyle* giving credence to the possibility of such a mixture, certainly goes far to free those persons from the charge of credulity, who are believers therein at the present day; of which there are many; and they, also, men of science and genius!

THE FAMOUS ELIXER OF LIFE.
Prepared from Balm.

"In the proper season of the year, when the herb is at its full growth, and, consequently, its juices in their whole vigour, gather at the fittest time of the day a sufficient quantity of *balm*, wipe it clean, and pick it; then put it in a stone mortar, and, by laborious beating, reduce it into a thin pap

"Take this glutinous and odoriferous substance and put it into a bolt-head, which is to be hermetically sealed, and then place it in a dunghill, or some gentle heat equivalent thereto, where it must digest for forty days.

"When it is taken out, the matter will appear clearer than ever, and have a quicker scent. Then *separate* the grosser parts, which, however, are not to be thrown away. Put this liquid into a gentle bath, that the remaining gross particles may perfectly subside. In the meantime, dry calcine, and extract the *fixed* salt of the grosser parts, separated as before mentioned, which fixed salt is to be joined to the liquor when filtrated.

"Next take *sea salt*, well purified, melt it, and, by setting it in a cold place, it will run, and become clear and limpid. Take equal parts of both liquors, mix them thoroughly, and having hermetically sealed them in a proper glass, let them be carefully exposed to the sun, in the warmest season of the year, for about six weeks. At the end of this space, the *primum ens* of the balm will appear swimming on the top like a bright green oil, which is to be carefully separated and preserved. Of this *oil, a few drops taken in a glass of wine* for several days together, will bring to pass those wonders that are reported of the Countess of Desmond and others; *for it will entirely change the juices of the human body,* reviving the decaying frame of life, *and restoring the spirits of long lost youth.*"

The author who records this curious and wonderful discovery, remarks, "If after the medicine is thus prepared, any doubt be had of its efficacy, or of its manner of operation, let a few drops be given every day on raw meat to any old dog or cat, and in less than a fortnight, by the changing of their coats and other incontestable changes, the virtue of this preparation will sufficiently appear."

This is the preparation of balm which Mr. Boyle (the celebrated chemist) mentions in his works; and in which he tells us that *"Dr. Le Fevre"* gave him an account of it, "in the presence of a famous physician, and another virtuoso, to whom he applied, as knowing the truth of what he said, that an intimate friend of his, whom," says Mr. Boyle, " he named to me, having prepared the *primum ens* of balm, to satisfy himself the better of its effects, made a trial upon himself, and took of it according to the prescription, for above a fortnight; long before which, his nails, both of his hands and feet, began to loosen themselves from the skin, (but without pain), which, at length, falling off of their own accord, this gentleman keeps yet by him in a box for a rarity; but would not pursue the trial any farther, being satisfied with what he had found, and being in no need of such physic; but having given the same medicated wine, for the or twelve days, to a woman that served in his house, and who was near 70 years of age, without letting her know what he expected it would do, her 'menses' came upon her again, in a sufficiently large quantity to frighten her so much that he durst not prosecute the experiment any farther. And when I asked, "says Mr. Boyle, "why he made no trials upon beasts, it was answered, that though he had but little of the medicine, yet he put apart an *old* hen, and moistening her food with some drops of it for a week, about the sixth day she began to moult her feathers by degrees till she became stark naked; but before a fortnight was passed, she began to regain others, which, when they were come to their full growth, appeared far and better coloured than at first."

And he added, "that besides that her crest was raised, she also laid more eggs than she was wont to do before." —*From "Hermeppus Redidivus," a scarce work.*

NATURAL MAGIC.

THE SYMPATHETIC VIAL;

Whereby may be immediately ascertained the Health or Sickness of an absent Friend, although a thousand Miles distant; and whether they are Alive or Dead.

It is tolerably well known that Nature has a secret communication within herself, through all her works; and the occult *principle* thereof is found in human nature, as well as in animal and inanimate bodies. Upon this reasoning the following curious experiment is founded.

If you wish to know how any relation, absent friend, or acquaintance, does, during their absence or travelling into any other country, in respect to their health, you must possess yourself with some of their *live* blood; and, while it is warm, infuse into it a small quantity of *white vitriol* or spirits of wine, and keep it close stopped up, in a glass vial, from the air. Now, if your friend is *well*, the blood will look lively, fresh, and florid; but, on the contrary, if he is ill, or the least thing indisposed, you may perceive it by the changing colour of the blood, which will immediately happen according as he is diseased in his body. If the blood gain a redder hue than usual, you may pronounce him in a fever; but, if it grow paler, and seem mixed with water, and to part in different colours, his sickness is dangerous, and he is reduced to the last stage of weakness.

After this indisposition, if he recover his health, the blood will again look fresh and lively, as at first; but, should *death* unfortunately ensue, the blood will putrify and stink accordingly, just as the rest of the body decays. This has been proved several times, as Dr. Blagrave, in his Astrological Physic, reports; and the same effects have been produced by Sir Kenelm Digby's sympathetic powder, which was said to cure wounds at a distance, being applied to some of the fresh blood collected therefrom.

THE MAGICAL CANDLE.

This candle is spoken of by a learned philosopher of the last century.* It is compounded after the following manner:—"they take a good quantity of the venal *blood* lukewarm, as it came out of the vein, which, being chemically prepared with *alcohol* and other ingredients, is at last made up into a candle, *which, being once kindled, never is extinguished till the death of the party, whose blood it is composed of;* for, when he is *sick* or in *danger*, it burns *dim* and *troubled;* and when he is *dead, it is quite extinguished.*

The Famous Unguent,

OR

The Wonderful Ointment for Wounds.

COMPOSED OF THE FOUR ELEMENTAL PRINCIPLES.

"Rebuke the company of spearmen; scatter thou the people that delight in war."

PSALM LXVIII. 30.

THE INGREDIENTS,

Sympathising with the Seven Planets.

1. The moss of a dead man's skull....... 2 ounces.
2. Of man's fat .... 2 do.
3. Of mummy.................................. ½ do.
4. Of man's blood............................ ½ do.
5. Oil of linseed............................... 2 do.
6. Oil of roses .... 2 do.
7. Bol-ammoniac............................. ½ do.

The three last ingredients are added unto it, because it helpeth to bring it unto a subtile ointment, and without question there is also great virtue in them.

---

* *De Biolychino*

All these things before mentioned must be mixed together, and beaten well in a mortar until it becomes an *ointment*, then keep it in a close thing, from air, for your use.

The way to use this unguent, whereby to cure, is as follows: Take the *blood* or matter of the wound upon the weapon,* or instrument that made the wound, or otherwise dry it upon a piece of wood; then put the wood into the ointment, or else anoint the blood, being kept dry upon the wood, with the ointment, and keep it from the air, after which you must every day wet a fresh linen rag, with the urine of the patient, and so bind up the wound,† do it early every morning, also you must be careful that the ointment which is applied to the blood, be not cold, but that it be kept warm. With this sympathetic ungent, wonderful things may be done, if it be rightly managed, according unto the directions aforesaid. I shall quote one example concerning the trial of this unguent, as follows:—

"One day, being at dinner with Sir H. Forrester, of Aldermaston, Berks, the female who usually waited on his lady, was extremely tormented with a toothache, we caused hereto prick her teeth with a toothpick, and to bleed it; immediately we put the toothpick into the ointment, and she had present ease, after some time, we took the toothpick, and put it into vinegar, whereupon she was presently in extreme pain; we then took it from out the vinegar, and again applied it unto the ungent, and she was immediately well, and so continued."—*Blagrave's Practice of Physic.*

---

* Another remarkable property of this famous ointment is, that a wound may be healed without the presence of the patient, only by taking a quantity of the warm blood which issued from the wound, and applying the ointment to it, which soon heals the wound.

† Sir Kenelm Digby relates upon his own testimony many surprising instances of its wonderful efficacy, as also the celebrated Van Helmont and others who lived in the seventeenth century.

AN EXTRACT FROM THE TRANSLATION OF
Ruben's Latin Manuscript.*

Communicated by Philadelphus.

EXTRACT I.

"If, then, love, in union with humility, is, in an inferior sense, perfection in this world already, it must needs be that which is perfect in the highest fulness of perfection in the world to come: when this mysterious and prophetical character (said to have been the seal of David, that great warrior, and of Solomon, that prince of peace, and that eminent lover of wisdom,—when this character, *denoting*

hieroglyphically the spiritual signature both of David and of Solomon; denoting the two eternal principles *in union*; denoting the creation of the *third principle*; denoting the six working properties of *eternal* nature in their everlasting *rest*; denoting fire and water in an harmonious union; denoting the *two tinctures* restored into ONE, who is ALL in ALL, or without whom there can be nothing; denoting that all whatever was, or is, or shall be, is of, and through, and to, that ONE; denoting *almost the whole* instance of time and eternity, as the same, in our age, is laid open by Jacob Behmen,

---

* A translation of the famous Latin MSS. by Sir P. Rubens, annexed to his treatise on the Proportions of the Human Figure, Cabalistic Principles, &c. &c. This valuable morceau of antiquity was sold at Hugier's famous sale at Paris, and purchased by the late Richard Cosway, Esq. R. A.

that blessed instrument in the hands of the Spirit of God; on which account, I may justly call this seal or character *prophetical*:) when this character, I

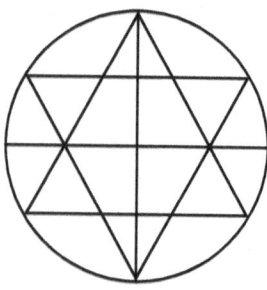

say, spiritualized, and only with *addition of a cross*, which is not expressed therein directly (and no wonder that it was not in those days), shall be the broad seal, not only of the eternal King of kings, but also of *every one* of his subjects; and not only of that everlasting kingdom of Light and Glory, but also of *every individual* inhabitant thereof; although *not in all of the same size*, but in some broader, and in others narrower, yet, *in all of them*, from the highest to the lowest, the very same, as to its spiritual shape and figure. Amen, Hallelujah!"

EXTRACT II.

Being Part of an Explanation of three wonderful Tables, representing the three States of Man, viz. his Perfect State, his Fallen State, and his Restored State.

"Though Adam was really created in this world, even upon earth, and introduced into Paradise, which was upon, or was greening or budding forth through this earth, yet still his distance from, and his height above it, was so great, that no spirit of reason—no, not in the best mathematician, shall ever be able to measure it; for that paradisaical earth, of which his body was made, was so distant from, and above, what we now call earth, as Paradise (which is still extant in the same place where it was then, and is not destroyed by the deluge, as reason fancies, but is only *covered by the curse*) is distant from, and as high above, the beastlike body of an earthly man that is to be turned into dust, though he may be buried upon the same spot of ground which Paradise did formerly green upon. So, therefore, what is here meant, is not such a distance, nor such a height, as may be measured by measuring lines, and may, nevertheless, be justly so called; but it is such a one as runs (in an inferior sphere) parallel with that superior sense which we take in mind, when we consider the *three principles* in a mutual relation. The first principle is still in the second, and the second in the first; and we may truly say, that heaven is in hell, and hell in heaven, seeing they are *both within ourselves*; and yet the second is at such a height above the first, and the first at such a distance under the second, and such a great gulf is fixed between them, that none (as Abraham said to Dives) can pass, neither from the one side nor the other. The *two eternal* principles are both together in *this temporal third* principle (or outward world), and in everything therein; and yet this third is in the same distance under them, and they in the same height above it in which time is under eternity, and eternity above time; and GOD himself, 'in whom we move and have our being,' *is nearer to us than we are to ourselves*; and is yet at such a distant height above us, that only the *true spirit of the soul* can attain to a *real perception* of Him; and that the Scripture calls the earth his footstool, and says that heaven, and the heaven of heavens, cannot contain him. The place of man's nativity in the middle, between time and eternity, wherein he was touched by this or that, is the only thing, on account of which it was said in the beginning, that this (the first) table did represent him in his primitive state of his integrity. For all his graces, perfections, virtues, powers, and glories, he was endowed and gifted with, and especially all those excellent particulars related and declared by Jacob Behmen, concerning the manner of his eating, drinking, seeing, never sleeping, &c. are all found necessarily depending hereupon, and flowing freely forth from this his standing in the middle, and being touched from that which was above, *as well as from that which was under him*. So that, by naming only this place of his nativity, all his perfections are named also implicitly, and want not at all to be enumerated distinctly to the spirit of understanding, to whom it is plain and clear that Adam could not have had them, if his station had been either higher or lower. For, if it had been lower, and he had not been touched by the Spirit of eternity, he must needs have been a creature belonging only to this third *temporal* principle, and a subject of the astral spirit of this world, though he might have been the noblest, and of the highest rank and quality among all his subjects; he could not have had such a dominion, as really he had, over all the creatures of this third principle, and over the astral spirit of this world: and, what is of the greatest consideration, he could not have had the *two tinctures* united in one in his own single person; but must, of all necessity, *have been made* male and female in two distinct and divided bodies, after the manner of all those living creatures that are subjects to the astral spirit of this world. And if his station had been higher, and he had not been touched by time, he would entirely have been cut off, or quite excluded from this third principle, and *could not have been an entire image of God, after his own likeness.* But here may be objected and queried—Are not the holy angels *entire* images of God, notwithstanding that they have nothing of this third principle in their created being?—*Ans.* The holy angels are *entire* images of God, as manifested then when they were created, viz. before the creation of this third principle, when God was manifested only in the two eternal principles of fire and light; but Adam was to be an *entire* image of God, as manifested in the three principles *after the fall of Lucifer*, not in eternity only, but also in time, which entire image of God, after his own likeness, he could not have been, if the third principle had not been a third constituent part of his being. Upon this account it is that Jacob Behmen rightly said, men shall, after the end of time in eternity, even excel the angels, whom we know the Scripture calls 'ministering spirits, sent forth to minister for them who shall be heirs of salvation.' The primitive state of integrity is commonly said, by the spirit of natural reason (human wisdom), to have been the state of Adam and Eve in Paradise; but, as this spirit is a fool *in these matters*, so he speaks both foolish and nonsensical things thereof.

"Can that be primitive which was not first, but had something antecedent to it, of which itself is but an appendix, or a necessary consequence? Can that be an integrum or a whole, which is divided into two, and so divided that these two can never more be made that whole or that one again, which they were before they were divided? These two here spoken of may indeed be joined and copulated together *from without*, and upon that account (yet in quite another sense wherein they were one before) they may be called one, as they are called in Scripture one flesh. But what is this state and condition to that wherein they were one in one only person? This primitive state of integrity was only then in being, when God (having made but one Adam) saw every thing that he had made, and found it very good. But when he said afterward, 'It is not good that man should be alone,' his state of integrity, alas! was faded away already, for he had already transgressed his limits, he was departed from his eminent station, he was sunk down into time, he had opened a door for the astral spirit of this world to come in; he had hearkened to his suggestions, he had stooped down with his will and affections to embrace the love of this third principle; and so he had already dealt treacherously against the wife of his youth, which had been his companion, and the wife of his covenant *within himself*, and had longed for a helpmate besides and without himself; he was infected with a desire after the knowledge of good and evil, and had eaten already of the forbidden tree of that knowledge, not indeed outwardly with his mouth, yet magically with his lust and imagination; and so he had really begun and carried on that same transgression, *which afterward was consummated* by that same helpmeet that was *made in this transgression* of his; and, therefore, first, it was now not good that he should be alone; *the plain reason thereof could be given distinctly*, but it is enough to say only, that he himself had made *not good* what God had made very good *before*. And therefore, secondly, like as afterward, the end of this transgression consummated was death, so the end of this foregoing preparation and disposition towards it was a 'deep sleep,' justly to be called a forerunner of, or a brother-in-law to, that death; and therefore, also, thirdly, when the transgression was consummated by his helpmeet, *he showed forth the inward signature of his own mind,* which he had in the beginning thereof, by calling his wife 'the mother of all living,' which certainly hath no manner of sense in it, except only with a close respect to this transitory world, wherein he had now settled himself according to his newly-framed own contrivance, and wherein, according to the Apostle's word, but contrary to his sense, he forgot the things behind him, and minded only that which was before him; for, if he had a sober serious remembrance of his primitive station, or a mournful sense of what he was departed from and was deprived of, he could not but call his wife the mother of all dead. But this denomination he could not reasonably have liked so well as that of the former, because, first, he was now for begetting children, which all were to have of him that life he now himself lived in, viz. in the region of stars and elements, when his former true life, which he now was dead unto, could not be propagated by him into any one of them. He must needs, therefore, be more pleased with such a denomination as denoted a life in this world, after his own likeness, and obvious to his senses, than by such a one as implieth, only tacitly, a life lost, gone, and vanished away, so that he could have no more any true sensation thereof, and expresseth downright and directly the very contrary of every life. And because, also, third, he must needs have likened better to please his wife, whom he loved, and to flatter her, than to make such an affronting reflection upon her, as to lay all the blame upon her alone, extenuating, at same time, if not quite denying, at least implicitly, his own fault and guilt, seeing especially that he could not be ignorant of the next immediate consequence thereof, which needs must have been this, that his own conscience would have risen and shown in his own face, and told him that *he himself had been the father of death* before ever his wife had got a personal existence. For this is true,—by one man (says the apostle, not by one woman, but by one man, even Adam the first, not by Adam and Eve, for, though this be true in a second posterior sense, yet it is not so in this chief original sense) sin entered into the world, and death by sin, which one man is always in the Scripture put in a diametrical opposition over against that other one man, Jesus Christ, for this very reason called the second Adam very frequently, but never the second Adam and Eve. And so, likewise, when God called to our first parents after the fall, he did not say in the plural number, 'Where are ye, Adam and Eve;' but he called in the singular only, 'Where art thou, Adam? Hast thou eaten,' &c. which-plainly showeth, that God called to an account chiefly, and in the first place, him whom he knew to have been the first author and original agent in the transgression, *before even the woman was taken out of him*, which never could have had a personal being in this world, if he, by his own lust, imagination, and desire, had not himself spoiled, perverted, and *caused to be not good*, what God had made very good in the beginning.

"In the primitive state of integrity, all the senses, thoughts, imaginations, and enjoyments of man, and all his magical operations in the spirit of his soul, could not but have been thoroughly pure, holy, and heavenly, because both the glass of his mind, and the eye of his understanding, were so too; and therefore, as this tree was, so must its fruits and products have been also. Accordingly, then, he could not have had any other sensations but such as could, and did, arise in the *spirit of the soul*, from a union with, and full obedience to, the spirit of God in his light and love, from an intuition and fruition of his infinite goodness, from a profound contemplation and deep understanding of the wonders and riches of his wisdom shown forth in the creation of this world, from an intimate acquaintance with the holy virgin Sophia (designated by Solomon, wisdom), from the mutual embraces of the two eternal tinctures of fire and light united in his own single person, from a familiar conversation with holy angels, from his own personal perfections, which he was endowed with as a sovereign prince ruling over all things in this whole third principle, &c. What those senses, sensations, and enjoyments were, in particular, no living soul can be found able to declare, because this primitive state is lost, and was never attained again,—neither can it be attainable by any during this mortal life; and Adam himself could not have declared it to his offspring, *after his transgression and fall*; for of that single primitive image of God, in which he was in the beginning, he himself knew nothing more after his 'sleep.'

"In the paradisaical or middle state thereof, all the former senses, or heavenly sensations, had left, and were departed from him, or rather he had left, and was departed from them, and had removed himself into a lower and more exterior station, wherein his senses were still indeed pure, holy, and paradisaical, yet no more so, as they had been before; for he, having now some other inferior objects before his mind, must needs also have had a lower and inferior understanding. Seeing that, instead of his former intimate acquaintance with the holy virgin *within himself* and instead of the loving mutual embraces of the two tinctures within his own single person, he was now wholly taken up, without himself, with such a visible helpmeet as he had longed for; which alone can show sufficiently an exceeding great difference between his senses in the primitive state, and his senses in this inferior state, wherein he was after he had awakened from his ' deep sleep.' But even these paradisaical senses also continued not very long with him; for, in the fallen state, when the transgression was consummated, all those paradisaical senses and enjoyments were *utterly extinct*, and, instead of them, all the sensations of Adam and Eve were no other but terrors, dread horrors, fears, anguish, trembling, and despair; and, although the promise of the woman's seed put a stop to the extremity of those terrible sensations, yet it did not restore them their lost paradisaical enjoyments, much less Adam's primitive heavenly senses; but it laid only in the inward ground of their souls a foundation of faith and hope, which they should keep up, strengthen, and corroborate in themselves, as a means to have this restoration performed in them successively, gradually, and always in the same proportion in which they should be found steady, faithful, and true to this *new-laid foundation."*

AN EPITOME OF THE ANGELICAL WORLD,

EXTRACTED FROM THE MSS. OF DR. JOHN PORDAGE, RECTOR OF BRADFIELD, BERKS, 1650.*

Communicated by Philadelphus.

THIS blessed world is called the heavenly Jerusalem and kingdom of love; it is inhabited in common by saints and angels. A heaven of a burning, flaming, sweet, rapturous fire; a clear, thorough-shining, crystalline, joyful light. The angelical world appears encompassed by a circle of infinity; having a firmament in which the angelical elements operate in harmonious unison and equal temperament, which makes a clear, serene, and eternal day. The angelical world is the metropolis of eternity, the temple of God, and glorious palace of his most high and mighty majesty, wherein he appears without obscurity to his angels, clear and plain in his holy Trinity, which they contemplate in the mirror of godly wisdom; and, through the love which is in them of God, they are united in humility and obedience to one spirit. The angelical world is but one heaven, inasmuch as Christ and his saints live together with the angels; but, with regard to its variety, there are *three heavens,* answerable externally to the Trinity, and internally according to *three degrees of glory,* the first, second, and third heaven.

In the angelical world, there is an *external transparent* Paradise to the angelical senses, and an internal understanding or mental sight; and it is by its most spiritual nature that it is *every where present* to the temporal world we inhabit, by which the communications and knowledge of it are given to men; and, as the time is at hand when the second advent of our Lord will *fully open the intercourse,* men will be justified, sanctified, and glorified, even in their earthly bodies, by having their conversation in heaven. And here appears the wisdom of God, that, although heaven is *every where present on earth*, it cannot appear but by his permission.

The nature of the angelical world is to draw the mind into it, so far as it is prepared, *by denying itself, and mortifying its hellish or earthly passions*. The saints in the lowest heaven may be compared to the stars, which are distinguished among themselves as to their size and splendour; those in the mid-heaven to the moon in its beauty, and those in the higher heaven, or most holy place, to the sun in its full glory. All these mansions are dwellings of purity. In the outward court or lowest heaven there is no selfishness in the saints or angels; all its inhabitants are in the life of love, peace, and righteousness. The saints in the second, or inward court, are in a more exalted glory: those in the most holy place are absorbed still deeper in the Deity, and consequently more gloriously sanctified.

The heaven, or the angelical world, is surrounded by a holy and pure element, which is an agreeable, sweet, quiet, and heavenly air.

The angels see, feel, taste, smell, and hear the heavenly sight, substances, odours, and delightful sounds, in their innumerable societies, in the empire of love in which they dwell; and there is no other beatitude than they may have outwardly in Paradise and inwardly in God; yet these are not divided, because *the outward is transparent*, and discovers the inward through it.

The angels, though spiritual, *are not without form and matter, with respect to themselves*; it is only with regard to the grossness of mortality, that they are accounted wholly spiritual, for they enjoy infinite and innumerable wonders and glories in food, entertainment, and pleasures, *springing newly forth* from eternity to eternity, in pomp and glory.

The government of the three princes of heaven is executed by seven angels or servants to the Trinity. The prince, according to the second person of the Trinity, is our Saviour, and has the most glorious throne: all these are in the harmony of the one only wisdom; and the lowest place of his dominion is a majestic glorious dwelling—a stately palace, an excellent building, a garden of delight, encompassed with the angelic principle, and enclosed in the cope of a pure and heavenly element. In the most outward court all is light and eternal day; the tree of life grows and greens in it, and the river of life flows through, pure as crystal. I truly advise all lovers of the truth to come to this school, *which the writer of this hath experienced and seen!* There is nothing but blessedness flowing from the influences of the Holy Trinity, in balmy strength, purity, and joy. There is no care for meat, drink, or garments; all these things are ready *at the desire of an angel, in a heavenly manner*; and their variety and wonderful distinctions are of such excellent curiosity, that the angels and saints of the *higher court* descend to look at and admire them. These wonders are so innumerable and past description, that I can only endeavour to relate the following, as *I have heard and beheld!**

1st. It is of the excellent variety of the lovely elements that the angels in the outward court are clothed, according to their will and pleasure, without work or trouble.

2d. The glorious fruitfulness of this Paradise, wherein grow divers trees, plants, herbs, fruits, and flowers, according to their species, coming forth of themselves in rapid growth and increase from the well-watered heavenly earth; they are transparent and crystalline, with divers colours, in goodly strength, power, and virtue. How pleasant, with a heartfelt boldness, strengthening look, and joy, are they to the spirit's

---

* PHILADELPHUS intends to furnish the Editor of "Urania" (a new interesting monthly publication) with many communications similar to the above, which will be regularly inserted in that work; and those who are desirous of possessing the most comprehensive and explicit books of this class are recommended to purchase "Bromley's Way to the Sabbath of Rest," &c. "Law's Spirit of Prayer," "Spirit of Love," "Appeal to all that Doubt," &c. "Way to Divine Knowledge" and "Address to the Clergy," "Roach's Great Crisis" and "Imperial Standard," "The Chevalier Ramsay's Philosophical Principles of Natural and Revealed Religion," and "Tryon's Mystery of Dreams and Visions Unfolded." These few volumes will form a choice philosophical mystical library.

eye beholding them, and how agreeable to the taste! They are all mere essences and self-existing things that grow in this delicious garden, and, seeing they are of an eternal substance, *like the bodies of angels*, they serve both for joy and pleasure to the sight, as well as for food and nourishment. I speak of the fruits of the garden. Angelic bodies cannot live without a nourishment conformable to their nature, which must be spiritual, heavenly, and impregnated with godly power. These fruits are such that the angels and saints who have reached the most holy place desire sometimes to eat of them, seeing they are full of the virtue of the Son of God, who is also the virtue of the most holy place.

3d. The great abundance of all necessary and agreeable things is remarkable in the angelic world: here is a continual day of superfluity springing up in a constant summer; eternal harvest or vintage; nothing rots; a fruit broken off brings another in its place; the soil is a multiplying strength and virtue of the white pearly earth, and of the balmy strength which penetrates all this outcourt. The

4th wonder is its beauty and joyfulness, consisting of manifold diversified colours, outbreathing odours, groves and walks in vistas, with the refraction of light sweetly mixed and tempered here and there in an excellent glory and majesty. No less beautiful are the plants and flowers, their variety of colours giving joy and exciting admiration: the leaves of trees and herbs are encompassed with golden edgings, and the fruits are of a granite red; they mix the colours together miraculously, charming the eye, which can only behold these amazing beauties through the divine light, fire. All things in Paradise are so clear *you can look through them*, but all colours rise with their pure transparency and splendour, through the mixture of fire with the other *heavenly* elements of water, air, and earth. Here are mountains that exhale aromatic odours, and abundance of houses, cottages, tents, and tabernacles of transparent gold, with majestic shades of vine-leaves and tree-covered walks, diningrooms, pleasure-houses, hillocks, mounts, and rocks of precious stones, low pleasant valleys, flowing rivulets and fountains, that augment the beauty and make it sweet and agreeable. The

5th wonder of the *lowest* heaven is its inexhaustible riches: here is gold, silver, and all kinds of pearls in abundance, distinguished by their extraordinary sparkling colours, for ornament, show, pleasure, joy, and merriment, above comparison with *our* gold, silver, and precious stones, which are infinitely *inferior* in appearance and virtue. All this belongs to divine wisdom for the use and pleasure of her children.

6. The wonders of this court, which spring up new, as if they never were known before, continually breaking out into manifold varieties, without end or measure. Here the eye feasts on the most glorious objects imaginable. Here the ears meet the most agreeable pleasures in the sweetest musical sounds, and the smell is regaled by the most enlivening virtues of perfumes, giving relish to the powers of taste and ecstacy to the sense of feeling; for, although all the wonders of this place appear in a godly heavenly essence, and as thin, rare, and translucent, *as the finest air*, most subtle and crystalline; yet they can be enjoyed by the senses of angelic bodies, which are suitable and proportioned to such subtlety and rareness. All these objects represent themselves to the blessed inhabitants of Paradise without their labour or trouble. *What would it be for a man to gain the whole world, and to lose this eternal place of joy and pleasure!* The

7th wonder is the union of the blessed through CHRIST with the DIVINE WISDOM, whereby the angels who never fell attain greater happiness since his incarnation and triumph in the redemption, whereby he has attained more than the first Adam lost. Of this no spirit can understand any thing *until it is purified* to enjoy this union: it will then know the experience of Solomon in the Canticles. The

8th wonder is the rest and stillness of all these wonders, since the inhabitants neither labour nor trouble themselves to lay up a store of any thing. All they want of food, clothing, or amusements, come at a wish. All is meek and satisfactory, still, soft, and clear; yet with unbounded power, pungency, triumph, and pomp. Here is a continual summer, cooled by sweet zephyrs, causing the balm of the celestial earth to exhale agreeable scents. The

9th wonder consists in the concretion of the *heavenly earth*, which hastens as it is moved *by the will of the angels*, under the influence of the *more spiritual* powers and virtues above it; for there is a *continual descent* of blessings from God, throughout the angelic deep or sky, falling upon the *earth* of Paradise, *which is a transparent, white, glittering, saline substance*, covered with all the productions of its fruitfulness, and their blessed influence from the *sphere of unapproachable light* passing *through Paradise*—reaching to *this external temporal world, thereby tempering* the harshness and wrath (or evil) of *our mortal elements.* PHILADELPHUS

City of London Coffee House, HIEROGLYPHICA PROPHETICUS. *Bucklersbury, Cheapside.*

[Raphael's(?) note on Pordage and Lee]

* Those who choose to refer to the third volume of Jacob Behmen's works, 4 vols. quarto, edited by William Law, A. M. (author of "The Serious Call," and several occult works, the most perspicuous extant), will be highly delighted at the sight of engravings of the "three wonderful tables," said to have been designed and drawn by Sir Peter Paul Rubens; and those who will take the trouble, critically, to examine them, will not, I think, hesitate to pronounce them three of as masterly pieces as were ever delineated by that eminent artist, and associate of illustrious and royal personages. The following extracts are from one of many extraordinary mystical works (never printed in English, but translated from the author's English and Latin MSS. into German) of the pious and learned Dr. John Pordage, rector of Bradfield, Berks, who was the contemporary and very particular friend of the celebrated Bishop Saunderson, Dr. Edward Hooker, and Dr. Francis Lee: the last-mentioned of these, his bosom friends, was a man of stupendous learning, and was most intimate with Robert Earl of Oxford, when lord high treasurer, to whom several proposals were made by him for the lasting honour and advantage of these nations. Dr. Lee's works are almost innumerable, but, as he never could be prevailed on to affix his name to any one, they have been made public under the names of others, or have come into the world anonymously. The greatest part of Nelson's "Feasts and Fasts" was found in his own hand, after his decease; he was the first that put Mr. Hoare and Mr. Nelson upon the founding of charity schools, upon the same plan as that of Halle in Germany; and he was continually promoting and encouraging all manner of charities, both public and private. Peter the Great, Czar of Muscovy, was exceedingly partial to him, for whom, by request, he wrote, in the year 1696, "Proposals for the right framing of his Government." —*Vide* Dissertations, Theological, Mathematical, and Physical, by Francis Lee, M.D. 2 vols. 8vo. 1752; also, Rev. R. Roach's "Great Crisis", 8vo. 1725. Dr. Lee was a member of "The Philadelphian Society:" I therefore recommend a perusal of "The Theosophical Transactions," by that Society (1 vol. small 4to. 1697), as it contains the most erudite and profound disquisitions ever written, both scientific and philosophic, as well as theosophic and divine magic. This singular work has been very rare for the last fifty years, and, as a proof of that, the copy belonging to the late Mr. Cosway was sold by a bookseller (Duke Street, Manchester Square), to a friend of mine, for ten guineas. This may serve to convince, *if possible*, the incredulous, that these sublime studies have not been, in any age, *confined* to men of little or no consideration in the world, but, on the contrary, it may be averred, that scarcely any, comparatively, but persons of liberal education and of distinction, have been the most earnest in those pursuits. As it is not generally know that the father of English astronomers and mathematicians, Sir Isaac Newton, was indebted for his transcendant knowledge to Jacob Behmen (who was certainly the prince of occult philosophers and astrologers), I beg to refer all who are disposed to "The Gentleman's Magazine" for July, 1782, where they will see an article very explicit on this point, written by a fellow of St. John's College, Cambridge.

But, to conclude, Shakespeare, Milton, Dryden, the author of "Junius", and numerous other great and good men, of all ages and nations, have reverenced these sciences, and benefited themselves and others by directing their attention to them. It is, however, fruitless to urge more, since those who "have eyes to see, and ears to hear," will both see and hear! whilst those who are blinded by vulgar prejudice (the offspring of ignorance), or by epicureanism or religious bigotry (which is the worst degree of superstition), cannot possibly either "see or hear;" wherefor it is truly "vanity of vanities" to attempt to convince them.

SINGULAR EXTRACTS

RELATING TO SPIRITS AND DEMONS, AND THEIR POWER OVER MANKIND,

Communicated by Philadelphus in a Letter to the Mercurii.

PHILADELPHUS TO THE MERCURII GREETING, SENDETH THEM WITH MUCH GOOD WILL—"A RELATION OF THE APPARITION OF A SPIRIT KEEPING THE TREASURES OF THE EARTH, AND OF HIS DELIVERY OF THE KEY OF A CERTAIN MOUNTAIN IN GERMANY TO A CONSIDERABLE PERSON, AND WHAT THEREUPON ENSUED."
—Abstracted from the Theosophical Transactions by the Philadelphian Society, 1697.

"We received advice about two months ago from the Marquisate of B—g, by a person of undoubted reputation and great worth, who was pleased to consult with some of us about what was best to be done in this matter. How that in a place called N—n, there was a little man, seeming of about 15 or 16 years of age, who came in the night to the bed-side of a certain person of quality, telling him he must go with him; and, as the gentleman refused, he was severely threatened by the other, menacing him that he would wring off his head if he still refused. Whereupon, being greatly terrified, when he had put on a coat which the little man had brought to him, the gentleman went along with him, and was led up out of the castle wherein he lived to a certain mountain;

the little man then proceeded to open the mountain, and having done so, gave the said person the key to it, saying,—'He would do' wisely to take great care of this key, for that otherwise it would not go well with him.' As the person awoke, early in the morning, he knew not whether it was a dream or a fact. But, nevertheless, he put his hand into his pocket, where he finds the key that was given him by the little man, and it was signed with three crosses. He looked also for the money which he had put in his pocket, but he remembers that he put it into the pocket of the coat which the little man had brought, and carried away with him again. He beheld also his shoes, which, according to his own boy's saying, the evening before were cleaned, but he found them now quite dirty. Now, after he had considered this a great while, and contriving what he should do with the key, he shows it to his companion; but, as he put his hand out of the window, the key slipped out of his hand; both of them saw where the key fell, but when he came down to fetch the key away, it was there no more. A little while after this, in the morning, when he was walking through a certain alley, he felt somebody give him a grievous stroke in the face, and yet he perceived none to be near him; but his cheek was swollen very much thereby, there arising up a great black and blue nob, and hereupon he sickened. But he is chiefly afflicted with the fallen sickness, wherewith he has been ever since troubled, notwithstanding all medicines and remedies used, yet not altogether so grievously as at the beginning. Likewise, as he not long ago was at prayers, in the church, (he being always very sedulous at the public devotions) he saw upon his hand these words—'He is dead!' No further particulars we have yet received; but, as it is already related, several questions may be put, that will deserve to be considered."

Query 1. What is to be thought concerning those treasures that are by many believed to be concealed in some mountains and caverns of the earth?

Q. 2. Whether there be any peculiar order of spirits that do preside over them, and of what rank?

Q. 3. What can be the end of keeping such treasures, and what must be their design in revealing them to any?

Q. 4. Whether this gentleman could safely have refused to attend the spirit, and what method he should have taken to have secured himself?

Q.5. Whether it is not possible that there may be *real* apparitions and transactions, both good and bad in sleep?

Q. 6. Whether the obedience to this spirit was voluntary or involuntary, and how far the liberty of the will may be supposed to be constrained, or let loose in this night action?

Q. 7. What was the meaning of the coat brought by the spirit? Was it a real coat, or only imaginary?

Q. 9. What was it that occasioned the loss of it, and gave such an offence to the spirit?

Q. 10. Whether natural distempers may not sometimes be caused from spirits? And whether evil spirits are not good natural magicians to hurt and destroy?

Q. 11. What is meant by the words—"He is dead," or "the man is dead?"

Q. 12. What is to be understood by Isaiah ch. xl. v. iii.—*I will give thee the treasures of darkness, and the hidden riches of secret places!*

An answer by Dr. Lee to certain queries proposed upon a relation of the apparition of a spirit, keeping the treasure of the earth, and of the delivery of the key of a certain mountain in Germany to a considerable person.

QUERY I.

What is to be thought concerning those treasures that are by many believed to be concealed in some mountains and caverns of the earth?

That there are really hidden treasures in several mountains, caverns, and other places of the earth, many relations do confidently attest. What ground there may be for such an attestation, and how far the evidence of the witnesses may deserve to be relied upon, will not, perhaps, be altogether unworthy of our present inquiry. These witnesses are not only dead, but there are also living ones, and some of them persons even of very great sagacity and penetration of judgment, as well as experience. The great mutations of the revolutions that have been in the world, but especially the terrible incursions of the barbarous nations, from the fourth century downward, and the dissolution of monasteries in the last age throughout the protestant part of Europe, may incline one to believe that much of what is related as to this matter may not be quite improbable, though intermixed with relations that are either wholly or in part fabulous, and set off with some unaccountable circumstances and superstitions. The writers *de Re Metallica*, may hereupon be looked into.

It is related in the life of Jacob Behmen, that whilst "he was a herd-boy, in the heat of mid-day, retiring from his play-fellows, to a little stony crag hard by, called the Land's Crown, where the natural situation of the rock had made a seeming enclosure of some part of the mountain, finding an entrance into it, he went in, and found there a great wooden vessel, full of money, at which sight, being in a sudden astonishment, he did, in haste, retire, not moving his hand thereinto, and came and related his fortune to the rest of the boys, who, coming up along with him, sought often, and with much diligence, an entrance, but never found any; though some years after, a foreign artist, as Jacob himself related, skilled in the finding out such magic treasures, took away the same, and thereby much enriched himself, yet perished by an infamous death, that treasure being lodged there, and it seems, laid covered with a curse to the finder and *taker away*."

And it is the opinion of some, that here, in England, there were formerly deposited such treasures in some of our churches and monasteries, with a curse upon whomsoever should find them, or should possess them, or any thing else appertaining to the said churches or monasteries, otherwise than by such a way of devolution as was originally designed.

It is also by some believed, that several of our monasteries were at first founded, either from such magic treasures, or from something of an equivalent, if not superior nature.*

And it has been said, that the walls of the fairest and richest monastery in the west of England were thus built by one who was afterwards brought to an infamous death; he having too much enriched himself by a treasure hid in the church thereof, which he was taught how to have access to, whenever he pleased, by a strange artist, who led him into it, and in his sight, carried away thence a jewel of an inestimable value, though with great hazard, because of the opposition that was made. And there is one known to our society, who doth aver, that when he was at Rome, in the year 1693, he was there told by a person of good intelligence, how that there died, then (in or about the month October), an unfortunate gentleman, in the hospital of St. John Lateran, whose death was chiefly imparted to a great fright, though the occasion hereof was said by him to have been concealed, till he opened the same in confession. Wherefore the name of the person was kept secret, but the matter of fact was said to be thus:—He having been engaged in a duel or rencontre, had slain a man, for which he was obliged to fly; and the fear of justice everywhere pursuing him, he absconded himself in very melancholy and lonesome places, and one night as he was endeavouring to rest himself in the porch of the church of St. John Lateran, he was suddenly terrified by the apparition of a skeleton, who commanded him to follow him, and to fear-nothing, for that he meant him no hurt, but a great deal of good, if it were not his own fault. So a little recovering himself, he said he followed the spectre into a certain ground belonging to the hospital, where the spectre stopped, and the earth opening, there was discovered to him six earthern pots full of money, which were encompassed about with flames of fire. Then, said the spectre unto him, "Friend, all this money that you see, I will now give to you, if you will but take possession of it; *be of courage, fear not the flames, for they cannot hurt you, fear them not, I say, they shall have no power over you, for therefore*

---

* See Dr. Campbell's "Hermippus Redivivus."

only do they appear, that you may be terrified from laying hold on what I now freely do offer you: But what you do, must be, done immediately, otherwise, I must deliver up this very hour all this treasure to the SPIRITS OF THE EARTH, *who are waiting just now to receive it; accept what is offered, if you are wise; it will not be longer in my power to transfer the same to any, and when it is too late you may repent.* But notwithstanding all the persuasions of the spectre, this poor man could not be prevailed on to accept the offer of the treasure at such a peril as presented itself. Only he made a mark where the spectre disappeared, and being left as it were half dead, was the next morning received into the said hospital, where he remained in a deplorable state for several days, being fully restored to his senses, in which time he made the aforesaid confession, with many other circumstances (some suppressed and others forgotten), for the truth thereof the curators of the hospital making a diligent search in the place to which they were directed, found just so many and such kind of pots as were named to them, but which were all empty.

That in Italy, there is great abundance of such treasures, some curious' inquirers do pretend to determine, from many reasons. And there is not wanting a catalogue or book that is kept very secret in some few hands wherein all the said treasures are said to be registered. And we are credibly informed, that some persons have been employed and pensioned for this cause, by those that are of a very high degree in the world, in order to make such a discovery. Accordingly some of them (the least guarded) we are told, have been discovered, and taken away by these artists, and particularly from out the ruins and antiquities of Rome, and also about Naples.

Now it may be demanded, whether all these hidden treasures be of the same nature and order? To which, it is answered in the negative, that they are not. For, according to what the persons were, unto whom they did originally belong, if they did ever belong to any, according to the manner and design of the concealment, and various other circumstances, and lastly, according to the secret laws, rules, and orders, of the divers inhabitants of the invisible worlds, to them any wise related so is the property and nature of these concealed treasures very much altered and circumstantiated.

QUERY II.

Whether there be any peculiar order of spirits that do preside over them, and what rank?

Some think they do enough when they cast all upon the devil that is of this kind. But let us do justice even to him; not ascribing to him more than he is rightly chargeable withal; or making him the refuge of our ignorance, as well as the butt of our ill nature. Yet, however, some cannot conceive or credit any intermediate orders and degrees of spirits, betwixt the blessed angels in the kingdom of light, and the adverse ones in that of darkness; others of an inquisitive and philosophical genius, both among the antients and moderns, do suppose that this would be to introduce a mighty chasm or breach into the creation of God, and therefore they do maintain there are many intermediate degrees betwixt these two, in the scale of the spiritual creation, and that there is no less variety in the invisible than in the visible system of nature.* Neither are they at all shocked herein by the objected silence of the Holy Scriptures; for they answer immediately, that by the things that are visible, those that are invisible are made clearly known. And therefore, say they, Moses had no need to describe the creation of the spiritual, and (to us) invisible world or worlds; for that, by having described that which is material and visible, we may thereby arrive to the discernment and knowledge of the other, which is in it shadowed forth; and they think that Moses speaks fully enough of this to any that are skilled in the oriental and symbolical way of writing.† They say, also, that David was not only a poet, but also a philosopher, or rather a theosophist,

---

* See Dr. Cheyne's "Five Discourses on Regimen," &c. also Dr. Nicholas Robinson's "Christian Philosopher," vol. 2.

† See the Chevalier Ramsay's "Philosophical Principles," 2 vols. 4to.

when he called upon all the creatures to praise the Lord. And indeed the ordinary interpretation of the 148th psalm, and some other places of Scripture, seems but flat and low, and very inconsiderable, if compared to that high and exalted sense which they would have given to the same with respect to the grand hallelujah of the whole creation.

Now they would give us to understand, that these middle ranks of spirits were all put into subjection under man, so long as he should remain in the Paradisaical state, that is, should be a true and loyal subject to God, his Creator, by virtue of the blessing pronounced upon him, Gen. i. 28. and afterwards prophetically renewed, Ps. 8th. wherefore they do suppose that not only the fowls of the air, the fishes of the sea, and the beasts of the earth were made subjects of man, in his original constitution (as he was the true *representative* of God, bearing his character and image) and were in all things obedient at his commands, as to their Prince and Lord; but *also* all the elementary spirits, or the natives, and spiritual *aborigines* of such or such class in the inferior or elementary worlds, whether they be of an aerial, aquatic, or terrestrial kind (according to the three grand divisions of these spirits there *typically* hinted at) were all made subservient to him from that word of blessing essentially spoken forth from the *central fountain* both of his and there being; though he be not after the same manner so to them as to him; whence say they, both angels and men, may not improperly be called the *offspring* of GOD, and the *sons* of GOD, but that neither of these expressions is at all appropriable or communicable to such inferior orders of spirits, who, by their birth, are put under the feet of Christ, and (consequently) of man also, before he was degenerated into a servile and *bestial form*, sinking into it from that imperial and divine one, wherein he was first constituted. And from this ministration, subserviency, and subjection of theirs to man, they may be called servants, or hired servants, as some that are learned in the Hebrew cabbalad—do think that they are called in the parable of the prodigal son. Now as the servant is not the heir, but the son, so likewise, these kind of spirits are not the heirs of GOD, neither can they be, being born under servitude; and as an hired servant receiveth his wages, so doth every one of these from their Supreme Master; and though they may not inherit with the son, yet may they possibly receive portions or gratuities, and be encouraged with suitable rewards, according to the fidelity and diligence of their service. These, say they, were to have been the *satellites* of the human race in their Paradisaical purity and power, and would thereby have been with them partakers of the heavenly favours and blessings which they enjoyed, as a good servant whom his master loveth is with him partaker according to his degree of the plenty which the master possesseth. But the fall of man (who was the master) was not only a tumbling down of himself into death and misery, but it has also subjected these subordinate classes of spirits (who were his servants) to the vanity and the bond which they now lie under, by constraint, and "not willingly." Whence there is hopes to them of a future deliverance from the bondage of the corruptability and impurity of the elements (wherein they reside) as man shall come again to be restored to his Paradisaic state and kingdom; wherefore, also, some do think that when the Apostle mentions the whole creation's groaning, and being in pains of child-birth for this *deliverance*, he might have, in the first place, an eye towards these ranks of intelligent creatures. And some relations there are that do seem highly to favour this interpretation.* Now as there is a very great variety, and even contrariety in the birds, the fishes, and the beasts, which we behold at this day, the which were yet created by God in a most beautiful and perfect harmony, so the like may be supposed concerning those invisible elementary inhabitants, that there is at present not only a great variety, but even a contrariety too among them. And though we are not able to behold them with our *outward* eyes, we may be allowed to judge concerning them, from that which is visible and sensible to us, when we shall consider all the orders of creatures that have terrestrial bodies. Some

---

* Particularly in the singular work of Count de Gabalis, from which Pope acquired the machinery for his "Rape of the Lock."

of which may seem to have partaken with man very little in the curse, others more, and some so much, as it may well be doubted, whether any particle of the divine blessing remain in them, and whether they be not rather generated wholly from the curse. In like manner some of these elementary *spirits* may have suffered very little in comparison of what others have done by the fall of mankind, whereas others may have fallen under an exceeding heavy weight by the entering of the curse hereby into nature. So that, being *naturally* the subjects of man, they stand with him in the corruption, discord, and wrath of the elements. And they must stand so, as long as the *elementary strife* shall remain, or until it come to be swallowed up into the holy heavenly quintessence, or *divine element*, the undefiled womb of the morning, the fire-water of life, which the Eastern Magi have named their HASSHAMMAIM.*

But if there be indeed such middle ranks of spirits, that do remain with man until the day of judgment in the contention of the elements and astral effluviums, it maybe queried in what rank of these do you place those spirits which are reported to guard the hidden treasures of the earth, whether in the mountains or in other places? To this it may be answered, that none of them are of the first or second, but all of them of the third grand division, and though amongst these there may be those of various kinds or tribes, yet that all are of a terrestrial generation.

Hereupon it may be further demanded, if there be such a peculiar order of spirits that do preside over the treasures of the earth, that of these there be various degrees, (some whereof are much better than others) whether upon supposition of the possibility, it may be lawful for man, while clothed with this gross and terrestrial body, bearing the marks of the fall, to maintain any kind of intercourse, society, or conversation, with all or any of these degrees? Some have earnestly endeavoured to converse with any of them indifferently, without examining first of what degree or station they might be. Others, not so easily satisfied, have yet

---

* See Law's "Spirit of Love," part 1.

consented to a correspondence with some of them who have appeared to be of the best sort. But whatever the practice of any may have been, either for a good or an evil end, we cannot but think such a correspondence, *of what nature soever it be, and after what methods soever it may be carried on, to be extremely dangerous;* for man being *naturally* their superior, and they *his subjects,* until man shall regain again his *natural* superiority over them, the danger may be exceeding great of passing away the right of nature, his true birth-right, and so of making *himself subject to them,* whose master he ought to be, and will be; if he be not kept down by a magnetical or magical force in some or other region below Paradise. Hence the rise of idolatry in the ancient heathens, who were much better learned in great part of the *intellectual system* of the world than the moderns are, under what denomination soever they may pass, or be called by. Hence the Egyptians, from whom *Polytheism* was derived to *other nations,* when, in their temples, they worshipped towards the image of a calf or of an onion that was made out of this or that metal, were not so stupid as to imagine that there was any deity either in a calf or in an onion; but through these images they had respect to some spirit, or perhaps order of spirits, that was figured or shadowed forth in visible and corporeal nature by one or the other of these; and that, in their sacred worship, was presented unto them in such or such a metal as might most aptly express such or, such a planetary influence, according to that *astrological* and *talismanical* knowledge in which they were most eminent.*

---

* See Gaffarel's "Unheard of Curiosities," but particularly the letter written by the Rev. Mr. Beford to a Bishop of Gloucester, respecting the great mathematician who had communion with the spirits of the earth. This letter Mr. Sibly has introduced into the 4th part of his "Occult Philosophy," and it was previously published in Beaumont's "History of Spirits," &c. a work of considerable merit.[Reproduced here, pg 408—Ed.]

QUERY III.

What can be the end of keeping such treasures, and what must be their design in revealing them to any?

Ans. According to the nature of the treasure kept, and of the spirits or demons that keep them, so must be the end of their concealment. And whereas these terrestrial demons can hardly be supposed to conceal them solely (if at all) for themselves, it has hence been concluded, by most, that they do it for man; for being in their *essence* somewhat allied to him (as has been declared) they desire that he should be caught into their principle; hoping hereby more to complete their essence, feed their life, and satisfy their nature, if they can but anywise make themselves masters of him, whose subjects originally they were. But as these are subordinate spirits, which are under the government of higher orders, so according to these, rather than the former, is the end to be sought for; and as this is extremely difficult to know, so likewise is the uncertainty of the end. For the invisible kingdom have their politics in like manner as the kingdoms of this visible earth, and they have doubtless as various designs to carry on, and may make use too of as different measures to compass them. However, there may be one grand end or design (under which many subordinate ones will be contained) common to the princes and subjects of this or that empire in nature whatever, whether good, bad, or mixed. And forasmuch as there is great reason to be afraid, that the *apostate* principalities and powers of the angelic world have here very far extended their usurpation, there may be a great design of them laid, which may not break forth till toward the latter end of this world.* Well, but what can they mean in offering to reveal these treasures to some particular persons? *Ans.* If the end and manner of their concealment, the laws, or pacts, respecting the same, and the qualifications of those persons to whom these offers are made were perfectly known, then might we be able distinctly to

---

* See Dr. John Pordage's Account of the Principalities of Hell, &c. in Beaumont's "History of Spirits."

resolve this query. But till this be, it is enough to be satisfied in general, that all such kind of offers are dangerous to the utmost to accept, or so much as listen to, without there could be such an impregnable armour obtained, as it were impossible for any evil (or mixed) spirit to penetrate. And further, it may not unreasonably be presumed, from the most deplorable history of our countryman, Dr. Dee, as also from some other relations of good credit, that *certain subtle Luciferian spirits have been carrying on, for above this hundred years past, some great intrigue, in order to grand alterations in the outward governments of the world, for the establishing somewhat that may run diametrically counter to the spiritual Kingdom of Christ, which they, foreseeing, do, and will continue, by all methods, to war against.**

But we know that Michael, the Prince of Israel, shall stand up to fight for the children of his people in the latter day. When the various centres and principles are unlocked, spirits of all kinds do go forth, *some to teach, others to deceive man; some to minister to him, others to domineer over him;* some for this end, and others for that, according to the great diversity of their nature, degree, or office. Wherefore it highly behoves all men to be exceeding careful in an affair of this nature; since the soul of man is so framed, that all are capable of being acted upon by them, visibly or invisibly, sleeping or waking, in one form or another. And if the *true spirit shall reveal itself towards the latter end of this world in a more than ordinary manner* (as many do believe,) *it may well be expected, that there will be sent out at the same time, from opposite and intermediate kingdoms, both wicked and lying, as also vain and*

---

* It will be discovered by this, that the spirits that inspired the late Joannah Southcote were of the *lowest* order of these elementary spirits, and those that taught Baron Swedenborge, of the *highest* order, both, however, under the direction of Lucifer, to mislead two orders of men, of very different signatures, thus mightily warring against the *true* spiritual kingdom of Christ, by spreading in many directions (gross and refined) false doctrine; and these infatuated spirits will now effect more than ever, on account of the near approach of that period when such wonders will be manifested in all nations, as were never before witnessed.

trifling spirits,* of various ranks, orders, and offices; and that, as the *true spiritual* Christianity shall begin more and more to exert itself, as in the most primitive and apostolical churches, so there may, on the other side, *start up along with it*, many impostures or delusions, whereby even well-meaning persons shall be captivated†; whence we ought to be very sober, and to examine into the grounds of all such appearances (if real) and constantly to hold fast to the true spirit of revelation *and of prophecy*, and by which alone the hidden treasures of the deity, and of the invisible worlds, are *manifested to the humble* and prudent of heart.

A perilous day draws nigh, *and is even now*, wherein the false prophet and his emissaries *shall exceedingly prevail!* And as it was in the days of the Apostles, some may live to see sundry Antichrists setting up themselves, and calling themselves "the mighty power of God," upon whom the God of this world will not be wanting to bestow those riches and honours which he claims as his own. However, the bank of wisdom, no evil or unclean spirit shall be able to draw near to ‡.

QUERY IV.

Whether this gentleman could have safely refused to attend the spirit, and what method he should have taken to have secured himself?

Ans. If his mind were already captivated with a strong imagination after such hidden treasures, it was then altogether impossible (though we should suppose him at the same time to have the perfect use of his senses) to refuse such an attendance as this demon did demand, at least without the imminent peril of life itself. But if his mind *were not before*

---

* To wit the followers of Joannah Southcote.

† As was most deplorably exemplified in that late excellent engraver, Mr. Wm. Sharp.

‡ A work has been recently published that will throw immense light on this interesting subject, entitled, "The Jugments of God on the Apostatized Gentile Church,"&c. It is a reprint of a book written originally by a friend of Dr. Lee.

thus captivated, it doth not appear but that he must have been at his perfect liberty either to obey or disobey this troublesome spirit. For though the exercise of will seems to be absolutely bound up in sleep, yet every one can more or less testify, that this is not perpetually so, but that they can perceive sometimes a liberty of following the free inclination of their wills, just as if they were awake. And it is the judgment of some philosophical and experienced heads, that could the imagination of man, (wherein the original evil and curse doth properly reside) come to be thoroughly defecated and cleansed, *all the scenes that pass before him in sleep would be real and substantial* and all his actions relating to them would be free and voluntary. But the apostacy and degeneration of the imaging part of the soul is so deep, that this is not to be expected of any, without a perfect renovation of the *lapsed* adamical nature. Wherefore, since this is so, and that the renovation and restitution of human imagination to its original seat, and subordination to the mind and wisdom of God is so great and difficult a work, it will deserve to be inquired what method he should have taken under the present imperfections of his nature, to have secured himself against the impertinencies and importunities of this terrestrial spirit? And the answer to this is very plain, that every one ought to free themselves from all covetousness *and the love of this world,* if they would expect to be secure from the machinations of all these orders of spirits, whether infernal or terrestrial, whether aerial, or else the inhabitants of the fountains of waters, who can take up various forms to act in, and are no less (if not more) dangerous when they transact their plots after an invisible manner, than when they do it after a visible manner. This is an effectual remedy against the insults and surprises of any spirit of this rank. And another remedy that is like to it, and not to be disjoined from it, is earnest and real prayer for the divine protection against all the illusions of darkness, with frequent aspirations, (after the custom of holy David) that so hereby there may be such an habitual delivery of spirit, soul, and body, into the hands of the Almighty, that it will be impossible for any other seizure to be made, either secret or open.

QUERY V.

Whether it is possible that there may be real apparitions and transactions both good and bad in sleep?

This is already answered in the *affirmative*. And not only this single instance, but many others do confirm the same, but especially the apparition of an angel to St. Joseph in a dream, warning him to fly from the intended persecutions of Herod, and the apparition of another angel to the magi, in like manner warning them which way they were to travel. Now here it ought well to be observed, that it is quite a different thing to *dream* that I see an angel, and to see an angel *in* a dream as this righteous man did: the former is phantastic, the latter is real. Here also a distinction is to be made betwixt substantial and symbolical apparitions, which last are, in some degree, real, but not so properly as the first. Of this kind were the dreams of the patriarch Joseph and of Daniel, and of several others mentioned in Holy Scriptures; whence the interpretation of these dreams was anciently a *divine science*, that was not bestowed upon any but such as were highly favoured and beloved of God. But as soon as man would go to make an art of it, it was presently defiled with a thousand superstitions, follies, and impertinences. Thus came in the Chaldean oneirocritics, which the Greeks afterwards mended according to their manner, *as the superstition of the vulgar in latter ages amongst us hath done since*, partly from their custom, and partly from strained allusions. Now it is certain, that these symbolical dreams are transacted in the soul by the ministration of angels (of one kind at least or other) and where the imaginative faculty is purified from drossy and earthly matter, there is an entrance opened for good angels to administer, and to step in at certain seasons for assistance and succour, many undoubted instances whereof are not wanting in history, but amongst which I know none to be more remarkable than that which is related concerning the deliverance of a certain congregation of Protestant Christians, in the reign of Mary I. Queen of England, by the timely securing of the catalogue of its members, which must otherwise have been seized, and would have involved them all in the peril of their lives; and it is not at all to be doubted but that if men did live generally better lives and more depend upon the providence and leadings of God, such sort of admonitions might be more frequent than they are. Though there be also some natural signatures, with which some are marked, *whereby they are rendered more apt for, and susceptible of such impressions* than others are, or can be.

As for the other sort of dreams (if they can properly be called so) *which are so very real and substantial* as to be transacted after the manner that in this narrative is recorded; they are much more rare than the former. But yet these real apparitions in sleep *are not so very rare as they may be thought*, which is because they are sometimes not heeded, or believed to be so. But were men possessed with a right notion of the manner of the soul's working during the sleep of the body, *many secret and hidden things might possibly come to be revealed to them by the apparitions of spirits* or demons connatural to them, and also of the *souls of their departed friends or relations*; for the state of the soul doth then most nearly approach to that which she finds after her solution from this elementary body, and is therefore most capable of a true and real intercourse with spirits and souls of *her own rank*, if she be fitly instructed for it, and be also rightly qualified and prepared *according to the instructions given*, especially if she have a strong magical signature, or a violent magnetic drawing of her will, which *to some is peculiar*, and is exceedingly dangerous, *until it be regulated*, for that it associates itself more easily with the inhabitants of the dark and middle worlds, which it also not seldom mistakes for the holy inhabitants of the light angelical world.* But such a

---

* Whosoever will be at the pains of reading the life and leadings of Joannah Southcote or Baron Swedenborge, will see how strikingly this applies to both of those well-intentioned, though

soul, *when it is brought into true order* and harmony by an *entire submission* to the divine will, is a vessel fitted for all the divine influences, and is itself such a wonder in the mystery of God, as requires the pen of an angel to describe.*

QUERY VI.
Whether the obedience to the spirit was voluntary or involuntary, and how far the liberty of the will may be supposed to be constrained or let loose in this night action!

This is already answered in the solution of the fourth query, for thence it appears that this obedience was partly voluntary and partly involuntary, and that the liberty of the will is not so constrained, or bound up even in sleep, as to endamage any one that has not *first by a previous consent,* some way or other, surrendered itself; upon which many reflections *might* be made relating to diabolical suggestions and temptations in dreams.†

MYSTIC ENCHANTMENT.
From the MSS. of Philadelphus.

The following is related by Eckartshausen, in his German work, entitled *"Magic."*

Eckartshausen was aquainted with a Scotsman, who was *not* given to the practice of incantations, but merely acquired the knowledge of an extraordinary process, which had been communicated to him by a Jew. *He made the experiment in company with Eckartshausen;*—it is extraordinary, and deserves to be related.

The person who wishes to see a particular spirit, (either of a living or dead person), must, for some days previous, undergo a state of physical and spiritual preparation. Very highly-deluded persons.

* See the last Discourse in Bromley's "Way to the Sabbath of Rest," and particularly Tryon's "Mystery of Dreams and Visions Unfolded."

† It is to be regretted that the answers to the other six queries were never published.

remarkable conditions and correspondencies seem required between the person who wishes to see the spirit, and the spirit itself, (conditions we can only explain by admission that a dawning of the spiritual world begins on our side of the grave). When these preparations are completed, a fumigation from certain ingredients (the knowledge of which Mr. E. very properly, from a fear of their abuse, declines to communicate) is made in a room. *The vapour forms itself into a figure which is the perfect resemblance of the person the operator wishes to see!* Magic lights, optical deceptions, &c., are here out of the question. THE VAPOUR PRODUCES A HUMAN FIGURE, resembling him we desire to see! The following are Eckartshausen's own words:—

"Some time after the departure of the foreigner (the Scotsman), I repeated the experiment with one of my friends—he saw and felt as I did myself. The observations we made were these:—as soon as the ingredients were thrown into the chafingdish, a whitish figure forms itself, and seems of natural size to hover just above the chafingdish. *It possesses a most perfect resemblance with the person to be seen, only that the figure is ashy pale.* Upon approaching the figure, a considerable resistance is felt, something like walking against a strong wind. If it is spoken to, no distinct recollection remains of what has been said; and when the phantom disappears, it seems like awakening from a dream. The head is stupified, and there is a great tightness felt in the lower parts of the body. It is singular, that the same appearance presents itself upon being in the dark, or looking afterwards upon dark bodies.

"The unpleasantness of this sensation was such that, however solicited, I was unwilling to repeat the experiment. A young gentleman came to me, and positively *insisted* upon seeing the apparition. As he was a man of a delicate constitution and lively imagination, I hesitated, and consulted an experienced physician, to whom I discovered the entire secret. He was of opinion that the narcotics used must powerfully excite the imagination, and might, under certain circumstances, be very dangerous. He thought the preparatory forms increased the power of their operation, and advised me to make trial of their effect in very small portions, *without* previous preparations.

"This I did, one day after dinner, when this gentleman, who dined with me, was present. The materials were all thrown into the chafingdish, when certainly *a figure showed itself*; but a shuddering, which I was unable to controul, overcame me. I was obliged to leave the room for three hours; I was extremely ill, and had the figure constantly before me. By the use of a great deal of vinegar, which I inhaled, and drank with water, I recovered, towards the evening; yet, for three weeks afterwards, I felt a loss of strength: and what is most singular, is, that, even to this time, when I think on the circumstance, and look upon a dark body, *a lively representation of the ashy-pale figure* presents itself before me. Since that time (adds he) I have never ventured to repeat the experiment."

The following note is added by a lady of erudition, who had read Eckartshausen's work, and remembers these particulars, viz.—"that certain previous forms and conditions are required before the operation takes place; upon omission of these, the operator is threatened with either loss of health, insanity, or the most serious derangement of his temporal circumstances. The particulars I do not remember distinctly, but I think *three days' utter seclusion* is commanded. During these days, the operator must employ himself in devotional exercises, he must often turn his thoughts to the subject he wishes to see, must have a particular regard to him in his prayers, must recollect and dwell on his good qualities, and be very certain that no impure view mixes with his wish to see him. The subject must have committed no crime; and if a living person, he must have no wound in any part of his body. This last condition is remarkable; the tendency of the other is obvious, when it is considered that they came from Arabia (where the Jew first found the secret), and therefore originate with a people not professedly Christian. I think it will be allowed that their piety is worthy notice."

Mr. E., in his second volume, says that he may venture to give the fumigating ingredients without fear, as the success of the experiment depends upon their exact proportions of *Opium, Saffron, Aloes, Henbane, Nightshade, Poppy-seed,* and *Hemlock.*

I most here regret that the author did not communicate whether his own experiments were made with a living subject, and what the state of that person might be during the operation.

From the same hand, Eckartshausen received another fumigation, which, used in a church-yard, would bring into visible existence the spirits of the persons there interred; and an ointment which, upon being applied upon different parts of the body, *would transport the spirit into any part of the world.* These, however, were composed of narcotics of such intense and fearful potency, that the author states he never considered it safe to use them.

Communicated by Philadelphus.

www.ingramcontent.com/pod-product-compliance
Lightning Source LLC
Chambersburg PA
CBHW021112300426
44113CB00006B/126